Ena and Bee

Ena and Bee

QUEEN VICTORIA'S SPANISH GRANDDAUGHTERS

ANA DE SAGRERA

TRANSLATED BY IAIN DORWARD STEWART

EDITED BY JOHN VAN DER KISTE

WITH THE ASSISTANCE OF SUE WOOLMANS
AND RICARDO MATEOS SÁINZ DE MEDRANO

FONTHILL

Fonthill Media Limited
Fonthill Media LLC
www.fonthill.media
books@fonthill.media

Ena y Bee: En defensa de una amistad first published by Velecio Editores, Madrid 2006
English edition first published in the United Kingdom and the United States of America 2022

British Library Cataloguing in Publication Data:
A catalogue record for this book is available from the British Library

ISBN 978-1-78155-854-6

Typeset in 10.5pt on13pt Sabon
Printed and bound in England

Acknowledgements

I would very much like to thank the many people who have helped me with their information, advice, and revelations, some of which I fear I had forgotten.

My most sincere thanks go to the princes and princesses of the House of Orleans: to Doña Geri, who was so close to her grandmother the princess, for her confidences; to Don Alvaro Jaime for the family journal the *infante* wrote on his journey from Madrid to Marseilles via Cartagena, which has never been seen before; to Doña Giovanna San Martino d'Aglie for her efforts in conserving the Orleans-Borbón archives; to Doña Elena Farini de Orleans-Borbón for the photograph of the wedding at Windsor; to María Angeles Tornos de Sáenz de Santa María, who presented me to the *Infanta* Beatrice, and who enjoyed talking about the *infantes*. I am grateful to her nephew, Alfonso Tornos y Zubiría, for his information from Vienna; to the marchioness of Santa Cruz, who always helped me with my books and this time to evoke echoes of the court of Alfonso XIII, where her paternal grandmother, the famous duchess of San Carlos, was Camarera Mayor in charge of the royal household, and to whose maternal grandfather, the duke of Santo Mauro, the queen, and the *Infanta* Bee presented the curious photograph of 'the two naughty girls'. At a luncheon in San Bernadino, Baby Santoña talked to me at length of the palace conspiracy against the *Infanta* Beatrice which her family called 'La Patraña' (the lie or tall story) as related in Chapter 10.

I have not the words to thank Rosario, the dowager duchess of Santa Cristina, for the loan of the two books dedicated to her parents-in-law by the British *chargé d'affaires*, the Minister Plenipotentiary, Mr John

Hurleston Leche. I equally wish to thank the four surviving members of the Rodríguez Pascual family, whose interest and dedication in telling me, sixty years later, of their exodus from the Nationalist Zone. Their recollections had to be omitted for reasons of space but can be found at the Orleans-Borbón Archives at Sanlúcar de Barrameda. I recall how in the summer of 1938, María and Carmen Primo de Rivera, aunt and niece, spent the month of August in my parents' home. 'Aunt Ma' as they all called her, spoke little of the prison in Alicante, where her nephew, Miguel, was held. He gained his liberty thanks to Queen Victoria Eugenia, arriving at Palma de Mallorca a month before the war ended.

I also wish to thank the good friends who have opened their family archives to me: Isabel de las Cagigas de Caruana and the brothers Manuel y Santiago Soroa y Suárez de Tangil, grandsons of the count of Vallellano, president of the Spanish Red Cross during the war; the director of the Antonio Maura Foundation, and his great-grandson, Alfonso Pérez Maura y de la Peña, who provided the information kept by the prime minister about the *infantes'* wedding; Manuel Burguete, grandson of Lt-Gen. Burguete; Don Alonso Herrero y Wallington and his wife, Blanca Nieves, in whose home they preserve memories of the *infantes* whom they and their parents served with such loyalty; the marquis of Selva Nevada, an unfailing fount of knowledge and wisdom; Air Force Col. Cecilio Yusta who has always helped me so efficiently; Beatriz de Lasuen, countess of Varea; two foreign friends of Princess Beatrice: in Coburg, doctor and history lecturer, *Frau* Gertraude Bachman of the Coburg State Archive and in America, Mrs Marlene A. Eilers of Alexandria, Virginia, author of *Queen Victoria's Descendants*, which provided us with so many interesting references; Ricardo Mateos Sáinz de Medrano for putting me in contact with his English and American friends, especially the historian John Wimbles who kindly lent me the correspondence he had from the Romanian Royal Family; my friend Chon Seco Ródenas for allowing me to enjoy her magnificent library of English historical books; Gerardo F. Kurtz for his patience and for the good advice he gave me; and Paloma Bermejo for her enthusiasm over five years' organisation, information, and data, with a true love I will never forget.

In Andalucía, my gratitude is more vivid and I fear forgetting so many people who have talked to me about the *infanta* with such realism and love. I shall begin with Pilar González de Gregorio, an old friend who spoke to me with true love for Sanlúcar and its people; Pilar Medina, dowager marchioness of Salvatierra who, with her husband, often accompanied the *infantes* in their later years; María Luisa González Gordon Díez, widow of Gonzalo del Río, who was so close to the Orleans family; Manuel Domecq-Zurita, who was close to the *infantes*; Encarnita Bustillo Ruiz de Somavia, her sister, María Dolores, and her cousin, Cayetana Bustillo Delgado (Tanuca), who I hope continue collecting data and anecdotes reflecting their 'city'. On my first investigative journey I had the help of Señor Don Vicente González Barberán and his charming wife, María Angustias, and on the following visits, Professor Doña María Dolores Rodríguez and Professor Don Manolo Ruiz Carmona were also most efficient.

Not wishing to go on too much, I draw attention to María Dolores Barbadillo Pardo, Cecilia Florido Álvarez, Manolo Argüeso Hortal, Elsa Astaburuaga Meade who played bridge with the *infanta*. Ramón Ageo Bustillo, José Sabio, the *practicante* (medical assistant) at the Maternity Home, Sebastián Piñuela, a veterinarian who told me of Doña Beatrice's interest in animals, José Guzmán Puente (the famous Pepín, son of Guillermo the cowman), Manolo Rey Cámera, employed for three generations at Torre Breva and Teresa Bermejo Ruiz, who told me about her neighbour Gener, the *infantes*' chauffeur who became ill and remembers, when she was a little girl, that the *infanta* wanted to visit him and as he lived in an attic, insisted on climbing a dangerous wooden stair.

Ana de Sagrera

John Van der Kiste, who edited the English version, would like to add his particular thanks to Ricardo Mateos Sáinz de Medrano and Sue Woolmans, for their indefatigable efforts in reading and checking at several different stages, and to Alan Sutton and Josh Greenland at Fonthill Media for their additional work at the editorial and publishing stages.

John Van der Kiste

Prologue

One day in the autumn of 1988, my brother, Álvaro, told me he planned to re-edit the memoirs of our great-grandmother, the *Infanta* Eulalia, inviting me to attend the book launch. That was when I came to know Ana María de Sagrera, one of the idols of my youth. I grew up in Rome and studied the Italian baccalaureate, and therefore know more Italian history than Spanish. So the biography of Queen Mercedes written by Ana Maria was my guide and also that which catalysed my awareness of belonging to a historic family, with the responsibilities and duties that entails. The thrill of knowing the author of the book that made such an impression on me was therefore considerable—and also the start of a great friendship.

I commented during one of my visits to Madrid that it saddened me that the history of such an interesting life as that of my grandmother, Beatrice, went unrecorded. Ana María surprised me by offering to write it herself. A few months later, she told me about her difficulties in finding sufficient material to allow her to write the story. And for me, from my unwitting lack of knowledge, it seemed quite normal that an unknown *infanta* who had decided to live out her life in a sunny, happy, little Andalusian town had not left sufficient traces to prepare the kind of exhaustive biography our author was accustomed to write. How little I knew Ana María and how little I knew of my grandmother!

The first thing she did was to talk to people in Sanlúcar and collect anecdotes about my grandmother. She also told me about her stay in the palace at Sanlúcar, telling me she and her family were the last guests at my grandparents' romantic home. Little by little, I discovered a life

fantastically rich in adventures, and misadventures, and which for me was
hitherto unimaginable.

My grandmother, granddaughter of Queen Victoria and Tsar Alexander
II of Russia, travelled throughout Europe and knew all the great and
powerful people of the time. She spent her adolescent years in Coburg,
Germany, where her parents were the reigning duke and duchess. At
seventeen, she began to study nursing, something unimaginable in those
times for a princess of her rank. She met her first love, a Russian first
cousin whom she captivated for a year. Passionate and impulsive, she
suffered greatly from her pride and from love, as she could not marry him
because of fundamental laws governing the Russian Imperial family. She
then decided to learn to paint seriously and gave classes of *bel canto*.

Although they had both known each other forever, the deep friendship
with her cousin, Ena, Victoria Eugenia, the future queen of Spain, began
during a fascinating journey to Egypt in 1904 and continued throughout
their lives, despite difficulties, personal tragedies, and exile. In 1906, she
accompanied Ena and attended her wedding. On this occasion, she met
her future husband, the *Infante* Alfonso de Orleans. In his memoirs, the
marquis of Villavieja, referring to Princess Beatrice and her husband,
wrote:

> Adversity made them into two independent spirits who suffered
> unjustifiable persecution with dignity and knew how to stay above the
> pettiness and slanderous accusations. Dedicated to each other, they
> worked, studied together and complemented each other through their
> common interests, understanding the secret of making life worth living.
> They seemed to always be on the same wavelength and were always an
> immensely happy couple.

Baby Bee, as her mother and her sisters called her, was a victim of jealousy
and conspiracies and knew the sadness of three exiles. The first, when
newly wed, was romantic but painful; the Spanish government reproached
her for not wishing to convert to Roman Catholicism. The second was
because of a shocking palace conspiracy, with courtiers approving of royal
seduction. As she did not submit, the punishment was alienation and exile.
Four years later, the queen of Romania visited her and found her thin and
emaciated, still very attractive but tense from worry, apparently hiding
much suffering 'and memories of different experiences which perhaps will
never be completely revealed to me.'

The third exile was heroic because, on the advent of the republic, she
and her son, Ataúlfo, remained in Spain to ensure that the invalid *Infanta*
Isabel could leave the country and die in France. During this enforced

exile, the *infanta* set to work as a labourer, selling her jewels and much beloved mementos to help her sons with their careers. The Civil War began five years later, and Beatrice and her husband dreamed of coming to fight for Spain. Denied permission to return, she sold more jewellery to create the Ambulance Service and organise an exchange of prisoners between the two zones. She and Queen Victoria Eugenia both worked with determination, suffering terrible frustrations from difficulties they encountered on the nationalist side in obtaining the freedom of prisoners. Faced with passivity, the frustrated *infanta* began to work on the front line with Frentes y Hospitales. Meanwhile, her husband and their sons continued risking their lives in the skies above Spain; one of them fell not long after volunteering. She lived in hope of bringing comfort to those who had been liberated, lived through the danger of entering Lerida, and appreciated the gratitude of the people of Castellón. In Tarragona and Barcelona, she saw their occupation with some difficulties, and cried with emotion on receiving an ovation when appearing before the people of Madrid.

After the war, our grandparents settled in Sanlúcar de Barrameda, where she founded the Maternity Home and a *bodega* or wine shop, and managed to make the Botánico Estate a model farm. In the 'years of hunger', they gave most of the harvests to the most emaciated of the expectant mothers and to the Gota de Leche, an organisation that fed the new mothers for six months. I remember making baby jackets and blankets, doubling endless tombola tickets, and writing letters for the El y Ella fiesta, asking for gifts for the charity auction. The fiesta became so famous that its profits covered 40 per cent of the expenses of the maternity home, and they also enlisted the help of Americans at the Rota base.

For us, she was a very loving grandmother, always showing us something new. We frequently wrote to each other, and our letters often referred to our hopes of returning to Sanlúcar to be with our grandparents. It was she who in the late 1940s, as a champion of local culture, encouraged us to learn basic flamenco dances such as sevillanas, rumbitas, and tanguillas, something then considered rather inelegant, showed us how to ride and taught my sister, Gerarda, to paint. My sister was the daughter she never had, and they always enjoyed a very special relationship. She took us to the beach, and when we left the sea, if she saw that we were cold, she immediately gave us a swig of muscatel. She organised picnics for us and swam with us in the swimming pool. Our grandfather taught us to drive when we were still children and showed me how to fly. My sister remembers the first time he let her take the steering wheel and, sitting on grandfather's knees, she headed rapidly towards a wall, with inevitable consequences. Gerarda climbed the palace stairs to our grandmother's study, which was on the third floor, and sat by her side as she painted and showed her how to mix and apply the colours. Gerarda says that when painting, she still hears her words from inside and that the lessons are still very useful.

I flew in the aeroplane with my grandfather. On returning, we circled over the house and within five minutes my grandmother came out into the garden to wave, a ritual without which we never finished a flight. On our return, we found her among the flowers in the garden: Madonna lilies, dahlias, agapanthus, plumbagos, which featured in her oil paintings. I remember her playing long games of cards and chain-smoking Camel-tipped American cigarettes. Only during games of mus, a very popular Spanish card game, did she stop smoking, the only ones in which my grandfather participated, and they exchanged conspiratorial signals and many laughs.

In the palace as in the Botánico, the family and guests enjoyed exquisite cuisine as varied as the knowledge of such a cosmopolitan lady allowed. The farm at the Botánico produced an ample range of milk from the Dutch cows, butter prepared in house by Alicia, pig and duck liver pates, caramel and blackberry ice creams, Russian borscht, and endless delights that she prepared. Breakfast was important, as much for the richness and variety of its dishes as for being an occasion to enjoy a long informal chat over the table.

My sister, who was very greedy, remembers a small plate of very white and desirable cottage cheese appearing at my grandmother's side and which she wished, without success, to try. Granny, as we grandchildren called her, was intelligent, well informed on medical matters and explained that at her age, lack of calcium, which she demonstrated by showing some stretch marks, required dairy products of which this supplied the element in an easily absorbed form. Famous for her advanced medical knowledge, she was consulted by all, as a letter from Ena in Lausanne attests in which she wrote: 'I tell you all this because you are like a doctor to me'. The statistics of the Maternity Home she published annually show the modernity of her thinking and would be worthy of scientific study.

The *Infanta* Beatrice was famed for being a distant person, although we remember her as accessible and humorous. Rather than distant, perhaps she was more reserved in the English manner. All the people of Sanlúcar who spoke to me about her, or who had heard their parents speak of her, told me she treated the needy sweetly and exquisitely. Her humanitarian actions certainly spoke for themselves of a heart as heroic as it was great.

Queen Marie of Romania wrote to her in 1937:

Your life has certainly been full of changes, difficulties, anxiety and heroism. I admire the valour with which you have decided to give up your small comfortable home which you have just finished arranging in Kent, England, to go to martyred Spain; and I admire Ali's reply to the call of your country. It must be extraordinary for him to be able, once again, to serve his homeland. I know that Spain has been the true love of your life, in that no sacrifice seems to you to be too great. But, on observing the path your life has taken, it seems tragic that you are destined never to have a stable home, something which for our family is so important.

Given that Ana María has allowed me to collaborate with her, investigating documents, photos, and collecting anecdotes, I have been able to admire her vast knowledge of the nineteenth and twentieth centuries. It is difficult to look at these centuries and to take in the names of so many politicians and so many families with their complicated inter-relationships which continue into recent times. Ana María is able to do this without devaluing an iota from her love of historic fact, which she manages to recreate after an exhaustive and through investigation. I have appreciated the diversity of her sources, her tenacity in studying them in depth and her delicacy in the treatment of topics which could have wounded the feelings of some people or the descendants of people, some of whom are still alive. Such tact never deviates from relating the true facts. She manages to get out of some thorny situations with positive results and avoiding the negativity that so stimulates the less generous part of our human curiosity. Despite renouncing all this, Ana María keeps her readers hooked, a talent that distinguishes her from many modern biographers. Without this talent, it would be impossible for the author to tell the history of a person such as the *Infanta* Eulalia, with whom she had such a deep friendship when she was young.

The *Infantes* Don Alfonso and Doña Beatriz met the author on the publication of her biography of Queen Mercedes, and offered her their help and friendship. This is reflected in an interesting exchange of letters which is kept in our archives.

Like the rest of my family, I feel a profound debt of gratitude to the author for allowing us to know fully the history of such a multi-faceted person as our grandmother for whom we feel such love, respect, and admiration without really appreciating so many aspects of her romantic life, Beatriz of Orleans-Borbón.

Beatriz de Orleans-Borbón

Contents

Acknowledgements		5
Prologue		9
1	Childhood	17
2	Coburg	26
3	Twilight of an Era	38
4	In Search of a Kindred Spirit	46
5	Sima	52
6	A May Wedding	60
7	History of an Engagement	75
8	A Controversial Marriage	92
9	Spanish Infanta	107
10	False Rumours	123
11	Hidden Exile	135
12	The Uncertain Return	150
13	Representing Spain	162
14	Glorious Days	176
15	Bitter Awakening	197
16	Forced Exile	221
17	Living the War	239
18	And Peace Came	263
19	Confined to Sanlúcar	283
20	La Señorita Infanta	308
Epilogue		329
Genealogical Tables		334
Bibliography		336
Index		341

1

Childhood

On 23 January 1874, Alfred, duke of Edinburgh, Queen Victoria's second son, married Maria Alexandrovna, only daughter of Alexander II, tsar of Russia, at St Petersburg. The first ceremony took place in the Russian Orthodox Church; the second under the rites of the Church of England, to which the bridegroom belonged, was celebrated by the dean of Westminster, Arthur Stanley. For the first time, the two most powerful families of the nineteenth century were united in matrimony.

While Queen Victoria distrusted the Russians in general, she had to accept that the choice of suitable non-Catholic brides for her son was limited. Alice, later grand duchess of Hesse, helped with the matchmaking, telling her mother that Grand Duchess Maria Alexandrovna was 'lovely and agreeable with her fresh and youthful face', loved children and life in the countryside.

The duke of Edinburgh had met Maria in Darmstadt in 1869 when she was sixteen years old, while he was a much-travelled twenty-four. The queen intended to meet the prospective bride before their betrothal, which took place in July 1873. When the tsarina suggested that the sovereign could go to Cologne to do so, the latter wrote witheringly to her daughter, Alice, who supported the tsarina, that she had 'completely taken the part of the Russians' and should not tell her what to do, since she had been on the throne twenty years, longer than the tsar, and was 'doyenne of the Reigning Sovereigns'. She did not go to Cologne, and thus did not meet her son's bride before the ceremony. It would be the only wedding among her children she did not attend, as she feared the long journey to Russia and the lack of security.

On their arrival in England six weeks after the wedding, in March 1874, Alfred and Marie went to Windsor to meet the queen. She found her new daughter-in-law, 'not affected, sensible and honest', clearly not afraid of her husband, and hoped she would be a good influence on him. The appearance of the new duchess caused some excitement at the Victorian court, still resounding with echoes of the Crimean War, and with English politicians regarding the politics of Russian autocracy in the East and the Balkans with apprehension. She brought with her a magnificent dowry, much valuable jewellery, a retinue including a Russian patriarch and two acolytes who celebrated Masses in a small chapel they had brought with them and which had served Tsar Alexander II in wartime. Until her marriage, Marie had been the central woman at the Russian court as her mother was too ill to attend palace ceremonies. At the English court, she never understood that, having married the second son of the sovereign, protocol demanded she walk behind the princess of Wales, wife of the heir to the throne. As daughter of an emperor, Maria resented her unmarried sisters-in-law preceding her as daughters of the queen at court, much to the latter's annoyance. When the tsar visited London in May, he tactfully calmed his daughter's aspirations and asked the queen that the duke of Edinburgh should come after the prince of Wales, as Alfred was the heir of his childless uncle Ernest, duke of Saxe-Coburg.

Maria Alexandrovna preferred German customs which were more familiar to her as her mother was a princess of Hesse, and had little sympathy for her husband's countrymen. She spoke admirable French, which she preferred to English, thought London 'horrible', and the atmosphere there 'awful'. English food was abominable, 'the hours late and very tiring, and the visits to Windsor and Osborne unspeakably boring', the concept of parliamentary democracy alien, and hunting parties utterly tedious. At one palace reception, wishing to take revenge on her in-laws, she 'adorned herself with some of her marvellous jewellery which caused such admiration from those present'. The English princesses were very envious, while the queen stared at the diamonds and gemstones with marked disdain, 'shaking her shoulders like a bird whose plumage had been dishevelled'. That first year they lived in Buckingham Palace. Accustomed to magnificent heating, comfortable bedrooms, and modern bathrooms in the Russian palaces, she found the draughts particularly annoying. Nevertheless, here on 15 October 1874, she gave birth to her firstborn, named Alfred after his father.

Relations between sovereign and duchess became tense, and when the young couple sought a home in the country, the duke of Edinburgh took a twelve-year lease on Eastwell Manor in Kent. Owned by the earl of Winchelsea, the house was a grandiose, grey mock-Tudor building, surrounded by fine gardens. The 2,500-acre estate included rich woodlands with deer and cattle, and a magnificent artificial lake. Every autumn, the duke invited family and friends there to large hunting parties. The duchess was bored with endless gossip and tales of hunting prowess, and most of her visitors shunned her conversations on art, literature, or philosophy, which were much more to her liking. They spent the summer in Russia, returning to Eastwell where, on 29 October 1875, she gave birth to a daughter named Maria after her maternal grandmother and her mother, known as 'Missy' and later queen of Romania.

In February 1876, the duke of Edinburgh was appointed commander of HMS *Sultan* and stationed at Malta, and the family went to live in the San Antonio Palace. Here, on 25 November, the duchess gave birth to another daughter, Victoria Melita, the latter denoting her Maltese birth, and always known as 'Ducky' in the family. When the children were small, their father was often away from home on duty. His eldest daughter recalled that he was almost a stranger to them, and mama was the main figure in their lives. She and Ducky were inseparable, although different in character and looks: 'She had dark hair and although we were only a year apart, looked older than I, as she was taller. According to the grown-ups, she was a difficult child'. Missy was the best-looking of the sisters, blonde with perfect features, good complexion, and colour.

After a wonderful Mediterranean winter, they returned to England and settled in Clarence House, which Queen Victoria had offered them as an official London residence. Expecting that her mother the tsarina would visit them there (which she was never able to do), the duchess had expensive renovations made and ordered comfortable furniture. They all spent the summer of 1878 in the Edinburgh Palace, Coburg, and on 1 September a third daughter was born. Blonde, quiet natured, and plump, she was baptised Alexandra Louise Olga Victoria, better known as 'Sandra', her godparents being the reigning duke and duchess of Coburg. After their return to England, the duke returned to his naval duties.

On 13 October 1879, Duchess Maria had a stillborn son. Saddened but undaunted and much in love with her husband, taking advantage of his home leaves, she pursued him whenever he was onshore to be with him and to make his life more agreeable, yet privately she sometimes reproached him for her loneliness. A sailor at heart, Alfred loved his career, and his returns home always cheered up 'the abandoned wife' who never forgot the first vocation of a princess of royal blood was procreation.

One morning in March 1881, at Clarence House, the children found their mother in tears on her knees in front of her icons. She had just learned that her father the tsar of Russia had been assassinated. Less than a year earlier, she had gone to St Petersburg to see her dying mother, lying on her bed in the Winter Palace, prostrate, unable to talk but still hearing the noise of her husband's children by his young mistress Princess Catherine Dolgoruki, playing on the floor above. The emperor's insensibility angered his daughter, and a bitter row ensued. When Princess Catherine and her three children left for Tsarskoye Selo, Alexander followed her without a farewell to his wife, who died in her sleep on the night of 3 June 1880. Her funeral was celebrated quickly, mourning lasted just over a week, and six weeks later her father married Princess Dolgoruki. Yet granting liberty to the serfs and plans to introduce constitutional government to Russia could not save him from the nihilists. On 13 March 1881, after several unsuccessful attempts on his life, he was assassinated in St Petersburg. Alfred and Marie attended the funeral. Twice daily during the funeral ceremonies, lasting a week, the imperial family and entire court had to kiss his forehead. On the eighth day, a procession took place through the streets of the capital, and he was buried in the Peter and Paul Cathedral. Devastated by her loss, the duchess of Edinburgh received condolences and visits, while having to face interminable ceremonies and gatherings. Afterwards the duke returned home separately while she remained in Russia, unable to attend the parties that spring season because of mourning.

The return to Eastwell Park was not as difficult as anticipated, as she was accompanied by her children. Alfred, the firstborn, had the conformist character of his father, while the girls were more free-spirited. The youngsters' early days there were happy and carefree, 'the childhood of rich children, protected and separated from the realities of life'. Both parents were enthusiastic amateur musicians, and the music room had two pianos. Missy often recalled the famous pianist Anton Grigorevich Rubenstein, wanting to please his illustrious compatriot, playing Russian music, and how she and Ducky, in their dressing gowns, listened from the hallway. The duchess and Lady Randolph Churchill, so dissimilar in many ways yet great friends, also played together on the two pianos. Once the young sisters put two tinplate toys that made the sound of frogs croaking under the piano stools; while the ladies were entranced by their music, the duchess had to excuse her daughters' mischievous conduct. Outside they loved the lake, which froze over so the duke and duchess could skate there with their friends in winter. During summer, they organised picnics, with tables and chairs laid out by the lakeside.

On 20 April 1884, the duchess's youngest child, a fourth daughter, was born. For a long time, the duchess of Edinburgh had felt sympathy for her youngest brother- and sister-in-law, Leopold and Beatrice, and she wanted them to be godparents to the baby whom they had expected to be a boy. The haemophiliac Leopold, duke of Albany, a lover of learning and the fine arts, had married Princess Helen of Waldeck-Pyrmont in April 1882 but died on 28 March 1884, after a fall downstairs, three weeks before Bee's birth. He left a small daughter, Alice, and Helen had a baby son, Charles, posthumously that summer.

That spring, Duchess Maria was keen to leave Eastwell for Germany. In April 1884, Victoria of Hesse and the Rhine, the eldest daughter of her sister-in-law, Alice, who had died of diphtheria in 1878 aged thirty-five, married her cousin Louis of Battenberg at Darmstadt. Intelligent, hardworking, and eager to serve, he had entered the British Navy in 1868, and the duke of Edinburgh took him under his wing. He and his brothers belonged to a morganatic branch of the Hesse family, their parents being Prince Alexander of Hesse and by Rhine and Countess Julia von Hauke, who changed her surname on marriage in 1851. Seven years later, they and their children were given the title of princes. The union was unpopular in Germany, but as Queen Victoria wrote to Crown Princess Frederick William, who shared her mother's admiration for the Battenbergs, 'great alliances' did not necessarily make happy marriages.

Princess Beatrice was so upset by the duke of Albany's death that she did not want to accompany the queen to the wedding in Darmstadt. She was now twenty-seven years old, and the prince of Wales hoped to arrange a marriage between her and Alice's widower, Louis, the grand duke of Hesse and the Rhine, who had four surviving unmarried children, but she preferred to remain at home as her mother's assistant. The latter's will prevailed and she arrived at Darmstadt very downhearted. The bridegroom, Louis of Battenberg, hoped to present her to his younger brother, Henry, who was keen to meet her. Despite the German royal family's strong opposition to another marriage between the queen's family and the son of a morganatic marriage, they fell in love. Initially, the angry queen refused for some months to speak to Beatrice, whom she had hoped would be her permanent spinster companion until the end of her days, but her daughter proved as obstinate as her mother. The sovereign then gave her consent to their betrothal, on condition that they would live with her until her death. They married in July 1885, and Prince Henry of Battenberg became a British subject. During the ten years that he lived near the queen, he was always the most cheerful and amicable of the 'guests', a model husband, and loving father to his children, three boys and the girl who grew up to be queen of Spain.

The baptism of Queen Victoria's new granddaughter was celebrated in the Eastwell Manor library on 17 May. She received the names Beatrice Leopoldine Victoria from Prince Alfred's chaplain, the Rev. William Lloyd, accompanied by the parish priest, the Rev. G. F. Gwynne, in the presence of her parents and godmother, Princess Beatrice. In the family she was always 'Baby Bee'. A nanny spent many sleepless nights with the child in her arms walking up and down the galleries, singing her lullabies. Although suffering from cancer, she remained in service almost until the end, dying soon after retirement at her home on 15 November 1884. According to Missy, 'Ducky said that Baby Bee was bad because she did not have a nanny. Perhaps this was true but not as bad as we thought.' Their mother did not want to look for anyone, and decided to bring the child up herself with the help of two maids.

Always close to his brother, the prince of Wales often visited the family. Missy found 'Uncle Bertie' jovial and friendly, 'generous and amusing', while his wife, Alexandra, was 'charming and [knew] how to dress admirably'. Each spring, the duchess was invited to Marlborough House by the prince and princess of Wales, and attended various London theatrical productions. The Russian uncles and aunts often came to visit their sister. Although argumentative by nature, the Romanovs felt extraordinarily attached to their own, and she in turn adored her brothers. The three eldest were Sasha, now Tsar Alexander III, married to Dagmar of Denmark, to whom he was devoted; Vladimir, ambitious and intelligent and whose worldly, frivolous German wife detested the English; and Alexei, three years younger, a lifelong bachelor. But she was closest to the two youngest: Sergei, four years younger, married to Ella of Hesse; and Paul, seven years her junior.

From an early age, the Edinburgh princesses were attracted by beautiful countryside, a spirited horse, and a delicate flower. They disliked London, and loved going to the Isle of Wight in summer, where their grandmother gave them Osborne Cottage so they could enjoy the beach, sea bathing, and pleasant excursions.

The sovereign received her grandchildren at the house and invited them to tea. At first they were served by Scottish servants, presided over by the indomitable John Brown. After she became empress of India in 1876, she surrounded herself with Indian servants in their colourful costumes, serving impassively and silently. Years later, as a Spanish princess, Bee would tell of their departure from England in October 1886 when her father was appointed commander of the Mediterranean Fleet and based at Malta. Before embarking, they had to say goodbye to the queen. For days the governesses taught the elder ones to practice their obeisances as well as the way to sit correctly, to have their feet together, and not to speak or ask anything until she asked them to speak. Baby Bee, only two and a half years old, was allowed to approach with a little curtsey and kiss the hand of the grand lady. But on the day, the queen had her hand covered with a black glove. On seeing it, the child stopped dead and the governess gently pushed her towards the queen who awaited her with a smile. Suddenly Baby Bee, seeing the glove approaching, spat on it with great precision.

As the family sailed for Malta aboard HMY *Osborne*, Baby Bee had her own cabin, next to that of her mother. Arriving at Valletta, they were received with salutes from the forts around the capital. As they disembarked on the quay, their reception was so enthusiastic that the princesses were open-mouthed. For the first time they became aware of the importance of Britain and what their father represented on the island. That autumn, they moved into San Antonio, the governor's summer palace where Victoria Melita had been born, a magnificent building with stone floors and great rooms, said to be haunted by ghosts. It seems that, as a girl, Bee who would be so valiant in her adult life, feared the possible appearances of restless spirits and could not sleep.

For Duke Alfred, these three winters spent near his family were the happiest time of his life. He enjoyed showing his wife and daughters what he knew and what interested him. They admired the forts and the great botanical gardens containing plants from all five continents. In the large park at their residence, there was a rockery and a small wood where they played hide and seek. The flowers included jasmines, chrysanthemums, violets, narcissus, and anemones and roses of every colour that, together with the verbena and honeysuckle, gave off a deep perfume.

Having left England, the duchess relished her new-found freedom. She prepared meals, arranged parties, and no longer had to worry about unexpected visits from Queen Victoria and her dictatorial advisors, or her critical sisters-in-law. Meanwhile, the princesses rode around the island on little Arab ponies. The adults found it difficult to separate them from the stables, where they were often found brushing the animals. Their mother often accompanied them in her horse-drawn carriage, accompanied by the two littlest ones 'along those atrocious and dusty roads'. At Christmastime, their brother, Alfred, and his tutor, Dr Rolfs, returned from Coburg. There were days of parties, horse races, pantomimes, dances on the ships, and great lotteries to give presents to the servants and, finally, the cutting and decorating of the tree.

In the summer of 1887, England celebrated the jubilee of Queen Victoria, who invited all her children, grandchildren, and great-grandchildren to the festivities. The duke, duchess, and their daughters left Malta for Coburg where they visited the old duke and duchess, collected Alfred and returned to London for the celebrations. Despite the long journey, Baby Bee, who was just three, did not complain and put up with everything. Her sisters commented that even as the youngest, 'she knew how to impose herself and enjoyed an enviable position'.

On their arrival, the family went to Clarence House where many alterations had been made, especially in the Chinese room containing the collection the duke had made on his travels. Another room held the

Fabergé collection brought by the duchess, who continued to collect the *objets de vertu*—jade carvings, malachite, rock crystal, lapis lazuli, enamels mounted in gold and adorned with diamonds and precious stones—that the Romanovs always appreciated. Maria Alexandrovna's jewel collection was kept in the passageway leading to her bedroom. The jewels were displayed in glass cabinets: emeralds, rubies, diamonds, and sapphires, considered among the most beautiful in the world, while the diadems, tiaras, necklaces, earrings, lockets, and bracelets were kept in a glass cupboard. It was a unique spectacle that Baby Bee took for granted as she went daily to her bedroom next to the duchess's.

For the jubilee, many guests arrived in London, all greeted enthusiastically, for the military inspections and religious ceremonies. The queen commissioned the Danish court painter, Laurits Tuxen, to paint a large family portrait of the reunion at Windsor. She appears in the painting alongside her eldest daughter, and behind her her husband, the German Crown Prince Frederick William, destined to become emperor and empress all too briefly the following year. The Edinburgh family are on one side, the duchess playing the piano, Ducky and Missy standing beside her, the duke in naval uniform, his arm affectionately around his kilted son looking at his two little sisters seated on the floor, playing with a black dog. While Tuxen just outlines the face of Sandra, beneath her hair, held back by a crimson ribbon, Baby Bee has her doll in her arms, her hair in a fringe, a necklace with a single pearl around her neck, her white dress adorned with pink ribbons.

The *Infanta* Eulalia, then aged twenty-seven, aunt of the infant King Alfonso XIII, was sent to represent the Spanish royal family. Coincidentally, she and the duchess of Edinburgh both became mothers-in-law of the same couple. In January 1909, Maria Alexandrovna would write that it seemed (Eulalia) 'liked me after the Jubilee in 1887, when I was very affectionate towards her and helped her against her severe brother-in-law (the Count of Paris) who would not let her do anything.'

Returning to Malta that summer, the princesses found it hard to resume their studies after the celebrations, after having occupied a carriage in London, been acclaimed by the crowds, much courted and honoured by so many cousins and friends. However, they soon the forgot everything in their passion for horses, so fearless that their governesses became quite alarmed. The duke admired his daughters' prowess and especially that of Missy, who under the guidance of David Beatty, an excellent polo player from Malta, had become a consummate horsewoman. Her father preferred being on the bridge of a ship rather than on a horse, as did his brother, the prince of Wales. He was surprised one day to see Baby Bee (who always wanted to do as her sisters did) mounted on a pony in the paddock, only four years old but following her instructor's orders attentively. She enjoyed a gallop until the end of her days.

Later George, second son of the prince and princess of Wales, arrived in Malta, where he was welcomed with great affection by his uncle, as they shared passions for philately, hunting, and the Royal Navy. The duke, it was observed, 'seemed to prefer talking with him than with his son, who was separated from him at the age of nine to be educated at Coburg, where he would one day reign'. The Duchess Maria received her nephew 'like a second mother', as she knew that the princess of Wales and her children were very close and that he was homesick. San Antonio became his temporary home, and he had his own room and office there. Despite the age difference, he loved playing with his cousins: they rode together, and went on picnics with Cocky, a chestnut pony, who pulled a little cart. George was ten years older than Missy, whom he gazed at spellbound. She found him 'an adorable companion', while he thought Missy was so wonderful that she should be queen, yet he was too timid to declare himself. In January 1892, when his elder brother, Albert Victor, duke of Clarence, died and he became second in line to the throne, it was too late. Missy was about to become betrothed to Ferdinand of Romania, heir to his uncle, King Carol. For the duke of Edinburgh, to have 'Georgie' as a son-in-law was the dream of his life; but he never said so. The duke, recalled his eldest daughter, 'said little and on occasions was somewhat taciturn'. It would be Baby Bee who tried to understand his silences and to find out what he wanted; as soon as he arrived, she got up, waiting for him to kiss her. There was mutual understanding between the old sea-wolf and his five-year-old daughter.

On one of Queen Victoria's visits to her son, she marvelled at the Russian antiques and other exquisite objects that filled Clarence House. As for her granddaughters, Missy she thought 'outstanding with her golden hair and her perfect features', while the good-looking Ducky was as tall as her mother. Sandra was blonde and very pretty 'although not as outstanding as her sisters', while Baby Bee had 'marvellous blue-green eyes which contrast with her dark hair, and is a most intelligent child seeming older than her years'.

The four sisters would always be very united, which, despite destiny keeping them apart, living in different countries and in very different conditions, made it possible for them to help each other and to get together despite revolutions and wars. They were not four hearts which beat in unison, but one heart divided into four. It was about this time that Bee came to know Ena, who was born at Balmoral in October 1887.

2

Coburg

A small German duchy of 572 square kilometres, situated in the Thuringian Forest, between Saxe-Meiningen and the kingdom of Bavaria, with 70,000 inhabitants, Coburg became famous in the nineteenth century for its princes who became major figures in European politics. Their good fortune, intelligence, hard work, and good looks opened the doors of the courts of Belgium, Great Britain, Portugal, and Bulgaria to them. The first was Prince Leopold, born in Coburg on 16 December 1790. He joined the Russian army and fought in the campaigns against Napoleon. In 1816, he married Princess Charlotte, heir presumptive to the British throne, but the next year, she died in childbirth after producing a stillborn son. After their brief marriage, his wife's uncle, Edward, duke of Kent, was betrothed to his sister, Mary Louise Victoria, widowed with two children. They married in July 1818, and on 24 May 1819, Princess Victoria, the future queen of Great Britain, was born at Kensington Palace. The duke died in January 1820, leaving his widow and her brother, Leopold, to oversee Victoria's upbringing.

The British government gave Leopold a life interest in the estate at Claremont, where he had lived during his marriage. In 1829, the Greeks offered him their vacant crown, which he declined. A year later, he accepted the throne of Belgium, and married Louise of Orléans, elder daughter of King Louis-Philippe of France.

As king of the Belgians, Leopold had considerable influence over his young niece, Victoria. On seeing her Coburg cousins when they visited her in October 1839, she was much drawn to Albert, better-looking than his elder brother, Ernest. On 10 February 1840, they were married in the

Chapel Royal, St James's Palace. Their family would comprise four sons and five daughters. Ernest, who succeeded his father as duke of Saxe-Coburg Gotha in 1844, had married Princess Alexandrina of Baden. As they had no children, it was agreed that his second nephew, Alfred, made duke of Edinburgh in 1866, should become heir to the duchy. When he and his family returned from Malta in 1889, the queen decided they should attend to their German interests, but he asked his mother to let him remain in the navy until the death of Duke Ernest.

In the summer of 1889, the Edinburghs were invited by the tsar and the tsarina to Finland, for the official opening of the tsar's fishing lodge at Langinkoski. As usual, Baby Bee accompanied her mother, bringing back fond memories of her stay at Kotka and of how charming 'Uncle Sasha' was to her. His youngest daughter, Olga, then aged seven and still very childish, was annoyed that Baby Bee was so lively and, although two years younger, confidently replied to the tsar's questions.

When the duke and duchess went to Coburg, they stayed at the Edinburgh Palace in the main square near the official residence of the dukes of Coburg. Faced with the bad conduct of Ernest II, a notorious libertine—the opposite of his virtuous late brother, Prince Albert—the strait-laced Maria Alexandrovna, anxious to defend their family life at all costs, decided to stay that autumn in the countryside four miles from the city in the castle of Rosenau, Prince Albert's birthplace. The building on a hill overlooking the town was surrounded by gardens, and from the study windows, the princesses could see the houses of the village across the park. It was Bee who enjoyed that memory-filled place most and, on marrying, later converted it into her living room.

The duchess felt no inclination towards her only son and hardly spoke to him. According to Missy, Alfred was not particularly good-looking, but very sensitive with a heart of gold, 'lazy and shy, and she was brusque with him because he made her impatient'. Sandra, a plump child, with fair hair, innocent and with a sweet character, always following the older ones, was 'humble and shy, always fearful of reproach'. Her elder sisters regretted that, though she was six years older than Baby Bee, 'she was unable to enter into her circle, now that our mother was completely occupied.' The duchess, an excellent conversationalist who loved the company of 'intelligent and interesting people' and preferred diplomats and politicians to soldiers, sailors, or sportsmen, told her daughters that a princess should be 'amicable, chatty and entertaining. When she receives an invitation she has to eat everything that is offered to her'. Always healthy, she found anyone who complained of illness irritating. She believed princesses must marry young, as once they reached the age of twenty, 'they begin to think too much and have too many ideas of their own, which complicates matters. Besides an unmarried princess has no position at all. Princesses must marry'.

In the spring, Aunt Beatrice and the Battenberg cousins came to stay at Coburg. The elder, Alexander, was three years old, his sister, Ena, only two; Baby Bee, five. Both sisters-in-law complained that their husbands were always away, and grumbled about their loneliness. On fine summer nights, they would eat in the garden. The tall trees were lit and a small string orchestra, hidden behind a hedge, played while food was served.

As they travelled and moved around so much, the princesses' education suffered, especially with regular changes of teachers and the different languages they spoke. Missy and Ducky studied together but the latter had a good memory and was a better learner than her elder sister. Sandra, the slowest, always studied alone. Baby Bee was a better student, 'more ambitious, and with more modern ideas of what a young lady should learn'. As for their teachers, they tolerated Professor Rieman, who taught history and geography, 'without liking him', Professor Beck taught literature, and Dr Heim, botany and natural history. Professor Neuman arithmetic and M. de Morsier, Alfred's second tutor, took them for French, 'but we escaped to the trees rather than do dictation.' They loved walking in the woods, and in summer, they would take a nap in their hammocks. Croquet was the preferred game, played on a grand esplanade at the home of Uncle Philipp of Coburg. In winter, the snow and frozen rivers gave them an opportunity to skate. Baby Bee, who was fearless, began to learn while small and became very proficient.

Unlike her daughters, the duchess loved speaking French. Their teacher, Mademoiselle, was from Strasbourg and hated Germans, which they found strange. Yet Marie always spoke to them in English, and never taught them Russian, as she said she did not wish to see her beloved language mutilated. At the theatres in Coburg and Gotha, there were concerts, comedies, dramas, and Italian and German opera, particularly that of Wagner. Ducky and Baby Bee were the main music lovers.

As Christmas approached, festive preparations always kept them busy. At the charity bazaar in November, the ladies wore fancy dress. The duchess and her daughters did needlework, crochet, and embroidered garments using Russian patterns, and sometimes she played the piano or read aloud while the girls worked. Every December, they made small presents for the family, such as teacloths for their grandmother the queen, or embroidered slippers for their uncle the tsar. Christmas was their favourite time of the year, as there was always a Russian uncle coming to visit his sister and bringing news from St Petersburg or Paris, and beautiful presents for adults and marvellous toys for children.

In August 1890, the duke of Edinburgh was appointed commander-in-chief at Devonport, where he served for three years. That autumn, the duchess and her daughters moved to England to be with him and settled in the official residence, Admiralty House, close to that of the general-in-command, Sir Richard Harrison. His daughters were the same age as Missy and Ducky, and became their close companions in games of croquet and on maritime expeditions. It was the first time that they had had contact with girls who were not princesses. A Plymothian contemporary, Hilda Picken, thought the duchess felt she had come down in the social scale: 'having married a mere Duke, [she] was obliged to come into contact with the likes of us'. The contrast between her daughters' cheerful faces 'and Mama's glowering looks was quite remarkable'.

While they were in Devon, six-year-old Baby Bee learnt to swim, an activity she enjoyed the rest of her life. The princess of Wales, who felt a special affection for her husband's nieces, wrote to her son, the future King George V, that she was saddened his cousins had to be educated as Germans, as they seemed to speak with a strong accent: 'after all, they are English'. They returned to Coburg for the winter where they were together for the last time. Separation would soon follow as Alfred would be sixteen years old and begin his military studies. He never went to school, and followed the same studies as his comrades, with the same masters, but at home, which Missy thought unfortunate. On him rested his parents' hopes, and his education was carefully planned. Nevertheless, he grew up with an exaggerated idea of his own importance and was easily led astray. School would have taught him the measure of his strength against others.

At Coburg, they met several young contemporaries, who came to their skating parties. The one they liked best was 'Löwel the giant', a friend of Alfred, whom Baby Bee admired. She 'blushed like a peony when she slipped her small hand into his'. For the first time the girl discovered that she was pretty and that the boys liked her, as they did her older sisters.

The duchess knew George was in love with Missy, and that both her mother-in-law and her husband would welcome such a match, but she recalled her loneliness and her heartaches, and knew the life of a sailor's wife too well. Although fond of George, she did not want Missy to suffer at court as she did—'always in second place'. His elder brother, Albert Victor, was destined to reign.

In order to keep them apart from the English family, the duchess had the two eldest confirmed in the German Lutheran Church and asked the German emperor to look after the future of her eldest daughter. Wilhelm II was delighted to help, and at the time of the autumn manoeuvres, he spoke to King Carol of Romania, who told him confidentially that his nephew and heir, Ferdinand, was in love with his wife's lady-in-waiting, Helena Vacarescu. The king immediately sent the queen away to her mother's home and the lady-in-waiting into exile, while the prince received a clear ultimatum that such a liaison was incompatible with his status as heir to the Romanian throne.

After the army manoeuvres, Wilhelm held a grand banquet in Wilhelmshöhe Castle. Missy was seated next to Ferdinand, crown prince of Romania. On her mother's advice, she began the conversation and she realised that, although ten years older than her, he was unnaturally shy and could hardly say two words without faltering, which she found rather trying. Afterwards, her mother angrily reminded her that it was not appropriate to sustain a conversation with one's neighbours and she should be patient. In fact, she returned to find Ferdinand smiling in admiration, and he recalled that his mother, Antonia of Portugal, was, through her father, a Saxe-Coburg like her.

After spending Christmas at Rosenau, Missy was invited to visit the Berlin court for the first time, and stayed with her cousin 'Charly', Charlotte, hereditary princess of Saxe-Meiningen and sister of Wilhelm II. Every time Ferdinand of Romania appeared he was invariably friendly, but timid and tongue-tied. The kaiser therefore summoned him to Potsdam immediately, and he appeared trembling before his emperor and commander-in-chief. Knowing he was enchanted by Missy, the monarch advised him not to waste time, as George was also in love with her.

In March, the duchess invited her relations to Munich and Ferdinand, impatient to declare his love, was among them. Missy found him excruciatingly shy, laughing 'more than ever to mask his timidity'. This was what attracted her most; something in him aroused her motherly feelings—'in fact, you wanted to help him'. Relishing her triumph, Duchess Maria had to be first to tell the kaiser, neither consulting her husband nor allowing Missy time to consider. Her telegram announcing the betrothal formally caused Duke Alfred such embarrassment that he considered withholding his consent, but as future heir of the duchy of Coburg he had to submit to his nephew the German emperor. He confided in tears to his mother that he had wanted a better future for Missy. As for Victoria, it was said that the union between Maria and Ferdinand of Romania was the only marriage among her descendants that was 'pulled-off without consent'.

In May, Wilhelm II organised a grand banquet to celebrate the engagement at Potsdam. There was no lack of congratulations and the passionate toasts of the Romanians, who saw for the first time the girl destined to be their queen. The gathering only lacked the father of the fiancée, simply because of the British royal family's deep disappointment.

The duchess went to visit Sigmaringen in the Danube valley, where Ferdinand's parents lived. To accompany her she had chosen her son,

Alfred, and Baby Bee, who at eight years was delighted by everything. Missy always remembered the first great family tea party, where Princess Antonia received them all at a large round table generously laden with food. Nando enjoyed showing her his old home, and shyly presenting his bride to old family servants and retainers and tutors. Despite this Marie always harboured a certain anxiety, a touch of dread. She instantly gathered that he was afraid of his uncle, King Carol, who had gone to England that summer to thank Queen Victoria for having thus honoured Romania. The king disliked travel, and only went to Berlin when the kaiser invited him. On arriving in London, he was delighted to be awarded the Order of the Garter, the queen's way of showing Missy that she was still interested in her. Nando, she considered, was a 'good boy; but there was something which she did not like'. Some of Missy's cousins tactfully teased her by telling her that in Romania (an old Ottoman province) she would have to live in a harem and wear a veil over her face, and she noted that 'on seeing her, cousin George could not hide his annoyance'. She was also upset as she did not feel her conscience was clear. The previous year, her mother had ordered her to write him a formal note announcing that 'there had never been anything definite between them'.

From the first moment, Missy had liked her future father-in-law, Leopold, who treated her with admiration and tenderness. However, his wife, Antonia, was cold and jealous towards her, fearing this radiantly beautiful, intelligent young woman would exert a powerful influence on her weak, insecure son. As well as getting to know Nando's parents, she had to meet Elizabeth, the queen aunt living in retirement in Neuwied, the capital of the principality of Wied, a simple protocol visit that put the future bride in a dismal mood. On arrival she was embraced by the queen, an eccentric woman of mature years, who wrote poetry under the *nom de plume* of Carmen Sylva, whose hardly-combed white hair fell over her shoulders, 'surrounded by a swarm of servants or vestal virgins who began to gather around her as if they were at a dance rehearsal'.

Her sisters knew they would miss her terribly, 'but we shall try not to think about it and try not to sadden our last weeks together'. Baby Bee hid so that they never saw her crying. There was a great affinity between the eldest and the youngest, both born at Eastwell Manor. They spent their last Christmas together with Missy at Rosenau, holding back the heartache they all felt. To their young eyes, Romania seemed mysteriously far away.

The wedding was arranged for 10 January 1893 in Sigmaringen Castle. Missy was to give her consent in three ceremonies: in her own Protestant church, in Nando's Roman Catholic church and then at the civil ceremony, but nobody remembered that Romania is Orthodox and that the children were to be educated in that religion.

Meanwhile, in the spring of 1892, Queen Victoria had made her grandson George, duke of York. In May 1893, he became betrothed to Princess Victoria Mary of Teck, the daughter of Princess Mary of Cambridge, cousin of Queen Victoria and granddaughter of George III. The wedding was held on 6 July in the Chapel Royal, St James's Palace, a serious and formal ceremony only being interrupted by five-year-old Ena of Battenberg who, knowing that one should be quiet in the church, protested loudly on hearing the priest say, 'speak now; or forever hold your peace'.

In August, the duke of Coburg caught a chill while out hunting, and died a few days later, aged seventy-five. His heir Alfred, duke of Edinburgh, had just ended his naval career two months earlier on being promoted to admiral of the Fleet. Since infancy he had been trained to rule in the duchy, but took up his ducal inheritance with little enthusiasm. The bad-tempered Ernest, indifferent to the feelings of others, especially those of his wife, Alexandrine, was barely mourned.

According to the new duchess's sister-in-law, the Empress Frederick, 'Aunt Marie loved being number one'. Alfred paid off his uncle's debts, and kept his predecessors' estate at Nice, acquired by Ernest, so his widow could spend winter there, from the end of November to the beginning of May. Alfred planned to continue living in Villa Fabron, but Alexandrine wanted to put it at the disposal of Ferdinand and Marie of Romania. Soon she gave up the journey from Coburg, and Alfred gave the villa to his mother the queen empress during her stays at the Hotel Cimiez, and to his wife's Russian family, converting it into the Château Fabron.

The duke knew he had to remain at Coburg until the education of his heir was completed and, above all, because of an obligation to marry off his daughters. That autumn, the duchess, Ducky, Sandra, and Baby Bee left for Romania to be with Missy, now expecting a baby. The first part of her marriage, far from being happy, was very lonely. While her sisters accompanied the duchess to Russia and were being fêted there, poor Missy, confined to the palace, sadly overcame the first months of her pregnancy and her lack of independence. She now had to live near the king, who only thought about governing without letting the crown prince show his young wife her new country.

In 1892, Maria wanted Baby Bee to accompany her to Sigmaringen to get to know Nando's family. Although only eight years old, she immediately distinguished herself as an amusing and clever child. In Romania she captivated the king, whose only daughter had died at the age of four. Baby Bee extended her stay and that of her sisters at Sinaia, letting the sovereign take her on walks together through the forest. Their departure was set for 17 October, but the birth was premature and nine-year-old Baby Bee came to know the facts of life, to the duchess's disgust. Missy, not yet eighteen, had a boy who would one day become King Carol II of Romania.

That autumn, Queen Victoria, ever the matchmaker, took advantage of the absence of her daughter-in-law Maria Alexandrovna and her daughters in Romania to arrange a marriage between Ducky and her cousin Ernest, who had succeeded his father as grand duke of Hesse in March 1892. Both cousins had been born on 25 November, one in 1868 and the other in 1876; it was all they had in common. The queen was particularly fond of Alice's children, and believed there was nobody better than Ducky, who was responsible, artistic, and very pretty, to marry her cousin and take the place of her late aunt, Alice. She had always been aware of the health problems of her Hesse grandchildren; one, a haemophiliac, had died after falling from a window and another from diphtheria. Her doctor, Sir William Jenner, who told her there was no risk if Ducky married the grand duke 'because the young Princesses of Edinburgh are like their mother, fit and strong'.

Although Ernie loved Ducky as a cousin, he was not attracted to her, preferring the masculine company of boys his own age. Alarmed, Victoria decided to advise her grandson to show interest in Ducky, advising him that 'George had lost Missy by waiting and waiting'. Thus encouraged, after a visit to Coburg, Ernie wrote to her that Ducky had been 'so loving and kind towards me during those last few days that I have the highest expectations that if I ask her she will say yes. But I have not done so because I wished to tell you first.'

Missy stayed at Rosenau that Christmas. On 9 January 1894, the new duke of Coburg sent a telegram to his mother, telling her that their great wish had has been fulfilled that night; Ducky had accepted Ernie's proposal. The next question was in which country they should celebrate the wedding. Everyone knew that Queen Victoria wanted her grandchildren to marry in England, but Ernest felt obliged to hold the ceremony in Coburg. Taking advantage of the fact that Duke Alfred was in his first year of his rule, he wrote to her tactfully that his uncle was 'now a German Prince and is doing everything so admirably well that all his subjects truly appreciate him'. For the wedding to be in England would not be practicable. It would do him (Duke Alfred) much harm, disappoint his people, and be very unpopular. Magnanimously, the queen concurred with his views.

It was considered a good match, but Duchess Marie took the news of the engagement coldly, and in a long conversation with the grand duke, she referred disdainfully to 'the English family'. Commenting on the matter to Missy, she insisted that 'we are not fond of them, as they have been disagreeable and spiteful towards me so many times.' Ernie, she went on, 'should not always drag Ducky to England in perpetual adoration of his grandmother and he has to understand the reasons why we should never revere her excessively.' However, when she knew the wedding would be in Germany, she was pleased because her mother-in-law would have to travel to Coburg. The ceremony was fixed for the third week in April, as the queen wished, because she feared it would be too hot in May. She would attend, as would the prince of Wales, the duke and duchess of Connaught, Beatrice and Henry of Battenberg, and his brother, Louis, whose wife was the groom's eldest sister, and bring a large entourage, including her Indian servants. Germany was to be represented by Kaiser Wilhelm II, his mother the Empress Frederick, and her other son, Henry, husband of Irene, the bridegroom's other sister. From Russia, Tsarevich Nicholas attended with his uncles, Grand Duke Vladimir with his wife Miechen, Grand Duke Sergei with Ella of Hesse, and Grand Duke Paul. Queen Victoria enjoyed returning to her adored husband's birthplace and praised the changes made to Rosenau since her last visit.

Hundreds gathered in front of the palace to see royalties entering the chapel. At 11 a.m., the short civil ceremony took place in Queen Victoria's sitting room, and the wedding party then went directly to the church. Just before midday, the dowager duchess of Coburg appeared with her six ladies-in-waiting and sat in a small gallery. The prince of Ratibor, grand marshal of the Prussian Court, struck the floor three times with his cane, announcing the arrival of Kaiser Wilhelm II, attired in the uniform of a Hessian general, with the duchess of Coburg on his arm. They were followed by the Empress Frederick, and behind came her brother, the prince of Wales, walking alongside his nephew, the tsarevich, in Russian uniform, followed by several princes and princesses. Finally, the bridegroom entered, resplendent in the same uniform as the kaiser, his helmet adorned with red and white plumes. After a long silence, Queen Victoria arrived on the arm of her son, the duke of Coburg, who took her to her golden throne in the front row. A little later, the bride appeared in a simple white satin wedding dress and her Aunt Alice's lace veil, accompanied by her bridesmaids, her sister, Beatrice, and Feodora of Saxe-Meiningen, the kaiser's niece. The wedding breakfast was served in the throne room, after which the couple left in a phaeton adorned with spring flowers, while the well-wishers' clouds of rice fell upon them.

Another forthcoming wedding would have much deeper consequences for Russia and for Europe. Nicholas Alexandrovich Romanov was heir to the throne of Russia. Physically, he resembled his mother, the enchanting Tsarina Marie Feodorovna ('Minnie'), born Dagmar of Denmark, sister of Alexandra of Wales, and also the latter's son, his cousin, George. He was unaffected, very agreeable, but terribly shy and insecure. Nicky knew he had to marry a princess, and had set his heart on Alix of Hesse, sister of Ella, married to Grand Duke Sergei.

Princess Alix did not meet with the tsar's approval, as she was also very shy and tongue-tied, but seeing his son was infatuated, the tsar gave way. Nicky went to the Coburg wedding with the intention of proposing. Initially reluctant to give up her Lutheran religion, at length she accepted, and Nicholas wrote in his diary that it was 'the most wonderful and unforgettable day in my life.' Some observers recalled that Alix had been indignant when the engagement was announced between her brother and a cousin whom she had never liked and would thus be filling the role once taken by her mother, and that she had had to be persuaded to write Ducky a card of congratulation.

The family left for Romania that autumn, because Missy was again pregnant, and stayed again with her and baby Carol in Pelesch Castle. A princess, born on 12 October 1894, was baptised Elizabeth, in the Orthodox faith, named after the queen. Around this time, the duchess learnt that the tsar was seriously ill. Leaving Missy in the company of Sandra, she and the duke left for Russia with Baby Bee (henceforth referred to as Bee), confessing she 'could not do without her'. In 1888, the imperial family had been involved in a serious train crash and the tsar single-handedly held up the ceiling of the compartment to prevent the others from being crushed, until they could be rescued. Twenty-one people were killed and many others were wounded. Although he was apparently unhurt, later the doctors diagnosed kidney trouble, perhaps a direct result of his heroic action.

The tsar was failing and had been taken to his Crimean seaside palace of Livadia. On entering his room there, and seeing him seated by the window, so gaunt and aged, Marie embraced him, exclaiming, 'Thank God I've arrived in time to see you again!' Having allowed Nicholas to let his fiancée Alix come, she arrived in time to receive the tsar's blessing, just before he died on the morning of 1 November. The following day, Nicky was proclaimed tsar. He was surrounded by the sons of Nicholas I, who all physically towered over the young sovereign, and his uncles, Vladimir, Alexei, Sergei, and Paul, ready to advise and guide him, but he refused their help. All he wanted to do was to be alone with his fiancée Alix, who urged him to remember that he was tsar and to stand firm.

Despite the sadness of the occasion, Bee enjoyed her stay in the Crimean Peninsula. The rooms were of vast proportions, with an immense garden, extending from the mountain on one side to the other with an English park, beautiful exotic plants, and monumental fountains.

During the tsar's final journey through cities, town, and villages, the train passed through packed stations. They observed the gaunt young new successor and his bride-to-be, old villagers murmuring that she would bring them bad luck, as they watched her following a funeral cortège. Alexander III had been well-respected, because throughout his thirteen-year reign Russia had remained at peace. A man of upright character, natural simplicity, and frankness, everybody had trusted him. He had preserved family unity, with every member respecting his orders. Duchess Maria was desolate, especially as she had no faith in the ability of her nephew who succeeded him. After his father's burial in the Peter and Paul Cathedral, and the foreign representatives had left, the wedding of the new tsar to Princess Alexandra of Hesse took place on 26 November 1894 in the Chapel of the Winter Palace. Attending the Orthodox ceremony were his brother the Grand Duke Michael and his three cousins, Kirill, Boris, and Andrei. As the court was in deep mourning, it was a sad occasion without any festivities.

Bee had a niece and nephew in Romania, but rarely saw them, as they were virtually isolated in Bucharest. As a result, there was joy on 11 March 1895 when Ducky gave birth to a girl, also named Elisabeth, who was born in Darmstadt. She was to become her favourite niece.

Queen Victoria wanted to get to know her Romanian and Hesse great-grandchildren. As rumours grew that Missy and Ducky were unhappy in their marriages, she invited them to spend Ascot week in London, and then lent them Osborne Cottage on the Isle of Wight for a month. The two sisters, still not yet twenty years old, enjoyed the beaches and the woodlands as they had as girls. Carol was eighteen months old and his sister only six months. They had both inherited Missy's good looks, while Ducky's daughter was a baby of three months. Bee wanted to accompany them, but her mother would not allow it as Sandra would be seventeen on 1 September, and they were preparing for her wedding in Coburg to Ernest of Hohenlohe-Langenburg, aged thirty-three, the only son of Prince Herman VI and his wife, Leopoldine of Baden. As a diplomat well acquainted with the courts of London and St Petersburg, he had studied at the universities of Bonn and Baden and served with the cavalry, being promoted to captain. He was also a grandson of Feodora, the half-sister of Queen Victoria, though she disapproved of the marriage. Missy and the duke of Saxe-Coburg did likewise as they did not consider him sufficiently bright, and because Sandra, on marrying, would become a serene highness—inferior rank in the *Almanach de Gotha*. Duchess Maria countered this by saying that she 'was the least interesting of her four daughters'.

The wedding, celebrated on 20 April 1896 in the chapel of Ehrenburg Palace, was simpler than that of Ducky, although the couple were well-matched. They spent their honeymoon at Langenburg Castle, near Hesse, where they would live.

Bee celebrated her twelfth birthday that same day, remaining in Coburg with her parents, looking forward to Alfred's holidays from his military service at Potsdam. Yet she dreamt of returning to Russia, whose family and country fascinated her. Meanwhile, her mother had projects in mind for the future of the daughter who, with her intelligence and beauty, was fit to be a queen.

3

Twilight of an Era

The death of Tsar Alexander III heralded grave uncertainty for Russia, as the diffident Nicholas II had been poorly prepared for his responsibilities. In March 1896, the dowager empress and her younger children visited the south of France. Her sister, the princess of Wales, joined her mother-in-law, Queen Victoria, staying at the Grand Hotel de Cimiez. Maria of Coburg and Bee went to Nice to greet her sisters-in-law, nephew, and niece at Chateau Fabron. After several weeks on the Côte d'Azur, they returned to St Petersburg for the tsar's coronation in May. The duke of Coburg suggested that Bee should remain at home because the Russian ceremonies were interminable, but his wife disagreed. Many years later, Bee would comment:

> I owe having attended the coronation of the last tsar to my mother's insistence as she prophetically repeated, 'It will be the last time!' I was just twelve but I remember everything as if it were yesterday. It was in springtime when Russia enjoys its most beautiful season of the year, when nature awakes with new life and one can see from day to day how the trees open their buds and the flowers grow in the gardens.

The dowager empress was only forty-eight years old. She and Tsar Alexander had had three sons, Nicholas, George, and Michael, and two daughters, Xenia and Olga. Alexander III had four brothers and a sister, Maria Alexandrovna, who was married to a duke, but was still treated as an imperial royal highness, with all its prerogatives, by concession of her father and brother.

Vladimir, her eldest surviving brother, was married to Princess Marie of Mecklenburg-Schwerin, the unofficial queen of St Petersburg society, with four children, Kirill, Boris, Andrei, and Elena. Alexei was unmarried, while Sergei, married to Ella of Hesse, was childless. Bee had only eleven cousins on her mother's side: five belonging to Uncle Sacha, as they called the late tsar; four belonging to Vladimir; and two to Uncle Paul who married Alexandra of Greece. Maria, almost six, and her brother, Dmitri, four, would be her companions at the coronation ceremony. Bee felt strongly attracted to her Russian relations, who gave her splendid presents and treated her like an adult. The English family all seemed oblivious to her, and some of its members even pretended not to know her. As her father had eight siblings, all married, there were forty-eight cousins.

Grand Duke Vladimir, commander-in-chief of the Imperial Guard, held a special position at court. He and his wife, 'Miechen', had great affection for Germany and a real dislike of everything English, partly because of perceived slights that his beloved sister, Maria Alexandrovna, had received. The intelligent, energetic, sharp-tongued Grand Duchess Vladimir did not enjoy favour at court and maintained her independence, gathering the elite of the country around her, and foreign diplomats who came to St Petersburg. When Maria Alexandrovna arrived there with her family, they were always Vladimir's guests at Tsarkoye Selo, or at the beautiful Florentine-style residence in the capital next to the River Neva, known as the 'Vladimir Palace'.

In May 1896, the imperial family moved to Moscow, staying in the Nicholas Palace in the Kremlin for the coronation. Bee, who still hardly knew Moscow, loved joining her cousins and Uncle Vladimir who acted as guide, explaining the beauties of the Kremlin, where the fifteenth- and sixteenth-century rooms remained well-preserved. Moscow looked brilliant, its streets and houses decorated with special archways and structures erected for the occasion. On the day of the 'grand entrance', the grand dukes met in the Petrovski Palace to accompany the tsar on his arrival in the city, bringing their horses, carriages, and servants. Mounted on a white horse, he was followed by more than twenty grand dukes in their richly coloured uniforms, royal delegates from other countries, and a group of Asiatic subjects in their sumptuous oriental costumes.

Bee told of how she saw the procession from one of the Kremlin windows, while Missy was struck by how slight the tsar looked alongside his uncles with their strong voices and imposing presence, always talking quietly in a soft tone. From the day she became empress and received the name Alexandra, and changed her Protestant faith for Orthodox, the new tsarina submitted herself to its dictates and became a fanatical daughter of the Russian church. In the first of the golden eighteenth-century coaches came the dowager empress, wearing a magnificent diadem, her neck adorned with jewels, resplendent in a gown with a golden mantle as she nodded to her right and left. The empress, in the second coach, was luxuriously dressed but without a crown as she would only obtain her rights after the Sacrament. More beautiful than her mother-in-law, she showed great dignity but did not smile. Throughout the long ceremonies, her attitude was the same, 'and in her presence the enthusiasm of others came to a standstill'.

Tragedy marred the festivities four days later at the customary festival in which people were given food, clothing, and a commemorative souvenir cup. The tsar always attended the distribution of these gifts to the thousands gathered at Khodynka field. Because of poor organisation, there was a terrible crush when the crowd surged towards the same point, and around 1,400 men, women, and children were killed in the resulting stampede. Alexandra was particularly affected. That night, a ball was held in the French Embassy, and she begged for postponement, asking that the night should be free of celebrations. She was overruled, for France, Russia's only dependable ally, had made expensive preparations for the reception. The dowager empress and the duchess of Coburg spent that night visiting the wounded in hospital. In accordance with protocol, royalty went in pairs. Missy, being quite tall, was amused at being placed beside the diminutive Prince Victor Emmanuel, heir to the Italian throne, who looked even smaller next to her. Grand Duke Kirill considered that among all the princesses, the daughters of the duke and duchess of Coburg 'were the most radiant'.

Bee and her parents returned to St Petersburg and then to stay at Tsarskoye Selo, in Vladimir's palace surrounded by parkland, including an enchanting private garden for the children, sloping gently down to a lake dotted with little islands containing miniature pavilions, and temples. Rather to the annoyance of her cousins, Olga Alexandrovna and Helena Vladimirovna, both two years older, at twelve Bee was so quick and intelligent that she seemed the eldest of the three. In the gardens at Tsarkoye Selo was a little house in which the grand duchesses learnt the culinary arts in childhood, and where Beatrice and her cousins, Olga and Helena, began cooking, particularly simple French dishes and Russian blinis.

After a long absence, they were delighted to return to Coburg and see their new nephew, Sandra's son, Gottfried, born on 24 March 1897 in Langenburg Palace.

In April, Grand Duke Kirill and his brother, Boris, accompanied by the duke of Coburg, went to the south of France, where Queen Victoria received them at the Hotel de Cimiez in Nice. She invited them to lunch and to attend her diamond jubilee festivities in London that June with their parents. They all stayed at Clarence House, with Kirill occupying rooms on the same floor as his cousin, Alfred. They had similar musical tastes; Kirill played the old piano in the sitting room and Grand Duke Sergei the flute. This delighted Bee, who had inherited her parents' love of music, and who saw very little of her brother for whom she had always cared deeply. She always tried to be near him when she could, perhaps sensing his unhappiness.

For the jubilee procession to St Paul's Cathedral, the weather was splendid, while enormous crowds lined both sides of the streets as the procession rode to the city. In attendance as ever was a great representation of royal houses with their brilliant uniforms, mixing with the exotic clothes of the Indian princes, jointly representing the glory of Great Britain at its time of greatest splendour.

It was natural that for a receptive child like Bee, this pageantry through the frenzied, cheering crowds would greatly impress her, feeling as she did, as at home in Moscow as in London and forming part of a unique lineage. While her parents, uncles, and brothers attended parties, dances, lunches, and dinners during the celebrations, Bee, her Battenberg cousins, and their cousin, Elisabeth of Hesse, went to the zoo and Kew Gardens. While 'Drino' of Battenberg once argued about her plans, the three younger ones followed her blindly, especially the sensitive, affectionate Ena, only nine yet already showing promise of becoming a beauty.

Missy could not attend the festivities, as Nando was seriously ill with typhoid and suspected pneumonia. She nursed him devotedly, later joined by her mother and Bee. They could not go to Romania until the king and queen went to Switzerland for their annual cure, as the king and the duchess of Coburg, both authoritarian characters, did not get on well together. Once he was convalescent, Nando could leave his bed for a few hours a day and sit in the sun on the balcony, playing games of patience or being carefully entertained by the few people allowed to see him. Missy was glad to have two of her family for company, Bee proving 'a delightful and intelligent companion'. She thought it 'was ecstasy to have a young and enterprising sister with [her], particularly in her rambles about the forest, regardless of the weather'. Their mother knew it would do them good to enjoy themselves, almost as carefree children again, and she cheerfully sat beside Nando's sickbed while they were out. At length he made a full recovery.

In January 1899, the duke and duchess of Coburg celebrated their silver wedding at Gotha. She invited her Russian family and members of the 'British clan', as well as Kaiser Wilhelm II and his relations. This time she did so as reigning duchess, blind to an impending tragedy that would mark her and her family for ever.

Unlike his four sisters, young Alfred was never robust. As the next duke, he had to become thoroughly Germanised, and was sent to join the army in Berlin. Contemporaries saw only a sad, lonely, venereally infected youth, missing his sisters' companionship as well as the advice of an ever-absent father, weighed down by a discontented mother incapable of showing him any love. His death at twenty-four was shrouded in secrecy, alternatively attributed to tuberculosis, or a brain tumour. In fact, he had shot and seriously wounded himself, ironically during his parents' anniversary festivities. The furious duchess insisted on moving him away, despite the doctors' insistence that he was too weak to travel. He was sent to Meran, in the Italian Alps, to convalesce, but died on 6 February 1899, attended only by Dr Bemkart and his servant.

Bee undoubtedly suffered most from her brother's death, from an illness she never understood; all she knew was that her father held his wife partly responsible. Both parents were stunned by his death. Dr Bemkart later said angrily he had told them that if they moved their son, he would not last a week. Yet they still sent him away, noted Marie Mallet, maid of honour to Queen Victoria, and were wracked with guilt 'because he had died almost alone [from] paralysis of the larynx, caused by the state of the brain, which was a result of the terrible dissolute life, which he had led in Berlin since the age of sixteen'. The duke of Coburg, a lifelong heavy drinker, was already stricken with throat cancer. With less than eighteen months to live, from then on he had very little contact with his family.

Young Alfred's funeral took place on 10 February 1899. Missy was astonished to see her mother crying in front of the coffin when it arrived for internment, the normally undemonstrative duchess sinking to her knees during the muffled tones of a funeral march, crossing herself many times. Some commented what a shame the youngest princess had not been born a boy, now that the succession of the dukedom had opened up dramatically. Once the duke had recovered a little, he left for Nice, arriving on 15 March. Queen Victoria found him 'terribly cut up about his son's death'. Marie Mallet suspected her elderly mistress was 'rather overwhelmed by her family and the Coburg succession problems', and hoped that for her sake a decision would soon be reached. The duke and duchess of Connaught were next in the succession, but desperately wanted to renounce it altogether in favour of their nephew, Charles, the young duke of Albany. In return for a handsome sum of money and a good position at his uncle's death, he would have to become a German, enter the German army, 'and give up his happy healthy English life'.

Bee went to London that year with her mother and her niece, Elisabeth, and they stayed at Clarence House. Queen Victoria, who was eighty in May 1899, had a special preference for this great-grandchild, perhaps knowing that her parents' marriage, which she had arranged, was so unhappy. The four-year-old girl appreciated her love in a special way and showed great confidence in the little old lady, wrapped in shawls, seated in her armchair, who could provoke terror in her older children and grandchildren.

From an early age, Princess Bee adored sports, especially riding and swimming. In a letter of 1960 to Arnold Lunn, she noted:

> These are things that happened many years ago, as I am a very old woman. At the beginning of the nineties I received a Christmas present of three or four pairs of wooden objects called skis, from my Russian cousins. I was much surprised by the fact that, although they looked like ordinary skis, they had a kind of fixed leather slipper into which one put one's foot, and also had leather pads fixed to the bottom faces which allowed one to go up the mountains and to slide down, because of the way in which the fur was fixed. My friends and I began to practice this noble sport at Coburg—to the surprise and delight of the local populace. Actually it horrified the young sportsmen to know that we wore long skirts and red flannel underskirts, which undoubtedly contributed greatly to our falling. I should add that each pair of skis had a perfect pair of sticks.

She also liked cycling, which gave her independence, had her first bicycle as a gift at the age of sixteen in the spring of 1900, and rode around the town to see it from a distance. It was a difficult time for her; she missed her married sisters, and the lonely death of her brother while Coburg was celebrating angered her so much that she could barely face her mother. The duchess was overwhelmed by what had happened and seriously preoccupied by the illness of her husband, who did not wish to see her. She suffered her youngest daughter's rebellion in silence, receiving news only from her older children.

On hearing that her husband had smallpox, Ducky left immediately for Darmstadt, where she was inoculated. She was not allowed to see Ernest until the end of June, when he recovered and she could telegraph the queen on 27 June that they were 'so happy to be able to be together again'. From all appearances, they seemed united once more.

Meanwhile, a bored Missy was having an affair with a young army officer, Zizi Cantacuzino, and the child she conceived at this time was probably his. She had just been obliged to employ a highly recommended governess for Carol, her elder son, with whom she did not get on at all. There was clearly a clash of personalities, and Missy accused the governess of spying on her when she was merely doing her duty. King Carol solved the problem by exiling Zizi and sending his nephew's errant wife out of the country indefinitely. Missy later admitted that she had been careless about how her actions might appear to others, saying it never struck her that her high spirits and behaviour could be misinterpreted. The duchess of Coburg had planned to spend the summer at Peterhof, taking Bee with her. However, she was so angered by the attitude of the king of Romania towards her daughter, pregnant for the third time, and perhaps feeling remorse for having married her off so young, that instead she arranged to await her at Gotha and then they would return together.

Missy was overjoyed to return to Germany, reunited with her mother and some of her sisters. She and Bee went to see performances of Wagner in the *Prinzregententheater*. Both were great lovers of his music, and the atmosphere of that theatre had a special quality, almost like going to church. They liked to sit in the front row near the stage if possible, so they could see the singers. Her youngest sister made 'a perfect and enchanting companion, very witty and full of fun'. It was a magnificent time for them together, 'our good humour causing us to laugh at the most trivial things.' Already a lifelong music lover and an authority on Wagner's music, after her marriage to Prince Alfonso of Orleans and Borbón Bee became a fervent Bayreuth-goer: 'there was not a single note of music nor a single word of the libretto that she did not know by heart'.

After their brother Alfred's death, Bee dedicated herself to her father whom she idealised. Although he had in general been distancing himself from his family, he became calm in his daughter's company. The four sisters spent Christmas 1899 together, and on 6 January 1900, Missy had a second daughter in the Friedenstein Palace, Gotha, where the duchess was living. Named Marie after her mother and grandmother, but known as 'Mignon', she would later become queen of Yugoslavia.

Duke Alfred was living at Rosenau, near Coburg, where his father, Prince Albert, had been born and where he wished to die. By May 1900, he could only be fed through a tube, news the doctors kept a secret even from his wife. On 30 July, he died suddenly in his sleep. At Osborne, the queen received the news in tears early next morning. She asked that a simple service should be held in the chapel, while in Coburg a magnificent funeral on 4 August was presided over by the German emperor and attended by most of the imperial princes.

As previously agreed, the young duke of Albany succeeded to the duchy of Coburg-Gotha. Charles Edward was the son of the first duke, Leopold, Queen Victoria's haemophiliac youngest son. He was only fifteen years old and Sandra's husband, the prince of Hohenlohe-Langenburg, became regent.

At forty-six, Maria Alexandrovna had to decide where to live for the rest of her life and the consequences that this would have for Bee's future.

Clarence House, which had been decorated to her taste, was available to her, but living in London did not appeal. She preferred to remain in Coburg, close to Rosenau Castle which she and Bee loved, but they had to leave the ducal palaces which now belonged to the young duke. She therefore acquired the estate of Tegernsee, in Bavaria. The young duke and his mother, Princess Helen, preferred to live in Berlin during the five-year regency of Prince Ernst.

Later that year, Grand Duchess Maria, accompanied by Bee, visited the various German courts to thank them personally for their condolences on her husband's death. They began with Kaiser Wilhelm II, who was delighted by their plans to stay at Coburg, rather than return to England. Then they left for Kronberg, near Frankfurt, home of his mother, Empress Frederick, Queen Victoria's eldest daughter. Passionately English, she could not understand how her sister-in-law, having the opportunity to live in London, preferred to remain in Coburg now she was no longer reigning duchess. Although the duchess was normally undemonstrative, the empress remarked, she made no secret of how much she had suffered. The elder woman commented approvingly that Bee had become 'a surprising and delightful young lady with a beautiful figure and a highly spirited demeanour'.

As usual, Queen Victoria spent the autumn of 1900 at Balmoral. She had suddenly aged, and Marie Mallet was shocked to see how thin and weary she looked. On arriving at Windsor *en route* to the Isle of Wight where she usually celebrated Christmas, she learned that Duchess Marie was in London with her daughter, Beatrice, and her granddaughter, Elisabeth of Hesse. They were packing up their home at Clarence House to move their possessions to Coburg. Feeling that she had not always been fair to the family of her late second son, she called his widow to her side. Marie and Bee came at once, arriving at Osborne on 15 January 1901, little suspecting that the final days were approaching. During her daily carriage drive through the gardens, the queen asked Marie to accompany her.

Surrounded by most of her family, Victoria passed away early in the evening on 22 January 1901. In accordance with custom, all her descendants, including the youngest, filed past during her lying in state. The three Battenberg boys entered, followed by Bee and Ena who held the hand of little Elisabeth of Hesse; her aunt wanted to bring her to pay her respects to her dead great-grandmother. On seeing her, the disappointed four-year-old exclaimed, 'She does not have any wings!'

4

In Search of a Kindred Spirit

At the end of the Victorian era, there were few royal houses not linked with the Queen Empress, and only two European republics, France and Switzerland.

For the widowed Princess Beatrice of Battenberg and her children, the death of her mother was a devastating blow. The queen had bequeathed her Osborne Cottage on the Isle of Wight, she also received a small income, and the right to live with her children in a wing of Kensington Palace, London. Yet it was a sudden change for them, according to the eldest, Alexander ('Drino') of Battenberg. Some fifteen years later (27 September 1916), he wrote to his brother-in-law, King Alfonso XIII:

> I think that you know that I do not feel the same blind admiration for Bee as Leo does. Ena has been her best friend since her youth and Bee was, indisputably, excessively kind and loving towards her, especially in those first difficult years when we left our home on the death of our grandmother.

Keen to paint landscapes and memories recording her travels, Bee bought a red leatherbound album, in which she recorded the most important events of those years. On the first page, she drew Maurice and herself bathing, mischievously annotated: 'Ena (waits) on the three steps leading down to the lake, dressed in her swimming costume, and does not seem to enjoy it'. With her mother's support, Bee decided to cheer up the little Battenberg children with excursions to the mountains, lakes, and attending local fiestas and dances, which Ena loved. She enjoyed a summer of freedom with her English cousins that was unforgettable as it would be the last under a peaceful sky, far from the court intrigues that would darken her youth.

The widowed duchess of Saxe-Coburg, who had long wanted a painting of her daughters, commissioned one from the Hanoverian artist Friedrich August von Kaulbach. He portrayed them in a garden: Ducky, wearing a dark dress, holding flowers; Sandra seated in the background; Missy, in white, seated in the centre, turning to greet Bee, dressed in tulle, also with a bouquet. Much praised at the time, the painting now hangs in Löwenstein Castle, Amorbach, the property of Sandra's descendants. In 2005, when Mila Ageo restored Kaulbach's pastel sketch of Bee for the portrait, she found an envelope attached with a note written by the princess and inside a negative showing the painter with the almost completed sketch. Bee took the photograph herself, intending that it should accompany the picture. After being stored in the stables for many years, the portrait was covered with mould. When Ali died, Duchess Carla took charge of the Botánico, removed the picture from the stables and gave it pride of place in the palace sitting room.

Among all the queen empress's granddaughters, the one perhaps most relieved by her death was the grand duchess of Hesse and the Rhine, whose marriage was beyond salvation. On 25 May 1900, she had given birth to a stillborn son. In the autumn, she went to Balmoral to convince her grandmother of the necessity of a divorce from Ernie. She had already discussed with Sir George Buchanan, the British *chargé d'affaires* at Darmstadt, how to explain everything to the queen. During the audience, the latter listened, then admitted sadly that she had arranged the marriage as she wanted it, but from now on would no longer attempt to arrange any more. She suggested that, as they were still young, they should continue living together.

In October 1901, Ducky returned to Coburg, insisting on divorce. Although the family knew, the duchess was surprised, but still received her daughter. Ernie agreed, writing with relief to his eldest sister, Victoria of Battenberg, that the last five years had been 'a living hell' and it was impossible for them to remain together, 'as it is killing Ducky and driving me almost crazy.' Victoria fully understood, knowing them both to be complete opposites. Meanwhile, Nicholas II, whose wife, Alix, disliked her Edinburgh cousins, wrote in astonishment to his mother to tell her of 'a terrible and unexpected event'. Although rarely in agreement, Edward VII and Wilhelm II were united in condemning Ducky for her actions. She was denounced at both courts for criticising her husband, who had stated that he would prefer the company of grooms and stable boys, and whose conversation was more intellectual than that of those surrounding his wife.

On 21 December, the duchy's supreme court dissolved the marriage. The couple's daughter, Elizabeth, now aged six, would spend six months of the year with her father at the court at Darmstadt and the other six months with her mother at Coburg. She completely took the side of her father, who had always adored her.

In the autumn of 1903, Ernie and his daughter were invited by the tsar to Skierniewice, his hunting estate in Poland. Elizabeth was the same age as Olga, the eldest of the tsar's four daughters. They walked together through the woods every morning looking for mushrooms, and in the afternoons played hide-and-seek in the palace. One morning, Elisabeth awoke with respiratory problems. A telegram was sent immediately to Ducky, who was in Coburg, informing her of her daughter's illness. It was followed by another explaining the symptoms, and just over an hour later, a third announcing her death came just as Ducky and Bee were about to board the train. It was rumoured that she had eaten poisoned food destined for the tsar, although an autopsy confirmed that she died of typhus. Prince von Bülow commented on the grand duchess's attitude when she returned to Darmstadt to bury her child, observing that she had formerly been so popular in Hesse, but now wanted to cut all ties with her past. Although received with all honours as she arrived for the funeral, at the end of the ceremony she put her Order of Hesse into the coffin, as if intending to forget for ever the place that had been her home.

This affair had some bearing on the destiny and marriage of Beatrice of Coburg. In the hypocritical and puritanical society of the Victorian age, the rebellious attitude of her two elder, beautiful, and attractive sisters had several detractors. In Russia, Tsarina Alexandra did not forgive her cousin and former sister-in-law for making her brother look ridiculous. Ducky was too honest to try and conceal that she had been in love with her cousin, Kirill, for some time. It is difficult to say when the idyll between them began as, being first cousins, they had always known each other. Grand Duke Kirill of Russia, the eldest son of Marie's brother, Vladimir, was tall, dark, and arrogant-looking, an officer in the Imperial Russian Navy. Highly respected by Russian society, according to Missy 'he was made of marble'; he reportedly 'froze people and treated them with disdain'. Even before Ducky's wedding, they were fond of each other. He told of meetings with her in his memoirs, and during the tsar's coronation festivities, he had commented enthusiastically on the prettiness of his three Edinburgh cousins, Missy, Ducky, and Bee.

After being invited by the duchess of Edinburgh to Clarence House, where the grand duke and duchess of Hesse were also staying, he attended the jubilee celebrations in London. Returning to Russia on leave, his brother, Boris, encouraged him to come to Darmstadt, where he was invited by Ducky. Over the next few months, at family gatherings, there were ample opportunities for both to meet. Their friendship gradually turned to affection, and after that they tried to see each other as often as possible.

Kirill's sister, Elena, persuaded Ducky to go to Paris with them, and they enjoyed themselves greatly 'with all the joy and liberty of youth'. On a subsequent visit to Wolfsgarten, Kirill noticed 'the way in which [she] kept the castle and the land so admirably', and called her 'the most consummate, intrepid and elegant horsewoman' he had ever known. Later, on one of his naval journeys, he visited her, her mother, and Bee at Chateau Fabron, near Nice. They came on board his ship for tea with the officers, and he showed them around the ship. Back at the Chateau Fabron, the duchess decided that Ducky and he should dine alone together, as it was his last night there: 'she was an exile and I had an uncertain future'.

In London, the coronation of Edward VII and Alexandra was scheduled for 26 June, with the duchess of Coburg and Bee among those invited, while newly-divorced Ducky was excluded. Because of the deaths of Bee's brother and father casting a shadow over the last years of her childhood, she had not yet 'come out', but was presented to society during the 'season' of 1902. Manolo Escadon, marquis of Villavieja, later recalled that during a ball at Buckingham Palace he met the marquis of Soveral, as they were admiring a group of young ladies chatting at the end of the ballroom. The marquis, the Portuguese ambassador at London, told him they were a group of English princesses, and as he knew the different members of the royal family very well, he offered to present them to him. 'As you are a very fine dancer,' he said, 'I am sure that they will be delighted to dance with you. Which is the one you like the most?' He replied that he would prefer 'the very distinguished looking one with the small head'. This was Bee, who danced with him a few minutes later. She was only eighteen and her manners greatly impressed him, even though they talked little as her reserve intimidated him, and he thought there was 'something very remote about her'. When their dance finished, he accompanied her to the group with her cousins. As he left that night, he never imagined that the day would come when she would be one of his most faithful friends, and that in her house at Kew he would later write most of his memoirs.

Two days before the coronation was due, it was announced that the king had appendicitis and the ceremony was postponed. After a successful operation, it was rescheduled for 9 August. The crown princess of Romania remained in England, and Bee enjoyed going around London with her, visiting the home of their friends, the Astors, where she was staying. The duchess of Coburg was anxious to leave London for Russia and travelled a few days later. Bee wanted to spend the summer in St Petersburg where, in mid-August, she met all the family at the wedding of Elena Vladmirovna, then aged twenty, to Prince Nicholas of Greece, ten years older.

Beatrice seemed to have fallen for her cousin, Michael, or Misha, though when is uncertain. It may have been when she was twelve, during his stay in Nice, before the coronation celebrations in Russia, or perhaps during the coronation festivities. From then on, she watched him carefully.

Grand Duke Michael Alexandrovich was born on 4 December 1878 at Anichkov Palace, the youngest son of Tsar Alexander III. The illness and death of his father was a heavy blow as he was only a timid youth of sixteen. When he was twenty, in December 1898, a solemn *Te Deum* was celebrated. Eight months later, his elder brother, George, heir to the throne, died suddenly, and Michael now took his place.

In the autumn of 1900, when the tsarina was again *enceinte*, Nicholas II became ill with typhus, and his life was briefly feared for. Some politicians thought Grand Duke Michael should be appointed regent. The tsarina maintained that if the tsar died, they should wait on his posthumous child and she should be regent, but the tsar recovered, and on 18 June 1901, she had a fourth daughter, named Anastasia. Misha remained heir, although as brother (not son) of the sovereign, he did not hold the title of tsarevich. Physically he was over 6 feet tall, with dark blue eyes and a kindly personality. He preferred living in the country to the city, was fond of children, horses, and dogs, and hated pomp and ceremony, spoke good English and French, played piano, flute, guitar, balalaika, and loved theatre, opera, and ballet.

He and Bee had much in common, both having suffered the deaths of their respective parents at only sixteen years old, and lost their beloved brothers. The latter left his fortune to Misha, making him one of the richest men in the world. Beatrice was eighteen, Misha twenty-four, and it was undoubtedly the first love for both. They had very dominant mothers whom they had to obey like good children, and their siblings were all married.

Bee was independent, although when small she missed her sisters who, apart from Sandra, lived far from Coburg. She liked being alone as she could sing, paint, and play the piano, but deep down, she was a romantic youngster seeking a soul mate. Additionally, both Misha and she were 'intendeds' to the same family, that of the great matchmaker, Grand Duchess Anastasia of Mecklenburg-Schwerin. Her elder daughter, Alexandrine, married the future Christian X of Denmark at Cannes in April 1898, and she wanted her younger daughter Cecilie to marry Grand Duke Michael. The grand duchess wanted Bee to marry her son, Frederick Francis IV, who succeeded his father in 1897, under his mother's regency. On his majority in April 1901, he assumed the reins of government. Bee could not stand them, and in his letters, Misha asked jokingly, 'What is happening with our fiancés?'

Misha was the man with whom Bee would fall madly in love. The hundreds of letters he wrote to her revealed how the relationship between the cousins began. He reminded her that they had met previously on different occasions, and paid her no attention, never imagining she would become so special to him. He remembered seeing her in the year of Queen Victoria's death, though not her being at Windsor, and he went to visit her mother in London but she was not at home. They saw each other again during the 1902 coronation festivities and talked, when he found her 'pretty but nothing more'. Their various meetings over the previous few years, activities and games played together, from riding and billiards to pouring over family albums and rides in the car, were all faithfully detailed. Misha was very self-effacing, insisting that he knew she was much more clever than him, 'though I am not so stupid as not to take account of it. I remember that I once asked you, while out riding, if you had ever thought of marrying and you said that you had never thought of it and were not interested at all.'

Perhaps she felt no inclination for matrimony after her sisters' unhappy marriages, but on the eve of the wedding of her cousin, Elena, and Prince Nicholas, she changed her mind. The ceremony was to take place on 29 August 1902 at Tsarskoye Selo, with many guests from throughout Europe, in particular the bridegroom's family, led by his father, King George, and his wife, Queen Olga, a Russian grand duchess by birth.

At the wedding, Beatrice, seated next to Olga and Misha, was deeply moved by the Russian singing. Four days earlier, Misha had called her 'Sima', as it was a Russian name and he liked it more than Bee, which meant 'honey bee' in English. Three days after the wedding, there was a ballet performance at which the ballerina Maria Kschessinska made her reappearance after a long absence. Two months earlier, she had given birth to a son, supposedly by Grand Duke Andrei, and named him Vladimir after his paternal grandfather. It was rumoured that she had retired on reaching the age of thirty, but that night the public was still enthralled by her performances. Beatrice was delighted to meet her, and long after the revolution, she would visit her at her studio in Paris. She was accompanied by her sister, Ducky, by then married to the youngest of 'the Vladimirs'.

The ice was broken and time passed quickly, with the horse riding, meals, and dinners breaking their moments of privacy together. Misha went to Poland on a hunting expedition with his brother, and to Denmark to see his grandparents as he did every year, but the regular correspondence with Bee continued. Accounts of his activities were interspersed with his memories of how their romance had developed, his sadness at their being so far apart, and his eagerness for them to be reunited as soon as possible.

5

Sima

Christmas was a sad time at Coburg for Beatrice, still deeply missing her father and brother. Her mother and two of her sisters were there for the festivities: Ducky, 'the one with the bad marriage' (they had to avoid the word 'divorced'), and Sandra with Ernie. Bee lived for Misha's letters and dreamed of seeing him again. Uncle Sergei and Aunt Ella were also in Coburg to consult the duchess about the plight of Grand Duke Paul, who had left his children to marry his lover and live in Paris. Maria and Dmitri had been left with Ella and Sergei and felt utterly lost.

Beatrice had planned to learn Russian. Misha was delighted, and looked forward to speaking to her in his language when they next saw each other. Before leaving Copenhagen, he bought her a porcelain cat and for Christmas he sent her a mantel clock so she could 'count the happy hours'.

Ducky was as preoccupied as Bee in choosing presents for the 'engaged cousins'. The first she sent was a Swiss clock to Kirill in Singapore, where he was sailing with the Eastern Fleet, while Bee sent Misha a porcelain inkwell.

He continued writing to his beloved 'Sima', saying that 'nothing will change'. She did not believe it, as she had had a premonition in October, telling him that in a dream he told her he would 'only love her for a year'. Astonished, he replied that his feelings for her would never alter. She was more brave than him, he told her, and though six years younger than him, she was much more self-confident. His 'greatest desire' was that she should be happy and he would be with her as much as possible: 'When you live in Russia, you will never be unhappy here'.

At the beginning of 1903, the duchess of Coburg, anxious about Ducky's situation, wrote to the dowager tsarina, asking her to bring influence to bear on the tsar and permit Kirill's 'secret marriage' with her divorced daughter. The young lovers were pining for each other, but neither Beatrice nor her mother was invited to Russia, and they missed being in St Petersburg during the bicentenary celebrations in May.

At the start of the relationship, Bee had declared that the sorrow of their being separated was nothing compared to the sensation of pleasure they had because they loved each other. Yet though she assured him that his letters made her 'cry with happiness', she was becoming impatient, convinced that Misha was so afraid of his mother that he did not dare tell her how much he wished to see his cousin. In each letter, he merely renewed the memories of what they had done the previous year. On 9 April, Misha managed to discuss his feelings about her with the tsar, who asked him if he was writing to her, and if so how often. When told that Misha wrote around twice a week, he said he feared it had gone too far and that nothing good could come of it. What he really wanted to say, Misha thought, was that he suspected such a marriage could mean great unhappiness for her in the future.

Weary of waiting, Beatrice tackled her mother to ask her plans for the summer. They had been at the Château Fabron in Nice since 15 March. Missy was expecting her fourth child that summer, and Prince Nicholas of Romania was born at Peleş Castle on 18 August 1903. Grand Duke Paul told his sister that he would visit her in September, having his children sent to him there from Moscow.

Bee then allowed Misha to ask his mother if she planned to invite them, and assured him her heart would break if they did not see each other that summer. He told her that the thought of not doing so was too terrible to contemplate. The following day, he reflected on what stopped them from seeing each other. Was it the fear of others 'that we might get to like each other even more?' On 3 June, he wrote to her that if she would let him talk to his mother about her coming to Russia with her mother, he would do so if he could.

Bee sent him a telegram, which he answered on 8 June, saying that when they gave it to him he quickly hid it, afraid his mother would ask who it was from: 'It is very stupid to be afraid; but I suppose that you will understand me when we speak. It feels like an electric shock that passes through my heart and body'. On 17 July, he wrote again that Anastasia had arrived at Peterhof 'with your fiancé and my fiancée. I have no wish to see them.' A few days later, he explained that he had been to Peterhof to visit them, found it 'very boring—knowing all the time what Anastasia was thinking'. He was adamant that he did not want her for a mother-in-law 'for all the world', insisting he would never marry her daughter, Cecilie.

Around this time, Kirill obtained an audience with his cousin, the tsar, who gave him permission—without which no member of the imperial family could leave Russia—to visit Coburg, thus giving him only vague hopes. Kirill, who knew Bee well, became the postal service between his two cousins. On 15 June, Misha telegraphed Bee asking her if she wanted to receive letters in this way, and she said yes. The correspondence continued. On 23 July, Kirill had returned from Coburg. Bee had sent Misha one of her pictures, a landscape of the forest showing a tree with their entwined initials. He was enchanted with 'the painting of the forest and with our MB 1902 on the tree and how well drawn it is!' According to Kirill, who went back to visit Ducky, Bee was more tranquil and less impatient. Misha envied Kirill, being able to see Ducky so much, as Nicholas was too timid to prevent him. Appalled, the dowager tsarina told Misha that she thought it folly to let Kirill and Ducky still meet each other.

Military manoeuvres took place in August, and Misha, who cared deeply for his military vocation, was busy with preparations. On seeing him on parade during a review the previous year, Bee had impulsively thrown him her glove. Nevertheless, now she could stand no more and approached the duchess of Coburg, by now very preoccupied with her new house at Tegernsee. Her beloved brother Paul had come alone to meet Grand Duke Sergei and his wife Ella, who brought the children. Marie, who was twelve at the time, found it 'a delightful place'. She also saw another side of the widowed duchess, who 'despite her intimidating brusque manners towards those around her, was a very happy person, rather ironical and gifted with a certain sense of humour. She did not hide her opinions and said what she thought, a rare thing among us.' The young grand duchess also noted that while her aunt's siblings 'laughed at her great airs, they held her in great respect'.

Meanwhile, the correspondence between Bee and Misha drifted towards an increasingly inevitable conclusion. At the beginning of October, she was alone at Tegernsee, as her mother had gone to Munich to say goodbye to her guests. A very long letter from him arrived, much of it about his visit to Denmark and activities with the rest of the family. Only after this did he tell her that he was sure mama did not want them to meet. If she and the family 'could understand that we are, after all, reasonable, and that we both understand that what we wish will never happen, because it will never be allowed, and that we only want to meet occasionally.... Life is so complicated.' At length, he admitted that 'they do not want me to care for you; but they want me to marry and naturally they do not wish that I occupy myself too much with you.'

At last, she had the information she had bitterly dreaded but probably long expected. Although she did not break off the correspondence on her side, she was heartbroken, took it very badly, and the stress made her physically unwell. Incredibly, nobody in Coburg remarked on Beatrice's illness after they broke up, even though the Russians did. On 3 January 1904, her cousin, Grand Duchess Xenia, mentioned in her diary receiving 'a terrible letter from Ducky about Misha and Beatrice in which she shows that he acted in an ugly and dishonest way towards her.' She fervently believed that after Misha's letter from Denmark, in which he said that he could not marry her, it would have been better if they had stopped writing these letters about their feelings for each other altogether. 'Lord preserve us from the uproar which he has caused on his side!' As a result, a 'very ill' Beatrice had been sent to Egypt 'where she cries and grows thin'. Ducky, she said, insisted 'that her sister never dreamt of being able to marry him' (which turns out not to be true) and that she never imagined such a thing, for which reason Misha's letter offended her so much: 'They say that it is saddening to see her: she has grown thin and is ill. Poor little thing! It seems that Aunt Maria is terribly angry with Mama over it and only God knows what has happened. One thing is clear: that they had set their sights on matrimony'.

Later that month, on 27 January 1904, Xenia recorded their arrival at Nice and going straight from the station to the duchess's house for lunch. She was living in Fabron with Ducky, and after eating, they went to the gardens among the orange trees, where the duchess brought up the matter of Misha and Bee. Afterwards, Xenia noted that all she could report was that Misha could not marry her 'because Nicky roundly stated so and that Misha has given in and now believes it to be impossible'. Then the duchess left her with Ducky and went to see Sandro (Xenia's husband) who explained Misha's actions very clearly: 'He returned with the impression that she (the Duchess) had expected, and desired, that the marriage should go ahead. Ducky said that she found Bee in such a frightening state that she feared for her and it seemed to her that she was losing her mind'. They found the dowager tsarina's attitude very offensive, with Ducky telling her that 'she could stand it no more' and wrote Xenia a letter, hoping she could help to ease matters.

Grand Duchess Maria did not consider the relationship broken, and was confident it could be resolved. Bee spent several weeks in Coburg severely depressed, tearful, plagued by insomnia, and a poor appetite. Aware that forcing her into company would change her frame of mind, her mother sent her to stay with her Battenberg cousins at Osborne, where they were delighted to see her. Meanwhile, the widowed Beatrice of Battenberg had received an invitation from the khedive (viceroy) to go to Egypt and spend the winter there with her children.

Princess Beatrice advised her sister-in-law that a change of air might cheer Bee up. Marie of Coburg agreed, and offered to contribute towards travelling expenses. Leopold, a haemophiliac and the most cultured of the Battenberg brothers, and Ena would be there too. They thought the expedition would be very informal, but soon realised that the khedive insisted on treating the daughter and granddaughters of Queen Victoria as illustrious visitors. While the trip was being arranged, Bee returned to Coburg and told Misha about her sadness. He thanked her for her congratulations on his birthday, adding that he believed they should be happy, he hated himself for having caused her such sadness, and he was sure that some day he would 'be punished for it'.

On arriving in London, Bee immediately wrote to Misha of their embarkation on the steamer *Moldavia* from Tilbury Docks in December 1903, passing through terrible storms in the Bay of Biscay before reaching Marseilles and later the North African coast. Fortunately, unlike her aunt and cousins, she was not seasick. Having brought an album to record her impressions, in this and in her letter, she drew a vivid portrait in words of the great demonstrations of friendliness that greeted them from the moment of their arrival at Alexandria. There were flags, musicians, and Arabs with their red tarbushes bowing formally, and the splendours of the Gezirah Palace Hotel in Cairo, where they were guests of the khedive. They said that the distinguished lady missed oranges and on hearing this, the khedive ordered the planting of a field of trees, and next morning she awoke to the smell of orange blossom. The young princesses marvelled at the hotel, visited the pyramids, rode on dromedary camels, toured the mosques, and were fascinated by the mummies in the museums. Each evening, they went to the opera or the theatre, and sometimes after dinner they danced with English officers.

After returning to London for the 'Season', Bee attended several parties, and Ena's 'coming out' ball at Kensington Palace, where they danced so much that her cousin admitted that she 'did not want to marry as she loved dancing'. Bee was present at the Russian Red Cross where a group of elderly ladies invited her to chair the meeting, she made a donation on behalf of her mother, and learned how ill-prepared they were for the conflict in the Far East, with a demoralised army that could not support its troops. Accompanied by the Battenbergs, she returned to Coburg where they stayed in Tegernsee. Faced with increasingly grave news about the campaign, Bee swallowed her bitterness and contacted Misha, who hated war, and busied herself looking after young Leopold of Battenberg who had suffered a painful fall. In October, he left for the Isle of Wight, filled with gratitude and a love for Bee that would stay with him until the day of his death.

Meanwhile, the correspondence between Bee and Misha continued. In a letter of 7 September, he thanked her for her congratulations on the birth of Alexei, heir to the throne, at Peterhof on 12 August. He admitted it was a relief not to be heir himself any more, and was not pleased that she had started smoking since her visit to Russia, saying he would prefer her to desist. Either because of her nervous condition which called for it or because she liked it, she ended up becoming a real chimney.

Alexandrine, widow of Ernst II of Coburg, died on 20 December 1904. Her nephew, Prince Gustaf Adolf, second in line to the Swedish throne, attended the funeral at Coburg. Beatrice had adored Alexandrine, who had inspired her love of gardening and passion for painting flowers and left her a generous sum in her will. But the prince's visit, which so thrilled Maria of Coburg, did not interest her daughter, and the Swedish prince married Daisy, the duke of Connaught's eldest daughter Margaret, in June.

In July 1905, at the age of twenty-one, Charles Edward became the reigning duke of Coburg, thus ending the regency of her brother-in-law Ernst. Charles Edward planned to marry in October. The duchess went to Nice for the winter, to be among the Russian diaspora there. At the Château Fabron, they awaited news of the war with Japan that, unknown to them, was proving a disaster. The harvest had been poor, and hunger bred increasing discontent among the people.

In January 1905, Father Gapon, a young radical Orthodox priest, had organised a workers' procession to present a written petition to the tsar at the Winter Palace, demanding better working conditions, fairer wages, a reduction in the working day, an end to the disastrous Russo-Japanese War and the introduction of universal suffrage. A peaceful march at which they sang 'God Save the Tsar', carrying flags, icons, and imperial portraits, attracted a huge crowd of people hoping their 'Little Father' would receive them at the palace. Nobody warned them that the tsar was at Tsarskoye Selo, or that armed soldiers were waiting to fire at them as they drew near. Men, women, and children fell on the snow, which soon became a carpet of red. Unaware of events, the tsar did not know how to react, nor did his government. The people were utterly disillusioned, a mood the revolutionaries eagerly exploited in what was remembered as 'Bloody Sunday'.

The news arriving in Nice steadily worsened. At the beginning of February, half a million workers were on strike. Nicholas II replaced Prince Sviatopolk-Mirskii as minister of the interior with Alexander Bulygin and his increasingly inflexible uncle, Grand Duke Sergei, with the more liberal Gen. Trepov, as governor of Moscow. A few days later, the duchess of Coburg received a telegram from Moscow, signed by her sister-in-law, Ella, to say that Sergei had been assassinated. She immediately decided to go to Moscow to be with the widow and whole family. Deciding Ducky should not attend as the grand duke of Hesse, her former husband, would go to his sister's side, she thought Bee should accompany her, never suspecting the difficulties and sorrows her choice would bring.

Leaving immediately on the Paris train, they met Grand Duke Paul, who lived in Boulogne-sur-Seine. He told them he had telegraphed the emperor for permission to attend his brother's funeral. Assuming all the family would gather in Moscow to keep the unfortunate widow company, Maria of Coburg decided to send a telegram announcing she was on her way. As she had been married for so many years to a foreign prince, she was not considered a subject of the emperor. After two days and three nights on the train, they arrived at the Moscow station to find none of the family were waiting for them. They said that even the authorities considered Bee *persona non grata*, and the widowed Ella had to seek permission from Governor Trepov for her niece to enter. It was conjecture, but Misha's last letter said that if he had foreseen so many difficulties, he would certainly have consulted his mother to ask that no difficulty would be put in her way. If she needed to come to Russia again, she would have to tell him beforehand and everything would be arranged.

They found the city half shut, but although travel-weary, they made straight for the Kremlin to embrace the poor widow. Ernest Louis had also arrived with his new wife. Under the circumstances all was forgotten, and he was very circumspect with his ex-mother-in-law and young sister-in-law. Grand Duke Constantine Constantinovich, cousin of Sergei and grandson of Nicholas I, organised everything. An intelligent, very cultured person, he tried to solve the difficulties that the horrible event had provoked. As soon as they arrived, they had to go to one of the Kremlin chapels, where Serge's coffin rested on a black covered dias.

Maria Pavlovna the younger wrote that she and her brother, Dmitri, received Bee and her mother with genuine satisfaction. Soon afterwards, Grand Duke Paul announced his arrival, and his children met him at the station.

The duchess of Coburg was told the funeral would be on 23 February. Grand Duke Constantine advised that neither the tsarina, who was ill, nor the tsar, fearing strikes and disorder in Moscow, should attend. Bee waited, confident that Misha would represent the emperor, but as days passed nothing was said. She received a very affectionate letter from him, redirected from Nice, dated 12 February, six days before the murder. In view of the situation in which they found themselves—less than a night by train from St Petersburg to Moscow—she wrote asking him to return all the letters she had written to him. Neither Misha, his mother, nor his sisters, nor the Vladimir family attended the burial but stayed in their Tsarskoye Selo palaces, saying at the last minute that it was impossible to attend. Nevertheless the church was packed, with wreaths of flowers piled around the catafalque guarded by the sentries. During the long and solemn service, Maria Pavlovna Jnr was sick and her father had to take her outside. At the end of the funeral, the coffin was carried to one of the monastery's small churches, where prayers were recited for forty days and nights.

Four days later, Misha broke his silence with a letter (25 February 1905) from Gatchina, addressed to Princess Beatrice of Coburg, the Kremlin, Moscow:

> I have not written before because I did not know and continue not knowing how to write you. Besides, I have not done what you asked me (about the letters). Why do I have to return all your letters? I heard nothing of your coming to Russia. Do you believe me?
>
> Sima, I am now going to say goodbye. My heart feels so heavy and I do not know what to say.
>
> Perhaps you could write me two words and explain to me something more because I do not understand this sudden change.

Those days within the Kremlin walls, unable to go out, were the saddest days of Bee's life, waiting for someone who should have come but did not arrive. Meanwhile, in Russia, the first sparks of revolution rumbled. Sima's hopes disappeared, while the figure of Beatrice, the strong and responsible woman, arose.

6

A May Wedding

Returning from Russia, the duchess of Coburg and Bee went to spend Easter in Nice. Château Fabron was again filled with guests, including Grand Duke Kirill, convalescing from the sinking of his ship, the *Petropavlosk*. On 8 February 1904, the Japanese had attacked the Russian fleet and the latter, proud of their navy and superior numbers, declared war. The flagship sailed towards base at Port Arthur when, on 13 April, it struck a Japanese mine and sank with the loss of the admiral and over 700 officers and men. Grand Duke Kirill was one of the eighty survivors. The water was freezing, and he was wearing a padded coat with a fur-lined jacket and an English woollen sweater underneath as he swam to a nearby whaler.

Beatrice was delighted that her sister was so happy, saying he had been saved by a miracle. Kirill had arrived on the Trans-Siberian Railway at St Petersburg where he was acclaimed as a national hero. A few days later, he had an interview with the tsar, who annoyed him by asking nothing about the *Petropavlovsk* disaster, the admiral, the war, or of any progress being made—only about his health and the weather. He then went for a holiday at Rosenau where he and Ducky planned their future. On returning to Russia, his health deteriorated, and he left for Munich for treatment, returning to Coburg whenever he could. The cousins were very much in love, and both approaching the age of thirty, knew they ought to marry; however, it was difficult to find an Orthodox priest to do so as the emperor had given orders forbidding the marriage of first cousins.

When Beatrice returned to Nice, she was much more relaxed, ready to forget Misha, when she suddenly received his letter (10 April 1905), written at Gatchina. After assuring her how preoccupied he was that he had made her worried or unhappy, and begging her not to be so sad, he reassured her that he would always be her friend. If she still wanted him to return her letters, he asked that she would likewise send him his.

That spring, Ena arrived in Nice to spend time with Bee, and they went to London to enjoy themselves together for the 'Season'. It was some two years since Boris, Kirill's notoriously womanising brother, had met Ena on the Isle of Wight. Now, after seeing her every day, he considered himself deeply in love and asked for her hand in marriage, but she was not ready. What she knew of Russia did not reassure her. Moreover, she was still very young and too attached to her mother and young brothers.

That year, the most outstanding event of the 'Season' was the five-day visit of the nineteen-year-old King Alfonso XIII of Spain, arriving from Paris after an attempt on his life and that of the president of the Republic, and a bad sea crossing. On his first night in London, Edward VII gave a dinner in his honour at Buckingham Palace where he presented his nieces. It was rumoured at court that he was seeking a bride, possibly an English princess. One possible choice was Patricia ('Patsy') of Connaught, younger daughter of Edward VII's brother, Arthur. However, she considered the people and customs of Spain 'detestable', had for some time been in love with Alexander Ramsay, son of the earl of Dalhousie, and would marry him in 1919.

Now aged twenty-one, according to the marquis of Villavieja, 'with her small and distinguished head, [Beatrice] looked more alert and regal than ever'. He thought her different from the rest; more independent, and with more personality than most people of her age. She appeared more sophisticated than her cousins, probably as she had spent part of her youth in Coburg, and her visits to the Russian court had given her self-confidence. Yet if anyone thought for a moment that she was a possible bride for the king of Spain, that night it was evidently not Beatrice on whom his gaze fell. First to enter were the British princesses, Helena Victoria (Thora), daughter of King Edward's eldest surviving sister Princess Christian of Schleswig-Holstein, then Bee, Patsy of Connaught, and her sister, Daisy, betrothed to Crown Prince Gustaf Adolf of Sweden. Behind them were the serene highnesses, including the tall and very pretty Princess Ena of Battenberg. From the moment he saw her, it was love at first sight.

They went to the great dining room with its shining golden dinner service for thirty-six. During the dinner, King Alfonso struck up a conversation with Princess Christian, whom he had visited at home that afternoon, asking her questions in French about the other guests. Ena, who was almost at the end of the table in eighth place to the left of the queen, noticed that the king was enquiring about her and heard him ask, 'Who is the young lady with the silver-blonde hair?' Instantly, she thought, 'Oh my God, he thinks I'm an albino!' As he stared at her, she blushed and later she could barely exchange a word with him.

Next day, after attending Mass at the newly consecrated Westminster Cathedral, the king went to Clarence House where he sat for breakfast beside Patsy. She was so offhand to him that he asked his other neighbour, 'Is it because I am so ugly that my neighbour on my right does not like me?' It had rained continuously, he had a cold and left in a bad mood. After attending the Royal Tournament at Islington, he visited the Spanish Embassy to see the London-born ambassador, Luis Polo de Bernabé, assisted by his minister, the marquis of Villaurrutia. The candidature of Patricia of Connaught ended forthwith.

That night, the king and queen and their nieces attended a banquet held by the Diplomatic Corps. After the dinner, Alfonso approached Olga, daughter of the duke of Cumberland, asking her, 'Who is that very pretty blonde princess?' 'You're talking about my cousin Ena of Battenberg,' was the reply. Until then, he had thought she was called Eva.

Next day, the king had few opportunities to talk to her. He visited the Natural History Museum, the Albert Memorial, and bought a present for his sister, Maria Teresa. While he was in the shop, his car burst into flames. His speed in reacting and presence of mind in extinguishing it won him the public's applause. He lunched at the Guildhall with the lord mayor of London, where his linguistic abilities were much commented upon. In the evening, he was the guest of the secretary of state, Lord Lansdowne, a supporter of his marriage to Princess Patricia, who was not present. Warily, the host went to look for her and found her in the flat above speaking to a young guardsman. He insisted that she come down and sat her at the side of the king of Spain, but he hardly batted an eye on seeing her.

The following day, he returned to chat to 'his blonde' at a performance of Gounod's *Romeo and Juliet* at the Covent Garden Theatre. They met in the Royal Box, conversed in French during the interval and he realised he was in love. The following evening, a farewell court dance in his honour was held at Buckingham Palace, and Ena was astonished when he asked her to dance. In her modesty, she could not believe that he had chosen her; she thought her older cousins were much better prepared, above all Bee, who seemed the cleverest and the most cosmopolitan. While they danced for the first time, the king asked her if she collected postcards. Although unprepared for this, she shyly told him she did. 'Good, in that case I'll send you some on the condition that you reply to me.' She related that 'He (the King) with his irresistible smile added, "I hope that you will not forget me."' Some seconds passed and she replied carefully, 'It is difficult to forget the visit of a foreign sovereign.'

They did not meet again. Next morning, she saw his car enter Kensington Palace for him to bid farewell to Beatrice, the widowed Princess Henry of Battenberg, and he gave her his photograph to pass on to Ena. Thrilled, she placed it on the table in her room. When Ena's brothers kept asking her about Alfonso and jokingly called her *Reine*, she replied simply what she would repeat years later, 'He was very slim, very southern, very cheerful and charming. He was not handsome, but on the other hand he was distinguished.' He was a disappointment for Bee, who was not interested in him. Like her sisters, she preferred tall well-built men.

Politicians and diplomats immediately began to plan the wedding. On the English side, Lord Lansdowne helped Ena, and the Spanish ambassador, the marquis of Villalobar, favoured the scheme. On 15 June, Daisy of Connaught married Crown Prince Gustaf Adolf of Sweden. Eleven days later, the three cousins—Bee, Ena, and Patsy, the bride's sister—met again. One of the postcards Ena sent was a photograph of the bride, groom, and bridesmaids, accompanied by a note: 'I think that it is very difficult when one leaves one's family and country. It was terrible at Daisy's wedding. Patsy merely whispered, "Ena, tell me, do I have a red nose?"'

Ena became nervous when the postcards, to which she should have replied, began to arrive; and it was Bee who completed them. On one dated 10 July 1905 that Ena sent the king from Kensington, she wrote: 'It is here that Beatrice and I go riding every morning'. The two cousins left for Coburg, and Bee sent a postcard from Lake Tegernsee where they were staying: 'Thank you for the postcards. This is the view from our house. A thousand greetings, Beatrice'. Another was a picture of Ena in the garden on which Beatrice wrote: 'I took this photograph myself. Isn't it good! It is so hot here; it could not be more so, even in Spain. We still talk of your visit. Beatrice. 18 July 1905'.

At first it was Beatrice who chose and wrote the postcards. The second was of Rosenau Castle, and the third 'our house in Coburg', showing the square where Edinburgh Palace was situated. The fourth showed Schloss Ehrenberg, and the fifth the Maximilian Palace in Munich. Bee wrote: 'Thank you for your letter. Ena is lazier than I am; it was I who asked for your news. A thousand greetings, Beatrice'.

Alfonso had been to Vienna and Berlin, where he saw other princesses whom he did not like. For this reason he complained to Ena, reproaching her for her silence and coolness. She replied in English, 'Do not think that I am cold, because I am not. Not a bit, dearest', and continued in French, 'I have deep feelings and I find it difficult to express them in writing.'

Ena was about to fall in love. Almagro San Martín stated that while Villaurrutia was minister of state, he tried to divert King Alfonso's feelings by sending him negative reports about the Battenberg family, which Empress Eugenia's faithful shield-bearer, the marquis of Villalobar, ably intercepted. Eulalia always insisted she had warned the king of the threat of haemophilia, which the women of Queen Victoria's family sometimes transmitted to their male children. She told him of the fates of her youngest son, Leopold, and of her second daughter, Alice, grand duchess of Hesse, one of whose sons had likewise died after a fall. Of the four Hesse sisters, the two younger ones were carriers. Irene, who married her cousin, Henry of Prussia, had two haemophilic sons at this point and Alix, married to Tsar Nicholas II, would later have a haemophiliac son. Bee knew Ena's brother, Leopold, was a haemophiliac, but she never mentioned it as she loved Ena and wanted her to be happy. The knowledge was probably concealed from Alfonso himself. Eulalia knew Irene of Prussia, and had written her a touching letter on the death of her little haemophiliac son, Henry, in 1904.

When Bee returned to Coburg, the Russo-Japanese War seemed to be almost over. Before the treaty was signed, Ducky and Kirill decided to marry; despite the tsar's opposition, the duchess of Coburg persuaded her chaplain, Father Smirnoff, to give them the official blessing. On 8 October 1905, the young couple arrived at the home of Count Adlerberg at Tegernsee, near Munich, who had offered them his Orthodox chapel for the ceremony. Apart from the bride and groom, the only ones present were the duchess, Count Adlerberg, her two ladies-in-waiting, and the count's housekeeper. Grand Duke Alexei, who was in Munich, had been invited to Tegernsee as their witness but without being told why, and he appeared half an hour after the start of the wedding breakfast. Kirill thought it curious to see this giant who reminded them so much of his brother, Alexander III, chatting and laughing at the proceedings. On seeing him, Father Smirnoff had feared the anger of the Holy Synod and above all that of the tsar. Alexis's arrival immediately reassured him.

A few days later, Kirill went alone to St Petersburg to inform his father of their wedding, and next day he planned to tell the tsar. However, after dinner on the day of his arrival, he and his father were playing bridge with some friends when Count Fredericks, a court minister, arrived to order him to leave Russia within forty-eight hours, deprived of all his honours and cashiered from the army and the navy. The following day, Grand Duke Vladimir, infuriated by the tsar's high-handed attitude, resigned all his imperial posts. Exiled from Russia, the newly-weds took refuge in Coburg, and spent part of the winter in Nice. Bee, like their mother, was especially delighted, particularly as Ducky was so happy at last.

Also very much in love, Alfonso XIII was forgetting or else dismissing the warnings of his Aunt Eulalia and the politicians, and intended to continue his relationship with Ena. She was invited to the reception for King George of Greece's stay at Windsor, and Edward VII told her that the king was 'a charming boy' and she would be very happy. He was very pleased about his niece's forthcoming wedding. Having always been fond of Alfonso, he was determined to make the Spanish marriage happen, though he would have preferred Patsy to Ena in the first place. While he could foresee the difficulties ahead, he did his best to help Ena and Alfonso in every possible way.

The first to raise the alarm were her marriageable cousins who exclaimed as one that Alfonso was 'so boring!' 'He is still very young!' Bee reported. In the future she would always take Ena's part, despite knowing the many gaps in the future queen's education. Ena knew English and spoke German, although not very well. French, of which she found the grammar difficult, was the language the king used as he did not speak English. Bee attributed these gaps in knowledge to the Princess Beatrice of Battenberg's indulgence towards her children. She recalled how on returning from Egypt, she and Ena wanted to invite two boys who had been very kind towards them to tea in the study, where every member of the royal family made an appearance, last but not least being the queen. 'A disorderly flight was all that remained of our Khartoum friends.' The Battenbergs lived very much apart from society, said to be the fault of Princess Beatrice, who was always very shy and as economical with her words as with her spending.

The year 1906 began with Ena and the king meeting at Biarritz. Princess Frederica of Hanover invited mother and daughter to her lakeside property, Villa Mouriscot, to meet the king of Spain who had come from nearby San Sebastian. Ena brought her cousin's album of drawings one of which showed her dancing with the Spanish Ambassador Polo, who looked like a dwarf in the presence of his future queen.

The king's mother, who had been regent for sixteen years, reportedly did not like her son's choice, commenting that for the first time in history a king of Spain would be marrying a 'Serene Highness!' On hearing this, Edward VII raised her to the rank of royal highness, something that pleased Princess Beatrice greatly. She wrote to her future son-in-law saying how kind it was as she thought it might be a difficulty.

It had not yet been decided how and where the princess's conversion to Roman Catholicism would take place. Although she was not very religious, the change in confession seemed such a violent act that Bee, on hearing how they treated her cousin, Ena, found it terrible, not because Ena did not wish to change, but because of her 'having to renounce her previous baptism as it was not valid'. It took place on 7 March in the Miramar Palace chapel. Although it was not a public ceremony, there were several witnesses to hear her say in English that she declared herself to belong to the Holy Catholic Apostolic and Roman Church, acknowledging it as the only true church, and apologising 'for having held other doctrines contrary to it'.

Ena sadly returned to London, her journey to Spain having given her a glimpse of reality. She knew that in future she would have to live in the same palace as her mother-in-law, who had always been in charge. Commenting on the situation with Bee, Ena exclaimed, 'She will always be the Regent!' Wanting a period of freedom, she had asked her cousin to come to London with her while she chose her trousseau. For a few days, the two cousins enjoyed visiting shops where Ena could buy everything she liked. She was delighted to be able to make purchases in the Bond Street jewellery shops because she had loved such items since childhood.

Princess Beatrice of Battenberg asked King Alfonso XIII for a special wedding invitation for her sister-in-law, the dowager duchess of Coburg and her daughter, Bee. The king sent it, adding a note saying he hoped they would stay at the royal palace. This pleased Maria greatly, as she wanted to see the capital, which would be difficult if they stayed at El Pardo, outside the capital. However, she was annoyed when she heard Misha was to represent Tsar Nicholas II in Madrid. He was said to be in love with his sister Olga's lady-in-waiting. Maria immediately asked her sister-in-law, the dowager empress, to prevent her son from attending, as she feared a reaction from her daughter who was 'almost well again'. The empress agreed and Grand Duke Vladimir, who knew Spain well, represented the tsar instead.

Ena left London on 24 May, Edward VII taking her by the arm to the station as the future queen of Spain. Beforehand she had had to sign papers renouncing all rights to the British throne. Uncle Bertie also warned her that if things went badly in Spain, she would have no right to return. Public criticism of her conversion to Roman Catholicism annoyed him, and the king had retorted that they were talking about a German princess from the Battenberg family. Nobody referred to the danger of her transmitting haemophilia.

Ena was accompanied by her mother, Princess Beatrice, and her brothers. The king waited for his bride at Hendaya, on the Spanish border, and they took another train to Madrid. Along the way, people waited at the stations to see their future queen. They arrived in the afternoon at El Pardo, and the family installed themselves in the palace. On the afternoon of 24 May, Duchess Maria and her daughter, Bee, left Coburg and reached Madrid five days later, bringing trunks, suitcases, and hatboxes. The dowager duchess of Coburg's entourage consisted of two ladies- and a gentleman-in-waiting, two ladies' maids, and a guard for the jewels. Also lodging at in the royal palace were the young Princess Alice of Albany, sister of Charles Edward, Bee's cousin, and the prince and princess of Wales, George and Mary, the most important guests. Ena's wedding cake, weighing 300 kg, was sent separately from London.

On 29 May, there was a performance in the theatre in El Pardo where Bee reportedly made a sensational entrance on the arm of Prince Albert of Prussia, the regent of Brunswick, representing Prussia at the wedding. The following day, Ena and Bee went incognito to the reception. There was a rehearsal and Bee met the count of Villamarciel, who was to carry the train of her blue dress at the wedding.

The king had granted Ena no dowry as he regarded her as his niece and not as an English princess, the dowry she brought with her to Spain being the £30,000 her mother gave her, excluding jewels and clothes. However, he and Queen Alexandra gave her a magnificent necklace with matching earrings in diamonds and turquoise which she thought far superior to anything her other cousins had been given, and £20,000, more than double the value of the jewellery. As the ceremonials began early next day, the guests went to bed before midnight.

The prince of Wales wrote in his diary for 31 May:

A magnificent day, with a very hot sun. Breakfast at 8.30. We gathered at 9.15 in a room in the palace and the procession set off in nineteen magnificent carriages drawn by six or eight horses towards the Church of San Jerónimo. The streets were decked out, full of people, with troops lining the way. The ceremony in the church was most beautiful, and the service lasted from eleven until one o'clock. Our coach went just in front of that carrying Queen Maria Cristina and Aunt Beatrice, behind whom (preceded by a spare coach) went the coach of Alfonso and Ena, which ended the procession. Just before our coach arrived at the palace, we heard a loud noise and we thought that it was the first of the gun salutes. We later heard, however, that a couple of hundred yards from the palace, in the Calle Mayor, a narrow street near the Italian Embassy, a bomb had been thrown from one of the balconies high above the street as the King's carriage was passing. It exploded between the wheels, the horses and the front part of the coach, killing twenty people and wounding between fifty and seventy, mainly officers and soldiers.

Cardinal Sancha pronounced a benediction at the scene before the guests were provided with undamaged carriages. King Alfonso XIII also recalled the attack:

Just as the procession was reaching its destination, I called the Queen's
attention to a group on a balcony who were waving flags, causing her
to turn her head to the left. At that moment, we came to number 88
Calle Mayor on the right-hand side. Alone and leaning out over the
fourth floor balcony, Mateo Morral threw a great bunch of flowers
which landed near the coach. There was a bright flash—an explosion—
windows shattered—screams—cries. I noticed a strong smell of acid
and for at least two minutes, I was blinded by thick smoke. When this
cleared, I saw that the lilies and roses of the Queen's wedding gown
were stained with blood. She was unharmed; but a number of our
guards had been thrown in pieces from their horses. Men and horses
bled profusely. Calle Mayor was a terrible sight. Twenty-eight people
died and forty were wounded. Everyone was shouting frantically. 'They
have killed the King and Queen!' Thanks only to the superhuman
discipline of my regiment, which guarded the procession, the line was
not broken. Among scenes of horror and enthusiasm, I took the Queen's
arm and walked to the spare coach (number 16 which was in front). If
it had not been for my desire that the Queen should reply to the cheers
from the official buildings, she would not be alive today. The bomb fell
to the right of the carriage.

The prince of Wales's diary continued:

Thanks to God, Alfonso and Ena were untouched although they were
covered with glass from the broken windows. The Marquis of Tolosa
and his niece were dead. They were found on the balcony just below that
from which the bomb was thrown. The carriage, however, went thirty
yards. Sir Maurice de Bunsen (British Ambassador), Captain Morgan
(Royal Navy); General Sir Cecil Lowther and four officers of the 16th
Regiment of Lancers (of which Don Alfonso was Honorary Colonel)
who were in a nearby house ran to surround the coach and to help Ena
get out of the carriage. Both she and Alfonso showed great courage and
presence of mind. They entered another carriage which immediately
left for the Palace amid frenzied cheering. I feel so sorry for poor Aunt
Beatrice who was enormously shaken by the shock. Naturally, the bomb
was thrown by an anarchist, presumably Spanish, and they let him
escape. I think that the Spanish police and detectives are perhaps the
worst in the world. They had taken no precautions; here they are much
happier believing in luck. Naturally, on returning, Alfonso was as much
down as Ena after such a horrible experience. I toasted their health, not
an easy thing after the emotions caused by such a terrible event.

Maria of Coburg, undaunted, exclaimed that it was 'common in Russia!' The *Infanta* Eulalia said that the explosion made a harsh, dry, and not disproportionate sound, while her sister, the *Infanta* Paz, had assured her it was scaffolding that had fallen down.

The *Infante* Don Alfonso de Orleans wrote:

I heard the bang of the bomb in Calle Mayor from the Palace. At that moment I was with Grand Duke Vladimir who was representing the Tsar of Russia. The King and Queen returned in the spare coach. Everything went very well once the moment of the explosion had passed, and the King and Queen were able to proceed without difficulty. However the other carriage wobbled when it went over a dead horse. Among the many things that happened, I remember that the bomb caused lacerations to the face of a footman called Belver, whose hair actually turned white in forty-eight hours. The Queen took him as her personal footman.

Alfonso XIII liked to say that many married at twenty, 'but the truth is that few are able to say like me, that they were married on the same day on which they were born.'

Early on 1 June, the morning after the wedding, Ena awoke to the sound of people below the windows on the Plaza de Oriente. When she saw the king was already dressed, and had left the royal apartments to receive the cheers, she put on a dressing gown and went to meet him on the central balcony dominating the Plaza. Alfonso loved his wife's familiar gesture, as did the Madrileños who cheered her, but she was criticised in the palace for her spontaneity.

After breakfasting together, *Infante* Don Alfonso de Orleans (henceforth Ali), accompanied the king to the garage. The latter called Antonín, his French mechanic, to fit four new tyres and said to him, 'Should a tyre burst in the street people would be injured because they would start to run, thinking that they were dealing with a bomb.'

A bullfight was held on 2 June. The Waleses, the prince and princess of Teck, and the English retinues declined to go, but Maria Alexandrovna and Bee attended. It is not known if she enjoyed the spectacle, but during her life, she and her children went to numerous bullfights when she lived in Sanlúcar.

The palace was filled with light, and guests milled around the small garden until they formed groups to go into the dining room where dinner was served. A ball took place later in the grand salon. In the corner of the doorway, Grand Duke Vladimir was chatting to a 'tall, athletic young man with fair hair and blue eyes, who looked splendidly like a Viking'. On

seeing his niece, Bee, the grand duke called her over and introduced her to
Ali, who soon led her to dance. He also spoke English with an excellent
accent. While they danced, she saw in the room's ten mirrors that they
made a fine couple. Suddenly the young man, looking at her fixedly, asked,
'Princess, will you marry me?' Startled, she slapped him with her gloved
hand, interrupting the dance that was finishing. Ali took a lively interest
in the young princess whose history he more or less knew, while Bee knew
nothing about him.

According to the marquis of Villavieja:

> Life had not been easy for the young prince but a deep human
> understanding had developed in him: domestic circumstances had
> carried him from one place to another. He was an intelligent man and
> his honesty surprised me, although I was then unable to judge all his
> extraordinary qualities, qualities which later would become greatness.

Ali, *Infante* Don Alfonso de Orleans and Borbón, was born in Madrid on
12 November 1886 and spent part of his childhood in Paris in the Palais
de Castille, with his grandmother, Isabel II. He would write in Bee's album
how annoyed she had been with him, as he asked if she would marry him
after knowing her for only ten minutes. Years later, he commented that
he had done so because that way she would not forget him and, 'as she
danced with so many, that would have been easy'.

On the morning of 5 June and the following day, the duchess of
Coburg, her daughter, and their entourage left on the *Andalusia Express*
to explore southern Spain. They visited Cordoba where they were
overawed by the mosque, and then took the mail train to Granada, but
neither the suffocating heat of Seville nor the dirty inns deterred her.
She even wanted to climb the Giralda to see the view. Arriving in the
Peninsula, Bee sketched the River Bidasoa entering the sea and wrote:
'The first view of Spain from the train'. Before leaving Seville, she drew
a 'View of the rooftops from our window in the Hostal Madrid, Seville,
11 June 1906'.

Returning to Madrid they were received at the station by the queen
mother, the *Infanta* Maria Teresa, Ferdinand of Bavaria, and Don Carlos,
enthralled by tales from the duchess who was most enthusiastic about
Granada and Andalusia. That night, Bee left for La Granja as she wanted
to tell Ena about her impressions. Next morning, they went horse riding
but were taken by surprise by a downpour on the Valsaín road and
returned to the palace wet through. Meanwhile, on 10 June, the *Infanta*
Eulalia and her sons, Ali and Luis, left for Paris on the *Sud Express*, and all
the other guests returned to their respective countries.

On 14 June, Corpus Christi, they attended Mass in the Collegiate Church. From a window, they saw the procession led by the king. Later the fountains played, a spectacle which surprised Bee with its beauty. One courtier remarked that Bee had been with the new queen and adapted immediately to the ways of the court. Years later, he would be her enemy.

Bee wrote to her sisters:

I accompanied the newly-weds to La Granja, where they were allowed to honeymoon something which they tried to achieve. Ena and I have been more united than ever and they always had me with them, although I tried to keep myself apart as much as possible. They have given me a room here, which is near to theirs, and they come and go all the time. They are madly happy to be together and are not embarrassed about it in the slightest. They are living almost all my theories about matrimony, which I love.

The son of *Infanta* Eulalia declared himself to me. I quickly closed the matter. I want to occupy myself with my own things and keep my future in my own hands.

The duchess of Coburg, who had become a friend of the *Infanta* Isabel, spent several days at La Granja. A fiesta in Segovia was held on 15 June. Mother and daughter visited the Alcázar and the cathedral, then met the princess in the La Suiza patisserie in the Plaza Mayor, and returned to La Granja to lunch at the palace. In the afternoon, accompanied by the king and queen, they went round the gardens in a coach pulled by mules, which amused Bee because she had never known how slowly they walked. The king had returned from Madrid and she declared that it had been a journey at 'vertiginous speed'.

Queen Mother Maria Cristina had returned to Madrid, accompanied by Maria of Coburg, leaving Bee at La Granja. Bee was dreading the approaching separation from her cousin, as they enjoyed going out riding together. On 17 June, the day of departure, the king and queen accompanied Bee to Alto de los Leones. After having tea, the two cousins left each other tearfully. The duchess of Coburg and her daughter left full of gratitude for everything they had enjoyed in Spain, especially for the good weather.

In her album, Bee drew various pictures of the stay, accompanied by various comments: 'Bee and Ena preparing to mount their steeds; but are close to desisting, on seeing how Alfonso mounts his. La Granja, June 1906'; 'Mountain scenery, a coach bounces Bee about'; 'Ena is abandoned by Bee, who leaves Spain in tears. She must do her duty as wife and as Queen. June 1906'. These made evident the pain of her separation from

Ena, of whom she was so fond. She had to return to the monotonous
life at Coburg, where Ducky was keen to hear her impressions of Spain
and her successes at court, which she found hard to believe. Suddenly
the *Infanta* Paz sent them an invitation to attend the kermis to be held
in Nymphenburg in aid of the poor. Maria of Coburg remembered (4
October 1904) how that autumn they were visited by Eulalia and her
sister, Princess Ludwig Ferdinand (*Infanta* Paz), whom she had never met
before: 'She is very ugly and small. Her husband fell for Baby at the opera.
He was so enchanted by her that he insisted that the two ladies visit us.
We even thought that the ugly woman was jealous. We returned the visit
at Nymphenburg but as they were at table, we did not wish to bother
them'.

Ali was Eulalia's eldest son. He was determined to pursue the woman
of his dreams, wanting to see her before his aunt and cousins dominated
her time in Nymphenburg. He arrived in a Minerva car he had bought
the previous year in Belgium, and drove it from the factory at Amberes to
Heidelberg, where he was studying at the university. Accompanied by his
French chauffeur, he arrived on 30 December 1904. Ducky and Kirill liked
the young Spaniard, who proved an amusing companion, with a passion
for anything mechanical. Marie of Coburg liked him at once, according to
Missy, who wrote (Edinburgh Palace, Coburg, 9 November 1907) that Ali
was very cosmopolitan:

> … and really I cannot determine to what nationality he really belongs.
> His grandfather Montpensier became Spanish on marrying the sister of
> Queen Isabel. The bitter pill to swallow in his case, are [*sic*] his shameful
> parents, who although separated, are not divorced. The father misspent
> his money in a scandalous manner and Eulalia—well, we all know how
> she is. I do not think that she will oppose and will even be contented
> if her son establishes himself. Ali thinks that his father could become
> disagreeable when he has to find the money and I fear that not being rich
> is a very serious matter, I cannot give Baby more than we receive.

Nothing is known of Bee's attitude towards the young pretender whom
she had certainly not rejected. She enjoyed excursions in his company such
as taking part in the musical life of Munich, something both found most
amusing. With September came separation, with Ali leaving for Spain
to enter the Infantry Academy at Toledo. Eulalia advised him to take a
furnished flat in the city so he could attend morning and afternoon classes
at the academy, while enjoying some liberty in the evenings, time he spent
studying in order to attain better marks on leaving. On 11 October 1906,
he entered the academy, knowing the duty incumbent upon him as an

infante of Spain: rectitude, sacrifice, and loyalty, attributes that would follow him through life. Because of his good character, he was soon accepted by his classmates, and as raw recruits, they had to put up with the senior pupils' superiority.

In the autumn, the Battenbergs called Bee urgently as Leopold was ill again. This infuriated the duchess because she was annoyed that her daughter was called on to be a nurse, but she managed to go to London with the excuse that Maurice was to be confirmed. The two brothers particularly liked Bee and were very pleased. Soon afterwards they went to Munich, and Prince Heinrich of Bavaria was evidently attracted to her after seeing her at the opera.

'It seems that he suffered a *coup de foudre* and would not leave her alone. He was not ugly,' said Maria of Coburg. 'However Bee thought that he was an idiot, because he was so friendly, which is something absolutely modern. To be liked, princes should be dumb and shy. I saw that he was always looking at her in the theatre.'

Ducky was nearing the end of her pregnancy, and to please Kirill, she was studying the rites of the Orthodox Church, into which she was received on 7 January 1907. On 2 February, a girl was born and named Maria after her two grandmothers. They had wanted a boy, as her father was fourth in succession to the Russian throne.

In the spring, the duchess of Coburg decided to spend some time in Rome with Beatrice, especially to see the works of art. After a while in the Eternal City, Bee asked if she could meet the Pope. An audience was arranged, and they were received by the Holy Father, Pius X. He blessed them and they kissed his ring while they curtsied: 'Baby did admirably and was a great success with the Holy Father who was looking at her continually'.

Soon after returning to Coburg, they left for London. Bee was perhaps seeking a husband and her reactions were feared by her mother who she knew wanted her to marry. The duchess admitted to being 'terribly afraid of arranging something, even a meeting, because she would immediately turn her back on it and I would be compromised. She, on the other hand, can be so charming and friendly when she wants to be, and it troubles me; people try to approach her but she immediately rejects them all, or most of them.' One of the Prussian princes came to meet her and declared himself at dinner, Sandra and her husband tried to foster the relationship, but Bee decided she did not like the kaiser and certainly had no desire to belong to his family.

Beatrice's thoughts frequently went to Spain, and above all to Ena who was about to give birth to an heir. Alfonso, prince of Asturias, was born in the royal palace in Madrid on 10 May 1907. Meanwhile Bee desperately wanted to return. On 15 September 1907, she replied from Tegernsee to an invitation from Alfonso XIII, assuring him she was greatly looking forward to her much-delayed visit to the country and getting to know the prince of Asturias.

7

History of an Engagement

On 22 September 1907, the Spanish newspapers announced that Princess Beatrice of Coburg had arrived at San Sebastian from France 'and was received at the station by the two Queens'. She was accompanied by Sophie de Passavant, a lady-in-waiting to the duchess of Coburg. In her album, Bee reflected on her joy at meeting the prince of Asturias: 'San Sebastian 21 September, 1907. Bee and Ena meet again and Bee finds that Ena has fulfilled her duty as wife and Queen. She is even aghast at the size of her son and heir'.

Early next morning, both cousins went shopping. On 24 September, Queen Victoria Eugenia, the little prince, and Bee left San Sebastian by train to visit La Granja for a few days. The king arrived next day from military manoeuvres at Galicia, and spoke for a long time with Bee about Ali, who was at the Toledo Academy, and who he had invited to spend the weekend with them. The young cadet had written to his cousin to extend his leave to Saturday evening, as he explained in a letter from Toledo (15 September 1907):

As you have been so kind as to invite me to La Granja on Saturday, I should like to know if you will be there next Saturday 21st or if you will be on manoeuvres.... I am going to ask you a great favour. In the afternoon, in Toledo, the only class I have on Saturdays is English from four to five o'clock.

If I attend this class, I will arrive at La Granja at nine o'clock, which is very late and besides, I will have to drive very fast to do it. As the class is English, I will lose nothing. Would you give me permission to leave immediately after lunch ... no doubt you will pardon me for asking this.

Despite heavy rain on 26 September, the queen went out riding. Then the *Infanta* Maria Teresa arrived to talk to Bee about Ali who she loved like a brother, and to encourage her to look favourably upon him if he proposed. Two days later, the king arrived just after teatime in Ali's car. First they went to Mass at the collegiate church and then went to the Riofrío hunting lodge where the king, Ali, and Bee went shooting. That night after dining, they made music, with Bee playing the guitar and singing. As the weather improved they could go on excursions to Riofrío, where they usually lunched, returning on horseback in time for tea at the palace. Ena and Bee enjoyed talking together, and Ena was happy to encourage the closeness that was evidently developing between Bee and Ali.

During clay pigeon shooting in the afternoon, the queen lost a a valuable ring, with a ruby surrounded by diamonds, that her husband had just given her. While she was tearfully looking in the grass, the furious king made a scene, repeatedly saying that she was not very careful and that it had cost 5,000 duros, equivalent to nearly £800 in sterling. Knowing how much Ena appreciated gifts, Bee was surprised and disgusted. Fortunately the ring was found before darkness fell and the king ordered that the finder should be rewarded.

They returned to Madrid on Monday to say goodbye to Queen Maria Cristina, who was leaving on Friday for Vienna. It was decided that they would travel by train, but at the last minute the king thought the little prince of Asturias and the entourage should go by train while they went by car. There was a race between the two cars, won by the king and queen who arrived first, while Bee and Ali had been 'held up', as the sovereign mischievously suggested to his cousin.

On 7 October, *La Época*, the monarchist daily newspaper, published news of the forthcoming wedding of the *Infante* Don Alfonso of Orleans to Princess Beatrice of Coburg. The young princess had made such a good impression and it commented that 'she hid a bright intelligence from the eyes of the courtiers, and a deeply cultured and artistic spirit. While appearing regal, she hid within her a very passionate character'. Queen Maria Cristina had taken to her because she was so fond of music and a good pianist, and loved hearing her singing some of the *Lieder* of her childhood. On leaving, the queen asked her again about her intentions regarding Ali, and Bee repeated that she would not change her religion for love: 'As for the children that may come, they would be Catholics being Spanish'.

Next day, the king went hunting with Ali at Casa de Campo. Meanwhile the two cousins went shopping, visiting the Tapestry Factory where Beatrice wanted to make an order for the following Christmas, a Spanish knotted carpet for her mother. Ali arrived from Toledo in the evening, and after dining, the king and queen went to the theatre to see *La Viejecita* and *Gigantes y Cabezudos*, two zarzuelas that they enjoyed greatly. In her album, Bee later wrote of having painted the scene of Ali's arrival. She also noted that 'Ena and Alfonso think that it is time for Bee to marry. At first Bee does not quite like the look of Ali but Ena and Alfonso soon persuade her to change her mind and contemplate matrimony'. Later she added that 'Alfonso put forward some points of view in respect of the wedding to the Prime Minister. This was so unexpected as Bee was not abreast of the situation, and saw herself being forced into a pressured isolation'.

Bee painted Alfonso XIII in his uniform jacket in this album, and in the margin on the opposite page there is a picture of Ena and Bee in tears and the inscription, 'Here endeth the second book of adventures of Bee and Ena! It is their saddest parting as for the first time they did not know when and how they will meet again. Madrid Station, Sunday the 14th October 1907'.

The original of this document written in English by Beatrice of Coburg on returning from her journey to Spain in October 1907, now in the Orleans-Bourbon Archive, lacks a beginning so I have transcribed the translation made by Ali, which he sent to his old teacher, Comandante Burguete:

I arrived in San Sebastian on the 21st September (1907). The following morning Ena spoke to me about you and said that they want us to marry. I talked about religion and she said that it would not be necessary for me to convert. On the afternoon of the following day I was singing to entertain Aunt Crista. Later she said to me, 'Ali loves you. He is a good boy. I love him very much as I do you, my great wish is to see you married.' I said, 'You know that I will never change my religion.' She told me that there is not the least problem if the children are Catholics. 'If I have understood correctly, a second son married a Protestant and it was necessary to send a signed paper about the children.' 'Yes, but there is a sentiment against this in Spain and I would feel miserable being unpopular.' She then pressed me saying, 'Oh no! There will not be the least feeling against it as everyone likes you both, and I long for it (tears and hugs, and complaints about Maria Teresa and Nando).'

We followed a detailed description of how to sign the paper and celebrate the wedding in Coburg. There was more pressure on her side, and more objections on mine. She denied each one of my objections about what would not sit well in Spain. Finally I said that I should not take a step further nor do anything here without my mother. She said, 'Do not worry yourself, my dear. Go and see Ali at

La Granja and, if you wish, I shall always be there and I will be by
your side like your mother until you accept him.' Then more pressure,
tears and kisses. Finally I promised to see you at La Granja. She asked
me to accept you and that I tell her of my impressions. Ena, who was
present during the conversation, joined her in saying, 'We want it and
we all long for it to happen. Kisses and promises on the part of Aunt
Crista.

I have written it down word for word in a letter to Mama, and Ena
can testify to every word now that Aunt Crista insists over and over
again that there will be no difficulties.

Alfonso arrived at La Granja on September 25th and came straight to
my room with Ena. I asked, 'How are you?' and without any hesitation
he spoke in French, 'Firstly, I wish to talk about the task I have been given
by my cousin Ali. It is *to ask you*, in his name, *if you will marry him*.
He is tall, strong and good-looking, and besides he has never touched a
woman. In the past I have said bad things about him. I was mistaken and
there is not a word of truth in it. Ali will come here and will speak to you
himself.

I have promised your mother that I will see him; but I fear the question
of religion. I have your mother's word on the matter, but I have a number
of doubts.

And I give you my *word of honour* that there will not be the slightest
difficulty.

There followed a chat in which Alfonso tried to persuade me to accept.
Every day, the same conversation took place. I protested and he sorted
out the smallest details about what he was going to do. What I would
have to stop doing (going to my church, etc.). You know my difficulties
in stopping him from declaring that we are engaged (because Mama was
not there).

In Madrid they knew the difficulties. I said that if they were found to
be insupportable, I would leave for Ena's happiness and never reproach
him and never return to Spain when I knew he was in the country. I
offered him the choice. He insisted, however, that considering we were
engaged, he promised to arrange everything. I even protested about
it and said that I would not come to Spain by the back door, but they
persuaded me not to think in these terms. The only one who did not push
the marriage was Ena, because she did not want me to be pressured and
perhaps marry a man that I did not love. She was the most clear about
the difficulties. I would like everyone to know what happened so as to be
fair to her.

I am able to swear to everything that I have written here, word for
word, as Ena can testify.

In a letter to Burguete, Ali reflected on events during Princess Beatrice's stay in Madrid in October 1907:

> The King wanted to announce our engagement in Madrid when the court returned from La Granja. We were impeded by not yet having written the Duchess of Coburg. I returned here.
>
> Everyone (King, Queens, etc.) was delighted. The King explained the situation to Maura who said that the wedding could not be, because the Liberals would ask for more religious advances (such as freedom of worship, etc.), the Carlists would protest, etc. Princess Beatrice said to the King that she did not wish to cause so many serious difficulties and that she would sacrifice herself for the Queen and go without seeing me. The King said no; he would arrange everything. I received a letter from my desperate fiancée. I went to Madrid immediately. I found the family to be troubled and distraught. The King said to me, 'What are you going to do?' I replied, 'Even if it were not for love, and I did not want my fiancée at all—as a gentleman, I could not go back. I will marry her. If, as a gentleman, I could go back, I would not do so.' The King said, 'That was well said. I, as Alfonso of Bourbon, approve and I will do what I can for you two. As King, I will also do what I can; but I am a constitutional monarch.'

Ali's determination, sense of humour, and his open, simple way of speaking had made a deep impression on Bee. No haughty, stiff prince, he was an intelligent man with his own mind. Deeply in love with him, she also admired his honesty, direct looks, and masculinity. In November 1907, they decided to become engaged. The duchess of Coburg, who had immediately liked him, wrote glowingly to her daughters that he was the kind of man who would 'know how to tame and dominate her, which was something which worried me so much, and to know that she has accepted him freely, and of her own free will'.

Bee did not intend to change her religion, feeling comfortable within the Protestant church, although she would allow her children to be raised in the Catholic faith. Her fiancé, who had been educated by English Jesuits and was also very religious, stood by her. On the king's advice, he went to see Pope Pius X during the Christmas holidays in 1907 to obtain the dispensation necessary for a mixed marriage, generally given on condition that the children would be raised as Catholics. Yet the government had already intervened, and he was denied this until he had the king's consent.

Ali went to spend Christmas at Coburg. The duchess wanted to celebrate their engagement, so Missy and Ferdinand arrived from Romania; the newly-married Ducky and Kirill came from Paris; and Sandra and her husband from Langenburg. At the party on 27 December 1907, nobody suspected it would be twenty months until the wedding. They all returned home in January, Ali back in Toledo delighted with his holiday in Coburg, where his intelligence, learning, and personal charm had gained the affection and friendship of his future in-laws and reinforced in Bee the idea that she had found in him the 'soul mate' she had sought for so long.

While they waited for the *communiqué* from Madrid so they could fix the date of the wedding, the duchess began organising her trousseau. Although the prices of lace and fabrics had increased over the years, she let her daughter choose as she wanted. She also wrote of the difficulties the three Spanish majesties had not anticipated: ministers' protests against a Protestant princess; the young age of Ali and his military studies which would not be finished for two years; and Alfonso's fear of his present government: 'They should have foreseen this before pushing Baby into "a secret engagement" which they all so ardently desired'.

As the royal house of Spain had not issued any *communiqué*, and as the foreign press had published the news of the engagement at Christmas, the duchess indignantly wrote (11 May 1908) to Missy, asking for help:

> The matters of Baby are a great worry as they have not advanced at all and we have to act faced with such dishonesty and deceitful tricks, we really do not know how and where to go to ask for help and advice.
>
> Mr Sweenen ... says that it is hopeless as the Spanish Government and the Vatican are working together against this marriage and we cannot take for granted how much Alfonso is mixed up in it.
>
> Baby is very relaxed because deep down, she feels very happy and contented but it also annoys her because she knows how much Alfonso (the Prince) is loved by those around him.
>
> I think that Ena is desperate. Aunt Beatrice refuses absolutely to disagree on the matter, which is not very friendly on her part, after her pretence of extreme affection towards Baby, who is her goddaughter. Eulalia has now gone to Madrid to make a fuss. She does not care about anything and I think that she will 'give it' to Alfonso, as she does not hold back strong words or truths. But Alfonso is now refusing to allow Baby's engagement, which is really very offensive of him and shows a weak and frightened character when at odds with his government. As for the conduct of his mother, Queen Maria Christina, it is absolutely shameful because she swears that she has never talked to Baby about Ali. Fortunately I have Baby's letters with all the conversations on the subject.

Infanta Eulalia, who looked unfavourably on the wedding, wrote to her husband, Antonio of Orleans, from Paris (4 June 1908) of a meeting with the duchess of Coburg in Paris in the Hotel Astoria. She thought they would need to go and speak to the duchess, and not leave her alone to deal with matters. She suspected the king did not oppose the marriage:

I think that it will be best for them to marry and put an end to the story. As we have not intervened in the matter, we have no responsibility. I think that, once married, it will be *bon débarras* (good riddance) to Ali.

I know that Coburg has more money than they say. So if Ali marries he will then not need to bother so much about (his brother) Luis.

Alfonso wrote to me (on 9 April 1908) that he will marry next summer, and that you have given him your consent and you cannot withdraw it. As I see it, *it is certain that the wedding* will take place as the King and Queen desire it so much and are exerting pressure.

If *Coburg does not give them a house*, I cannot leave them on the street, as they do not have the means to take a house in Madrid where they want to live, near the King and Queen.

You now know that the King and Queen help Ali and Bee in everything.

I do not believe that the Duchess of Coburg will pay for the ménage and will only give her daughter forty thousand marks.

I will let my house in Madrid to Alfonso and his wife so that they pay the running costs and *find out* what they spend. I have no desire to stay in Spain other than in the little house at Las Navas (del Marqués) which I told you about. I am running away from the court and I understand that you flee also.

I hope that this summer the Duchess of Coburg lets them marry and keeps them, and I beg that you help, using your authority so that they may marry as minors.

There were festivities in Spain for the centenary of independence and the king wanted his Orleans cousins to accompany him to Zaragoza, the city of the sieges. On 13 June, he left Madrid accompanied by Ali and arrived at Zaragoza in the morning. They first visited the Virgin of Pilar after which the sovereign bestowed the title of 'Immortal' on the city in a solemn act, then attended a banquet and a bullfight, returning to Madrid on the evening of 15 June amid such festivities that Ali had little time to talk to his cousin and explain that he planned to go on holiday to Coburg after his exams. Alfonso XIII replied that they would talk when he returned in the summer.

After passing his exams at the Toledo Academy, Ali left for Coburg where he spent part of July and the month of August, to the joy of Bee who felt more in love each time she saw him. Faced with the duchess of Coburg's anguished letters, her daughter, Missy, now pregnant again, had obtained King Carol's permission to have a quiet time: life at home with her mother and sisters, Ducky and Bee, was most agreeable. The king and queen of Spain were expected to come in September.

Ali felt a deep affection for his Aunt Paz and his Bavarian cousins. The *Infanta* María Teresa wrote from Nymphenburg (19 August 1908) to her brother, Alfonso XIII:

> I suppose that Ena wants to see Bee at Tegernsee, which is a beautiful place. Bee and Ali have visited us with the Romanian (Missy) but we have, of course, not spoken about the wedding. We have seen nothing of her mother because she spent the day with her brother Vladimir, who arrived unexpectedly.

Many members of royalty had congregated in Munich, as the wedding of Bee and Ali had long been expected to take place that summer. Ali wrote from Toledo to Alfonso (1 September):

> As you know I went to Coburg where, as you can imagine, I had a good time. Then I went to Tegernsee and Munich where the family had gathered, Uncles Luis Fernando and Vladimir and Aunt Maria, Nando and Maria Teresa, Pilar, Missy and Gisela's two daughters, Ducky and Kirill, etc. Later, I went to Langenburg to see Sandra (Bee's sister).
>
> I have left them all in in good health and condition. Bee and Aunt Maria stayed for a while at Tegernsee. Bee will be delighted to see you and Ena in Munich when you go. On arriving here I have found out that I am a sergeant in the sappers. Bravo the bold lads from Madrid!

Missy was still at Coburg when the king and queen of Spain arrived. As she felt a predilection for Bee, and great friendship towards her fiancé, who would later became her most loved brother-in-law; she tried to contact Alfonso XIII and come to an agreement about the wedding. Fortunately, her mother had not shown too much hostility towards the young sovereign while he was in her house. However, Duchess Marie was like a judge examining a prisoner so much so that 'Ali could only remember that during the interview the Monarch appeared strangely nervous and seemed very ill'. Ena wrote the same to her brother, Leopold, who hastened to tell Bee. Ready to bond more closely with the Spaniards, Missy asked Ena to be godmother to the new baby, who was born at the royal palace in Bucharest on 5 January 1909, and named Ileana.

Although Alfonso supported the idea of a wedding between Bee and Ali, he insisted repeatedly that Spain would not accept 'a Protestant princess'. A little later, the king sent a decoration to the Romanian crown princess and she replied gratefully that 'although each one defends their point of view, there is no reason why we should not be good friends. We have pleasant memories of our meeting and we hope that we shall mutually broaden our relations'.

Ena was tired, having borne two sons and become uncertain of the fidelity of her husband with whom she was still very much in love. She was very conscious of his way of thinking and felt uncomfortable with his Nymphenburg cousins because they had not tried to finalise the marriage between Bee and Ali.

Empress Eugenia invited the duchess of Coburg to lunch at her Villa Cyrnos. After eating, she sent the guests into the garden and remained hand in hand with the duchess whom she needed to consult about the wedding. When they began to talk, Maria realised that the Spanish-born empress had been sent by the court in Madrid. No sooner had she had her say than the guests appeared from the garden, and the duchess was unable to reply because the empress stood up to say goodbye to them. Angered by her hostess's actions, the duchess quickly took her coach and left.

That autumn mother and daughter spent some time in Paris, where Bee took singing lessons with the teacher Jean de Reszke, and bought new items for her trousseau. Sometimes a feeling of melancholy entered her, fearing her marriage would never happen. In April, she would be twenty-one, and still unmarried. The trousseau had been complete for some time, but no news came from Spain about the wedding date, annoying the duchess of Coburg who was preparing for Christmas well in advance. Meanwhile in Toledo, Ali continued to progress in the final year of his studies. It was then that the *Infanta* Eulalia decided to go to Coburg and show her support for the marriage, resulting in a letter from the duchess to Missy (5 January 1909):

Imagine, now we are invaded by Eulalia. She insisted on coming; but wanted to go to a hotel, so I had to ask her to come to our home. Who would have thought that Eulalia would be under my roof?

Actually, touch wood, everything goes well and she is delighted and finds everything delightful. She insisted on meeting Ali before she arrived here, but he had left for Lichtenfels ten minutes before she arrived. So we had to quickly send a car so that he could return at top speed.

I have never seen more confusion, and imagine—we had even sent a telegram carefully showing the best trains that run from Frankfurt to Eisenach, as she came from Paris. Besides, she had lost her luggage which came by the goods train; but as she is such an unusual person and does not care. She was not bothered. She is crazy about exercising—every morning she drags poor Ali along and after lunch she took us to

Rosenau to go skating, something she adores and does very well. I have invited people to dinner, wishing to make things livelier naturally for the engaged couple. Eulalia's presence is quite conflictive, as she does not like to sit alone and complained to us yesterday from teatime until seven o'clock. But she becomes most amusing when talking about her past and present friendships, among whom one finds most unusual people. She also claims to love Bee and is always talking of the future grandchildren before the engagement.

I have to stop to get dressed for lunch, because I hear the car bringing Eulalia back. She is staying until next Sunday and then goes to Munich and wants Ali and Bee to go later to visit Nymphenburg before she goes. Ali is very happy but, naturally, somewhat subdued in the presence of his mother.

Another letter from the duchess at Edinburgh Palace (11 January 1909), returned to the theme:

I have had no time to write until today. [Beatrice] very much wanted to go on a sleigh and was very pleased because we had a heavy snowfall. I was even photographed with her on the Bandach sleigh, which is rather good. She insisted on being photographed with me. Those photos which were taken in the teahouse in the little conservatory did not come out. As soon as she saw them, she took them, so I have to send them to you next time because they will amuse you, as will those of Baby and Ali in the little sleigh.

This winter with its fine weather has been a source of immense pleasure for the very youthful Ali who is also crazy about exercise. We are occupied eating all kinds of good things because he seems terribly thin after the bad Spanish food at his Academy.

As for Eulalia, she eats enormously and we presume that, for economic reasons, she is dying of hunger in Paris. For example, she served herself three pieces of roast venison, two servings of chicken or pheasant and generally repeats the sweet plate, having begun lunch with a double portion of the first dish. The result is that her digestion was very active because of this and she had to get up once in the middle of bridge or on other occasions. What an eccentric creature! I can hardly believe that her visit has gone so well, without explosions or her making a scene with Ali whom she adores, but whom she generally attacks in an unjustified way. We all breathed a sigh of relief when we saw her leave for Munich.

When *Infanta* Eulalia returned to Paris she wrote to tell King Alfonso XIII how pleased she was with her visit to Coburg, adding that she had spoken with Ali about the wedding and was pleased that his king, his career, and his country were his main preoccupations. Time passed and the king of Spain continued without giving the authorisation, which the Vatican and the royal house needed to announce the wedding. In June, the *Infanta* Eulalia went with her son, Luis, to La Granja hoping that Ali would go to see her at the weekends, but he was studying hard for his exams and remained in Toledo.

Queen Ena gave birth for the third time in the spring, her mother and her brothers were also at La Granja, and the queen enjoyed the entertaining chatter of the *Infanta* Eulalia. Some English newspapers had reported that the young King Manuel of Portugal had become engaged to a granddaughter of Queen Victoria, and specifically mentioned Princess Beatrice as the future queen. A few courtiers remarked on the duchess of Edinburgh's old friendship with the Orleans family, but the duchess, who had known Queen Maria Amelia since childhood, was only thinking of the happiness of her youngest daughter, wanting her to marry the man she loved as soon as possible.

On 27 June 1909, the baptism took place at La Granja of the baby princess, given the name of Beatriz. 'The ceremony was celebrated at half past two in the afternoon and the baby cried throughout the brief service,' Ali wrote. 'All went down to the gardens and the fountains were turned on.' He spoke to the king, about his intention to visit Coburg and see Bee after such a long separation. The king said that he approved, gave his consent for the wedding, and was very sorry about what had happened. That night, Ali, his mother, and his brother returned to Madrid by car. Their joy was shortlived. The following week, Ali wrote to Lt-Col. Burguete from Toledo (6 July 1909), telling of his disillusion about the attitude of the Maura government.

Pardon me for writing you as I did when you were my teacher. Firstly a thousand million thanks to the Chiclana Battalion for the honour that they have bestowed upon me. The King told me that he wanted me to go into the 1st Regiment.

I am going—well I have already said so to him and to various friends that I have in the Regiment and who were my companions here.

The King has now promised that I will go to the first war that arises, I will go even if it is in Morocco.

It will be hard if they now throw me into a boring place for three or four months in charge of water and not to have the pleasure of firing a shot.

I am not going if there is not a war for the following reasons: I want to marry in a few months having had a fiancée for almost two years.

Here is the story: When the King married, Princess Beatrice of Saxe-Coburg turned me down. I did not give up, as that is not my custom. The King, with whom I had spoken, and who has been very good to me, went to see her and asked for her hand on my behalf. Princess Beatrice said to him, 'I have promised your mother to see him again but I fear for the matter of religion. I have said so to your mother and I have many doubts.' The King replied, 'I give you my word of honour that there is not the slightest difficulty.'

In the end, they convinced her that she should not be so inflexible and should at least see me. I went from here various times to La Granja to see her. Everything went well. The King wanted to announce our engagement in Madrid when the court returned. But we were stopped because of not yet having written to the Duchess of Coburg. I returned here.

When I come of age, I will marry.

How? I do not know. I write all this because if some day, by fault of the Government, I have to marry without the King's official consent (because as a cousin, he approves and is very sorry for what has happened) and they throw me out of the Army and of Spain, you know that I have worked like a gentleman, and have no shame in saying that if I lose all that I have it is not for some dishonourable thing nor from not doing my duty as a gentleman towards a lady. Besides, this is not a marriage of convenience. No! We love each other, and we will work as hard as we can to get married. She will not change religion because she finds it vile and dishonourable when it is not done with conviction and in good faith. Saying and swearing that you believe; renouncing and repudiating your religion when you have faith in it is immoral, unworthy and cowardly. The wife of an infantry officer cannot do this. I fear that I am losing my career, although few have more love and enthusiasm for the Infantry than I; but faced with losing my honour and my self-respect is losing that which makes me an officer. Now I am not worth anything neither as an officer nor as a man. But if I conserve my honour unblemished, although I will not be an officer, I will be a man—a gentleman … do not say anything about what I have written other than to those who are worthy of your confidence. I do not want my wedding talked about before it happens, as the Government might create new difficulties for me.

His mother, *Infanta* Eulalia, was also worried about his wedding and the possible loss of the career on which he had worked so hard, and she confided in Burguete (Madrid, 9 July 1909):

On Monday, the King gave Ali his officers 'stripes' and we then went abroad, because Ali was in a great rush to see his fiancée. The King wants Ali in the King's Regiment. I am sorry that he is not going into the Cazadores de Chiclana which Ali likes as much as I. Unfortunately Ali's military career has to suffer for marrying a Protestant princess and I think that, in November, Ali will have to leave his country and his career, long term, unless he receives a pardon, and if not, he will remain in his wife's country.

While dining at the palace one evening, Ali asked the king to appoint him to the Chiclana Battalion, but the king had said that he was to go to Melilla—in the Alfonso XII Battalion.

At 8:45 a.m., Eulalia was awaiting the king's arrival at Mediodía Station in her best Paris finery, accompanied by her lady-in-waiting. After reviewing the troops, the king boarded the royal train with the *infanta* in one carriage and the minister of war, Gen. Echagüe, and the entourage in the others. As the train did not stop at any station during the journey, they arrived at Toledo in ninety minutes, and went immediately to the Alcázar, where the patio was adorned with magnificent tapestries lent by the cathedral for the ceremony. The upper galleries were full of people waiting to see the royal party.

The Students' Regiment received the king with due military honours and, followed by the *infanta*, he made his way to the throne and Doña Eulalia sat in an armchair. The 240 new officers formed a line while the minister of war named them individually, and they came forward and stood to attention before the king to receive their commissions from him. He congratulated each one and they noted that he was the same age as many of them. When Gen. Echagüe arrived at student number thirty-five, he paused for a moment to name the Serenísimo Señor Don Alfonso of Orleans and Bourbon, prince of Spain. The king wanted his aunt to give him his commission, but Doña Eulalia emotionally refused the honour, saying simply, 'He is still Spanish!' Years later, she remembered the day with great pleasure, saying that at that moment all the bad memories were erased for her. She had felt ashamed that Antonio was not allowed to go to Cuba as he was the only man in the royal Family, although she had happily allowed her son to be a soldier.

With the ceremony over, and in front of the expectant crowd, the king approached the monument to Carlos V and spoke to them, saying that after three years of study, they were now expected to serve in a regiment whose valour and discipline were legendary. Their comrades have often had occasion to demonstrate with their gallantry these virtues that the Spanish Army kept alive, and he was sure they would always achieve a great level of satisfaction and pride from your king: 'As proof of this all shout out with me: Viva España!'

At the end of his speech, frantic and enthusiastic cries of '*Viva!*' broke out. Afterwards the Students' Regiment paraded again and then a lunch was served in the academy's library. The king left the Alcázar at 12 p.m. to public cheers, a real demonstration of affection towards the *Infanta* Eulalia, and of friendly affection towards the prince who had lived among them for three years.

When they boarded the royal train and could speak to the king, Ali asked him about the situation in Morocco, which he had mentioned in his address. The king explained that on 10 July, a group of Moroccans had attacked some Spanish workers in Melilla, there had been a fight, and that the previous day shots had been heard. The king had no idea how this situation would develop. Ever loyal to his king, he was always willing to serve the Spanish army. Moreover, nobody would dare to argue with any orders from Ali, even if often contradictory or given without warning. As soon as Ali knew of the problems, he proceeded to Africa.

That night after returning from Toledo, the *Infanta* Eulalia and her two sons left in the *Sud Express* for Paris, while Princess Beatrice of Battenberg was returning to the Isle of Wight with Leopold and Maurice, after spending the spring in Spain with her daughter. They were happy enough and Ali was planning his stay at Coburg, well away from the duchess of Coburg's imminent telegram offensive. The first message was directed at the *Infanta* Eulalia: 'Letter received. How can the marriage be questioned when Alfonso is going killing in Morocco? My indignation has no limits. Marie'.

At 8 a.m., the king was in his office at La Granja with his secretary, very upset by a similar missive from the duchess: 'I request that you explain the sudden departure of Ali to Morocco and why no one has spoken of it previously. Marie'.

The king understood the spirit in which the words were said, though in fact Ali would occupy a position of honour in the expeditionary force to Melilla, and replied by telegram (Madrid, 12 July 1909) that the Moroccans had not advised that they were going to attack his troops. As head of the army, he was unable to tell her what plans he had for his officers. Ali had volunteered to proceed to Melilla, and he could not refuse to let a prince of Spain go.

In Coburg, the king's telegram of the evening of 12 July reduced the duchess to tears. Seeing her mother cry and on re-reading the king's telegram, Bee angrily wrote to him in French (Coburg, 13 July 1909):

The news of Ali's leaving has pierced my heart like a knife; but I say nothing as his duty calls and I cannot complain. Our luck is in the hands of God. But you have replied with an insult to the telegram from an old, sick woman broken by the pain of seeing a boy who she loves like her own son, who she lost, going to war and she asks for news … I found it, and everyone finds it, like me, to be unworthy conduct from a man and a king. May God forgive you.

Alfonso XIII never replied to this; but later he wrote to his cousin, Ali, of his annoyance at receiving 'a very impertinent letter from Bee and, as she is your fiancée, I bring it to your notice, as I cannot permit that she treats me in this manner. In spite of everything I have a clear conscience. They amuse me when they insult me.' Bee became calmer on receiving the news that Ali would visit her before leaving for Morocco. He planned to travel to Coburg arriving at 8 a.m. on 15 July. The king was still at La Granja, and during dinner, on Tuesday 13 July, he received another telegram from the duchess, which his mother had redirected to him from San Sebastian:

What nameless cruelty to suddenly and unnecessarily send Ali to Morocco! Alfonso wants to get rid of Ali to prevent the wedding. It will be disgrace if his blood falls on your heads. I have suffered enough in silence these two years for me to keep quiet when the happiness of my daughter could be broken from one day to another.

In a further telegram the next day, the duchess of Coburg wrote:

I have never put the Royal Prerogative in doubt nor the veneration of Your Majesty. I do however reserve every right as a German Princess and a Grand Duchess of Russia, as well as being your aunt, my dear cousin, of posing all totally justified questions as well as discussing your decisions, knowing that there is not the slightest possibility of you changing them. I beg you to consider this telegram as the last which will refer to this sad episode.

The king replied that he thought it better if she did not telegraph him. When he took a decision, he warned her, 'it is not permitted to discuss it'.

On the night of 14 July 1909, as telegrams crossed and Ali dozed in the train to Coburg, the reigning duke, Charles Edward, invited him to dine at Rosenau with his wife, Victoria Adelaide, who liked Bee and wanted to arrange the wedding quickly. She thought that as the fiancé was leaving to fight in Morocco, they should take advantage of the Catholic Church's dispensation 'Partida de la Mort' marrying Ali before he left for the front. They discussed the matter and before nightfall, the duke called his minister of state in Gotha and promised to go with him the following day to celebrate the civil marriage.

Early in the morning, Bee went to see the chaplain of the royal house, asking him to shorten the religious ceremony by not repeating the questions and by limiting himself to a sermon and a blessing. She then went to the station where Ali, 'who was only thinking about saying goodbye to his fiancée', was expected to arrive a little later. While they were on their way to Rosenau for breakfast, she explained matters. At 11:30 a.m., they heard the arrival of the royal coach, from which Charles Edward alighted, accompanied by the minister of state and a second witness, the court's grand marshal, Hans Friedrich von Rüxleben. They entered the room where, around a large table, the bride and groom exchanged promises, and they and the witnesses signed the papers. 'They are royally united forever!' exclaimed a triumphant duchess of Coburg.

Immediately afterwards, Charles Edward and the bride and groom returned to Coburg, and went to St Augustine's Roman Catholic Church, where they asked for the parish priest, the duke explained everything and asked him to marry the couple. The priest replied that he saw no difficulty and immediately telegraphed Bamberg for a licence. The duke made it clear that he expected a reply that afternoon, and that the wedding should be celebrated as soon as the licence arrived at his home. They then parted, and Bee and Ali went to Rosenau for lunch.

At 3 p.m., they were advised that the licence had arrived from Bamberg. Bee and her mother immediately changed, the bride choosing an ivory and gold evening gown and carrying a crown of heather picked from the garden, while Ali was still in his travelling clothes. Fifteen minutes later, at top speed, they arrived at the church, and entered the sacristy immediately to sign the documents. In the priest's house, his sister helped Bee with her hair, placing a small crown of heather on her head, and using a lace mantilla as a veil. Following the English tradition for the bride to have 'something old, something new, something borrowed and something blue', the mantilla was borrowed and came from Spain.

The priest, Georg Wohlparte, assisted by a boys' choir, celebrated the Catholic rite in German, asking if the couple wanted to marry, if there were any impediments, and blessed the rings. At the end, the newly-weds and the duchess of Coburg and Duke Charles Edward thanked Father Wohlparte and the deacon, Francis Ott, for the ceremony they had improvised. They all immediately left by car for Callenberg Castle where a third awaited them, held in the old castle church in the presence of the reigning duke and duchess, Duchess Maria, the grand marshal, von Rüxleben, the minister of state, Ernest von Richter, Princess Feodora of Holstein, and the ladies-in-waiting to both duchesses. At 5 p.m., the duke and duchess offered tea in the tower room where Bee was so happy that she wanted to telegraph Ena immediately.

As evening fell, the bride and groom, accompanied by the duchess, returned to Rosenau. There the upstairs room was prepared with twin beds. It was unfortunate for her that her wedding night coincided with a time 'in which she was not well' as her mother delicately described it. She advised Bee to explain to Ali, but he was well prepared, assuring Bee that his mother had always spoken of such matters.

That night, before supper, the duchess gave Bee her wedding gifts, an emerald diadem and a collar. She therefore came down to dinner, wearing the diadem with a low-cut dress. Afterwards, the three played bridge until 1 a.m., something they had always planned to do on their wedding night.

The following morning, Sandra of Langenburg arrived with Leopold of Battenberg, somewhat disturbed on learning of the sudden marriage. In the evening, the duchess gave a lively dinner attended by the reigning duke and duchess, and Charles Edward told them he had telegraphed King Alfonso XIII, announcing the celebration of the wedding. A little later, he received a cable, saying that it caused him 'great sorrow' not to reply to the news of the wedding with his cordial congratulations as he had to comply with his inescapable duty, 'something which Ali has not respected'. He would have preferred the marriage to remain secret, while this confirmed the couple's desire to make it public.

Ever manipulative, Alfonso had always encouraged Ali to marry Bee, but would not disclose his plans to his prime minister, in front of whom he always pretended not to know anything about his cousin's wedding. Ali and Bee believed Alfonso and decided to marry in Coburg, away from the limelight. They thought that they had Alfonso's backing in doing so, and after the marriage ceremonies, the duke of Coburg wrote to Alfonso with official confirmation that the couple were now man and wife. This was not expected by Alfonso, who had wanted the marriage to be kept secret until he could manipulate his government (which was unaware of the marriage) to arrange everything in a proper manner, as Bee was a Protestant marrying a Catholic prince. Ultimately, Ali and Bee were blamed, and Alfonso always unfairly accused them of having acted on their own initiative.

Next morning, 17 July, in a car adorned with white flowers, the happy couple were photographed before leaving on their honeymoon, which began in Munich, after which they went to England. Despite the dark clouds gathering, they felt, as Bee said, 'immensely happy, because they were going to live together as a loving couple for more than half a century'.

8

A Controversial Marriage

Queen Victoria Eugenia was at La Granja that afternoon when she received Bee's telegram in English, 'Married today. Incredibly happy. Coburg 15 July, 17.10 p.m.' Ali telegraphed the king an hour and a half later of his 'enormous pleasure in informing you that we have wed civilly and Catholically. I leave for Paris on Tuesday. I hope that you will allow me to serve King and Country in the campaign. Ali.'

Early next morning, the queen, accompanied by her sister-in-law, the Infanta María Teresa, went to the telegraph office to contact the king, who was with his mother at San Sebastian in the Miramar Palace. He advised that he was not responding to telegrams from the newly-weds. On telegraphing him again, the queen said, 'Very well, I will not reply to Bee's telegram. We are amazed. And you? Love, Ena'. However, Ena must have written something to Bee because the latter replied: 'Loving thanks for the telegram. Bee.' on 18 July at 8:20 a.m.

Overwhelmed by news of the marriage he had wished to keep secret, Alfonso XIII contacted the prime minister, Antonio Maura, who was spending the summer at Santander. The Spanish Constitution forbade the king to sanction a royal marriage without the government's consent. The prime minister, a profoundly religious man, was unwilling to do so. As leader of the Conservative Party, he believed the wedding would be most unpopular.

The king's telegram said:

I wish to inform you that the *Infante* Don Alfonso of Orleans has just contracted marriage with Princess Beatrice of Coburg without my knowledge or consent. Given the gravity of the situation, I believe that we should talk and I would be grateful if you would come at once.

Maura then telegraphed the members of the government:

Leaving for San Sebastian to deal with the consequences of the marriage of the Infante Don Alfonso. The *Minister of Public Education should prepare the text of a decree removing all dignities and honours from the Infante,* and await decisions from His Majesty's office and my subsequent telegrams. *I do not know how harsh he wishes to be.*

Maura's last phrase reveals his great concern, as he knew the love the king felt for his cousin. He left for San Sebastian at once, but as the coastal road was dangerous and he did not like going fast, the journey took time. It was nightfall before he arrived at the palace. The king was anxious to tell his family and the other European courts what had happened, and his private secretary issued a *communiqué:*

I wish to inform you that the *Infante* Don Alfonso of Orleans, having contracted marriage with the Princess Beatrice of Coburg, has today been stripped, by decree, of the title of *Infante* and of all honours and related prerogatives. Alfonso Rex. Given at San Sebastian the 16th July 1909.

Maura stayed at the Miramar Palace until late, then went to spend the night at the Hotel Londres. The bridegroom's father, *Infante* Don Antonio of Orleans, telegraphed his son to tell him he had 'not taken into account the duty of honour and the sacred obligation that God places upon a good son. For this reason, all is finished between us.'

Infanta Eulalia replied to the king:

I have just heard of my son's marriage. I have had nothing to do with the matter nor do I know how it happened. The couple are coming to Paris on Wednesday. I beg you send me your orders. What attitude are you and the government taking? His father has not given his consent and my son is a minor. Let me know if, in spite of everything, the marriage is valid and if my son remains in the Spanish Army.

Eulalia wrote to Maura from the Spanish Embassy in Paris, asking the government not to terminate her son's career in the army. The countess of Paris, Don Antonio's elder sister, and the most important members of the

Orleans family, replied to Madrid saying that they were aware of what had happened.

Prince Bernhard von Bülow, who was about to resign after eight years as imperial German chancellor that same month, later recalled how he bid Kaiser Wilhelm farewell as he was going down the Chancellery staircase. His sovereign told him 'in some agitation' about the marriage to his cousin Princess Beatrice of Coburg, and that the Spanish had removed the *infante's* military ranks and the Order of the Golden Fleece as he had married a 'heretical bride'. Meanwhile, Edward VII discussed the wedding with his nephews, Tsar Nicholas II and Kaiser Wilhelm II, all of whom were critical of King Alfonso, his government, and the decree:

> Don Alfonso de Orleans and Bourbon, having contracted matrimony without complying with the requisites, nor obtaining the necessary consent according to his rank, and in accordance with the Laws of the Kingdom, I, in agreement with my Council of Ministers, hereby decree that:
>
> *Article One.* Don Alfonso of Orleans and Bourbon be deprived of all positions, honours and other distinctions corresponding to his position as *Infante* of Spain which were conceded upon him as a Knight of the Order of the Golden Fleece, and as a holder of the Grand Cross of the Royal and Distinguished Order of Carlos III, on the 18th November 1886 and the 13th May 1907 respectively, and all other gifts and favours which he may have received from me.
>
> *Article Two.* The respective ministers will adopt all necessary resolutions for the efficient and immediate compliance with this Royal Decree.
>
> Given at San Sebastian, 16th July 1909.

It was published by the newspaper *ABC* two days later. A photograph of the couple appeared on the front page, with Bee dressed in travelling clothes and Ali in the uniform of an infantry lieutenant, wearing his decorations. That afternoon, Queen Ena at La Granja received telegrams from her family regarding the infantes' marriage. Her brother, Leopold, pleaded with her: 'Try to do something. Bee half dead. Telegraph her. Leo'.

Ali soon knew that not only had he lost all his titles including that of *infante*, but also that all the gateways to Spain were closed to him, and his hopes of fighting in Morocco would not be realised. Nevertheless, he still thanked his cousin the king (17 July) for his telegram, to express his sadness at not being able to join the campaign, and remind him that he still hoped to fight one day for his beloved country. He showed his loyalty by neither commenting on nor attacking the king, especially as he was under pressure from Maura and his government. The king had openly favoured the Orleans-Coburg wedding and had even sent the petition 'for those who marry their cousins in time of war without reading the banns' to the bishop of Bamberg, knowing the staunchly Roman Catholic Ali would not be content with a civil and Protestant wedding.

The newly-weds left for Munich by car on 16 July to visit the *Infanta* Paz. She received them affectionately as Ali had spent much of his childhood at her home of Nymphenburg, and her family was very close to him. Despite official ostracism, he received several letters of congratulation on his wedding, sent by some of his companions at the academy. He was especially moved by an open letter from his teacher, Infantry Captain A. García Pérez, addressed to Ali, in the press:

> The Infantry respectfully salutes and gratefully acclaims you. During your three years of academic life, obedience was your norm and comradeship your incessant desire. You were liked by your superiors, and valued by your equals. The most complete modesty always dominated your actions.

Although comforted by a valiant defence from his teacher, he was sad to hear that García Pérez had been suspended from his position. A year later, when Pérez was put on trial and thought he would lose his career, *Infanta* Eulalia wrote to the king from Paris (30 September) 'to beg your benevolence in pardoning this poor man if it is that he has broken military law. You know how much it would please your aunt.' Her plea was successful.

Suddenly the Moroccan situation intensified. On 18 June, the Moroccans launched a sixteen-hour attack on the redoubt of Sidi Amet, where Gen. Marina was based. The reinforcements he requested from Melilla arrived by nightfall. There were skirmishes during the following days, but on the morning of 21 July, the fighting intensified and 'converted itself into a formal and hard campaign'. More reinforcements were necessary, and the Maura government decided that troops from Barcelona should embark for Melilla. This gave rise to terrible scenes on the docks, and to the so-called 'Tragic Week' in which the mob burnt the Church of St Jerome and the convents of the Salesians and Poor Clerics. Crowds stopped the reservists leaving, telling the soldiers that they would not be defending the honour of Spain but the furthering of their politicians' interests. On 4 August, the government proclaimed obligatory military service. The news greatly affected Ali who still could not join the campaign. He constantly telegraphed the king, who replied (13 August 1909):

On the afternoon of the 12th July in Madrid, full of goodwill towards you, I talked to you and told you everything that I had to tell you. However, I also remember that after having discussed the pros and cons, I then said to you that this was the moment to go on campaign and marry later or, if not, marry in secret and ask for forgiveness from the field. Thus opinion would have been on your side in respect of anything that you had asked for and all would have sorted itself out in the best possible way.

But if I knew about your wedding in advance, there would have been no other option than to have proceeded as I did. I do not think that it is necessary to say that, on learning of the event and having received your telegram and another official telegram from the reigning Duke of Saxe-Coburg-Gotha, I had no alternative but to take action even although I did not wish to. You are cashiered from the Army as an officer, and so you cannot serve as a trooper and besides, you renounced the honour which you had requested and received.

I am very sorry that I am unable to accede to your request.

That summer, the king was deeply depressed, unable to control matters, humiliated in front of his Orleans cousins, and dismayed by the Moroccan war, as it had caused such hardship. Faced with alarming news from Barcelona, he had gone to La Granja to join Queen Ena, and then to Madrid on the afternoon of 20 July. As he was dressed in ordinary clothes, he changed at the palace into infantry uniform to bid farewell to the Figueras Regiment, which was to leave for the front that night. Alphonso reviewed the troops lined up in the barracks square, and Lt-Col. Ibáñez Martín addressed them: 'See the flag which has been placed in your hands. In it you carry the honour of our institutions and of the Fatherland'. He finished with a *Viva el Rey*! and a *Viva España!* to which they responded enthusiastically. Arriving at Melilla, they were in the thick of the fighting.. The lieutenant in charge and his men were killed by guerrilla Moroccan troops, and Lt-Col. Burguete took command of the battalion after his comrade's death. On learning of the situation, and knowing his teacher would have to reform the 'Glorious Battalion', Ali wrote to the king (Tegernsee, 30 August 1909):

What do you think of my going to Melilla, by my discharging myself as an officer and asking to take my place in the ranks as a soldier? I await your reply with impatience and God willing I will be in this campaign in the Figueras Regiment. I will write no more so as not to bother you.

Bee wrote to the king from Tegernsee (30 August 1909) to tell him she was the wife of a soldier who only asked to go to war:

I realise that my letter, written before my marriage, hurt you and I am infinitely sorry. Ena will have explained that I did not know the details of the telegrams which you have exchanged with my mother. We had no news and I asked my mother to telegraph you and ask. You can understand how your ironic reply has wounded me because I did not know that your mother received a telegram from Mama.

I do not wish to raise the question because my letter would be too long. I have asked Ena to explain it all to you and I am sure that she has done so. Everything that has happened since our wedding has taken into account all the things you have been forced to do, and I am sure that you have made great efforts because I cannot believe that an old and good friendship, such as that which existed between us, ended at some moment because of a sad misunderstanding and word said in anger. I have thought much about you and Ena at this sad time for Spain. God willing all will now go well.

Ali and I are more than happy; but Ali is desperate about not being able to go to Morocco. I, as a soldier's wife, suffer with him. Although the separation would be terrible for me, I wish with all my heart that he could go.

Is it not possible for him to go as a soldier? It has often happened in all countries that a disgraced officer has gone on a campaign as a simple volunteer soldier. No doubt there are protests believing that this is a manoeuvre on Ali's part to return to Spain, but he only wants the honour of fighting for his country and then to return abroad without saying a word and without the question being raised.

This letter reassured the king and his wife, who still worried about the plight of her cousins. On 17 September 1909, the king and queen, who were spending summer at Miramar, invited Grand Duchess Vladimir who was in Biarritz to visit, and she arrived with her son, Boris. The king and queen took them to Ondarreta, where a horse race was taking place on the beach that morning. They then went to the palace for lunch during which the grand duchess broached the subject of her niece, Bee, in French, blaming what had happened on her sister-in-law, the duchess of Coburg, and the king agreed. Then, remembering her great friendship with the *Infanta* Eulalia, she declared that Ali was not to blame: 'a young man of twenty-two years, deeply in love with his fiancée, and on the point of going to the front, and they offered to marry them the same day. He could not have refused!' Faced with this, they all agreed, much to Ena's delight.

Four days later, there was a government crisis. According to the newspapers, the king had accepted Maura's resignation, which the latter had not tendered, ensuring he was 'fatally wounded politically'. He was suçceeded by Segismundo Moret, an old Liberal politician who had served Amadeo I and Alfonso XII and whose government only lasted a few months. Next came José Canalejas, who governed from December 1910 until his assassination in 1912. He would however help Ali greatly in his wish to return to Spain and above all to fight in Morocco.

The *Infanta* Eulalia had no intention of going anywhere quietly. She sent the Spanish colony of St Moritz a message:

> Tell Mme Yturbe, the Count of Sedano (known as Pocholo) and all the Spanish colony on my behalf that I am sorry not to be among them.
>
> Ali and Bee are very happy in Tegernsee. The King had said to Ali when he left Toledo that he should get married and *he has done that*, and now the King as well as Queen Victoria Eugenia are in constant affectionate correspondence with my children. The only thing that I am sorry about is that the King has not permitted Ali to go to Morocco, even although Ali has asked to go as a simple soldier.
>
> I should like that all this news is known, and say to Pocholo from me that I wish all this to be known in Spain.
>
> Because of Maura, the King does not dare to pardon Ali and allow Bee to enter Spain, but I hope that will change soon.

On publishing this message, the *infanta* allowed the true course of events to be known—that Ali had received 'verbal permission' from the king to contract a Catholic marriage. Under ministerial pressure, the king changed his mind and followed the line taken by President Maura.

Bee knew that her husband liked an active life, and she feared Coburg was too small for him. One day she told him he should become a nurse. That autumn he went to the Central Hospital and was immediately sent to the mortuary 'to block up bodies'. Always ready to undertake disagreeable and difficult tasks, he fitted well into his new job and soon distinguished himself for his attention to and care of the patients. He was profoundly compassionate and some of them told him of the doubts 'they had about life'. They also enjoyed their journeys and excursions with Ducky and Kirill, whose expulsion from Russia allowed them to divide their time between Coburg and Paris. Ducky had a little dog that she spoilt greatly. With no responsibilities, the days and weeks passed quickly. Bee was soon pregnant which delighted them, as Ali also loved children, and Ena asked to be the godmother. When they asked *Infante* Don Antonio to be godfather, he agreed, if it was a boy he would be baptised in the Catholic faith.

Bee had a boy on 20 April 1910. Like his father, he was born at eight months and given the name Álvaro. 'The last to know the news are Ali's parents,' wrote the dowager duchess of Coburg. 'She was in Lisbon yesterday, and she should know by now. The baptism is fixed for the 24th May and we are waiting for Eulalia and Philipp (of Coburg).'

The duchess was very excited by the birth of her new grandson who, having been born in the Edinburgh Palace, seemed even more hers. The invitations were already prepared for relations and friends when, on the morning of 7 May, they heard of the death of King Edward VII just before midnight. The funeral in London on 20 May was attended by his nephew, the kaiser, his son-in-law, King Haakon VII of Norway, his brothers-in-law, King Frederick VIII of Denmark and King George I of Greece, the kings of Spain, Bulgaria, Belgium, and Portugal. In a family photograph, King Alfonso stood on the right of the new British king, George V. Yet he was criticised for going to London and leaving his pregnant wife who had a stillborn baby on the day of the funeral, the fourth child in less than four years of marriage.

Although Bee mourned the death of her paternal uncle, she had more love for his successor, remembering their shared days in Malta and how he was more like a brother than a cousin.

In Coburg, the Roman Catholic baptism was simple. The child did not appear in the photograph. Surrounding Bee were the two grandmothers, Maria and Eulalia, Ali, his brother, Luis Fernando, and the reigning duke and duchess of Coburg, Crown Prince Ferdinand of Romania, Prince Philipp of Coburg, and Leopold of Battenberg.

José Canalejas had been prime minister since 9 February 1910. Yet there was no peace in Morocco, where the Moroccans were still attacking isolated Spanish positions. Ali bought many Spanish and foreign newspapers. He was a great reader and took a great interest in aviation, having once gone up in a balloon. Although the English had good aeroplanes, flying schools began to appear in France. In the summer of 1910, Ali enrolled in the Mourmelon flying school, near Châlons-sur-Marne, 44 km south of Rheims.

As Ali and Bee did not want to be separated from the baby, they installed themselves with him and his nanny in the Hotel d'Angleterre. Their arrival caused a sensation as it was not normal to receive such distinguished guests, and the young couple asked for the manager to treat them as M et Mme d'Orléans, as they called themselves when in France. It was even believed that they wished to celebrate the baptism in the air and not go on a flying course. The head of the school kindly directed the princess to go up first, but Ali wanted to dissuade her until Bee insisted, 'If you don't let me go up first you're a coward!' When she got down after making the flight, she was radiant.

Then Ali got into the plane and at once fell in love with what became his vocation. He was not bothered by the early mornings, the difficult training on the ground, or the time in the *tonneau d'apprentissage* training simulator that seemed eternal, because the future pilot felt he was flying when told he was 'in the air'. He listened patiently and obeyed the instructions of his tutor M. Latham who gave him his pilot's certificate on 23 October 1911. Although Beatrice did not take the course, she loved the simple atmosphere of the school and always remembered their stay at Châlons, touring around the castles and churches of this corner of France. That winter, they returned to Coburg.

After that, Ali studied the importance of aviation in time of war. He decided to go to England, where one of his closest friends was Thomas Scott-Ellis, 8th Lord Howard de Walden. He had married Margarita, only daughter of the Van Raaltes who were great friends of Eulalia and with whom they had spent many summers as children on Brownsea Island. They arrived there in June. Bee was pleased, as the news from Spain offered them no likelihood of an imminent return. They were there with their son and his nanny when preparations for a new offensive in Africa were suddenly launched.

Ali wrote to ask for the honour of fighting for his country and for his king, and Lt Alfonso of Orleans was called to the ranks. Bee wanted to accompany him to Paris, where her mother-in law was staying at Boulevard Lannes. The separation was sad, but she was brave enough to see him leave dry-eyed, even though she thought she was expecting again.

The *Infanta* María Teresa wrote in her diary (27 September 1911) that Ali arrived at the palace at 2.30: 'He has asked to be sent as a volunteer to the war in Morocco and leaves for Melilla with the San Fernando Regiment under Miguelito Primo de Rivera'.

The same day, Eulalia wrote to Queen María Cristina from Paris:

The reason my daughter-in-law does not travel alone is so that I can see my grandson. So we are all going to Russischer in Munich at two o'clock tomorrow and my grandson will be coming too.

I do not have to tell you what a comfort it is for me to have Bee, who is behaving as a good and true daughter, by my side.

Of course I do not see this as a moment to reason with Paz that Ali should fight, or that the men of the royal family should all work. Giving permission to a twenty-three year old *Infante* serves no useful purpose [her younger son the *Infante* Luis Fernando]. How terrible it is to fight with someone who lacks intelligence!

Álvaro is running around me and I have to attend to him. I am stupid with love for him! As I have to go to Madrid in January to see my house before Ali and Bee move in, I will speak to you then.

Queen Victoria Eugenia, knowing her cousin well, knew she would not complain and put up with as much as possible. During the Moroccan offensive, she wrote to her almost weekly. The queen's loyalty towards her disgraced cousins was admirable. She paid no attention to her mother who pretended not to know about the matter for fear of her son-in-law, Alfonso XIII, writing to Bee (9 October 1911):

> I have not written to you because I had no satisfactory news about Ali until late last night. He is well and I telegraphed you instantly even though I was in bed. They have fought a terrible action and the battle on the 7th lasted ten hours because the Moors fought desperately and then they attacked our soldiers again at nine o'clock at night. Thanks to God, all passed happily for Ali although his regiment suffered heavy losses: an officer, the son of our administrator in Seville, is dead. I will send you the best article that I have been able to find in this morning's newspapers. They will tell you better than I all that Ali's regiment has suffered. You, poor darling, all this worry that you are going through. It must be awful and I cannot bear you suffering so. Your letter made me cry because I also realise that you are expecting. If I could only take your fears upon my shoulders, I would do so. I would prefer a thousand times that Alfonso was in the war rather than Ali because I have been married for five years and you only a short time. But I am sure that God will care for your loved one and you will have many happy years. Maria Teresa asks lovingly about you every day. She will write you as soon as she rises. Her little daughter was born a week ago, tomorrow. Aunt Isabel and my mother-in-law are also full of sympathy for you. You may be sure that you will receive a warm welcome from all the family when Ali returns and you come here. Please ask me for anything you want, darling. I would be so happy to be useful to you at this so terrible time in which you feel so far away and so alone without Ali and without news of him. Alfonso hopes to receive a telegram from him tomorrow.

Ali also wrote to the king from Morocco:

> On the night of the 10th to 11th October there was heavy fire from twelve thirty to quarter past two. I escaped from the tent and had to cross some fifty metres under heavy fire before reaching the trenches where my company was. Later, although bullets were whistling past, there was little danger.
>
> I am telling you this in case you are considering coming here to be under fire. There was one death and three wounded. The Moors, although in great number, dared not attack.

The regiment should have thirty-six stretchers. There are six here, as the rest have not come from Melilla.

This last phrase showed Ali's interest in the smallest details. He knew how to plan ahead, believed fervently in order and discipline, and reminded the king that while the daytime temperature could be hot, it dropped to two or three degrees when night fell, and felt very humid. Soon he fell ill with serious colic, and was hospitalised in Melilla. Ena explained in a letter (Madrid, 2 December 1912) that Loriga had just received a letter from Ali who was now much better. Almost all the officers had the colic but were fine when they returned to Spain, and she hoped he would be as well.

The queen, who was about to give birth, mentioned her worries. She wrote of the arrival of her son, Jaime, from Switzerland, and hoped his hearing would improve. In her letters, she tried to cheer up her unhappy cousin, telling her that when the campaign finished, Ali would come to Madrid to serve as first lieutenant with his titles, wife, and child: 'Please keep this to yourself my dear sister, because the rest could fall if this news is told before it should. I am so happy to think that the sad part has passed so quickly, Ali returns to his country!'

In another letter (2 December 1911), the queen mentioned her plans for Bee to join her and her husband for Christmas. Alfonso, she said, would invite Ali to her new baby's baptism and then send him immediately to Coburg: 'The doctor says that I will not go longer than the 15th December, so Ali should be able to be with you by Christmas or as soon as possible. I am thinking of doing violent exercises, although they tire me, because I do not want you to be separated a day more from Ali because of me'.

All went according to plan. On 12 December, *Infanta* Maria Christina was born, her godparents *Infanta* María Teresa and Tsar Nicholas II, represented by Ali who had arrived that day from Melilla. His brother, Luís Fernando, came from Cuenca. That night, they left on the *Sud Express* for Paris, arriving at 9 p.m. the following day, to change train for Coburg. Bee informed Ena by letter (Coburg, 16 December 1911):

I hope that Ali will soon be pardoned and that it will be possible for little Álvaro and me to go to some city in Spain, perhaps Malaga, to be near him.

I want to follow Ali as any woman should follow her husband. You can imagine that my meeting with Ali was very sad. God has protected him from all harm. It was as if all the sacrifice and sadness was for nothing. I feel that it is God's will that in another battle, Ali will fall.

My position in my family is impossible just now, as you can imagine I cannot admit that Ali serves in the Spanish Army, as they would criticise it...

If you believe that Alfonso would prefer not to know that I am going to Melilla. I leave it completely to you whether to tell him.

I am sorry to bother you with my affairs—we have now been separated for three months—it is said that I could go in March. (The thing with his mother could upset everything.) I have suffered so many worries and humiliations that my situation has been very difficult without Ali.

Bee also learned of the publication of *Au fil de la vie (The Thread of Life)* by *Infanta* Eulalia, which caused a sensation at the time in the intellectual circles in which she moved, and where her admirers were appalled at the attitude of the *Infante* Antonio of Orleans. That autumn, Eulalia was humiliated when her husband paid 250,000 pesetas to reinstate the title of viscountess of Térmens for his lover Carmen ('Carmela') Giménez Flores Brito y Milla, an extraordinary sum for the time.

Duchess María of Coburg commented (Edinburgh Palace, 23 November/12 December 1911):

[It was] stupid of Eulalia for nearly ruining the matter of Ali by her rudeness towards Alfonso, who behaves like a ill-mannered schoolchild. But now everything has been smoothed over again, and the whole episode was simply idiocy on both sides.

She sent her book to Baby. It is full of current events in French, but she was mistaken in publishing such a long chapter about the divorce. The rest is absolutely inoffensive.

She loses all measure in relating the matter to the newspapers and to some more than doubtful friends.

Plans were made for Christmas. Ducky and Kirill, who had arrived from Paris, Leopold and Maurice of Battenberg all loved spending the season at Coburg before going to Madrid to celebrate Epiphany. With the arrival of the two Orleans, there was no lack of fun in the old palace. Ali used to say that in Coburg in winter, there was no more than 'hunting, skating or skiing, and music at night' in the happy, fun-filled days. Little did Bee suspect that it would be the last Christmas they all spent together.

On 27 December, the Moroccans attacked again on the River Kert and Ali was recalled to his regiment. He immediately returned to Paris where, between trains, he was able to meet his father. Arriving in Madrid on 1 January 1912, he spent his time until taking the train for Morocco by eating at the palace, and meeting comrades from the regiment at the station. His sudden departure before the new year saddened Bee, who was greatly enjoying his leave. She was left with only the memory of those happy days and her strong desire to leave for Morocco, as she wrote to

Ena (Coburg, January 1912), confiding her future plans:

> I hope the New Year will be happy for me, beginning the year like you with a new baby. I am writing to tell you that I intend to follow Ali to Melilla. Of course I will not go via Spain, so that it will not be disagreeable for any of you.
>
> I am thinking of going via France or England. Alfonso cannot stop the wife of an officer going to join her husband but I do not wish to get involved in any way in advance discussions. I do not wish to do anything behind your backs. This letter is for you.
>
> It is not stupidity or selfishness on my part which now makes me want to follow Ali. I feel forced to do so. Previous occasions have demonstrated that there is almost no hope that Ali will be pardoned. Now all reason speaks of his rehabilitation. I thought that he would be pardoned in the first months!

The duchess of Coburg then wrote to her eldest daughter about their Christmas (30 December 1911):

> After a short time in which we have been able to breathe more easily again, we have returned to live a life full of worries because Ali leaves today for Morocco. He was thinking of remaining a fortnight more because a ceasefire had begun, but now he has to return quickly because all the officers have been recalled. Alfonso has done nothing for Ali. In addition he has said bad things about his cousin in order not to give him the title of *Infante*. He claims that Ali became ill in Melilla so as not to be in a battle.

Bee had planned to take the best medicines and new instruments to the Moroccan hospitals, and all kinds of clothing for the soldiers. She knew from Ali how bad conditions were in the hospitals behind the lines, and at the front. Her experiences caring for the haemophiliac Leopold of Battenberg showed she was a born nurse. In mid-January 1912, she went to Spain via England where she sailed for Malaga, accompanied only by her son and his nanny, Irene Collenette.

On arrival, they installed themselves at a house in the mountains run by an English lady. At length, the princess received permission to go to Morocco, and arrived in Melilla on the morning of 14 February on board the *Sister*. Ali had left the front the previous day, and accompanied by Gen. Jordana, the naval commander, and Capt. Sánchez Miñana, sailed out in a *falúa* to meet her. They drove in a car supplied by the commander in chief, followed by another with a vast amount of luggage, to the hotel where they stayed during his time in the city. That afternoon, they visited the Docker and Buen Acuerdo Hospitals. Bee spent some time in the Docker to chat with the soldiers who were former prisoners in the camp at Bu Hermana. The ladies of the Melilla Red Cross received her at the door of the Hospital of the Buen Acuerdo, and she issued them with medical supplies. Accompanied by the ladies, she visited various rooms, including those reserved for Moroccans wounded in recent combat, talked to everyone and took a keen interest in their convalescence.

On 17 February at the Central Hospital, the *infantes* visited the widow of José Esgleas who had been assassinated in the town of Frajana. She was recovering from her wounds, and as Ali had told her the sad tale, Bee spoke comfortingly to her in almost perfect Spanish, then made her a substantial donation. They also visited Melilla, accompanied by Gen. Marina. Although she was six months pregnant, it did not stop Bee from visiting the hospitals daily to explain about the medicines and materials she had brought. At the end of her visit, she returned to Malaga, while Ali returned to Issafen to rejoin the San Fernando Regiment. Her two-week stay in Morocco left behind pleasant memories. She was particularly glad to have been able to talk to the wounded, hear their worries, and offer words of comfort, as well as congratulate them on their heroic conduct.

In Malaga, Bee found her son waiting to hug her. Leopold of Battenberg wanted to come from Madrid to join her at her Malaga retreat. On 4 May, they heard from Issafen that Ali had led his company on a reconnaissance of the nearby heights and protected the return of a convoy. Later, seventy-four soldiers of his company were awarded with the Cross of Military Merit, presented to them by the commander at the taking of Ifratuata. A few days later, Ali acted as interpreter between the military *attachés* who had come to visit the front. They were very pleased with the treatment received from the new captain who could speak to them equally in French, German, English, or Italian.

At last the day of rehabilitation arrived: 'Yesterday, the 12th March 1912, H.R.H. Don Alfonso of Orleans Bourbon is rehabilitated to his high title as proposed by Don José Canalejas'. It caused great satisfaction in the San Fernando Regiment. On 18 March, Ali bade farewell on being promoted to first lieutenant and was posted to the king's 1st Immemorial Regiment in Madrid. The colonel addressed the officers, commending the conduct of Ali, who replied gratefully and emotionally. On the eve of his departure, a banquet was held in the Hotel Victoria with all the chiefs and officers where they toasted Spain and the king in champagne. Accompanied by his cousin, Ferdinand of Bavaria, he left for Spain on the steamer *Lázaro*. On 22 March, now in Madrid, he lunched at the palace, thanked the king for his benevolence, and they talked about Morocco.

At last he went to Malaga, accompanied by a convalescent Prince Leo who wanted to stay in the Andalusian city. Bee was eager to see him again. Before returning to Madrid, they had to set up their household. It was very easy for Ali because, among his friends at the academy, the closest was Luís Moreno y Gil de Borja, whom he named as his assistant and palace manager, and whose friendship and loyalty never wavered. Later he appointed César Sáenz de Santa María, who formed part of the entourage on his visit to Japan, and stayed with Ali until his death.

The *infanta's* household was more difficult. According to historian Melchor Fernández Almagro, 'in the narrow and closed court of Madrid she did not find anyone with a title who wanted to be her lady-in-waiting'. She sought out Doña Belén Rojas, the widow of Ruata, who accepted the position. The queen received her in an audience on 10 April before she left for Malaga to meet the *infantes*.

During the long journey from Malaga to Madrid, Bee felt unsettled and spent a bad night. She asked one, then another, how the royal family would receive them. They had borne their exile of twenty-one months with fortitude. Ena would surely show her affection, but how would the king behave towards them? From some things said by her brother-in-law, Luis Fernando, who was very observant, she knew he had once treated Ali cruelly. She realised she could never stand seeing her husband unjustly treated.

On 15 April, she looked out of the window, saw they were entering the Mediodía Station, and noted the red carpet in the distance, a sign that Ena had come to meet them. Drawing nearer, she saw the royal couple, behind them the *Infanta* Isabel, and next to her the queen mother. The whole royal family were on the platform.

9

Spanish Infanta

King Alfonso and Queen Ena left the palace early on 15 April to meet Bee and Ali, arriving by train from Malaga. Ali immediately jumped down onto the platform and helped his wife, still agile despite advanced pregnancy. Embraces and kisses were exchanged, and then two-year-old Álvaro appeared, a charming child with blond hair in ringlets. On leaving the station, they went straight to their new home, *Infanta* Eulalia's house at No. 5, Calle Quintana. Ali was delighted to be back in his home city. They soon discovered that the house had many reception rooms but few bedrooms with bathrooms. Bee disliked the kitchen, which was on the lower floor so that the smell of cooking pervaded the house, and decided to renovate it later.

Bee's twenty-eighth birthday and little Álvaro's second was on 20 April. The family assembled for lunch, followed by a concert by the Madrid Symphony Orchestra and the Orfeón Catalan, featuring the music of Wagner.

Duchess Maria's letter from Château Fabron (9–12 April 1912), written a week after the new *infanta*'s arrival, noted that she was very satisfied with their reception and happy in her new house, even though she was not used to so many visitors, audiences and courtesies: '*Good for her*. This painful episode has drawn to a close, and now she can create a good position in Spain, which will depend upon her tact and her *savoir-faire*'.

In the mornings when there were no audiences, Ena took her cousin to show her the shops, then they would chat until lunchtime. Because of the heat, they generally went by car to the Casa de Campo after tea. Now in her last month of pregnancy, Bee tried to go on the long walks recommended by the doctors. She saw her husband was happy in his new post in the king's 1st *Regimiento Inmemorial*. His job was to train new recruits, and he showed such enthusiasm that the squad made great efforts to follow his lead.

Everything seemed to be going well until Bee was surprised to receive a letter from her mother-in-law, Eulalia, who was very upset as she wanted to return to Spain to be godmother to her new grandson. This letter is missing, but instead one received by Queen Cristina (29 April) tells the story:

> As I do not know if they have told you about the situation, I wish to tell you that I have just written to the King and my daughter-in-law to tell them that I will not accept being godmother to my new grandson (or granddaughter) because in my *position* as a *mother* I object to my being represented (even by the Queen) at the baptism of a grandchild of mine. *I will hold my grandchild in my arms or I will not be godmother.*
>
> I know that they want me to know that my presence in Madrid would be harmful to my son's position and I know that they want me to be godmother by proxy. I have forgiven Ali for marrying without telling me. I have sacrificed my personality for Ali, although it means more to me than my title of *Infanta*, which only makes me a 'satellite'. I have given Ali everything that I possess, and now they say that I cannot enter my own house but that I can be *godmother* (why?...) but I cannot go.

As Bee and Ali had been made so welcome by the royal family, Eulalia had forgotten the furore caused by the publication of *Au Fil de la Vie*. She was supposed to have sent the king a copy before it reached the public, but never did; he was very unhappy with it, and Prime Minister José Canalejas had advised him to maintain a distant attitude. The letter caused Ali as much sorrow as Bee, as it had come at a time of calm and tranquillity. The royal decree of 21 May 1912 stated that the forthcoming son or daughter of the king's beloved cousins, the *Infantes* Don Alfonso María de Orleans-Borbón and Doña Beatrice of Saxe-Coburg-Gotha, and any others born from this marriage, would receive the rank of 'Royal Highness' and be *infantes* of Spain. Some thought the title of 'Royal Highness' did not apply to their first-born, Álvaro. The *Infante* Antonio of Orleans mentioned this to his friend and confident Ramón de las Cagigas, and the *infantes* later confirmed that Prince Álvaro was indeed also a royal highness.

Ali had attended the sovereign's birthday banquet on the evening of 17 May, and was very pleased by his reception from those close to the king. According to the doctors, Bee's confinement was due at the end of the month, and she regretted being without her mother's support this time. The duchess also still felt antagonistic towards Alfonso XIII and his mother, Queen Maria Cristina, making it difficult for Bee to choose them both as godparents. Fortunately, Ali decided to tell his mother-in-law that his cousin had offered to be the godfather and as 'he had as good as said' that as it had been Ena last time, this time it was the queen mother's turn.

On 28 May, just before going to lunch, Doña Beatrice felt unwell and the Count of San Diego, the doctor who brought the royal children into the world, was summoned. That evening, she gave birth to a healthy son who was given the names of Alonso María Cristino Justo, and the baptism was arranged for 5 June. Some thought the procedure would be altered as the mother was not a Roman Catholic. Nevertheless, she was always very respectful of the customs of the Spanish court and royal family, who would never have altered such an important ceremony.

Afterwards, the king and queen visited Calle Quintana to give the new mother various presents, including the Sash of the Order of María Luisa with the insignia in diamonds, and a gold and diamond medal for the child. In order to re-establish Bee, the queen had invited her to go with her and her children to La Granja, a relief after the heat of Madrid. At 9:30 a.m. on 27 June, the two cousins left for La Granja in the royal train accompanied by Ali, who had to return later to his regiment in Madrid. During their conversations, Bee mentioned her husband's interest in aviation, adding that she was worried about the number of pilots who had died practising at Cuatro Vientos aerodrome. Soon afterwards, Alfonso XIII arrived at La Granja, having come from San Sebastian where he was spending the summer with his mother.

When Emperor Mutsohito of Japan died, the king asked his cousin to represent him at the funeral. Ali asked for César Sáenz de Santa María, his contemporary, to accompany him as an assistant on the long journey— Ali would bear the travel expenses for his assistant. The king agreed, and from then on César would become the *infante*'s most faithful friend. While Bee went to stay in Coburg, on 20 August, Ali began his journey to Japan, passing through Berlin, arriving in Moscow eight days later, and continuing on the Trans-Siberian until arriving in Tokyo on 11 September for six days. He returned on the Trans-Siberian railway, remaining a few days in Moscow as guest of honour of the imperial family. He arrived in Paris by train where his wife and children met him, and they returned to Madrid on 18 October. They found a court in mourning, for *Infanta* María Teresa, who had married her cousin, Ferdinand of Bavaria, died a few days after giving birth to a daughter. Her death was a heavy blow for Bee and Ena, herself in the sixth month of pregnancy. As the family peacemaker, Maria Teresa was a great loss to the family. Bee wrote to her mother, who told Missy (16–19 October 1912), 'how depressed she is and how unhappy Ena feels!' On hearing of her niece's death, Eulalia went to Madrid to present her condolences to her sister-in-law. Deeply upset, the king went to Ali and Bee's home to meet his estranged aunt and thank her, but no reconciliation resulted and she did not return to Spain for many years.

One month later, the prime minister, José Canalejas, was assassinated. On the morning of 12 November, he was with the king in his office, returned home, and then visited the Puerta de Sol. While looking in a shop window, an anarchist shot him dead, and then fled through the crowded plaza. The funeral was attended by the king who walked behind the coffin without any bodyguard, followed by a great crowd. Ali was terribly upset because he admired Canalejas as a statesman, and as he had always been very good to him.

Bee wished to celebrate Christmas with her usual German and English customs. She enjoyed her new country, but it was not quite the same as home as her mother wrote to Missy (6 December 1912):

> What a strange life they lead in Spain! Naturally [Bee] found it somewhat hard and complained 'like Sandra' [her third daughter] ... imagining that nobody suffered as much as she.
>
> I would have been able to tell terrible stories about my first experiences in England and the extreme desperation I had to overcome. But what for? You will not believe me and at least she has a good friend there in Ena, which is a consolation I lacked intensely because my sisters-in-law were strange, incomplete, and jealous.

Bee accompanied the queen on her walks and shopping, as the king was constantly hunting and Ali accompanied him when he could. On Christmas Eve, the family met around the Christmas tree and the children received their gifts, although the adults had to wait until Epiphany for theirs. They attended a Christmas dinner, and on 31 December, a Te Deum was held in the chapel of the royal palace.

On 3 January 1913, Ali entered the Military Aviation School at Cuatro Vientos as a pupil. He went up in the dirigible *España* for fifty-seven minutes as an observer, and then took charge of training the squad of recruits in his company. As Leopold and Maurice of Battenberg were in Madrid, Ena invited Bee and Ali to accompany them on excursions. On 5 February (Ash Wednesday), the palace chapel was open to the public. Bee was not required to attend, so they played bridge, with Bee and Ali beating the king and Prince Ranieri of the Two Sicilies in a couple of games. Holy Week was approaching and Bee watched the Procession of the Holy Sepulchre from the palace balconies with great interest. She and the queen hid Easter eggs for the little princes to find.

On 26 March, Alfonso XIII fell during a polo match and was unconscious for about ten minutes, but recovered and he returned to the palace on foot. After a few days of rest, he resumed his duties. On 13 April, he presided over the Oath of Allegiance from recruits in the Paseo de la Castellana. As he was returning, a man fired a revolver at him and he calmly rode his horse Alarun towards him. The man tried to grab the bridle while shooting a second time, the flash scorching the king's glove and the bullet grazing his horse. He made the animal turn and knocked his assailant down. The previous month, King George I of Greece had been murdered in Salonika. The next day, a Te Deum was celebrated in the palace chapel. Ena, her sensitivity exacerbated by pregnancy, considered it ominous news.

The king and queen were up early to congratulate Bee on her birthday and brought presents for mother and son. The king spent a few days in Paris, and his wife went out with her cousin. They went to tea at the home of the countess of Casa Valencia, to the English and Russian embassies, and to an art exhibition.

In January, Missy had given birth to her youngest child, a son named Mircea. She was suffering from phlebitis, and the doctors recommended she take the waters at Dax in the south of France, travelling via Spain. Bee was thrilled to be reunited with her older sister, and Ena invited Marie to the palace on 16 May. The king and queen greeted her at the station. As the following day was Alfonso XIII's birthday, there was a Mass in the tapestry room, then a reception in the throne room and a banquet in the grand banqueting hall. Bee showed Marie round her house and wanted to discuss her projects to renovate it with her, now that they needed an ample and sunny nursery where the children could play freely.

The *Infanta* Isabel took Marie to El Escorial by way of a farewell, while Bee accompanied Ena on her walks. She wanted to go to La Granja to rest because Madrid tired her. On 5 June, the court installed itself there, with polo and games of bridge the main attractions. On 19 June, Ena did not go down to lunch. Bee stayed with her until the pains began that evening as the king was returning from Madrid. Next morning, the government and all the royal family were alerted to Ena's condition. At 1:15 a.m., Ali went into the king's office but moments later came out to tell the assembled court, 'Gentlemen, it is a boy', and Gen. Aznar left to give orders for the twenty-one gun salute. According to custom, a red light and the flag were placed on the facade of the palace. The king was satisfied because the baby was not a haemophiliac, and he and Ali also won the cup for polo.

The new baby's sister's birthday was 22 June, another *Infanta* Beatriz who, though only three years old, dressed in white and with a mantilla, made the traditional offering in church. The following day, her brother, Jaime, was four, and on 24 June, the baptism of the new *Infante* Juan was celebrated.

On 11 July, the queen, accompanied by her husband, attended the Mass of the Purification (Candlemas). She then lunched with the king and the *infantes*. That night, Ali left for San Sebastian, where the queen mother was awaiting him. A week later, the queen and her sons went to San Sebastian for the summer. That same day, the *infantes* of Orleans left by train for Paris and then to Coburg. According to Missy, it was the last summer the four sisters spent with their mother, and they always remembered it nostalgically.

During his military service Ali had trained on biplanes, so he volunteered to receive five Lohner aeroplanes from Vienna on behalf of the Spanish government. They were to arrive in the Peninsula in August for use in the future war with Morocco. Suddenly, on 13 September, the minister of war ordered Ali to rejoin his regiment and go with his battalion to Algeciras by train, and from there, to the Sierra Carbonera where he would train the troops until 29 September. He was then sent to Madrid to join the Aviation School to form part of the expeditionary squadron. Bee stayed in Coburg with the little princes, then went to San Sebastian and to Madrid, where Ali arrived on the morning of 30 July.

By the summer and autumn of 1913, the newspapers were announcing 'the conversion of the *Infanta* Beatrice which was to be celebrated with great solemnity'. One forecast that when the court returned to Madrid, around 1 October, Bee would receive the baptismal waters in the crypt of Our Lady of La Almudena, administered by the Papal Nuncio, to be followed by a grand banquet at the Alcázar. It would not happen for another fifteen years.

On 5 October, Bee and Ali received the king and queen, with Queen Maria Cristina and the *Infanta* Isabel, for lunch. They discussed the imminent arrival of Raymond Poincaré, president of the Republic of France, and the necessary protocol. Bee asked permission not to attend because of her advanced pregnancy, but she came to the palace with the queen and the *Infantas* Isabel and Luisa for the review of the troops. She attended the dinner in honour of the president, and on 15 October, invited all the royal family to a dinner.

Ali's departure for Morocco was now imminent. Bee hoped to have her child before her husband left, but she thought it might not be possible, and their third son was born on the evening of 20 October. The count of San Diego attended her, and the queen was never far from her cousin's side for a moment. Three days later, the king came in his car to collect Ali, who was to leave Madrid that night for Ceuta, and gave him the good news that from now he was to devote himself completely to aviation.

On 24 October, Ducky arrived in Madrid at the invitation of the king and queen. On her arrival they all went to Calle Quintana, where Bee was perfectly composed despite Ali's departure the previous morning. Six days later, the baby was baptised Ataúlfo Alejandro Isabelo Carlos. To keep Bee company, the king and queen went every day to take tea at her home and then returned to the palace to dine and watch films. The baptismal party was celebrated at Bee's house, although she was still in bed.

While Ducky was in Madrid, the king and queen showed her Toledo, El Escorial, the Armoury, and the Prado Museum. As her father-in-law, Grand Duke Vladimir, had died that year, her husband, Kirill, was now third in line of succession to the Russian throne. Bee felt herself in good company with her sister in Madrid. Unfailingly generous, Ducky had brought many gifts from the Russian and Coburg families for her and the little ones.

On 13 November, Bee visited Ena, who wanted to see her because she was embarking on an official visit planned to Germany and Austria. As she had a heavy cold, the queen had to remain in the Hotel Meurice in Paris where she was cared for by Ducky and Kirill, who had a flat on Avenue Henri Martin. Ducky kept Ena company until she went by train to England, where she was met by King George V.

Meanwhile Bee, very much alone in Madrid, dreamed of going to Ceuta with the children to be reunited with Ali, who was happy to be flying and living the war intensely with his comrades. She had listened to her husband's projects. When he left, he had said, 'If they allow you to go...', and she was determined to go to Morocco and spend Christmas with him. However, at the court, they had not seen a princess following her husband to war since the times of Isabel the Catholic, so they dissuaded Bee from leaving until the return of the king and queen on 15 December. They were full of the good time they had had in London visiting the family.

Both cousins went to Casa Madel toyshop to choose toys for Three Kings' Day (Epiphany). That night, a grand banquet was held in the palace for the diplomatic corps. Bee met the new British ambassador, Sir Arthur, and Lady Hardinge, who had been in Romania and had fond memories of her sister, Marie. At table, Bee sat on the left of the sovereign who was in a very friendly mood, telling her Ali could come from Morocco to the south of Spain for a short holiday.

The king nominated Ali to preside on the commission which was to present the uniform of honorary colonel of the 2nd Sappers' Regiment to the king of Romania and Bee, who was keen to see Missy again, accompanied him. On the eve of their departure, the king and queen went to dinner at their home and the king showed much interest in their imminent journey. Leaving Madrid on 15 April, they were received in

Bucharest with full honours. King Carol was especially affectionate towards Bee, remembering their walks in the woods when she was a girl. He also recalled when Queen Elizabeth signed her books and gave a demonstration of dance and poetry in honour of Bee. Missy enjoyed showing Ali the beauties of Romania on various excursions. She was happy caring for her youngest child Mircea, now sixteen months old, although concerned about the two older ones with their difficult characters.

At twenty years of age, Carol was intelligent but rebellious. Nineteen-year-old Elisabeth, a classic beauty, was engaged to Prince George, the Greek heir. She told her Orleans aunt and uncle she would love to see Spain, so they agreed to take her with them when they returned, but her stay in Madrid would prove a nightmare for them. Back in Madrid, they were met at the Estación del Norte railway station by the king and queen. Alfonso XIII immediately captivated Elisabeth with his friendliness, and Ena took her to the Prado Museum as she said she was very interested in paintings.

That evening, a grand ball was held at the home of the marchioness of Squilache. About 1,000 had been invited, including the king and queen and the other members of the royal family. The *infantes* of Orleans arrived accompanied by their niece, Elisabeth. Bee greeted her husband's aunt, *Infanta* Isabel, who entered out of breath having climbed the staircase briskly despite her seventy-two years. Finally, the king and queen arrived, and he greeted the marchioness who took his arm to climb the staircase between footmen with powdered wigs who held silver candelabras with lit candles, while the orchestra played the national anthem. In the hall lit by sparkling chandeliers, they danced the rigaudon of honour, the king with the hostess, the queen with the *Infante* Don Fernando, *Infanta* Isabel with her cousin, Don Alfonso of Orleans, Doña Beatrice with old Gen. Azcárraga, and the princess of Romania with the German ambassador, followed by other members of the diplomatic corps. The party finished after 1 a.m. Next day, the king took Elisabeth in his Hispano to the Sierra de Guadarrama to attend an automobile competition.

Later that week, there was a dinner and a dance at the royal palace, at which the king danced with Elisabeth of Romania until 2:45 a.m. The attitude of Missy's daughter, a self-centred young girl who constantly craved attention, annoyed Ena greatly as King Alfonso's behaviour with her verged on the flirtatious. A few years later, on her wedding, she wrote to Missy (Madrid, 1 April 1922) that as she had known her children since they were small, she had followed the great events in their lives with interest, and was 'pleased that Elisabeth is happy with George; it must be a great relief to you as she certainly had a strange and difficult character when she was a girl'.

On 7 June, accompanied by her lady-in-waiting, Elisabeth left by train for Andalusia. Meanwhile, the *infantes* went to Castellejo, an estate near Tarancón in La Mancha, which they had inherited from Queen Cristina. The king and Ali returned to Madrid for the birth of Princess Esperanza, daughter of Louise of Orleans and Carlos de Borbón Dos Sicilias. The baptism was celebrated on 22 June, and immediately afterwards the two cousins decided to return to La Granja where their children were staying. Pregnant again, Ena found that walking bothered her, and it occurred to Bee that they could go fishing; so they went trout fishing and then cooked the catch.

On 26 June, accompanying Elisabeth, who was leaving Spain, they went to El Escorial, where she took the night train which arrived at San Sebastian so she could say goodbye to Queen María Cristina. As the king had left for San Sebastian to be with his mother and Ali was in Madrid, Ena and Bee were looking forward to a rest, when on 28 June a telegraph brought news of the assassinations of the Austrian imperial heir, Archduke Franz Ferdinand, and his wife, Sophie, in Sarajevo. Ena remembered how he had represented Emperor Franz Joseph at her wedding. Nobody yet realised that the incident would lead to a European war.

For a while, life in Spain continued as before. Spain maintained neutrality despite the pressures from belligerents on both sides. Bee used to say that on crossing the French frontier, the scene changed and she felt portents of war, especially when they arrived in Munich. German mobilisation began on 15 July. Austria and Russia had already done so, and the kaiser declared war on Russia on 1 August. France, which was an ally, did nothing, but President Poincaré urgently asked King George V on behalf of the British government to inform the Central Powers that they should reflect before attacking France, which mobilised on 2 August. Next day, Germany declared war, occupied Belgium before invading France, and England subsequently declared war.

On 20 August, the already ailing Pope Pius X passed away. The troops of the Central Powers had taken the initiative from the beginning of August, and by 6 September, the advance stopped. A major battle was fought, with a front beginning on the outskirts of Paris and ending on the River Moselle. The enemy fled in retreat, Paris was saved, and the front stabilised. The *infantes*, who were staying in Coburg, thought the war might not last more than six weeks. In Madrid, the press reported that they and their children were spending the summer in Germany, and it was expected that they would remain there for the duration. Ali left Coburg and after several security controls reached Munich, took the train to Genoa, and arrived in Barcelona on 18 September, where he was met by his assistant Moreno Abella. Next he went to the royal palace in Madrid.

The king and queen were expecting him. During lunch, Ena asked him about Bee and the children and insisted 'that they return quickly, as she wanted to have her there at all costs for her next birth especially as her mother could now not travel from England'. The king asked Ali what he thought about the war, adding that he trusted Spain would keep out of the conflict.

The following day, Ali went to the Cuatro Vientos aerodrome, spending each day with his comrades and only returning to the palace in the evenings where he would walk and dine with the king and queen. Life at the palace was difficult, as the two queens' families were on opposing sides. Queen María Cristina, who was Austrian, had three brothers and several nephews at the front, and Ena's English brothers, Alexander and Maurice, were also serving, while the less robust Leopold was in the rear-guard as an officer with the king's Royal Rifle Corps. 'Most of the aristocracy and the military favour the Central Empires,' Ali told Bee when they met in Barcelona on 25 September.

The *infantes* arrived in Madrid on 1 October. Ena met them at the station and accompanied them to the Palace of El Pardo, which the king had lent them while alterations were made at Calle Quintana. The children were delighted with the size of the rooms and the surrounding countryside. Bee also felt happy far from the city, having spent a sad summer in Coburg seeing friends go to the front. That afternoon, the king and queen went to take tea and asked them how they were. The following day, as the king had a cold, the *infantes* went to the palace to visit them and to see Queen Maria Cristina, keen for news of Austria and Germany.

The king wanted to know how they had settled in, and on 6 October, he was invited to dine at El Pardo. He was interested in receiving news of Romania, which remained neutral although King Carol was born a German Hohenzollern prince and had studied in Potsdam. King Carol died at Sinaia Castle on 10 October, tormented by being unable to enter the war in alliance with Germany. At seventy-five, he had reigned for forty-eight years. Now aged thirty-eight, Missy was queen. Bee was delighted although she worried about the weak character of her brother-in-law, but she believed deeply in her sister's intelligence and *savoir-faire*.

On the morning of 16 October, Bee walked across the racecourse with Queen Maria Cristina, who wanted to know her views and to which side she was inclined. Four days later, Ena went to congratulate little Ataúlfo who celebrated his first birthday and brought him some toys. Next day, Bee broke the news to Ena that Álvaro had diphtheria, and she could not be with her during her coming delivery.

Early on the morning of 24 October, the palace called to tell Bee of the arrival of Ena's baby son, Gonzalo. The *infantes* did not attend the baptism because of Álvaro's illness. That same week, Prince Maurice, the queen's youngest brother, had fallen on the Belgian front, but as she had just given birth, the family did not tell her. He had gone to the front with his section, was wounded at Zonnebeke, near Ypres, and died from a haemorrhage while being taken to hospital on 27 October. He had left a letter, dated 18 September 1914, written in pencil, addressed to his brother-in-law the king, asking him not to forget to look after Camille, probably his lover, if anything happened to him, and adding her address in London. The *infantes* attended Maurice's funeral on 1 November at the chapel of the English embassy. Bee went into strict mourning and at the end of the ceremony received declarations of sympathy from various members of the Allied embassies.

During November, the two cousins saw each other every day. On 6 December, the king organised a hunt at La Granja, and the two couples went in the same car. Returning six days later, Bee wrote to her sister, the queen of Romania, telling her that in Spain the army 'and all decent people are strictly pro-German, although the Republican Party has French sympathies'. Ena, although English, 'is not uncomfortable: and I am neutral because I was born in England and educated in Germany. What can one say or feel?' They had returned to Madrid after a week at La Granja. She envied Missy, being in her position and to 'be able to be an influence for peace! One dreams of being able to help—to help with all the suffering people—and to ask that all those who are not involved stay that way!'

The *infantes* and their children went to spend their Christmas holidays at Castillejo, returned to court on 2 January 1915, and went to the palace at Epiphany with their cousins to receive the toys the 'Three Wise Men' had left for them. After attending a military festival in the throne room, Ali and Bee left for Sanlúcar de Barrameda. For Bee, the Andalusian town, filled with churches and palaces and with beautiful gardens by the sea, was a pleasant surprise. They got to know the Aladro Palace in Jerez and went round the more celebrated *bodegas*. Local society was very cosmopolitan and in Jerez many people spoke English, but she preferred to speak in Spanish, and in English or German privately with her husband.

After returning from the trip to Andalusia on 11 January, Bee went down with flu, while Ena had scarlet fever, which kept her in bed for a while, so Bee resumed her visits to the palace to see her cousin. They both particularly enjoyed going to painters' and sculptors' studios, and one morning called on Manuel Benedito, who was painting a portrait of the king.

Around this time, an anecdote arose that I heard from Bee herself. At the end of the 1950s, I finished a biography of the king and queen of

Savoy. She was very interested and commented to me, 'Did you know that Amadeo I left a child in Spain?' I answered that I knew, although I had scant details of the mother. She then told me:

> After the birth of the *Infante* Don Gonzalito, the Queen was much troubled by the phlebitis she suffered in her legs which made walking very difficult. As my husband was working at Cuatro Vientos, I often lunched alone with the King and Queen at the palace. Once the King asked me, 'Bee, would you like to go to see Savoy?'
>
> This consisted of taking a walk through the Casa del Campo to the house of a forest ranger who used to fix shotguns and other weapons. As I have always liked walking, I accompanied him. The ranger was the son of King Amadeo I, and his likeness to him was famous. He lived happily there with his wife and children in the middle of the countryside, because he did not like the court, unlike his brother, the ambassador, or the other brother who was a colonel in the cavalry.
>
> The mother of these three Saavedras was a noble and very pretty Portuguese, called Valentina Vinent y O'Neill. She was a daughter-in-law of the Duke of Rivas and bore a Castilian title.

The king and queen invited the *Infantes* Carlos and Luisa, and Ali and Bee, to spend a few days with them at the Alcázar of Seville. All three couples arrived on 5 March, and after lunch the king suggested to the *infantes* of Orleans that they come for a run in the new car he had just acquired. He took the wheel, 'left with the *Infanta* Beatrice by the Tablada road and the Cruz del Campo, then returned by the Paseo de las Delicias via Palomares and through the city centre'. The newspapers politely described the trip thus. But on the patio of the Alcázar, there were shocked comments by the rest of the party as, in full view, they were surprised to see the king leave quickly without waiting for his wife and his cousin to sit in the rear of the car as would normally happen. Without losing any time, Ali asked for his car, the queen got in, and they made their way through the main streets and avenues.

Ena and Bee both liked to walk through the narrow streets of the Santa Cruz district and, after hearing Mass in the cathedral, they visited the Hospital de la Caridad to admire Murillo's paintings. They then went by horse-drawn carriage to Triana, to the convent of the Encarnation to pray to the Virgin. They also visited the tile factory, where the *infanta* chose some tiles for the kitchen of her new flat being built in Quintana. When they told the king what they had seen, he decided to visit the museum with his cousin, Ali. The doorman did not recognise them and asked them for a peseta to enter the Murillo and Valdés Leal rooms. As the king never carried any cash, it was a most amused Ali who paid the entrance fee, telling him, 'You can go everywhere with money.' The same day, 17 March, Ali went to the Real Maestranza bullring in Seville, as he was a devoted follower of bullfighting.

At Jerez de la Frontera, the king and queen were awaited with impatience and warmly welcomed. In the Gonzalez Byass *bodega*, the queen tasted wine from a barrel dated 1887, the year of her birth, and added her signature to it. They left with Princess Maria Christina of Salm-Salm, and arrived the following morning in Madrid, where Bee offered to show the princess the Prado and Modern Art museums. As niece of the regent and first cousin of the king, the princess stayed in the palace where she was well respected. Nevertheless, some courtiers would criticise her frequent journeys to Spain during the war and her visits to the Austro-Hungarian embassy, presided over by the prince of Furstenberg, and above all to that of Germany where her kinsman the prince of Ratibor was ambassador.

On 22 March 1915, the *infantes* of Orleans gave a dinner in honour of Maria Christina of Salm-Salm, attended by most of the royal family including the king and queen. The *infantes* and their children left for Castillejo for Holy Week, and on returning to Madrid they went to visit Ena who was unwell. When she was better, she went to the estate of La Almoraina, where her elder brother Alexander was staying with the duke and duchess of Medinaceli who had invited him for the hunting. It was the first time they had seen each other for over a year.

On 6 May, Queens Maria Cristina and Ena went to the Cuatro Vientos aerodrome and were welcomed by Ali and Bee, who showed them around. They lunched there with the officers whose leader, Alfred Kindelán, was a sincere monarchist and a great friend of Ali, and would later be appointed aide to the king. Another day, the two queens went to have dinner at El Pardo, and Queen Maria Cristina said to Bee that she would like to see the work going on at 5 Calle Quintana before completion. On Alonso's birthday on 28 May, Ena, carrying many toys for him and his brothers, went to El Pardo to congratulate him. The king visited his cousin to show him the new car he had acquired and took him for a spin at high speed. The same day, Queen Maria Cristina went to visit the Rubio Institute and asked Bee to accompany her, as she knew she was very interested in its work. They both sat on the pupils' benches. Taking advantage of the king's being at San Sebastian, the *infantes* gave an informal dinner for the two queens at El Pardo palace.

On 13 June, they invited the Princess of Salm-Salm to tea, to which the king and queen also came. Three days later, at the Cuatro Vientos Aerodrome, little Prince Don Álvaro had his first flight. His mother and little brothers accompanied him and watched as Ali climbed into the

Farman biplane and placed the boy upon his knees, while an experienced friend accompanying him started the motors and piloted the aeroplane which landed after making a few circuits. The child did not turn a hair.

The queen was at La Granja for the St John's Day holiday and Ali was at Alcalá de Henares, taking part in manoeuvres with his infantry regiment, when it occurred to the king to go the Palace of El Pardo to visit the Bee who, according to *La Epoca*, 'was out', while other newspapers said, 'that as she was ill she could not receive him'. Two days later, the king accompanied by Ali, went to Toledo where the awarding of commissions to the infantry's new lieutenants took place at the Alcázar. The queen attended the ceremony with the princess of Salm-Salm.

On 27 June, Bee and Ali formed part of the retinue accompanying the king and queen on their visit to the monastery at Guadalupe. Returning two days later, the princess of Salm-Salm went to El Pardo to say goodbye, and the *infantes* gave a tea attended by the king and the marquis and marchioness of Viana. Four days later, the *infantes* left for La Granja with their children. The king waited to see the children, asking them many questions. It was a very pleasant time for Bee, who went riding with Ena from morning to night, walking and fishing in the streams. In the afternoons there were polo, and clay pigeon shooting championships, in the evenings theatre and cinema, and the occasional dance, which the two cousins loved.

Ena went to San Sebastián to congratulate Queen Maria Cristina, on her fifty-seventh birthday, but during the European war relations were still delicate between them both. Historians suggested there was a very close relationship and that María Cristina now never interfered in politics, having handed over the reins of state to her son, although a letter from Ena to her cousin Missy would later suggest otherwise.

Later that month, the *infantes* returned to Calle Quintana, Madrid. At La Granja, the king asked Bee if she would go to the studio of the great painter Sorolla to judge if the portrait which he was painting looked like him, and what she thought of it. She went to the studio with the marquis of Viana, 'Master of the King's Horse', and an intimate friend of the king, but was unimpressed by the portrait. The king was annoyed, as he believed that everything painted by Joaquin Sorolla Bastida, whose work he greatly admired, was the best.

On 26 July, the king arrived in Madrid. The *infantes* were waiting for him on the station, invited him to Calle Quintana, and then they dined at El Pardo. The *infantes* always went to Coburg after spending time at La Granja, but during the war they could not travel abroad and found themselves without somewhere to spend the summer. It was probably Ena who asked her husband if the Orleans cousins and their children could be their guests at Santander. The little *Infantas* Beatriz and María

Cristina loved playing with their cousins, and a photograph was taken that summer at La Granja on an excursion they made on donkeys with the children. The king also liked having his cousin, an excellent polo player, at the Magdalena palace, especially as he had recently had a new polo field constructed there. Bee was curious to visit the palace that the city of Santander had given the king and queen, with its wonderful peninsular location. They had decorated it with English furniture and large sofas covered in chintz. Ena was very pleased because the Cantabrian Sea reminded her of the Isle of Wight, and she commented to Bee that for the first time she felt herself to be 'in her own home'.

The prime minister, Eduardo Dato, an intelligent and cultivated man whose company Bee greatly enjoyed, used to come and work with the king. The 'Minister of the Day' was the marquis of Lema, an elderly diplomat who had held the portfolio of foreign affairs. They were also accompanied by more intimate courtiers such as the duke of Santo Mauro, the marquises of Torrecilla and Viana, as well as the queen's lady-in-waiting, the duchess of San Carlos, whose children often invited the king and queen to their lovely estate of Las Fraguas, near Santander.

The marquis of Viana was such a perfect courtier that when he played polo in the team against the king, the sovereign was nearly always on the winning side. Being devoted to sport, especially shooting and polo, Alfonso enjoyed being first at everything. He, Ali, the marquis of Viana, and the count of La Maza formed the purple team and the duke of Santoña, the count of Rincón, Joaquin Santos Suárez, and Ernesto Larios formed the white team. In yachting regattas, again he liked to come first, although this depended upon the wind and the state of the sea. That year there were regattas at Bilbao, where he took the helm of the seven-metre Mektouh, accompanied by Bee and the princess of Salm-Salm. He was sure of victory when just before arriving at the finish, Narria was a minute ahead and was classified first. It was crewed by the *Infanta* Luisa and her husband, Carlos, as well as Ena and Ali.

Thanks to the war, Vizcaya (Biscay) was enjoying a time of prosperity and the people of Bilbao, being very grateful to the king and the government, did not stop giving to the royal family. It was then when the relationships between the sovereigns and the high society of Vizcaya began, and soon they were distinguished with Castilian titles. Alfonso XIII and his family visited Guernica and its famous oak tree, an old symbol of the traditional and historical rights and liberties of the Basque provinces in the North of Spain, and the Casa de Juntas (Meeting House). They returned to Santander to plan an excursion to Covadonga, which the king and queen wished to make by car with Doña Luisa, Don Carlos, the princess of Salm-Salm, and the *infantes* of Orleans. Years later, Bee commented on how interested she had been by the long tunnel in the rock leading from the Chapel of the Virgin to the lake among the mountains with its lunar landscape.

The *infantes* went to the Sailing Club for another race on 9 September and the *Infanta* Luisa was again the winner. The days passed quickly and early on the morning of 10 October they left Santander, leaving the children to return by train with their nannies. Ali took the wheel of the automobile with Bee at his side and the chauffeur behind to look after the luggage. They stopped in Burgos to refuel and then later at 11:30 a.m. near Aranda de Duero to lunch on the provisions they carried, then continued on towards Somosierra and arrived at the palace at 5 p.m.

The next day, there was a hunt at El Pardo while Ena, accompanied by her lady-in-waiting Conchita Heredia, walked to Calle Quintana to see the new house. The queen continued to visit her cousin regularly, and Bee invited both queens to come and see her new home. They also accompanied the *Infanta* Isabel to the station to meet the king and see Ali participating in the great hunt at Mudela. Later they attended the festival of aviation at Getafe, where they opened workshops to carry out motor repairs and maintenance, and watched Ali giving a demonstration piloting his Lohner biplane to much applause.

Beatrice thought the new air force needed an emblem and designed one consisting of large feathers, with a golden sun in the centre to be embroidered on the aviators' green uniforms. The pilots came from the armed forces including the engineers and artillery, although like Ali, most were from the Infantry. Curiously, the Spanish Emblem would be copied by the British Royal Air Force and other countries. Seeing her design on the uniforms, Bee felt honoured and even closer to her husband.

10

False Rumours

Since that summer in Santander, a whispering campaign directed against Bee began among certain courtiers, who were devoted to the king and began murmuring about the power she had over the queen. Ena was much saddened, especially as it was the first anniversary of the death of her younger brother, and also because the doctors were certain her latest child was a haemophiliac. Alfonso XIII had reacted by distancing himself from his wife, and he told his intimates that 'these bitter words about the illness which my wife's family carries' were sentiments he would never forget.

On 25 November, the anniversary of Alfonso XII's death, a Mass was held in the Collegiate Church attended by the king, queen, and the *infantes*. They then went to Valsaín, to inspect the polo horses. That afternoon, they visited Segovia and the Alcázar, inviting the director, teachers and cadets to a dinner, returning to Madrid three days later. The king, notorious for driving as fast as possible, had planned to take his car, but the queen preferred travelling over the Pass of the Lions with her Orleans cousins, 'with the *Infante* proceeding at a moderate speed'.

A palace offensive to force Bee out of Spain began. In an official report of 6 July 1916, the British ambassador, Sir Arthur Hardinge, recalled what happened at a hunt at La Granja. According to him, the previous autumn, there had been a disagreement at court when the duke of Santo Mauro, the queen's secretary, and the duchess of San Carlos, first lady of the bedchamber, offered their resignations in protest against what they considered unworthy treatment during their stay at La Granja. The source of his information was admittedly a lady who had perhaps exaggerated matters. She told him that at dinner there was music during the intervals between each course. Ena and Bee left the table and danced, partnered by young men of little social standing, whom they themselves had chosen. After each dance they returned with their new partners to their places, making those who had been previously dining beside them, and who were customarily elder dignitaries and some 'Grandees', move in favour of the younger dancers. These requests to move were denied. Nonetheless, the champions of the old Castilian etiquette thought Bee a bad influence on the queen, and felt it desirable that this did not continue. They had apparently persuaded the king to accept their point of view.

Mariano Fernández de Henestrosa y Mioño was the 1st duke of Santo Mauro. On 24 March 1884, at twenty-five, he married Casilda de Salabert y Arteaga. Kindly and well-educated, he was appointed secretary to the queen, whom he worshipped. It was difficult for him to approve of Ena and Bee breaking protocol because of the resignation of the duchess of San Carlos. She was the mother-in-law of his elder daughter, and the duke also felt obliged to resign. Queen Ena, who valued him greatly, opposed the resignation and the king did not accept it.

A curious photograph was taken at Santander by the photographers, 'Los Italianos', in August 1915, showing the two cousins in the sitting room at La Magdalena. The queen wrote on the upper frame, 'To our dear tutor Santo Mauro'. On the lower part were the signatures of Victoria Regina and Beatrice, who added 'Two naughty girls!'

Bee was busy that December finishing woollen shawls for the charity Ropero de Santa Victoria. Ena, its president, took a great interest in the clothing being donated before Christmas. Bee asked her friends for all kinds of clothing. That year they distributed 51,045 garments, through the Ropero and the parishes of Madrid, to 21,226 families.

When the princess of Salm-Salm visited Madrid again, the *infantes* invited her to tea, also attended by the Austro-Hungarian and German ambassadors, and later dined with the American ambassador. King Alfonso XIII and his cousin went hunting at the home of the count of Gavia at Santa Cruz de Mudela, arriving in Madrid on the queen's saint's day, 23 December, their wives waiting for them at the station. Dinner at the palace was for ninety, and Bee bought toys for the Christmas tree which she gave to the *infantes*, the princes, and their children. The year ended with a solemn *Te Deum* at the palace.

On the morning of 20 January, Bee went to the station to meet Ena's brother and her cousin, Leopold, who had fifteen days' leave from the king's Royal Rifle Corps, where he was an officer. Ena was very pleased to see him and they walked together through the Casa de Campo Park. The king's saint's day was on 23 January, and at the banquet for 100, Ena sat with Ali on her left; Bee did not attend. Next day, she received her cousins at tea time and they reminisced about past times. The Day of the Purification was on 2 February with 'Public Chapel' at the palace, and Leo viewed the galleries, then went with Bee to spend the day at the Casa de Campo. On a subsequent afternoon, he went riding with Ena and the *infantes* de Orleans. One evening, after a function at the Palacio Real, they went to a dance given by the duke of Santo Mauro. The *Infanta* Isabel gave a farewell breakfast for Leopold who left for Paris that night.

In April, the marquis of Viana invited the king and queen to Moratalla, his estate on the banks of the Guadalquivir River, 51 km from Cordoba. He invited the *infantes* of Orleans to try out the new polo field he had just had constructed. Later, the *infantes* left for Seville where they took part in the April Feria. Bee loved the flamenco dancing, and years later she wanted her grandchildren to learn it.

In his report on the background to the 'false rumours', the British ambassador pointed out that 'the spiritual chief of the intrigue against them [the *infantes*] was said to be the Marquis of Viana'. He held a major position in the royal house, brought the king's horses from England, and generally kept him amused. He and his wife were said to be very pro-German, and great friends of the prince of Ratibor.

In May, the *infantes* accompanied the king and queen to Écija. On arriving at Madrid on the 3rd, Ena and Bee visited the studio of the sculptor Benlliure. Ali played polo with the king at Puerta de Hierro, and helped with the children on a visit to the circus. As they had adjacent boxes at the Teatro Real, they went to see *Aida* in the evening. On 29 May, Ali flew from Madrid to Cartagena in three hours, leaving the Cuatro Vientos aerodrome and arriving at Alcázares, averaging more than 60 mph. Bee held a tea for all the members of the royal family at Calle Quintana where they congratulated Ali: the most vociferous was his aunt, *Infanta* Isabel. It was the last time Alfonso XIII attended.

What happened then? A century later, we cannot be sure.

A few days later, the *infantes* and their children went to Castillejo, returning on 8 June. The following week, the marquis and marchioness of Viana invited the king, queen, and *Infanta* Isabel to their house, the *infantes* of Orleans joining them later. On 19 June, the queen was about to go to La Granja. Ena attended a lunch given by the *Infanta* Isabel for her nephew Prince Felipe of the Two Sicilies, brother of Don Carlos. After lunch, Ena said goodbye to Bee and Ali and returned to La Granja at 4 p.m. On 20 June, the newspapers announced that the *infantes* of Orleans were planning to visit Switzerland next. Ena took advantage of her husband and mother-in-law's stay in San Sebastian to visit them. On 12 July, the Palace of Medinaceli opened its doors for a grand ball which only the *infantes* attended; Bee wore a white gown with silver brocade and 'gave an example to the young ladies by dancing with various people'.

Alfonso XIII returned to Madrid, having left his mother installed in the Miramar Palace. On the morning of 5 July, he summoned Ali, whom he had not seen for almost a week. A letter from Ali in the archives of Gen. Burguete (Madrid 17 July 1916) told his teacher what had happened:

> I have appreciated your letter greatly but, as I know how much you care for me, I have to give you some bad news. I leave for Switzerland in a few days time, as I am obliged to go with all my family for an indeterminable time.
>
> Appearances will be kept up by my being on a commission to study the Swiss Army; but the reality is that I have been exiled. You now know that I have many enemies among those surrounding the King. I annoy them for two reasons. Firstly, the King was showing me friendship. Secondly, I tell the King the truth, disagreeable though it may be, if he asks my opinion.
>
> The first reason is paramount, since this tends to spoil the monopoly which some want to have over him. This will be very long to explain in a letter and I am sorry that I am unable to see you before going (I probably go on the 25th) but my assistant Moreno, and more so the archpriest, Padre Mudarra of Seville, can explain it.
>
> To summarise.
>
> The King called me on 5th July.

The complete letter does not survive, but that same day, they told the British ambassador what had happened. According to his report, he sent a telegram, which came into my hands thanks to some English friends. The report, numbered 250, marked 'Highly Confidential', dated 6 July 1916, is addressed to the Secretary of State for Foreign Affairs Sir Edward Grey. Sir Edward, a politician and diplomat, was a great friend of Ambassador Arthur Hardinge, who wrote:

> With reference to my telegram dated yesterday, I have the honour to inform you, and His Majesty, of more details relating to the visit made to me by H.R.H. the Princess Beatrice of Borbón and Orleans. I found Her Royal Highness in a really agitated state. She said that her husband, the *Infante* Don Alfonso, had been called by the King of Spain to inform him that his attitude and that of his wife and the *Infanta* Eulalia (his mother) in Paris had offended the Allies and that an official representation would be presented at the Court of Spain in this respect. His Majesty realized that this would, at least, put them in a disagreeable position and he

(the *Infante*) should leave Spain with his family for a time, leaving for Switzerland on the 9th July. Don Alfonso replied energetically to the King saying that his attitude towards the war had always been perfectly correct and that he was not responsible for what his mother said in Paris and that the French Government could act (as it wished) without resorting to the Government of Spain.

His Majesty's order was that he should leave for Switzerland on the 9th July however inconvenient that may be and that he, as an officer, should obey. But the *Infanta* and their children could not do so for numerous domestic reasons, and therefore they could not go with him nor leave before the 20th July and, as she was related by birth to various Allied Sovereigns, their representatives *here* had the right to ask for an explanation for such an extraordinary procedure.

'The King', said the *Infanta*, 'resented the reply and said to the *Infante* that he would consider putting him under house arrest.'

She came to me as an English Princess to ask for my assistance and that I should call my French and Russian colleagues.

Do you wish me to code and send a telegram from her to my King? And do you also wish me to ask the French and Russian Ambassadors to come at once to my house to see her?

I have to say to you that the matter is extremely delicate because she lost her British nationality on marriage and is now an *Infanta* of Spain, and as ambassadors accredited to the King of Spain, we should be very careful in mediating on a personal matter between his Majesty and other members of the Royal House.

I will, however, consult with my two colleagues since they allege that the exile of Don Alfonso was based on complaints by the Allied Governments and that certainly did not come from this Embassy. I will personally telegraph my Lord the King, through the official channel of the Foreign Office, to relate to him what Her Royal Highness has told me. I should add that as far as it concerns me, I could not be more grateful for the attention received from the very special friendship and courtesy which both Lady Hardinge and I have invariably received from the *Infante* Don Alfonso and from her. Because of the petition by Her Royal Highness, I will arrange a meeting with the Ambassadors of France and Russia at my Embassy before she leaves.

Monsieur Geoffray was out, but Prince Kudashev, on hearing what has happened, came immediately and after hearing what the *Infanta* had to say, said that he would telegraph the Emperor (Nicholas II) and Monsieur Sazonov (Minister of Foreign Affairs).

After her Royal Highness left, we went to the French Embassy where we met Monsieur Geoffray who had returned. He declared his

willingness to send a telegram to his government although France was
not personally involved as in the case of the Courts of England and
Russia, but he was willing to telegraph a report to his government. It
was found that what was said and done by the *Infanta* Eulalia was not
important, especially as the French authorities could, if trouble had been
caused, have required her Highness to leave France. Geoffray had not
received any insinuation nor dissatisfaction from the government in
Paris in respect of the *Infante* Don Alfonso or the *Infanta* Beatrice.

With the affirmations of his colleagues that the *infantes'* attitude had
given no reason for the campaign against them, the British ambassador
quickly let it be known in his report that he was inclined to think this was
an intrigue against them. Its authors had taken the names of the Allied
governments in vain with the intention of deceiving the king, and were
probably eager to cause them harm, as well as harm to Ali and Bee. The
Germans in Spain would like to be able to say that the Allies had been
interfering (as in Greece) in internal Spanish matters and to press for the
exile of a popular soldier prince, if only because he shared the view of all
Spanish officers about the German Army.

As for *Infanta* Eulalia, this was another matter. From his slight knowledge
of her, he could imagine that she was capable of any indiscretion. He had
been told that 'she now believes that the Emperor of Germany is madly
in love with her, and this could explain her language in respect of certain
victories by the German Army, which may have scandalized any Parisians
who have heard her'.

In 1913, the *infanta* had been a guest of Kaiser Wilhelm II, who had
assured her there would be no war during his reign. She was enormously
disillusioned by events a year later, as she regarded him as a firm friend,
and admired the order and discipline of the German Army. 'My neutrality
was absolute,' she confessed, 'and I would never go beyond the delicate
part which I have to play, although my fellow countrymen may say
otherwise.' In another confidential report, dated 6 July, Hardinge stated:

The French Ambassador came here today and told me that after my
Russian colleague left him the previous evening, *Señor* Quiñones de
León, came to see him and asked him to arrange a special train to take
the *Infante* Don Alfonso, and his wife and family from Hendaya station
on the French border to the Franco-Swiss border in the next two weeks.
A day had not yet been fixed.

Monsieur Geoffray observed that he had heard that the fact of their
Royal Highnesses having left Spain had supposedly been connected with
declarations made by the Allies and this surprised him because he could

not conceive that the representatives would have behaved thus. The situation was that Eulalia, always known for her pro-German stance, would undoubtedly have spoken in Paris against the Allies and in favour of Germany. Her comments inevitably reached Madrid and enraged King Alfonso, who used them when blaming Ali and Bee for having allegedly made similar pro German comments when he needed a reason to send Ali and Bee away from Spain.

Señor Quiñones de León smiled and said that he thought that 'the Allies had nothing to do with it; but that there were other reasons connected with what the *Infanta* Beatrice had done at Court.'

This confirmed the opinion which I held (and I told him so) that we were in the presence of a palace intrigue targeting the *Infanta* who is seen disapprovingly by some old and more conservative members of the Court, partly because of her adherence from childhood to her Protestant religion, and partly because they judge her to be too modern, and not being very friendly towards Spanish customs. They also disapproved of the influence which she is supposed to have over the Queen and the affection that His Majesty the King feels for her.

I should add that the *Infanta* mentioned to me that *Señor* Quiñones de León is an attaché at the Spanish Embassy in Paris but is also some kind of private agent and does business there for the King of Spain. He is a bitter enemy of hers because the *Infanta* made an unfriendly remark about him (which he found out about) and he declared that it would cost her dearly.

It is probable that he acts as an intermediary between the part of the Court which is unfriendly towards the *Infanta* and the King.

In a third confidential report, dated one day later, Hardinge stated that the *Infanta* Beatrice had paid him a second visit that morning to inform him that her actions had 'completely swept away the intrigues and hostility of the group at court [who were] working against her husband and herself'. She believed this had resulted from interventions by Prince Kudashev and himself and by her visiting the count of the Romanones, the prime minister, to whom she explained that the severe measures adopted against the *infante* had been inspired by the oversensibilities of the Allied Powers. She thought she had every right to ask her cousins, the king of England and the tsar of Russia, to ask their representatives in Madrid what charges they had against him, and then asked the count of Romanones if he did not think that she had acted correctly. He replied that as prime minister and therefore his majesty's representative, he could not approve her actions; but as a private person and a man of honour, he approved and thought it the most appropriate thing to do.

According to what she said, the count was most disconcerted that a stupid court intrigue, based on an imaginary intervention by the Allies, had caused such embarrassment and led to the *infanta* calling on the Allied embassies. However, after an interchange of points of view between the prime minister and the king, the situation had been entirely modified to the advantage of the *infante* and his wife, and his majesty was very angry about the intrigue and with *Señor* Quiñones de León. The order putting the *infante* under house arrest was cancelled. He and the *infanta* lunched at the palace and later went to the Royal Polo Ground.

Hardinge continued:

> As for her future movements, it is possible that she may go to Switzerland for a short stay. She has asked to do so for a few months to meet her mother the Duchess of Coburg, as she would prefer not to visit her in Germany; but it is believed that the King of Spain had by then consented and had entirely changed his position from not considering giving permission to leave Spain but ordering them to leave as it had been established that he, and she, had offended the Allied Powers. I asked her what the *Infante* had really said in his supposed hostility towards the Allies and she repeated from memory the exact words the King had used addressing his Royal Highness and they do not indicate that the Allies had really asked for the exile of the Prince.

The king told Ali that his mother had 'said stupid things in Paris and it may be that there are indications that if the matter is not dealt with, the Allies may take measures which will be disagreeable for Spain'. Bee thought that the king now saw it had all been a false rumour instigated by certain intriguers at the palace. She had said she wanted to go to Switzerland as she had asked before and was anxious to see the duchess of Coburg for a week or two, with the security of a document in writing from the king that she and her children could return to Spain when they wished, and this was promised. She was very angry with *Señor* Quiñones de León who, she said, had wanted to present the king to loose women in France. Bee had protested against this in front of the queen and, in condemning his conduct, had made an unscrupulous enemy. However, she now seemed content with the friendly help of the ambassadors and the count of Romanones, and had thus unmasked and defeated the plotters. In conclusion, he commented that the *Infanta* Beatrice had until then 'defeated her enemies, who, if the facts described by her Royal Highness are correct, have behaved in a gross and a stupid manner'.

With this, Arthur Hardinge finalised his three reports to Sir Edward Grey. Initially, it seemed that there was a truce and Bee had won the game. However, Ali's fellow aviators found it very strange to read in the official bulletin that Ali was to be sent as military attaché to Switzerland, where there was no aviation, and especially after his flight from Madrid to Cartagena which had been so applauded by the king and the royal family.

Remembering what trouble his first exile had caused, Ali wrote to his teacher Capt. A. García Perez, asking that his colleagues not to come to his house at Quintana because this time he only wanted to be alone. Bee had no support, and only a few people visited her, particularly the countess of Casa Valencia, a close friend—the rest kept silent. The view was that everything had changed since the arrival of Bee at the palace, some four years before. The queen had been happy to be accompanied by the lady-in-waiting on duty, usually an elderly woman, on her visits to centres of charity or shopping, to which she was very partial. When she went riding, which she loved and practised between her successive pregnancies, the only person to accompany her was a young lady in waiting, Conchita Heredia. On Bee's arrival, it seemed that Ena only enjoyed her cousin's company, and they saw each other at all hours. A celebrated courtier said that 'they were more like a couple of schoolgirls sharing secrets than two people of their rank'. Meanwhile, the king's absences were noticed more. He presented them as official business, and with the passing of time they became 'most amusing chats with that ineffable conversationalist, the Marquis of Viana'.

A rather discouraging letter by Arthur Hardinge (18 July 1916), to his cousin, Sir Charles Hardinge, Baron Penshurst, recounted events in detail:

> There are all kinds of strange stories about what happened. It is said that the King is in love with the *Infanta*, and she does not want him, through the loyalty she feels towards the Queen and towards her own husband, and she gives him no encouragement. Also, that the group at court hostile to the Queen wants the *Infanta* to go in order to put a more compliant lady in her place as mistress of the Royal Household, so that they could influence His Majesty behind the Queen's back, and that the Count of Romanones was with them for his own reasons ... we are in the presence of a plot like that of the Hydes to destroy the influence of Mary of Modena and her Jesuit entourage to establish Catherine Sedley as the lover of James II.
>
> Prince Kudashev (the Russian Ambassador) urged the *Infanta* to try to achieve an honourable reconciliation with the King; but this is easier said than done. Personally I have remained apart from all suggestions, avoiding all future questions, watching, and keeping my ears open. This is a delicate matter which could affect the Queen's future.

I write to say that the success that the *Infanta* Beatrice thought she had achieved has proved shortlived. The hostile band at court has managed to prevail despite the ending of the pretext of ill will towards the *Infante* on the part of the Allied governments. His short-term destination and that of his wife and children still appears to be a mission to report on the current state of the Swiss Army.

The spiritual head of the intrigue against them is the Marquis of Viana. For the moment he is wishing to be our friend as he is somewhat fearful that the cry for help, made by the *Infanta* to my Russian colleague and me, should prosper and that the forces opposing her would have difficulties. Yesterday he asked Prince Kudashev and me to dine at his house in order to meet our old colleague and his cousin, the Marquis of Villalobar, who has come on a short visit to Madrid. He tackled me before I entered with the subject of the *Infanta* 'insinuating that she had gone to the Allied Ambassadors seeking protection and advice' and that it was a great mistake on the part of a Spanish princess to be insubordinate towards the King.

I said to him that he was mistaken, that she only had been distressed by the insinuation that the *Infante* and she were seen in a bad light and mistrusted by the Allied Governments and she was anxious that they knew, through us, that there was not a grain of truth in what had been insinuated.

The *Infante* and the *Infanta* have asked me to go to a farewell luncheon. She said he has been ordered to leave on the 20th of July and he fears that after Switzerland they could send them on a military mission to Germany and, as a soldier, he cannot refuse.

She is completely tranquil and serious, but evidently very irritated by the plotters who have tried to put the Allied governments against them and, if it were not for us, perhaps they might have succeeded.

The *Infanta*'s agent in the matter of her own defence seems to be an odd priest who was previously a strange radical, an ally (in his younger days) of Romanones, in all kinds of politics and business negotiations and who now acts as a go-between with the government.

She is determined to obtain a written guarantee so that no obstacle is put in her way, nor in that of her children, to return to Spain after her husband has completed his report on the Swiss Army, and I believe that she will eventually obtain this. The King and Queen are presently at La Granja, but I imagine that they will go to San Sebastian at the end of the month.

Please show this letter to the King and to Sir Edward Grey. Although the matter of the *Infanta* has a remote connection with politics, it could influence them indirectly, and his Majesty may be interested in the present situation of his cousin and also that of the Queen of Spain.

Bee awaited written permission guaranteeing her return and that of her children, but it was denied at the last minute. Her enemies and the king's friends immediately produced unfounded rumours that Bee wanted to be the *bête noire* at court; that she talked badly of the queen to distance the king from his wife; and that she sought only her own pleasure. Throughout the years, her reputation remained despicable, but nothing could be further from the truth. In the Orleans archives are drafts that Ali sent to the king, ending, 'Do not upset her any more' and 'Leave her in peace!' Nothing was retained in the palace archives.

In 1967, Indalecio Prieto, a future republican minister, noted in his memoirs:

> Fifty years ago on my arrival at the Congress (1918) copies of adoring letters which Alfonso XIII had written unsuccessfully to the beautiful wife of one of his relations were going around in the hands of Republican Members of Parliament. Such was the ardour of his entreaties that he even invoked the Fatherland—the result of her contempt would be prejudicial for Spain because if his burning passion was not returned, it would prevent him from attending to grave national problems.

The historian Ricardo Mateos y Sáinz de Medrano researched the matter in 1996, published his findings in *Los Desconocidos Infantes de España* (*The Unknown Infantes of Spain*), and told me:

> I have to confess that the more I read, the more convinced I become that it was the jealousy and certain manoeuvres by Don Alfonso XIII (assisted by a faction at court supporting the Central Empires during the Great War) which led to the distancing and exile of the *Infantes* who, because of his actions, suffered severe financial loss. However they always remained faithful to the monarch.

Ricardo de la Cierva, also well versed in the era, wrote:

> The version that I have picked up, according to my own family tradition, indicates that a stormy final scene took place at the Campo de Moro and the Royal harassment was interrupted by the unexpected presence of Don Alfonso of Orleans who naturally defended his wife energetically.

Arthur Hardinge showed his interest in the *infantes* of Orleans staying in Spain. He continued in his post, and on his return to England, where he spent Christmas, he wrote in French (14 January 1918), requesting an audience with His Majesty King Don Alfonso XIII:

On my having had a conversation with His Majesty King George V on 22nd December, 1917 regarding Her Royal Highness the Princess Beatrice of Borbón and Orleans, the King (George V) wishes to inform Your Majesty of the contents of this letter and prefers that I deal with this matter personally, probably because of the delicate nature of the same, and that it would be better presented verbally than in writing. If such is the case, I respectfully request that you be good enough to designate the day and the hour at which I may have the honour of being received.

Having to follow protocol and hypocritically follow everything according to plan, the king and queen left San Sebastian for Santander the day before. That night, the *infantes* left Madrid in the *Sud Express*, and on arriving at San Sebastian found Her Majesty Queen Maria Cristina waiting at the station with the prime minister, the count of Romanones, and other authorities. The *infantes* went with the queen to the Miramar Palace, while their children went down to the beach. According to a press report, 'After lunch, which was also attended by the Prime Minister, the Count of Romanones and the Minister of War, General Luque, they continued to Switzerland. The lunch had been a strained affair and such was the brief newspaper summary of 'a hidden exile', lasting for eight years, in which Bee would lose her health, her beauty, and much of her fortune.

11

Hidden Exile

In the Royal Academy of History's archives of the count of Romanones, then prime minister of Spain, a confidential report in French records the journey into exile of the *infantes* and their children. From Paris, they took the train to Switzerland, reaching Geneva on the afternoon of 27 July 1916. They telegraphed the duchess of Coburg at 11:30 p.m., announcing their arrival at the Hotel Beau Rivage. Next day, all five went for an afternoon drive around the city in a horse drawn coach. On the morning of 30 July, they went by train to Zurich and were met by various members of the family at Arbon. From Spain, they had brought two manservants, one Spanish, one English; a German nanny; and a Spanish lady's maid. The English servant, Robert (Arthur Gower) Papworth, had left his employers in Arbon to return to Spain where his wife was expecting a child; while in Bellegarde, he had said he would return to Switzerland that autumn to accompany his employers on their return to Spain.

On 1 August, the *infantes* and their children sailed from Romanshorn to Lindau. On return, they were accompanied by the duchess of Coburg, her lady in waiting, and two German lady's maids. Their luggage was sent that day to the Hotel Baur au Lac, where they would stay, perhaps indefinitely. Next day, Ali left with an overnight bag to Romanshorn, then to Divonne and then finally to Lindau, returning the next day. On 6 August, dinner was organised in the garden of the Hotel Baur, attended by the *infantes*, the duchess and her lady-in-waiting, and the German and Spanish consuls. On 7 August, the *infantes* drove to Wädenswil, 25 km from Zurich, and returned to the hotel for dinner. Next day, they visited the mountains near Zurich and talked to the manager of the Dolder Grand Hotel, intending to stay there until the weather was cooler. Ali seemed nervous, speaking all the main languages, but very reserved when in contact with the public.

The duchess of Coburg had long been aware of the problems, foreseeing in 1910 what might happen, and could not wait to meet them. She had noted that year that Ali was 'a good person, a great soldier who follows his career, but he is certainly being treated badly just now'. Her youngest daughter was 'brave and her intense hatred for Alfonso makes her keep plotting some slow revenge. In this respect, I understand her perfectly and share it with her.' She thought King Alfonso was trying to blacken Ali's reputation any way he could because he resented his popularity in the army. His 'entourage' naturally shared such ideas and undoubtedly did not want the 'Alis' to return. Ali was 'energetic and intelligent', while Bee was 'feared for her sharp tongue. God knows how it will all end!' Six years later, she knew that nothing had changed. While she had no personal relationship with the king or his mother since Bee's wedding, 'I know that they fear me and there can always be a new outbreak.' Arriving in Switzerland, she wanted to stay in Zurich, where she met her youngest daughter. She intended to write to Missy explaining in detail what had happened to Bee, who on discovering her mother's intentions, implored her to destroy everything she had written about her story.

In another letter of 1916, the duchess revealed the reason why Bee and Ali had left Spain. Many lines were illegible, as she presumably did not wish it to be read by future generations. However, taking into account what she said in later letters, it was apparent that King Alfonso was making 'advances' towards Bee. At length, she could bear it no longer, and apparently everything ended in a great row. In order to hide the truth about the rupture between the king and Bee, his cronies spread rumours about Bee alleging that she was trying to exercise pro-German influence in Madrid, and ensured that in doing so, Ena remained in the background. On deciphering another part of the same letter, Maria of Coburg mentioned that her daughter was always on the best of terms with the Russian and British ambassadors. However, they had made clear that their life in Spain had become impossible in some ways, 'and their nerves were in tatters'.

The duchess's comment on the ambassadors indicated that there was never any reason for Bee to take a pro-German stance during the war. Returning to the central matter, she emphasised that it was 'a long standing personal quarrel, rather than there being a political reason for the scandal,' and she called Alfonso's conduct 'outrageous'. Full of indignation, she wrote to Missy:

H.R.H (King Alfonso) is ten times worse than any of us can believe. Morally he is a coward, but he is in no way stupid, although he never says a truthful word, and is under the influence of the worst clique imaginable, and the marriage is on the rocks.

She concealed nothing when talking about her youngest daughter, adding that there was no doubt she had 'a very difficult character and a sharp tongue which has made her many enemies'. Historians did not understand Bee's reaction in not wishing her mother to tell Missy about what had happened, as she was the sister in whom she had always confided intimately, unlike Ducky and Sandra. The quick-witted Bee had known from childhood how little in love her eldest sister was with her husband, and feared she would not understand her attitude to rejection, based on her being happy and deeply in love with Ali. If in the beginning it amused her that, though she was older than Alfonso and was the mother of three sons, the king found her attractive, she soon understood that she had to defend her position as Ena's cousin and Ali's wife.

Unused to refusal, King Alfonso dreamed of the conquest of a royal relation who inspired great desire in him and which she did not wish to satisfy, making him react with frustration and anger. Seeing himself being rejected, he decided to make Bee's life difficult. He included Ali at the same time, as another way of attacking Bee.

Was it jealousy that drove him to take these strong measures against Ali, with whom we know he had no quarrel? The *Infanta* Eulalia had said that when Ali returned from his English college with a new sense of maturity and confidence, Alfonso, six months older, was annoyed. After ten years of marriage, he had tired of Ena and allowed those in his intimate circle to call her 'the peahen'. While he had known about the danger of haemophilia long before as his mother had warned him, he still blamed her for the illness of their three sickly sons.

Ironically, Ali and Bee's three boys were strong and healthy. In the army, the king knew his cousin was very popular, and that his commanders in Morocco and comrades, praised his work and spirit of service.

It was difficult for Alfonso, who became king at birth, not to listen to the flattery of the clique around him, and he could not see that Ali's loyalty was so deep that he told him the truth. For this reason, his 'intimates' treated Ali and his family as they did and managed to expel them from Spain. Accustomed from youth to ordering people about and being obeyed, the sovereign could not understand that he had been rejected by a woman who, although a Protestant, resisted him as she loved her husband, and because of her loyalty towards her cousin who had been a friend since childhood.

From a letter the Grand Duchess Vladimir wrote to Missy (Petrograd, 14 October 1916), it was clear that the duchess of Coburg had been spreading the news around the European courts:

She has gone to Coburg again because she does not like life in hotels. I believe that she simply loves Germany so much that she cannot live in another country. Bee believes that Alfonso is in love with her and, as she does not want to give in to him, she and Ali are in disgrace and will remain for the moment in Zurich. But someone has told me that she had tried to influence Alfonso to favour Germany and that the government insisted that she should be sent away for a while.

This dealt naturally with the government led by the count of Romanones, who according to information held in the Spanish Legation, sent a letter by diplomatic bag to Ali. They knew each other and apparently had some unfinished business together. In October 1975, shortly after Ali had died in Sanlúcar de Barrameda, Agustín de Figueroa, the marquis of Santo Floro, told me: 'You who admired and knew them well, did they never speak to you about their expulsion from Spain?'

I replied, 'I knew that they were exiled because the wedding was not liked because of her being a Protestant princess.'

'This was before,' replied Agustín, 'What interests me is what the exile they suffered was like during the European War, and what was ordered by the King as my father (the Count of Romanones) was Prime Minister.'

As a minister many times, he lived through those years of intense political change. Apparently, at the end of his life, that 'stormy dinner' at the Miramar presided over by Queen María Cristina 'in honour of the *infantes* who were leaving Spain' was very much on his mind and he still felt strongly about it years later, speaking frequently of 'the grave injustice done to them'. As I did not know about the matter, I wrote of my surprise to my friend, Leonor Ceballos, to ask her husband what he knew about it, as he knew the royal family intimately. Eugenio Vegas Latapie replied that the count de Romanones helped Bee at first, 'but on knowing that the King and his friends were betting on her leaving, changed his attitude. According to the British Ambassador, the Count wished, as always, to be on the winning side'.

Eugenio Vegas was one of the first to comment on the matrimonial tensions between the king and queen:

I dealt with and knew the Royal Family well enough to be able to give an opinion on it. I have always believed that the Spanish people were most unjust with Doña Victoria, and never in the least, appreciated her extraordinary personality. Without dwelling on personal matters of the Royal marriage, I can confirm knowing that the cause of the marital tensions was always the character of the King.

Queen María Cristina and her sister-in-law, the *Infanta* Isabel, were such fervent admirers of the king that the former never said a word to her son about the scandal, and the latter left for Salamanca, as she did not wish to help. The princess of Salm-Salm, said she thought Maria Cristina was beginning to regret her lack of loyalty towards Ena. Queen Victoria Eugenia and the *Infanta* Beatrice were always very united and never stopped writing to each other.

On 23 September 1916, the minister in Berne, Reynoso, requested permission to send two letters from the *Infanta* Beatrice to the queen and to Robert Papworth and Lucie Brun, the faithful servants left in Madrid: 'Bern, 3rd November 1916: The *infanta* continues staying in Zurich'. Three days later, it was confirmed: 'The Legation sent a letter and a large folder for HRH the Princess Beatrice of Coburg from the Queen to the Dolder Hotel in Zurich'. Unfortunately, there is no sign of letters, invoices, or data on the stay in Switzerland in the royal palace in Madrid, or in the Orleans Archives in Sanlúcar. However, Ena again expressed her feelings towards her cousin to Missy (Madrid, 1 June 1917):

Bee is in Switzerland for now. Please do not think that my friendship towards her has changed because of the trouble and quarrels with Alfonso. I am a very faithful soul and when I love someone I never change. Poor dear Bee! She has so many enemies here who have done her great harm. But God will make everything better again. She should have a little patience now that the injustice and slander are dying down by themselves. I am in a difficult situation because Alfonso's word is law, and he does not allow any interference by anyone and even less from me. I am hoping she will return again soon but the best that I can do is keep quiet for a while as any movement on my part will have negative effects and it will be worse than ever...

Missy was now queen of Romania, a country that had proclaimed its neutrality at the outbreak of the war due to King Carol I's German ancestry. Unable to persuade his subjects otherwise, he died a few weeks later. His nephew and heir, King Ferdinand, intended to continue his policy, but Queen Marie, Brătianu's government, and the people wanted to join the Entente powers and lay claim to Transylvania. The Royal Commission met on 27 August 1916, and on leaving it, the king announced that Romania was at war on the side of the Allies. Although a member of the Hohenzollern family, he was above all king of Romania: 'I obey my subjects' wishes and have faith that Romania will conquer them as it has conquered me'. The queen took him by the hand in front of all the ministers and told them that nobody could understand as she did how much this had cost him, saying she was proud of him and Romania should be too. Seven hours later, at midnight, the bells pealed to warn that a German bombing raid was imminent. Angered by the attitude of the new king and queen, Kaiser Wilhelm ordered a full offensive against Romanian forces. On 22 October, the seaport Constanta fell to the Central Powers. The queen was personally distracted as Mircea, aged three, had typhus and died ten days later, and German troops entered Bucharest, three months after the declaration of war.

The duchess went first to Zurich to see her daughter, Bee, and find out at first hand what had happened, then on finding herself displaced in Switzerland went to Tegernsee. She was very angry that Romania had entered the war on the Allied side. 'Mama had decided not to maintain relations with me while the war continued, only the death of Mircea caused her to break her silence,' Missy wrote sadly to Bee, 'Can she really believe that I am responsible for the war?'

Bee wrote: 'It all seems to be eating at her heart and one feels for her; it is very, very, difficult'. She was very worried at having no news of Ena, who had been seriously ill at the end of 1916. Once again she had returned to be with her husband in the hope that this could help Bee. Her illness was misdiagnosed, and turned out to be an almost fatal attack of peritonitis. Months later, she explained to Missy that she did not write as she was also very ill at the time, in bed for almost two months after a miscarriage with complications 'and on top of everything I went through a bad spell which knocked me down completely, leaving me very depressed.' Because of his wife's serious condition, the king remained with her.

During the bitter winter, Ali, who had thoroughly studied the Swiss Army, wrote to the king (17 November 1916, Lausanne) that he had asked the chief of aviation to inform the authorities of the desirability of ending his mission there:

> ... as there remains nothing more for me to see and besides it has been almost useless from the outset, as there is, in general, very little aviation here and none of an advanced level and, also, my desire is to return to my destiny. You will understand that with the summer now over my absence could give rise to false interpretations.
>
> The exile applies to grave offences and as I have committed none, my honour as a gentleman and soldier demands my return, the only way of avoiding its being said, 'If he remains away, with no light being brought upon the subject, something has happened which he wishes to hide'. I am sure that you agree with me that this is something an officer cannot admit and I write to you in the confidence that you will look after the interests of one who has served you loyally for nine years, by ordering him to return.

Missy was overjoyed when Ducky arrived at the end of the year. Always practical and generous, she brought large supplies of medical aid and clothing, in what was the coldest winter for fifty years. The two inseparable sisters could talk about the situation of Bee, who had lost her position at the Spanish court, abandoning it for her husband. She, who seemed the least romantically inclined of the four sisters, was the one who had given up everything for love. As for Ali's letter, as restrained and as well written as it was, he never received a reply, although the original was kept in the archives of the royal palace.

With the arrival of Christmas, the *infantes* resigned themselves to waiting. They changed their plans, trying to stop their children from finding out what had happened, and went to St Moritz to enjoy the snow. Álvaro was six and a half years old, Ataúlfo just three, and here their passion for skiing began. As they went to a good hotel, the Christmas tree was enormous, better than the one they had brought with them from Castillejo, and superbly lit.

Years later, Ali would write to his wife:

I look back over all the years and I am filled with a feeling of great gratitude towards you. I love you. I have always loved you, and I love you still. But this is something which one cannot explain. It is simply there. You and I are beyond that. We are one. But in spite of or despite being one, an immense gratitude overcomes me when I think of you. In the endless battle, I always feel that my back is protected. Your mind sees it. Your intuition feels it. I will be advised of dark threats and I will receive your good advice in time. Should I need to rest, you will never shrink before danger like other weaker people.

It is strange I never need to explain myself to you. I hate myself when you become sad or are upset ... if I could make you see how I feel, I should be so happy! I look back over the years, and see that you have always helped me and fought for me. Wherever we had to go on our endless pilgrimage, in peace or in war, you made sure that we were always comfortable. Home is always where you are! The long battles with Pérez, the Moroccan wars, the return to Spain; you never complained. I was always away, my trip to America. 'I am strong,' you said. You are always strong and will always be with me, May God bless you my darling!

Bee always hoped each new year would bring better tidings than the last. The year 1916 had been very hard with the unexpected, hurtful departure from Spain. Early in 1917, a letter from Missy arrived for them, referring to Ducky's visit and plentiful supplies.

This meeting of the two sisters was moving. The grand duchess, with her resolute appearance and almost mannish energy, did much good for the queen. Since Mircea's death, she had worked ceaselessly, visiting hospitals and towns, trying to improve the lot of her people, who because of their distance from the Allied Powers could only rely upon Russia. However, the news Ducky brought was grim. Since 1915 when Grand Duke Nicholas was relieved of his position as supreme commander of the armed forces, the inexperienced tsar had replaced him and lived at headquarters. Alix remained at Tsarskoye Selo, advised by the peasant Rasputin, who had the gift of calming the pain of the haemophiliac heir. Preoccupied by her son's health, she was lonely in a court dominated by two very ambitious women, her mother-in-law, the dowager empress, and Grand Duchess Vladimir, 'Miechen', a German princess who had never approved of the marriage of Nicholas with a granddaughter of Queen Victoria. The tsar tried to compromise by taking more account of his wife's advice.

Despite the cold, the sisters drove around Romania in an open car. It was Christmas time and the peasants blessed them for the gifts they received. The grand duchess made a good impression on the king and the government, and she thought the queen should go to Russia and seek help from Nicholas II, who was at the front, at HQ. It would be a secret but very important visit. She then returned to celebrate Russian Christmas (thirteen days later than European Christmas) with her husband and the children. A little later, terrible rumours arrived from the Russian court. On 31 December 1916 (OS), Rasputin was invited to a party where Grand Duke Dmitri and fellow guests tried to poison him, then shot him, and threw his body into the frozen waters of the Neva, where he eventually drowned.

In January, Ducky returned again to Romania with more supplies and several railway wagons to serve as hospital rooms. She also told her sister how her mother-in-law, the Grand Duchess Vladimir, had brought together sixteen members of the imperial family one night in her palace to write a letter to the tsar asking him to pardon Dmitri, and rescind his exile near the Persian frontier in view of his tubercular condition. Nicholas II noted on the letter: 'Nobody has the right to kill'. Grand Duke Alexander, married to Xenia, the tsar's elder sister, also wanted to see the tsarina and suggest that he form a government acceptable to the Duma, but she retorted that 'an autocrat cannot govern with parliament'. Alexander reminded her that the tsar had ceased to be an autocrat when he granted Russia a constitution in October 1905, and told her angrily that she had no right 'to take the family to the edge of the abyss'.

When Ducky returned from Romania in the middle of February, St Petersburg was on the verge of revolution. Provisions were poorly distributed because of heavy frosts that paralysed transport, while the government appeared uninterested in what was happening. Mobs came out onto the streets to search for the police, while soldiers mutinied and killed officers in the barracks. Kirill was commanding the marine guard, with orders to remain in the capital, where food was scarce. Crime and violence grew daily, with the forces of law and order under threat. The French ambassador, Maurice Paléologue, noted in his diary that the tsar's cousin appeared to be disregarding his oath of loyalty as an officer and as *aide-de-camp* to his sovereign. In full uniform, he was seen apparently directing the marines under his command and putting their services at the disposal of the revolutionary forces.

Nicholas II might have saved his throne by signing a separate peace with the Central Empires, but did not wish his allies to doubt his loyalty and honour. On 15 March 1917, he abdicated in favour of his brother Grand Duke Michael. The king and queen of Romania immediately sent a telegram of condolence to which he replied, thanking them both as he wished them 'final victory and the realisation of all your aspirations'. Missy's feelings towards the tsarina never changed, although she tried to keep in touch with her cousins and later to save them. Her main worry was Ducky, who suddenly stopped writing.

The British cabinet immediately recognised the provisional government. Ministers were thought to be working for the tsar and his family's escape to safety through the Gulf of Finland, but the emperor would not leave without his family. The British ambassador's efforts were misinterpreted and the tsarists complained that he did not help them. Ducky wrote bitterly to Missy in April saying they had abandoned her in her hour of need and refused to help, her worries exacerbated by the fact that at forty she was expecting another child. At last Bee received another letter from her in May, and told Missy all (Savoy Hotel, Ouchy, Lausanne, 15 May 1917):

Goodness! In her curious and brusque manner, it was full of bitter reproaches against Mama and against me, and you have no idea what this meant for Mama. Not to mention me. Our hearts were consumed writing and telegraphing to get news of her. Even Ali was trying to arrange everything so that I, risking everything and leaving him and the children here, could be with Ducky when she gave birth.

Ali and I are so miserable interned in Switzerland and she, without ever thinking that it was the Revolution that stopped our efforts, was accusing us and saying that she detested and despised us. It hurts when these are the only things that seem to survive in this horrible war; the family's love being thrown to the winds.

Forgive this miserable letter when I should be trying to cheer you up, but sometimes the horror of everything frightens me.

The tsar's abdication had caused deep feelings at the front as well as in the capital. Grand Duke Vladimir's family stayed in the palace guarded by the marine force until on the eve of Holy Week, a delegation of Marines arrived at the house, and insisted that Grand Duke Kirill came to the barracks chapel to choose the liturgy for Holy Saturday. He was granted permission to leave St Petersburg by train with their two daughters, while Ducky would remain alone. Finally, they all left Russia at the beginning of the summer of 1917, during the first months of Kerensky's administration, planning to stay in Finland with friends until danger had passed. Thinking it was only a general uprising, they expected Kerensky's government would soon restore order. They arrived at Porvoo and the family, accompanied by servants, went to Haikko Manor, while the others stayed in a house rented by the grand duke. Ducky wrote to Missy to assure her that all was well, although she had cramp in her legs and could not stand. After two weeks at Haikko with the Von Etter family, they returned to Porvoo and on 30 August Ducky gave birth to a boy, named Vladimir after his paternal grandfather. He was baptised in Haikko on 18 September 1917 in the presence of Russian exiles and Finnish friends. His godparents were his paternal grandmother, the Grand Duchess Maria, and his uncle, Boris.

King Gustaf V of Sweden invited the Kirill family to Stockholm but they preferred to remain in Finland, believing themselves safe, hoping the former tsar and his family would be liberated. They were living in the Alexander Palace in Tsarskoye Selo as prisoners of the provisional government, until it was decided on 8 August that they should go to Siberia for their own safely.

Bee opened her heart in a letter to Missy:

Mama and I are living in deep and desperate fear for you and Ducky. We are living in a kind of blind drama and there are times in which we can almost not talk for fear that we become even more anguished. You can imagine how all this affected everything that happened with Mama. As she feels that she should help Ducky, she organises crazy plans making appointments with Alfonso (XIII) and Georgie (V) understanding that both, in different ways, do not have as much power as Nicky (Nicholas II) himself.

All this seems to be undermining her heart and she is often very, very difficult; and I feel so sad in our rooms and I cry my heart out. Again, I try not to think about myself, because others are suffering so much more than I, but also I have run out of money. My address continues to be the

Dolder Hotel in Zurich.

I am worried about Mama and also about her matters. At present she does not have a penny to live on, everything was in Russia or in Russian investments. Ali is also desperately hard up because of the injustices which have been committed against him; but he will do what he can.

Unfortunately Mama has simply thrown away her best jewels behind my back and is so ashamed that she has asked me not to speak of it. To pacify Sandra, she gave her her complete ruby parure; something so unnecessary at this time. Sandra's grasping and envious conduct on one hand annoys me, but on the other the frightful anxiety I feel for you two devours my anger. Sandra has taken advantage so many times in these last years that she is in very good circumstances and without doubt it is she who is the best off of the four sisters; but naturally she does not think of helping Mama. It seems useless to write about it. Who cares if one dies of hunger when all these horrors are allowed to happen around us. Ali and I are trying to save the little that remains for Mama, in order to see if much later, if nothing is settled in Russia, it might be possible to raise a little capital for her, as now she has nothing. It is too tiresome to enter into details but it is heart-breaking.

Faced with revolution in Russia, Europe remained paralysed, and at the courts of both groups there was grave concern, as a letter from Ena to Missy confirmed:

When you wrote me, the terrible business in Russia had not taken place. How much you have suffered from it all! This revolution is such a serious thing for all monarchies! Above all, I think that it is a very dangerous time for Kings and Queens and one asks oneself what will happen in the different countries if this war continues much longer. And to think that Alix (the Tsarina) is greatly responsible for having brought ruin upon her family. I would not like to be in her position for anything in the world.

When revolution broke out, King George V desperately wanted to help his cousin, Nicky. Yet fearful of losing his throne, he disowned his German origins and changed the dynastic name, renouncing for himself and his family, the family name of his grandfather, Prince Albert of Saxe-Coburg Gotha, for that of Windsor. The German titles of his immediate family, Schleswig-Holstein and Battenberg, were likewise swept away.

At the beginning of 1917, Lenin was in exile in Switzerland. Anxious to remove Russia from the war, the Germans came to his aid, offering him a safe passage home. Accompanied by his comrades, he crossed Europe in a sealed train. The imperial family was dispersed, and the Romanovs who remained in the capital were the unluckiest. The Empress Dagmar, in Kiev, saw the former tsar after his abdication, but avoided accompanying him to Tsarskoye Selo where his children were ill with measles. She left Kiev in April 1917 and stayed with Xenia, and her husband, Grand Duke Alexander, in the Crimea.

At the end of the summer of 1917, Missy received a letter from her mother, who since the fall of Belgrade had changed her attitude towards her eldest daughter for the better: 'Darling Missy, I think of you all the time. May God bless and protect you from your terrible trials!' Missy had become a legendary queen—spending all of her time helping to nurse the wounded and support the troops. Bee had a deep admiration for the work her sister was doing.

Since the abdication of her nephew, the tsar, the Duchess Marie never stopped thinking of Russia and was horrified to hear how he and his family had 'been sent to an unknown destination in the middle of the night'. On signing peace with Germany, the Bolsheviks decided to move the imperial family away from Petrograd, fearing a possible monarchical restoration. Michael lived in Gatchina with his wife and son until March 1918 when he was arrested and sent to Perm, accompanied by his secretary, Nicholas Johnson. Just before midnight on 12 June, a group from the local Soviet burst into the room to capture the grand duke. Pretending to be monarchists who had come to escort both men to safety, they took them by car to a nearby forest and then shot them both dead. Michael thus became the first of many Romanov victims of the revolution.

During the spring and summer of 1917, the French Mission led by Gen. Berthelot began reconstruction of the Romanian army. Young recruits under the command of French officers were soon converted into hardened patriots. The offensive began in July and the Russians under the Kerensky government also battled against the Austrian and German troops, winning the battle of Marassechi (Mărăşeşti) during August and September 1917. From London, Lloyd George promised the Allies would never forget the Romanian soldiers 'who fought with singular valour'. But the Russian troops disintegrated when faced with the slogans of Lenin and fraternised with the enemy or fled the front, leaving the Romanian soldiers in a difficult position. The queen exclaimed that if Russia abandoned them, it would cause 'such a terrible disaster that it will be the end of everything!'

In September, the American ambassador arrived at Iaşi. King Ferdinand advised him not to unpack his luggage because he feared Moldavia was about to fall into German hands. The queen willingly received the forty Americans from Ambassador Vopicka's entourage made up of Red Cross doctors, medical experts, engineers, and technicians, coming with ample supplies of provisions, unfailingly practical and efficient in everything they did.

On 6 November 1917, the Russian Provisional Government ceded power to the Bolsheviks, who intended to make peace with Germany and Austria. They ordered the Romanians to do likewise, planning to imprison the royal family and the government. The Allies, far away, could not help them. On 2 December, Queen Marie received a telegram from King George V, informing her that she and her children would be welcome in England whenever they wished. Fortunately, the members of the French Mission helped the Russian general, Teherbatchev, asking him to curb his soldiers who wanted to sign an armistice with the Germans. For a few days, the troops remained quiet without attacking the Romanians. So many Russians deserted that the Romanian soldiers were left alone, most of them peasants with an extraordinary love for their country and, wishing to defend it, remained at their posts.

On 9 December 1917, Romania signed an armistice with the Central Empires. Two weeks later, Russia signed the peace of Brest-Litovsk, leaving the Russian front unprotected, while the Central Empires redoubled their attacks on Belgium and France. Miserable about her sister's terrible situation, Bee wrote:

> When and how will this letter arrive? Is it true that you are about to leave Iași? I hope and pray that it is not true. My heart is so full of sadness and desperation that I do not know how to pass on all my sympathy to you. Some calamities are so immense that one keeps quiet before them. As so many things have been lost, when you receive this letter, please, mention in your reply that you have known of my sympathy for you.
>
> I write all this and I do not know when you will receive it. I telegraphed constantly, and on receiving no reply, I have asked your Minister that you telegraph. He is always more than friendly and says that not even your telegrams pass normally.

Queen Marie was desperate when thinking about the abdication the king and his government had to sign before the armistice. The Romanians wanted the treaty to let the dynasty retain the throne, while the Germans wanted to take over the oil wells, communications, railways, and telephones, thus isolating Romania from the world. All foreign missions had to leave, and went to say goodbye to the queen. The king held a farewell luncheon on 7 March 1918. On the following day, Marie offered the British and Italians dinner. Addressing the former, the king asked them to 'swear that his so ruined and mutilated country should not be forgotten when peace came'. To make sure, he wrote to his cousin, George V, that they had been betrayed, surrounded by enemies, and had to give in despite the high morale of their troops and their total loyalty to the mutual cause:

'I did everything that my power allowed. You will fight and win; but on the day of victory, do not forget us'. Next day, the queen obtained a promise from the king that they would go to the station with the missions to say goodbye; it was midnight when the train was complete, with five wagons for the French. The train left for Russia, the only route to the west of Europe.

Since the beginning of 1918, everything had gone from bad to worse for Missy and Nando. On 5 January, Lloyd George had recognised the fall of Romania to the Germans. As for the Russians, on 31 January the Bolsheviks seized the gold and jewels of the Romanian crown, which had been sent there before the advance of the Germans, as Missy thought they would be more secure in the empire of the tsars. After the break-up of the Russian Empire, two provinces, Bessarabia and the Ukraine, wished to unite with Romania because they felt more secure under its government. This raised the morale of the Romanians, many of whom longed for Allied victory.

Confused rumours from Russia brought bad news about the Romanovs, and it was said that Lenin wanted to exterminate the dynasty. That summer, it was reported that the Soviet of Ekaterinburg had shot the tsar and his family in the basement of the Ipatiev House on the night of 16–17 July. Grand Duchess Ella, elder sister of the tsarina, had become a nun and dedicated herself to charity. Although upset by her brother-in-law's second marriage with Princess Paley, she was much involved with their son, Vladimir, during her imprisonment. They died together, thrown down a mineshaft at Alapayevsk, in the Urals, two days later, as were the Konstantin Princes, Ioann, Konstatin, and Igor, the sons of Grand Duke Constantin Constantinovich. Grand Duke Sergei Mikhailovich, supreme commander of the artillery during the war, was shot immediately without suffering the horrible agony of his relations.

Wishing to help her family, Queen Marie sent the Canadian Col. Joseph W. Boyle to Russia in November. He tried to contact her aunt, the dowager empress, sending her a boat, as she was with her children and grandchildren near Yalta. She replied that despite the king of Romania's entreaties, nobody would make her sail for Romania in such a small craft. Of the fifty-two members of the imperial family who lived in Russia, seventeen disappeared during the Red Terror and many waited too long to leave. By the autumn of 1918, the Central Empires, faced with the occupation of the territory they had abandoned, saw their troops diminish. The Americans' arrival was bearing fruit. Members of the French Mission as well as the Americans who lived through the abandonment of Romania remembered the country fondly, and talked of the queen who bid them farewell at the railway station.

Meanwhile, decrees were made in the name of the king which impressed the people: there would be universal suffrage and agrarian reform, giving land to those who worked it and had done so for over a year. The royal family had moved to Bicaz, a house in the mountains where the echoes of victory were late to arrive. Until April 1918, the Central Empires hoped for victory, but by August, the situation had changed. The American ambassador reported that the Germans intended to abandon the country completely, and it was necessary to withdraw a considerable number of occupation forces.

The king and Prince Barbu Stirbey went to Iaşi to negotiate with the enemy in September, the Turks surrendered at the end of October, the Dardanelles were opened, and Austria called for an armistice on 3 November. Meanwhile Lenin's propaganda in Romania was ceaseless, yet the peasants did not revolt. There were also doubts about the Allies' conduct in respect of the defeated nation. Fortunately the pro-German Marghiloman resigned on 6 November 1918. Three days later, the king mobilised the army on the American ambassador's advice, giving the Germans twenty-four hours to leave the country.

The armistice was signed on 11 November. That same day, the queen arrived at Iaşi, where the French awarded her the *Croix de Guerre*. Her enthusiasm was triumphal and she returned to Bucharest on 1 December 1918. King Nando asked her to accompany him on horseback, and they made their entrance surrounded by Romanian and Allied troops. They were preceded by their sons, also on horseback, while the three princesses travelled in a horse-drawn coach, accompanied by Gen. Berthelot. Missy promised to help those who had been treated unjustly, above all her unhappy sister Bee.

12

The Uncertain Return

Missy attended the Paris Peace Conference at the end of the war—doing much to promote Romania there and positioning it amongst the great Allied Powers who had defeated the Central Empires. She then left Paris for Switzerland with her eldest daughter, Elisabeth, and Bee came from Zurich to join them. It was five years since they had last seen each other at Tegernsee. Then she was a plump young mother, overflowing with happiness, her little son, Alonso, in her arms. Now she was thin and weak, looking very slight, her face showing worry and fatigue, her attire simple but very chic, her hands large and pale but her movements still graceful, her wit as quick as ever.

Missy told her sister about the death of Mircea, the failure of the Romanian offensive, how that in order to save the crown jewels they had sent them to Moscow, now in the hands of the Bolsheviks, and her efforts to save the Romanovs. Now she was in the front line of the Peace Treaty Commission, fighting for Romania, and deeply upset by her elder children's behaviour.

Bee was deeply moved. In her turn, Queen Marie was saddened by her sister's tragedies. King Alfonso, previously a great friend, now treated his cousins badly, forbidding them to return to Spain, leaving them stateless. Marie desperately wanted to lift Bee from the oblivion in which she found herself. Bee had arrived in Paris on 10 April 1916, on the eve of the luncheon they intended to give the president of the United States, Woodrow Wilson, and his wife. The president resented women's involvement in politics and treated the queen of Romania with reserve, but the two sisters managed to get him to talk. The queen asked him to expound his theories, and the luncheon proved most agreeable. At the Peace Conference, the queen put Romania on the table. Before leaving Paris, she wanted to go to Aix-les-Bains, where they spent a day visiting the American soldiers to show them the difference between democracy and communism.

The queen sent her eldest daughter, Elisabeth, to a finishing school, under the care of the duchess of Vendôme, Mignon to an English college, and Nicholas to Eton. She left Paris on 16 April, arriving at Bucharest five days later, leaving Bee to prepare the meeting with her mother. She (Marie) was going to see mama again after five years of separation. As she was on the side of the victors and their mother among the vanquished, it would be a delicate time for both. The Russia and Germany the duchess had loved and believed in had vanished. Their first stop was Lausanne, where Bee was waiting for her so she could discuss with her the best way in which to meet the matriarch. Although the queen's journey was unofficial, she found it strange that on her arrival Swiss soldiers paid her honours. Yet it was a joy to be with her younger sister again, now very settled in Switzerland as she had lived there for three years during the war.

Prince Barbu Stirbey, head of the royal household in Romania and confidant of the queen, contacted Bee before her sister's arrival. They spent ten happy days in Lausanne, and she also met her friend Maruca Cantacuzino there, living in a small apartment near their hotel. They were in the centre of a small group of artists, some friends of Bee and others of Maruca, and they arranged enchanting musical evenings at her home.

The duchess of Coburg seemed keen to postpone the meeting, which was to be in Lucerne, during early September. For Queen Marie, the meeting was as difficult as expected, and she was grateful that Bee and Ali were able to join them. Ali's presence helped to relieve the tension and bridge the gulf between mother and daughter. Being on the side of the victors, Missy only spoke of her own experiences and tried as far as possible to talk only about what happened to them. The tension between them lessened, but there was no heart to heart chat between them, something for which she had hoped: 'Mama still followed the old traditions separating the generations'. Once Bee and Ali had left, the queen persuaded her mother to let her take her to Florence, a city she always loved and very much wanted to visit again. It proved a successful bonding exercise, allowing them 'two happy weeks'.

Bee tactfully did not accompany them. Nevertheless there was always a special relationship between them, and the queen also loved and respected her brother-in-law. Ali, she said, was undoubtedly 'one of the most perfect human beings' she had ever known. She praised his intelligence and moral rectitude, and one whose advice she asked at difficult moments in her life, as she admired his loyalty to the king, his calm and commonsense amid the issues his parents and brother had caused him.

Ali's problems with his father had reached a crisis point. On the death of his paternal grandfather, the duke of Montpensier, Ali's father, Antonio, had appropriated his fortune. Antonio also administered the inheritance Montpensier had left to his grandchildren, and the considerable civil list his wife had, as sister of King Alfonso XII. But still in 1919 Antonio of Orleans y Borbón was in severe straits and had to ask the king for a loan of 7,600 pesetas to finance his stay at the Palace Hotel in Madrid. Previously Ali had written (27 March 1919) to the king from Zurich that he had received the most alarming letters about papa from mama, about the state of his finances as well as his personal life.

The Spanish embassy in Paris put an end to the problems. Ali was appointed administrator of his assets, together with a supreme court judge appointed by the king. The judge, Don José Ortega Morejón, was among the most intimate advisors of the *Infanta* Isabel, making it legally necessary for Ali to present himself in Spain to carry out the formalities required to curtail the activities of the prodigal Antonio. He had to keep silent for a long time, but faced with the atmosphere that surrounded him and, doubtless under his wife's influence, Ali wrote to the king (Paris, 17 August 1919):

On the 25th of last month it was three long years since we left Spain on your orders ... [I hoped] that you would contact me of your own accord without my having to ask you.

In your last letter dated the 11th August 1918, in reply to mine, you tell me that I have persecution mania because I wrote you that there is no doubt that my enemies speak badly of me and that here they invent new calumnies. I was right to fear this as they are again writing me from Madrid saying that you are complaining about us, and that instead of being thankful towards you we spend our time speaking badly of you. Whoever tells you that we speak badly of you lies with the intention of doing us harm and it remains to say that there is not a word of truth in what they tell you. There is nothing more convenient, nor more cowardly, to slander someone who is absent and cannot ask to meet the slanderer face to face in front of you. Anyway, I should be very grateful if when someone makes an accusation against us you let me know the name of those who accuse us. As for the financial part you can understand that we are appreciative of the money which your government gives us (some forty thousand pesetas I believe). But now that we are talking of money, I do not know if you have taken account of what all this has cost me financially. In your last letter, you told me that is a sacrifice and not a punishment. The matter of the benzol was the worst, and you know that it was you who advised me to set up the business as it was in the National Interest. Refusing me the leave given by Romanones to return for a few days undid everything, with the results that I have already set out in other letters. It seems to me that not being able to rent-out my house prejudices me by at least thirty thousand pesetas a year. I have explained the bad state of my fortune various times and why it is necessary for me to at least know the length of my exile so that I can take measures to sell or rent my house, for which it is imperative that I spend some days in Madrid. I have had to help my mother-in-law who has been totally ruined by the Russian Revolution. The most serious thing is that of the benzol and this, with the other circumstances, has reduced our wealth to a third of what it was. I think that this could be called a sacrifice and that our suffering in silence for such a time is a good test of our loyalty to the King. I believe that you take no account of the fact that we live in Zurich like poor people on a family pension, that we eat in my dressing room, and taking a taxi is something almost unknown, so we go on foot or by tramcar. Remember that I have formed a family, and we keep a home which the boys cannot now remember as they have not been able to enjoy it. Yes, we do go to St Moritz in the winter (we do not travel in summer), but this is because it is absolutely necessary for the health of the boys and it's only for forty days in the year that we live in a hotel like people of our class. Three years!

Bee told Quiñones everything about this when she was in Paris so that he can tell you about it in full detail and for this reason I shall not write any more on the matter.

What is all this compared with my good name as a military man. If you know that I have not committed the slightest offence and you tell me that it is not a punishment but a sacrifice, my exile with all my family for more than three years without any fixed end, is a punishment for most people. Those who know me well consider it a tremendous injustice and those who do not know me say, 'Something very serious must have happened for such a heavy penalty to be imposed,' and they of course try to find out what the crime was. There are things that I do not understand. Given that I am not suffering a punishment, why was my adjutant, Moreno, not allowed to come and see me as I wished, not even after the accident that almost cost me my life? Why can you not give me a reason why you ask us to make such a great sacrifice, when I could be of great use to the fatherland? I am sure that you would not have demanded it of us without a reason. As much as I think, I can find no reason. But when you refused to allow me go to fight in Morocco as

I asked, to hear from you that 'at this time your intelligent management is necessary in your current location' seems that you are making fun of me. All over the world, prisoners and the defeated are returning home, do you not think that it could be that we are the only ones who are to be excluded from the current spirit of concord and goodwill. Will you allow me to return so that I may put some order into my life and so that, little by little, the situation which has been bitter and insupportable for us, and not advantageous for you, will disappear before too long.

The near-fatal accident was when Ali hit a rock while skiing near Brunnen on 7 May 1919, after which the king telegraphed him, wishing him a rapid recovery. This letter apparently went unanswered, but at the end of the summer means were made to reinstate Ali. Bee was eager to return to Madrid, now that Ambassador Quiñones de León informed her that the war was over and her possible return would be a question of months.

That autumn, meetings were arranged to consult with Ali who arrived in Madrid on 17 October, and found that the king and queen were absent. The king was in Paris, where he was popular after his magnificent work in locating prisoners from both sides and repatriating those who were ill. From the president of the Republic to the most humble French mother, all wished to embrace him. He toured the trenches, the theatre of bloody battles, and was acclaimed by the people. On 21 October, he went to London to take care of the queen who was ill and who would arrive in England at the end of the month. The two cousins did not see each other as Bee arrived on 5 November. As the king and queen were absent, *La Epoca* did not publish its 'Palace News'. In the edition for 16 November 1919, it was reported that *Infanta* Doña Beatrice had recovered from her recent illness, and that their highnesses would probably remain in Madrid until after Queen Victoria Eugenia returned from London.

The *Infanta* Isabel's Saint's Day was 19 November, and Ali and Bee visited her. They talked about the family of the *Infante* Don Carlos, who had a son, Alfonso, and a daughter, Isabel Alfonsa, and four more by his second marriage to Louise of Orléans, and about Nando of Bavaria with two sons and a daughter, who two years after the death of the *Infanta* María Teresa, had married a lady-in-waiting of Queen Cristina, the daughter of the count of Pie de Concha. She was short, fat, and not pretty, and four years older than the good-looking and elegant prince, yet it proved a happy marriage.

As Ena was extending her stay with her mother in England, the *infantes* decided to return to Switzerland. A curious letter from Merry del Val, Spanish ambassador in London (15 November 1919), noted:

> [The presence of the *Infanta* Beatrice in Spain caused] the worst possible effect on this Royal Family, beginning with King George because he fears her intrigues, and given the sincere love that they all profess for our Royal Highness Princess Beatrice [of Battenberg]. He appears to be particularly worried, and has not hidden this from me, and hopes that His Majesty the King of Spain will insist with all necessary firmness that the *Infanta* cuts short her stay and returns to Switzerland as soon as possible without having occasion to try to exercise her influence over her distinguished daughter.

While in Madrid that October, the king and queen of Spain went to England, a visit recorded in Grand Duke Dimitri Pavlovich's diary. On 25 October 1919, he was at a party at the Spanish embassy in London to celebrate the arrival of King Alfonso XIII. Merry del Val led him to the sovereign, who was most friendly, talked to him for a long time, and insisted that he sat beside him. When he returned to the Ritz after midnight, he found Alfonso waiting for him upstairs, and they chatted for hours, mostly about Russia and the assassination of Rasputin. Then the king told him, among other things, the complete story about Bee (which he had already heard many times before), and how she tried to attract him (illegible word) and then went and told the queen everything. Four days later, Dmitri attended dinner at the home of Lord Curzon of Kedleston for the king and queen of Spain, sitting between Ena and the duchess of San Carlos. The former was 'enchanting' and reminded him much of her brother, Drino (Alexander): 'Naturally we talked about the weather and did not discuss serious matters. The food was disgusting. After the dinner there was a professor telling the most boring stories. Alfonso and Ena left after an hour'.

Several months earlier, on 24 February 1919, he had dined with the Spanish ambassador and Merry de Val. He noted that the duchess lived 'only to gossip and spread rumours about other people' and spent an hour telling him the story of Bee and Alfonso. His diary also mentioned Ena's movements in England during the first two weeks of December 1919. One day she arrived for afternoon tea with them, in the company of her brother, Leo. The grand duke found him very likeable, but 'so unhappy and so ill', discontented with living at home as he did not like his elder brother, Drino. As for the queen, he said he would be very sorry to see her leave. She 'talks a lot and almost exclusively about the family drama in Madrid which is the result of the strange and amazing conduct of Baby

Bee, who seems totally lacking in tact'. The duchess mentioned that she wanted to know why Drino was so critical of Bee; meanwhile, Leo blamed Alfonso.

Bee left Spain, saddened not to have seen Queen Ena after so many years of separation. She returned to Zurich with her mother, who did not return to Coburg because of the revolutionary atmosphere in republican Germany since the abdication of the kaiser and his flight to Holland. In May 1917, King Constantine and Queen Sophia of Greece had been obliged to abandon their throne under pressure from the French government. It considered them pro-German as the queen was the sister of Kaiser William II, apparently unaware of the long-standing antipathy between them almost since her wedding in 1889. After staying briefly in St Moritz, the royal family went to the Villa Wehrli in Zurich, where some old friends arrived to support them. The Swiss government made them live in the German part of the country, where they could be watched more carefully. There they enjoyed the company of Ali and Bee, a first cousin of Queen Sophia. It was a particularly hard exile for Constantine and his family because of their lack of funds, and because they were forbidden to contact the new king, their second son, Alexander. The *Infanta* Eulalia said that Queen Sophia's 'patience in adversity was marvellous and her stoic philosophy allowed her to see her entire life as a state of *omnia vanitas* in which nothing lasts for ever'. Although Bee was fourteen years younger, they enjoyed a close friendship, and in a letter to Queen Marie of Romania, she wrote:

> Poor people! They are in a terrible position. Sophia and Tino (the King and Queen of Greece) have experienced real horrors and meeting them was really sad. Georgie, their first-born and future king, must have a true affection for your eldest daughter (Elisabeth) because he comes to talk to me about her and never finishes. It is all so sad. Those wasted lives!

Bee felt sorry for Prince George, whom Elisabeth initially rejected and gave full support to the idea of their marriage. The *infantes* did everything possible to help the family, and Ali even sought work for Prince Paul during the latter's fourteen-year exile. During their time in Switzerland, the friendship between both families increased with the arrival of Queen Olga of Greece, born a Russian grand duchess, very proud and profoundly Russian and, as granddaughter of Nicholas I, hated democracy. She left Russia as the sovereign of another country, ordering those in her way, 'Out of my way! I am the Queen of Greece!'

It was all good company for the duchess of Coburg who, in the last winter of her life, was greatly cheered at seeing Ducky again. After three years of exile with her family in Finland, preoccupied with the end of the Civil War and the triumph of the Soviets, King Gustav V of Sweden wanted to get Grand Duke Kirill and his family out of Finland. They left Borgo in May 1920, spent two days in Berlin where they met Sandra, then saw the duchess in Munich and went with her to Zurich.

At the end of the war, many of the Romanovs remained in Russia, reluctant or unable to believe that Nicholas II and his family had been killed. Nine days after their murder, the White Army entered Ekaterinburg, found the Ipatiev house empty, and began to investigate what had occurred. Meanwhile, the Spanish ambassador in London wrote to King Alfonso XIII to see if he could take in the tsarina and her children, still thought to be alive, and the dowager empress in the Crimea with her daughters. The king offered to grant the latter asylum, although she was not of his family, but she would not leave Russia at first. Convinced that she was safe as the widow of Tsar Alexander III and as a Danish princess, she knew her sister, Queen Alexandra, would not abandon her, which inspired her nephew, King George V, to help.

Missy had already asked her cousin, Xenia, repeatedly to entreat her mother to leave the Crimea before the Bolsheviks arrived. Finally Xenia, her family, and the dowager empress sailed in April 1919 and arrived at Portsmouth a month later. Grand Duchess Vladimir, Kirill's mother, did not want to leave Russia either, as she hoped the Allies would help the White Army against the Soviets. At length she was also persuaded to depart, staying first in Venice, then Cannes, then Contrexéville where after a short illness she died on 6 September 1920, surrounded by her three sons and Ducky.

Meanwhile, Missy visited her mother again, and found her suffering from heart trouble, thinner, and more tired. She was relieved that her mother had her four daughters and grandchildren close beside her. It had emerged earlier that year that her brother Grand Duke Paul, the youngest and her favourite, had been shot in the Peter and Paul Fortress in Petrograd. Bee tried to prevent her from reading the newspapers as they only contained cruel articles about the Russian Revolution. On the night of 24 October 1920, she died in her sleep.

Bee was with her at the end and her sisters joined her as soon as they could. Reunited at the Hotel Dolder Waldhaus, they planned to take her to Coburg so she could be laid to rest in the mausoleum at Glockenburg beside her loved ones. The queen of Romania was not allowed to join the cortege as she was disliked in Germany for her actions in the last war, and had to remain in Switzerland.

Despite its revolutionary republican atmosphere since the end of the war, Coburg received its old duchess with respect and even devotion.

Notwithstanding her brusque character, she had been much loved in the duchy. The same day on which she passed away, the young King Alexander died in Athens from a monkey bite. As he only had a daughter, Venizelos again summoned King Constantine to occupy the throne.

The *infantes* wanted to live in England so their sons could study in one of the colleges in or near London. They decided to settle in the country as life in the capital was very expensive. Moreover, Ali had studied near Windsor at the Jesuit school, Beaumont College, and still had friends there. The two elder boys went to St Mary's School, Winchester, and thus they looked for a house near Esher and Claremont where King Louis-Philippe and his wife, Marie-Amelie de Borbón, died in exile. The estate belonged to the English crown and on her death her sons had to leave it.

In July 1920, Ali viewed various properties in Surrey, chose a house in Esher, The Chalet, and three months later signed the rental contract for £33.12s a month. It was well furnished and comfortable, but lacked household linen, crockery, and cupboard space for a large family. Robert Papworth, Ali's butler and *aide-de-camp*, was transferred there, and three maids were employed at £1 weekly. The *infanta* and her sons did not stay there until the end of February 1921, as they were attending two family weddings. At first they did not have a car, and as The Chalet was some way from the town, they usually took a taxi to the Catholic Church and station.

A good friend, Luisa Rich y Paulet, daughter of Fernando Rich, military *attaché* at the Spanish embassy in London, told me about the *infantes'* time in England:

> I remember that we arrived before my 'coming out', now that I was eighteen, at a fiesta given in the Embassy on the occasion of the visit of the King and Queen of Spain to London and, as the only young lady from the Embassy, King Alfonso XIII asked me to dance. As much as I try, I cannot remember the *Infantes* being there. On the other hand, I well remember the day when Don Ali came to the house for the first time. He was a friend of my father's and stayed to eat. He was tall, well built and very handsome and he immediately won over my brothers and me. He loved to talk of Spain and to eat simple food: paella, fried eggs with chorizo, potato omelette, etc., etc. We had a Basque cook who made these tasty foods.
>
> We lived in the north of London in an old large, rambling house which soon had a room dedicated to the *Infantes'* things. Don Alfonso used to come punctually at the beginning of every month to visit my father and to receive his pay. He generally stayed to eat with us. The meal was great fun, as he was a good storyteller. After coffee my father accompanied the *Infante* to his office and they enthused over a map of Morocco.

It was 1921, the year in which the Moroccan offensive took place and the disasters of Annual, Monte Arruit, etc., etc.

Infanta Beatrice also came once. She was very elegant and distinguished, and although we spoke amicably, we felt more inhibited with her. We were more at ease with the *Infante* because he had a gift with people and an unpretentious way of speaking that included everyone. He went to his 'box room' and selected what he wanted to take to the train, as he rarely came by car. He was not a man who enjoyed criticism, but he had a keen sense of humour and laughed at anecdotes about people at the Embassy.

In springtime, when the weather was good, the *Infantes* used to invite us to spend the day at Esher. The journey by train was very short, less than an hour (it was only about 15 miles) and as we arrived punctually, we walked around the lovely garden, then we lunched in the open air if the weather allowed and invariably, after coffee, the *Infante* indicated to my father that they ought to retire to the office where the map of Morocco was. Don Ali had made the map even larger by joining various maps together.

For me the moment I most feared had arrived, when the Infanta showed me her albums and asked me for news from Spain which I did not know how to answer. Then she said that she was going to play the guitar, and then she sang *lieder*. I was happier when she showed me the gramophone and left me with records so that I could listen to what I wanted. Sometimes we also went to visit Claremont House, a big square building with a Grecian peristyle, situated in a lovely park with a pretty view over the River Thames and the county of Surrey. It should have been lived in by the Duchess of Albany, widow of Queen Victoria's youngest son Leopold, the much loved aunt of the *Infanta*. However she was generally absent because she was German and preferred to live in the Tyrol, where she died.

I knew the three Princes of Orleans and when a weekend coincided with them, I enjoyed myself greatly as they were boys who were full of life, very good looking, very likeable, and they always spoke at the same time.

Before arriving in Esher, Bee and her sons attended the wedding in Bucharest of Elisabeth and Prince George of Greece who, after the death of King Constantine in Palermo was called to reign as King George II. The marriage did not last long, they were dethroned in 1924 and went to Bucharest. There they parted, largely due to Elisabeth's aversion to having any children. The king lived in exile in London. In July 1935, he divorced Elisabeth, who lived in Romania, and returned again to Greece as king.

The wedding between Carol and Princess Helen of Greece in March 1921 was a match for which Queen Marie had fervently hoped. She had persuaded the Orthodox Church to annul the crown prince's morganatic marriage to Zizi Lambrino in 1918 on the grounds that King Ferdinand had not given it his permission. A son, Mircea, had been born on 8 August 1920. On 25 October 1921, Princess Helen also had a son, Michael, the future King Michael of Romania.

In the summer of 1921, Ducky, who had just bought a country house in St-Briac, Brittany, invited her sisters to enjoy peace and tranquillity by the sea. They had still to address the inheritance of the duchess of Coburg, which although somewhat diminished, still left a fortune in jewels. Missy arrived from Romania with her youngest daughter, Ileana, aged twelve. The *infantes* arrived with their sons from England, and that summer was one of the happiest in the sisters' turbulent lives. The absence of court etiquette, the simple country life with the minimum of clothes (normally swimming costume and a string of pearls), the company of a few faithful friends and the best of golf, made for a much-needed carefree holiday. The jewellers had recommended that the duchess's collection of pearls, kept for so long in a Swiss bank, should be in salt water and fresh air, so the sisters wore them even with bathing costumes. Various photographs showed Bee walking on the rocks of the Brittany Coast in espadrilles and pearls.

On 22 February 1922, they attended the wedding of Princess Mary, only daughter of King George V and Queen Mary, to Viscount Lascelles. Bee met her cousin, Xenia of Russia, who was living at Frogmore, lent to her by King George V, while her husband, who had difficulties entering England in 1917, stayed in France.

Ena wrote to Queen Marie of Romania (Madrid, 1 April 1922):

I often think that destiny awaits my daughters and ignores which country they marry in. I have the same idea as you. I would not find it disagreeable if they marry Spanish Grandees, but I infinitely prefer a prince of similar rank. A marriage like Mary's, which should have been extraordinarily popular, I simply cannot understand.

Mignon's [Marie's second daughter] engagement moves me. Personally, being Queen when one is very young is not my idea of happiness, it is too hard a role for a young girl to play, because later in life one finds great satisfaction in doing things which are really useful for one's adopted country. Happily Mignon will be at least alone with her husband without having a mother-in-law criticising everything she does.

I have received lots of news about poor Bee from my family, because they met her at the festivities for Mary's wedding. How I hope her health improves! The agonies of headaches surely cannot be normal. How I hope that she becomes happy again, but it may not be possible with her strange character. Poor darling. She may say now that she was happy but she was not happy here either. I can assure you of that.

Perhaps Bee suffered from an early menopause during her stay in Switzerland, with migraines which kept her to her room for days at a time in darkness, and frequent attacks of neuralgia.

That summer, Mignon married King Alexander of Yugoslavia. Bee's favourite niece, born in Coburg in 1900, always a sweet, loving child who quietly followed her mother's advice, married King Alexander, a man of simple pleasures and a born soldier. They had three sons: Peter, who was king under the regency of Prince Paul, a cousin of his father, Tomislav, and Andrew. The wedding was celebrated on 8 June in Belgrade, and many royalty attended, including the *infantes*.

A month later in London, they attended the wedding of Lord Louis Mountbatten to Edwina Ashley. The groom was the son of Princess Victoria of Hesse and by Rhine and the late Prince Louis of Battenberg, formerly first lord of the Admiralty, and subsequently marquis of Milford Haven. He was later viceroy of India, and later earl Mountbatten of Burma. The ceremony in St Margaret's, Westminster, was attended by 1,200 guests, including the entire royal family and the dowager empress of Russia accompanied by her sister, Queen Alexandra. How the meeting went between the Infanta Beatrice and the old tsarina, who had not seen each other for twenty years, was not known. As Misha's mother, she had changed the direction of Beatrice's life forever.

13

Representing Spain

On 20 April 1922, Bee's birthday, Alfonso and Ena were about to leave for Moratalla when a telegram arrived from London in which Prince Leopold of Battenberg told them of his forthcoming operation. As he was a haemophiliac, Ena instantly realised the danger, and asked to go to London and be with their mother. The king told her it was not serious, but she insisted she must remain in Madrid for news of the patient, knowing the English family would keep her up to date on everything. Alfonso was determined not to alter his plans, and the queen slept in Moratalla that night. On Saturday, the doctors reported that the operation had been successful though the prince had lost much blood and was very weak. He had improved a little, but that night he worsened and asked Bee to come at once. He felt that with her beside him nothing bad would happen, and she would nurse him again as she had years before. His mother and elder brother, Alexander, were present, as was his wife, Lady Irene Denison, whom he had married three years earlier.

Bee joined them, holding his hand to the end and closing his eyes on the morning of 23 April. It was of great comfort to Leopold, who had been so close to her since childhood. He shared her sorrow when Misha left her and they went to visit Egypt, defended her when she married, and enjoyed seeing her on his visits to Madrid. In 1916, defying his mother and older brother, he was a pillar of support to Bee and Ali. After the war and her stay in Switzerland, he had loved having her near in Esher, and she visited him when she was in London. With his death, she lost a bond with her English family. Princess Beatrice of Battenberg was invited by her son-in-law, Alfonso XIII, to spend the days of mourning with her daughter, and she arrived in Madrid at the end of April.

The Moroccan campaign was like a cancer for Spain. At times it seemed in remission, and at others it flared up with real fury. Knowing from experience that with good aircraft it would be possible to subdue the tribes, Ali was determined to join the campaign, but the king ignored all his requests. In February 1920, his most faithful aides, César de Santa María and Luís Moreno Abella, left him to take part in military duties and be promoted. Ali was hurt because they had been so loyal. At the end of that year, he asked again to return to the front via General Goded, and again in spring 1922, this time approaching the ministry of war, but received no reply.

Ena herself commented in April that 'life here and now [was] very sad'. The Moroccan campaign had caused great dismay, with many families mourning sons and husbands who never returned. She had worked hard, organising and visiting Red Cross hospitals at Madrid and in Andalusia. It had not been possible for her to leave Spain for over a year, but she hoped to visit England again before long.

It was said that Gen. Silvestre, having authorisation from the king, had advanced towards Annual (a camp 80 miles from Melilla), without the knowledge of his immediate superior, Gen. Dámaso Berenguer. He was defeated humiliatingly there, in July 1921. Among his papers they found two telegrams from the king, the first saying, 'I expect good news on the 26th', the second, 'Well done men! I hope'. At that time, the king was preparing to travel to Deauville and he did not suspend the trip despite the disaster in which 14,000 men died, including Silvestre, allegedly by suicide.

The *Infanta* Eulalia was at Deauville and met Alfonso for the first time since 1912. She claimed he was very affectionate towards her as they spoke about family matters which were taking time to resolve, such as the incapacity of the *Infante* Don Antonio and the 'secret exile' of her son, Ali. This meeting undoubtedly improved relations between them both. Alfonso suggested she return to Spain, and Eulalia decided to buy a country house at Igueldo, facing the sea. She liked living in San Sebastián in the summertime and visiting Queen María Cristina, for whom she always had a high regard.

On 21 May 1921, a decision of the supreme tribunal had declared the *Infante* Don Antonio de Orleans y Borbón a 'prodigal'. Matters were far from clear as *Infante* Don Luís (his younger son), who was very greedy and had accepted that César Sáenz de Santa María should be the administrator of Castillejo, had unbeknown to Ali requested a mortgage on the estate. When the brothers met in Madrid in June, the elder persuaded the younger to leave César to administer the estate unconditionally. Ali was very worried by all this.

Ali was in Paris by 27 September, where he received a letter from his cousin the king, ordering him to represent Spain at the coronation of King Ferdinand and Queen Marie of Romania, eight years after their accession. The ceremony took place on 15 October 1922, and Missy thought that Bee outshone everyone, dressed in gold with a long tailored train in coral pink from Russia and gold brocade trimmed in white fox, a headdress including an opaque golden veil draped around her face in Egyptian style, a diamond diadem placed high and on top a large pendant hanging on both sides of the face, complemented by emeralds and diamonds on the violet and white of the Great Sash of Spain. Afterwards there were various military parades, processions and other festivities, then the *infantes* stayed a few days to rest. Queen Marie showed them a letter from Ena, who told them that King Alfonso was very well and asked her to send his respects and, 'although he feels that you do not like him, is satisfied at least to amuse you, which he hopes to do on the first occasion he has the pleasure of seeing you again.'

While in Romania, Ali visited various aviation centres, all equipped with good quality aircraft thanks to French help during the war. On returning to England, he was commissioned to undertake tests with Vickers aircraft at Brooklands. From March to June 1923, he attended a course at Netheravon, and visited the RAF Staff College at Andover. At Coventry, he tested Armstrong Whitworth Aircraft, which Col. Fernando Rich, the Spanish military *attaché* in London, called 'a very dangerous, but very well paid job'. But even though he had represented the Spanish nation and his king in Europe, he could not freely enter his country. He therefore planned to go to Paris and see Pepe Quiñones de León, Spanish ambassador in France, to ask if his children could take advantage of the Easter holidays to get to know Andalusia. The reply was that they could spend the month of April in Sanlúcar, but difficulties were made to prevent Ali from going to Seville, Madrid, and other cities that were necessary for his business interests.

He detailed the journey in a letter, noting that Bee and the boys were delighted to be in Andalusia, despite bad weather. They went by sea, the Bay of Biscay was rougher than usual, and most of the passengers were seasick: 'Thank goodness Bee and the boys are good sailors'. The cruise delighted the little princes who made themselves very popular with the crew, as they excitedly explored all over the boat.

Carlos Delgado, a friend of Ali, took them fishing in the marshes of the Guadalquivir and found them horses to ride at Torre Breva, where they raced each other. Yet what surprised them most after living in England was the respect and friendliness shown them by the Sanluqueños, their interest in showing off their town, and readiness to invite them into their houses and *bodegas*. They enjoyed the Holy Week processions in the late afternoons, and the artistic floats in the lamplight. With songs, bands of musicians, siestas, rockets, and applause as Andalusia resonated before their eyes.

In a letter (23 April 1923) to his father, whom he was expecting to meet in Sanlúcar, Ali recalled his impressions of the town he had been unable to visit for six years:

> Bee as much as the boys and I are very sorry that you are not here with us and it is sad to see the empty rooms, but I hope that you will be here with us some other time. The house is very clean, but it is so many years since there has been any maintenance that some of the leaks are overwhelming and there is no option but to repair them. Besides, the timbers of the windows and the shutters have not been painted for God knows how long and some are now rotten. To summarise, there is a great deal to do and these are things that cost money. I understand that at your age you are too young to permanently bury yourself here and no doubt it is as sad for you as it is for me to see these ruins of a great fortune and a prestigious past.
>
> But as you are in the autumn of your life, I am sure that makes you want to return to spend some time with your grandchildren and return and regain the respect and love that this area would love to show for a son of the venerated Duke and Duchess of Montpensier. Above all I should like your grandsons to learn the concept of respect for their grandfather and this would be easily done by your giving up a few weeks from time to time.

On another page, he mentioned that there was almost no silver in the house, although much of the silver plate remained. Thanks to Quinones who said the *infante* should have liberty of movement to carry out his personal affairs, he managed to go to Madrid to arrange his father's involved legal claims with the family court. He went to live at his house in Calle Quintana and many aviators and military men visited him there, many of whom were worried about the continuing war in Morocco. In conclusion, he said that Bee and the boys would return to Esher one week later.

Bee usually sailed from Gibraltar to a port in England. They never feared storms in the Bay of Biscay, and always enjoyed the ship's menu to the full. Beatriz of Orleans, Álvaro's younger daughter, later wrote that they never liked returning to school at Winchester:

[Her father, the eldest of the brothers,] was intelligent and a good student, and had a *joie de vivre* which made everyone respect him. Alonso, on the other hand, had a very accommodating, helpful character. He was a bit timid and very loving, for which he was popular. They say that some teachers bullied him, and my father told me repeatedly that the two shared very bad memories of their stay there. He said that the system of punishment was iniquitous and unnecessarily cruel.

Ali returned to England from his stay in Spain, worried by news of many disasters and few solutions in Morocco and in Catalonia where there was major social unrest. The situation became so critical that on the morning of 13 September, the captain-general of Catalonia ordered the occupation of the telephone and telegraph building, confined the troops to barracks, and proclaimed a state of war. The king, who was in San Sebastian, left for Madrid to remain in contact with the government. Arriving next morning and, faced with the indecision of the prime minister, the marquis of Alhucemas, who knew of the uprising in advance but had done nothing to stop it, he telegraphed the captain-general of Barcelona to come at once, and gave him orders to form what he called the military directorate.

The co-ordinator of this uprising was Miguel Primo de Rivera y Orbaneja, marquis of Estella, an infantry general and friend of Gen. Burguete, Ali's much-loved teacher and hero 'because he gained his laurels at Cabrerizas Altas at twenty-three by saving a canon from the Moors'. In Toledo, Ali saw Rivera on various occasions. On returning in 1911 from his 'nuptial exile' and offering himself as a volunteer, Primo de Rivera was Ali's colonel and they shared a tent, mess, and various attacks in which the Moors had tried to kill them. He was promoted to general on 18 December 1911 for his valour at the Battle of Ifratuata, and in May 1913 sent a photograph of himself Ali with a dedication saying he was not sure if it was a breach of court etiquette to dedicate a portrait to a prince of Spain, but if it was, 'I know that Your Highness will pardon he who had the honour of being your colonel in the 1911 campaign and was able to appreciate the conditions of brilliance and bravery that adorned your Royal Highness as an officer.'

On learning of the *coup d'état*, Ali wrote from Esher (4 October 1923) to Primo de Rivera:

Among the thousands of congratulations which you receive, believe me, there is none more sincere than that from your old lieutenant in the San Fernando Regiment, although it feels ridiculous to congratulate a soldier who has the Cross which you wear, and your military record of demonstrable bravery. Gambling one's life is little compared with the things you have done but, at the same time, you have taken on a great responsibility.

I have a dozen years experience of flying and I have studied aviation in depth, especially in these last three years in England.

One of the problems which you have to resolve is that of beating the rebels and pacifying our zone in Morocco, and I am convinced that the rational and intense use of aircraft is the only way to achieve this with the minimum loss of life.

Some days ago, I again wrote to HM the King reminding him once more of my service in Morocco, and although I work as I can abroad, he understands that it pains me not to serve my country and my King more actively. I also drew special attention to studying the use of aeroplanes against natives in his colonies.

On 14 February, Ali notified the king that he had been at the Central Flying School for three weeks on an instructors' course to update him before giving a short course to the instructors in Madrid.

In the spring of 1924, the king and queen of Romania paid a four-day state visit to Britain, to cement their position as allies. The *infantes* were invited to Buckingham Palace, where they privately discussed the strange situation in which Ali found himself living in Esher, while he was officially a military *attaché* in Berne. George V understood neither Spanish diplomacy nor its king, whom he disliked for his treatment of Ena.

As the British royals were expecting the arrival of the king and queen of Italy, and Queen Marie wanted to remain a few days more, her husband left for Italy to wait for her. Meanwhile, Missy decided to stay at Bee's house and she was delighted to have her elder sister at The Chalet. While Queen Marie was there, Prince Stirbey arrived to attend to some matters. 'We were very happy to be together in England for once, as it had always been one of our dreams,' confided the queen in her diary, 'I took him to the woods to see the bluebells.'

From there they went to Cliveden to visit the Astors and then on to other friends at Plymouth. Far from Romania in the company of her sister, Bee, Missy seemed much younger. Incognito, they visited small villages buying seeds for flowers and bushes, and old copper pots. Stirbey usually advised on what he thought would do better in the gardens at Sinaia or in Balchik next to the Black Sea in Romania.

Luisa Rich told me a curious anecdote regarding the royal visit. Wanting the Spanish military attaché to meet her sister, the queen of Romania, Bee invited Col. Rich to lunch at Esher. That morning, he received a parcel for the *infanta*, marked 'Urgent' and 'Confidential' to give personally to the queen. He arrived punctually at The Chalet, where they indicated that luncheon would be served in the garden. Rich was in the drawing room waiting for Bee when Ducky arrived. Greeting him in a friendly manner, she took the package as if it was for her. Later the queen arrived with Bee who presented him and they went into the garden. They had just sat down when Ducky told Missy that she had a parcel which the colonel had brought. On opening it, she took out fat envelopes in white, grey, black, and brown, and threw them through the air to the various guests who followed her example by doing likewise. Rich was shocked! Then Queen Marie thanked him in English for bringing her the stockings. She had regularly ordered them from the factory since she was young, as she had straight, shapeless ankles and 'my sisters always annoy me by joking about my legs.'

A visit to Ashford, Kent, close to the Eastwell estate, was left until the end of Missy's visit. As they passed through Ashford, Missy noticed many of the shops were named 'Bishop's' after a large local family, many of whom had been in service with the duke and duchess. The façade of the house she had left when she was only eleven years old had been altered, and was no longer all grey but now rose-coloured as a wing had been covered with bricks. But the 'pretty side' still existed with its four floors and its circular towers. Now converted into a hotel with a golf club, the lounges had lost their charm, although the music room still had its two pianos. Full of curiosity, they explored the glasshouses, less beautiful than previously, but the lake was as picturesque as ever.

Ali went to Madrid to see Primo de Rivera and offer himself as a volunteer pilot. Rivera remembered their earlier conversations in which Lt Orleans had spoken of his belief in the role that aviation would occupy in war in the future, with aircraft having been used for the first time in battle in the new campaign in the spring of 1924. Rivera had ordered withdrawal from the Souk of Arbas, and the aircraft protected the vanguard and helped the ground troops.

Luisa Rich told me her father had arrived in London months before the *infantes*. Having completed five years there, her father was due to return to Spain, while the princes of Orleans had to remain. The boys continued with their studies, while Ali spent some time in Madrid preparing for the landing at Alhucemas. Bee was very much alone but, stoical as ever, did not show it.

At the end of June, Ena planned a three-week holiday in London with her daughters, Beatriz, just fifteen, and María Cristina, thirteen. On 29 June 1924, they left Madrid for Paris, staying at the Hotel Meurice before leaving for England where Princess Beatrice of Battenberg was awaiting them at Kensington Palace. Ambassador Merry del Val and his wife gave a dinner for Ena, her mother and brothers, and her uncle and aunt, the duke and duchess of Connaught. They sat at two tables, one presided over by the queen and the other by her brother, the marquis of Carisbrooke. Later a reception was attended by 300 guests, including the *Infantes* Don Alfonso and Doña Beatriz de Orleans, Prince Genaro of Two Scillies and his wife, Prince Paul of Yugoslavia, and Prince Andrew of Greece with his daughters. According to what Luisa told me, 'the two cousins embraced, and greeted each other with great naturalness'.

Bee wanted to spend the summer in Sanlúcar and do up the palace a little. She and her sons had spent the previous summer at the home of Lord Howard de Walden and his family. According to Lord Howard, Ali wrote to the queen of Romania, inviting her to spend the summer at Brownsea Island with her daughters. Lord Howard de Walden owned the island, where Ali and Bee were always welcome. He was married to Margaret van Raalte whose wealthy parents were very close to the *Infanta* Eulalia, and they had always enjoyed a close relationship with the *infantes*. Bee offered Ducky the same invitation. They both accepted, and photographs show the three Edinburgh sisters in dressing gowns accompanied by their children, Nicholas of Romania, Maria and Kira Kirillovich, and little Vladimir with his nanny. The children got to know the children of their hosts, John and Bronwen, who were twins born the same year as Alonso; Elisabeth (Ebite) who was younger, and the three little girls; Priscilla (Pip to her friends), Gaenor, and Rosemary. Bee then left for Spain for Queen María Cristina's birthday on 21 July, after which they went to Santander.

Queen María Cristina wrote to Ali (Miramar, 17 August 1924) about the meeting:

> My first letter after my return is to thank you again with all my heart for having come from England to see me. I was very pleased to see you and I thank you for the depth of love that you have always shown me. I shall be very pleased to see you this autumn.
>
> I arrived here yesterday. The journey went well but was rather sudden. Nino should come today to see Louise in Cauterets; but he has not been able to leave Seville because of the troop movements. Louise arrives tomorrow and on the 20th goes to Seville with Isabelita and Esperanza.

It was just over eight years since Ali and Bee and Marie-Cristina had had a stormy lunch at the Miramar Palace in San Sebastian, prior to leaving Spain.

Ali had been in Italy testing aircraft at the Centocelle Aerodrome since October 1923, and his old chiefs asked his advice on which to purchase. That year he attended the International Air Congress in London, visited the flying instructors' school at Upavon, the photography and aeronautics schools at Farnborough, and the school of mechanics at Halton, and completed a flight instructors' course at Upavon. On return to Spain in March 1924, he went to Getafe, completed a new course as lecturer in military aviation, and was back in England as *attaché* to No 25 Fighter Group of the RAF at Hawkinge aerodrome, where he made several training flights. Bee endured these separations and dangerous missions stoically. For Christmas, they returned to Sanlúcar, then Bee and their sons returned by sea to England where they continued at Winchester, and where young Ataúlfo, just eleven years of age, was sent.

The *infantes* spent the summer holidays of 1924 in Sanlúcar where they talked of the coming war, the Guerra del Rif or Moroccan War that began with the uprising of the Rif tribes in north Morocco against the colonial forces of France and Spain in 1909. It continued intermittently for many years. By 1924, it was expected that the problem would soon worsen. 'Although our bombing in Morocco,' commented Ali, 'was not the first (bombs from aircraft were first used in the Balkan wars), we Spanish believe ourselves to have been the first to have (after firstly having kept the bombs on our knees) perfected the system of tying bombs to the aircraft's fuselage; the gunner took aim then cut the cord with a pair of scissors.' He was referring to the Spanish army in Morocco, although he had not actually been there.

The retreat was completed safely on 13 December 1924. Nearly 200 positions had been evacuated, and for the first time in many years it was felt that Christmas would be more tranquil. Nevertheless, Ali and Bee were not fully restored to favour. He had not taken part in the Moroccan war, because their position was not yet assured and they had yet to be restored to their full rank and position in Spain though they could make short trips home. At last the family was allowed back to Spain. There was still no sign of a rapprochement with Alfonso, though Ali attended an audience with Queen María Cristina on 14 November, with *Infanta* Isabel and Princess Pilar of Bavaria. Ali joined the school of aerial combat and bombing at los Alcázares, to give a course for group and squadron leaders which he would finish on 2 February 1925.

On 7 May 1925, Ali and Bee went to Sanlúcar, to join their children. They attended the grand fiestas in the palaces of the dukes of Medinaceli, and of Montellano, attended by the king and queen and her brother, Drino. That afternoon, there was a reception in the throne room, attended by members of the family, top civil servants, the full diplomatic corps and various members of the army and the navy.

Dinner was held at 8:30 p.m. in the gala dining room for ninety guests. On the right of the king sat his mother, Queen Maria Cristina, followed by Prince Ferdinand of Bavaria and *señora* de Ruata, Bee's lady-in-waiting.

On the left of the king was the *Infanta* Isabel with Ali at her side and then the countess of Heredia Spínola, Queen María Cristina's lady-in-waiting. Ena had on her right the prince of Asturias, and at his side Bee, who was greeted with great kindness by the president of the military dictatorship, Gen. Primo de Rivera, followed by the duchess de la Victoria. On the left of the queen was the young *Infante* Don Alfonso of Bourbon (the king's nephew, son of Mercedes, his eldest sister who died in childbirth), and then the duchess of Talavera, wife of *Infante* Don Ferdinand of Bavaria, and Capt.-Gen. Weyler, duke of Rubí.

The king appeared delighted to see Ali again, who thought his sovereign now looked more like his mother, although he was thin and his fine hands reminded Bee of her Uncle Leopold. As for Primo de Rivera, Bee was very attentive to him as she knew how well he thought of her husband. She suspected that he was connected with this invitation on this memorable day, she also spoke to the duchess of la Victoria who fronted the Red Cross in Morocco. Before the king and queen left for Barcelona, the countess of Casa Valencia threw a party at her palace, attended by Queen María Cristina, the *Infanta* Isabel, and the *infantes* of Orleans, who chatted with the duchess of Somerset, who was guest of the British ambassador and his wife.

On 23 May, Bee was in the palace to bid farewell to the two queens as she was going to England to join her sons. Ali visited various representatives of the dictatorship, who decided he should remain in Madrid and prepare for the landing at Alhucemas, expected that summer. On 5 June 1925, he was appointed leader of the Fokker squadron, destined for Tetuán, and the expeditionary force organised at Getafe. Both units were to join with Ali in overall command.

The flight left on 14 July, arriving at Daimiel, then made the next stage to Seville, where Ali visited Capt.-Gen. *Infante* Don Carlos of Bourbon and his wife, Luisa of Orleans. The next day, they arrived at Tetuán. 'These operations,' Ali said, 'co-ordinated with the French Army, went like clockwork.' The French suffered from incursions led by Abd el-Krim. On 17 July, reconnaissance flights commenced, followed by bombing which continued until the end of October. Being an early riser, Ali arrived at the aerodrome promptly to help the mechanics examine the aeroplanes and take them from the hangers. The Fokker C IVs had been given more powerful engines than usual, so Ali complained to command, 'Carried out reconnaissance of lower slopes of Mount Semse. It was impossible to reach the summit. The mountain is seven hundred metres high!'

Ali then became seriously ill with a high temperature which baffled his doctors. On learning this, the king sent him a card (Royal Palace, Madrid, 30 August 1925):

I know that you are now well and that you return to your post, making the journey with the General in command. The first news of your illness was alarming, but then, fortunately, thanks to your robust health you recovered quickly. Some attribute your illness to bathing in the cold sea, something which does not surprise me, as I know your liking for going in and out of the water and perhaps your insides were not well and you started something. Take care and don't do anything careless.

As the king indicated, Ali was required by Primo de Rivera to participate in the conference held on 21 August in Algeciras between Marshal Petain and Primo de Rivera and their high commands, with the landing scheduled for the first week in September. Some thought the dictator wanted it to coincide with the second anniversary of his *coup d'état*; others suspected the dangerous Levante wind would make the action impossible, and other members of the executive suggested postponing operations until the spring. Some military leaders believed that aviation should not be a part of the battle as they doubted its efficiency. The general in command, José Sanjurjo, did not accept their advice, 'making them understand the important part which aviation will have in war'. On his orders, the bombers and the seaplane carrier *Dédalo* were to protect the landing at Alhucemas, due to take place on 8 September 1925, the fiesta of the Virgin of Regla.

Ignacio Hidalgo de Cisneros, the future commander of the Republican Air Force, observed:

They spent most of the day in the air, over the bay, and during advances made by the groups of legionnaires, they could see the officers directing operations from the front. There was a moment in which the resistance must have been very strong, as the advance was stopped with the troops seeking protection behind the rocks. The two companies that came to reinforce them advanced rapidly, though leaving many of their men on the way, and caught up with the force that had been halted, so they could carry out the final assault together. The advance progressed all along the Monco. The Moroccans could not escape, as the cliffs were high and the rocks sharp, and they defended themselves like cornered wild animals.

The landing had been a success. The first of the wounded arrived aboard the hospital ship *Barceló*, staffed by the duchess de la Victoria and Dr Gómez Ulla, and several doctors and nurses.

Years later, not long before he died, Ali told me, 'Aviation was acclaimed throughout the Rif,' a region in the north of Morocco reaching the Mediterranean, part of the Spanish Protectorate. The local Rifean tribes never accepted the Spanish Protectorate, resulting in continuous uprisings and skirmishes. He was giving himself little credit for his role in this action, although I knew he had participated in the heroic action. His service record just indicates that in the years 1924, 1925, and 1926, he was still military *attaché* in Switzerland.

After the landing, the battle continued, and on 22 October, the press reported that squadrons under Ali's command took part in the action and two squadrons of seaplanes bombed the enemy intensively, causing losses and starting fires in some Riffian dwellings. Tactical demands necessitated adjustments to the Axdir front to unite the position called Bescansa with Monte de las Palomas. Forces of friendly Moroccan infantry (Regulares) and the sappers set out from their bases early in the morning under the command of Gen. Saro whose superior officer, Gen. José Sanjurjo, was giving orders. The latter, who loved flying, went up in seaplane No. 7 and went to Monte de las Palomas, near Gen. Saro, and followed the development of operations: 'The work of fortifying new positions was carried out under conditions of complete normality. Sanjurjo returned in the afternoon in the same seaplane'.

On 2 November, the aviators held a farewell lunch for their comrades in Ali's squadron. The aircraft went to Granada, and then Madrid. Two days later, at Cuatro Vientos Aerodrome, Ali, who was returning with Lt-Col. Alfredo Kindelán, landed leading his squadron. In the afternoon, he was at the palace, accompanied by Bee, to greet the king and Queen María Cristina and tell them of his exploits.

A little later, the *infantes* went to Rome to obtain the Holy Year jubilee indulgence, the jubilee or 'Holly Year' (*Año Santo*) being a special year for the forgiveness of all sins in the Catholic church. If one travels to Rome as a pilgrim during the Año Santo, one is granted the 'Indulgencia Plenaria', the total remission before God of the temporal punishment deserved for sins, already forgiven with respect to guilt. They stayed at the Hotel Bristol, then went to the Vatican on 18 November, accompanied by the countess of Casa Valencia and her daughter, María Teresa. The count and countess of Viñaza held a banquet for them and invited Col. Francesco de Pineda, the Italian aviation ace.

In her will, the duchess of Coburg had left the Edinburgh Palace, in Coburg, to Ducky, giving her a home in Germany. She, Kirill, and their children moved there in 1924. The elder, Maria Kirillovna, born in Coburg on 2 February 1907, was now engaged to Friedrich Karl VI, prince of Leiningen, the eldest son of Princess Feodore Victoria of Hohenlohe-Langenburg, and thus grandson of the half sister of Queen Victoria. The wedding at Coburg was set for 25 November 1925. Diplomatically, because of the war, Ail could not attend, but Bee was determined to go as she had been at the weddings of Missy's children and could not disappoint

Ducky. The latter had become very embittered since losing so much in the Russian Revolution. Besides, María was very pretty and agreeable and was marrying for love. Bee was delighted to be back in Coburg as she had not been there for many years. The first, Orthodox, ceremony was held in Grand Duchess Maria's Orthodox chapel, filled with the icons Tsar Alexander II had given his daughter, followed by the Lutheran one in the town church. Kirill, the self-proclaimed 'Guardian of the Russian Throne', behaved like the emperor of Russia, but ex-Tsar Ferdinand of Bulgaria, seeing him coming, picked up his walking stick and overtook his host.

To her annoyance, Missy was not invited to the wedding of Ducky's elder daughter as the Germans had never forgiven her actions during the war. She was going through a bad time, as Ferdinand was gravely ill and Crown Prince Carol had returned to his old ways, having an affair with Elena Lupescu, a redhead who reputedly brainwashed him, driving a wedge between him and his wife, Helen of Greece, and son, Michael.

Queen Alexandra, widow of King Edward VII, died in November 1925. Prince Carol was chosen to represent Romania at the funeral, so he could collect his sister, Ileana, at college in England, and they could return together to Bucharest for Christmas. Ena was also there, and Carol asked to travel to Paris with her by train to spend some time there with Mme Lupescu. His furious mother tried in vain to persuade him to do his duty and return to Romania. Ali, Carol's favourite uncle, the mighty hero of the Moroccan war, was in Paris at that time, and Missy turned to Ali for assistance. She knew there was not the slightest chance Carol could return 'before he has purged the atmosphere of sin and degradation in which he lives', and asked her brother-in-law to help him 'be a man again. I know you are the beloved and clean creature who can perhaps manage to stop him from sinking into the quagmire.'

The meeting between Ali and Carol was a disaster. When the former asked his nephew if he wanted to return to Romania, he replied that he did, but only under certain conditions. Ali told him firmly that it was not up to him to demand conditions, but his parents, his king and queen, who could do so if they agreed to let him return. There was not one single person in a royal family, he warned, nor any person with monarchical principles, who did not 'look in horror and sadness at the damage you have caused to the monarchy in general and who does not now look at your present life with anger and contempt'. On 3 December 1925, King Ferdinand met the council of state at Sinaia to propose disinheriting his firstborn, making his grandson Prince Michael heir. Bee wrote to Missy after a conversation with Carol, telling her he was blindly in love, having 'fallen into a group which naturally says that he is a fine fellow, and he is treated unjustly by certain politicians in his own country'.

On returning from Rome, the *infantes* left Madrid for Esher. Surrey was very popular for hunting. Lord Arundel, who had a magnificent hunting estate and was a great friend of Ali and his sons, often invited them to his castle near Littlehampton. Ali was delighted with his sons' good marksmanship. He had taught them to manage and clean their shotguns, always 'breaking' them on entering Arundel Castle. They kept their ammunition there and Alonso put himself in charge of the cartridges, telling his older brother with great mystery that he had a debt to settle. Bee described what happened next: 'When the last day of term arrived, just before leaving school for ever, Alonso put powder in front of the pavilion door, blowing it up, without doubt to liberate himself from his bitterness'.

Bee arrived in Paris with her sons on 18 December 1925 on her way to Spain. As they had always gone by boat, it was exciting for them to visit the French capital. They arrived in Madrid on 23 December. Every year they put nativity scenes in the rooms, explained the *Infanta* Cristina, 'but Grandmother always put up a gigantic tree in her rooms, which I think they brought from Navacerrada, and in front large packages with the names of everyone written by her. At exactly 6.00 Grandmother switched off all the lights and then one could see the brightly-lit tree. Then she switched the lights back on and each one rushed to retrieve their package full of joy.'

Álvaro and Alonso were also invited to the private homes of the aristocracy for children's parties. The biggest party of that Christmas was held by Princess Hohenlohe. Her tree came from Bohemia; ingenious toy cars and boats that ran on gasoline were given as presents; and the boys had to dress like Santa Claus, with beards, whilst the girls became snowmen.

14

Glorious Days

Ali and his family quietly prepared to leave England for Spain. In June 1926, Col. Kindelán offered Ali command of Getafe Airport, 'not that it [was] the most desirable charge in the service', but because he thought him the best person for the job. Ali replied:

> I cannot deny that, thinking of my sons, this rehabilitation is an immense satisfaction after the injustices which I have suffered.
>
> Equally, I want you to be convinced that I was and I am fully satisfied with my position on the list of group commanders that Kindelán has sent me. I repeat this because the *Infanta* was very much saddened because they had credited me with only nine years of service while she has suffered the tension of watching me fly, without complaining, for fifteen years. She has suffered so much from the injustices that the military have committed against me on various occasions that she is very sensitive about it.
>
> As this month the credit for my mission here has run out, would you do me a great favour and, if for unforeseen difficulties my appointment to command Getafe should be delayed, give the necessary instructions so that they continue paying me here as usual through the Bank of Spain until my new appointment ends my commission. Because of circumstances which you know of on my side, and which do no honour to the Count of Romanones, and because of the Russian Revolution on the *Infanta*'s side, our financial situation is nothing like it was in 1916 and I cannot close up this house for an appointment in Spain, until my mission here ends.

If the idea of my appointment at Getafe excites my enemies in Madrid, they can calm themselves as the *Infanta* will live at Castillejo and I will live at the aerodrome at Getafe or at Cuatro Vientos, whichever you prefer.

After consulting a specialist, he has found that I am suffering so badly from malaria that I am obliged to spend some fifteen days at a clinic for treatment, after which he guarantees that I shall be completely cured forever. I have suffered from the ups and downs of fever for some time and life has been made impossible, as I never know when I am going to have an attack.

A month later, Ali wrote from the Nursing Home for Tropical Diseases at Putney, where he spent three weeks being treated for malaria. The doctors found he had the physique of a well-trained man of twenty-eight:

His Majesty the King was good enough to come and see me here and he said to me that he would soon approve my promotion to commander because of Alhucemas. They will have to hurry up as if many more months pass, I shall be promoted for length of service under the thirteen-year law.

The *Infanta* is having a bad time as she has to do all my work as tutor, and besides, she has a Russian niece, the second daughter of her sister the Grand Duchess Kirill, who is with us for 'the season' and thus has dinners and balls almost every night.

If God wishes, and you do not order otherwise, I am thinking of going by car on the 30th of this month to Sanlúcar, via Saint Malo, San Sebastian, and Burgos, arriving in Madrid on the 5th or 6th August. If possible I will leave the following day for Mérida where we will spend the night, arriving in Sanlúcar on the 7th, 8th or 9th, and leaving Sanlúcar on the 10th to be at Algeciras on the 11th when the *Infanta* arrives by sea with Alonso and Ataúlfo. Álvaro will go with me in the car.

It was a time of happy memories for Spain and the *infantes*, returning to court with the same honours they had before they left for their 'hidden exile', now greeted with warmth and friendliness wherever they went. The little princes behaved impeccably during their first family Christmas in Madrid. They seemed cosmopolitan in a way not seen since before the First World War. Cristina, impulsive and sincere, recalled that the Orleans family were their 'favourites, they adored us and we them'. Cristina, the younger of Ena's daughters, aged fifteen, immediately fell in love with Alonso, who was only five months younger. She treasured his memory for many years and did not marry till late in life. Her older sister, Beatriz, whom the family called 'Baby', was not quite so smitten.

The two *infantas* were very close and accompanied their mother into society after they came out. Beatriz came out in 1927 at the age of eighteen and was given a ball at which many of the 3,000 guests stole the silver coffee spoons as souvenirs. Queen María Cristina gave a dance for 100 guests in her rooms for Beatriz. It was so successful that in 1928 she repeated it for Cristina. At Cristina's big coming out ball, she referred to the spoons: 'at my party they put out tin-plated ones'.

The two princesses lived the same life as any young people of wealthy families of their age with walks, sports, horse riding, cinema, theatre, and dances. They accompanied Ena on hospital visits, often early in the morning, and became Red Cross nurses. Unaffected, friendly, often dressed alike, and very popular, they had two younger brothers to whom they were very close. The boys were good students and took their baccalaureates at public examinations at the San Isidro Institute. *Infante* Don Juan soon showed his independence and vocation as a sailor. His younger brother, Gonzalo, physically much smaller, was interested in law.

At charity functions, girls who sold raffle tickets always aimed to sell to Juan and Gonzalo. That year, 50-céntimos coins were put into circulation, the exact price of the tickets. I remember once watching, in the casino in San Sebastián, a girl of about six years old, timidly approaching Don Gonzalo. He said to her, 'You're too late! I'm broke'—and he pulled out his jacket pockets. 'I'm so sorry,' he continued, repeating, 'You don't know how sorry I am.' Then his teacher approached him and said, 'I could lend you two pesetas until next week.' 'Oh thank you!' replied the little prince, 'Please give me two tickets and that way I'll have enough for another commitment.' It was amusing to listen to his informal language contrasting with the word 'commitment'. The four *infantes* and the three princes of Orleans, all born between June 1909 and October 1914, were very close.

'The Prince of Asturias got on divinely with Mama who called him Alfonsito,' the *Infanta* Cristina said. 'We had lots of fun with Jaime. As he was deaf we learned to speak to him in signs and also by pronouncing the words with our lips but without speaking. And we also understood him from afar from his lip movements as he always spoke Spanish then; and he was more attached to Papa because Mama got tired having a long conversation with him. He was very likeable, poor thing, and always protecting Alfonso.'

In 1927, the Orleans family closed up the house at Esher and returned to Spain permanently. Ena had waited for this impatiently but had also become more independent, and sought new friendships. The king continued with his clique, presided over by the marquis of Viana. The latter had a reputation for being disagreeable, his obsequious manners towards the queen only increasing her aversion towards him. She knew he was her principal enemy at court, procuring women for her husband as well as his own amusement. Worse still was his way of poisoning minds against the queen, merely because she was a foreigner and apparently lacking glamour and sex appeal.

In 1916, during Ena's serious illness after a miscarriage and an operation for peritonitis, the king became involved with Carmen Ruiz Moragas, an actress. She was beautiful, and contemporaries said she looked extraordinarily like the queen. It had been love at first sight, she belonged to the upper middle class, her father was a civil governor and her grandfather had been a senator. According to *La Época*, 13 July 1925, Miss Ruiz Moragas received a generous contract of 30 duros a day and a profit share at the Fontalba Theatre. She seemed happy, but her friends thought she did not really love the king, despite bearing him two children, a daughter, María Teresa, and a son, Leandro.

Queen Ena was at the nadir of her emotional life in the mid-1920s, and the king's liaison with Carmen Moragas brought out the worst in one or two of Alfonso's intimates, particularly in his 'evil genius' Viana. Some thought they could get rid of the queen completely. A possible annulment of the king and queen's marriage was considered, and the necessary details were found to send to the Papal Nuncio. Those who learned of the plan were stunned, but Ena, who had calmly suffered so many humiliations, reacted quickly. Knowing the character of her husband as she did, she knew he could not have planned this alone. She perhaps felt that, from now on, she could not tolerate the marquis of Viana, whose treachery was largely responsible for what had become an untenable situation. That winter, the marquis twice invited the prince of Asturias and *Infante* Don Jaime to go hunting and Ena was worried, fearing the influence he could acquire over her sons.

When Princess Beatrice of Battenberg arrived in Malaga on 25 February 1927, Ena travelled from Madrid, accompanied by the little *infantas* to meet her mother. The prince of Asturias had also come to Malaga, accompanied by the marquis of Viana. The English fleet was in the city and the sailors visited the town. Viana upbraided Asturias when he stopped to chat to the sailors. Asturias complained to Ena that he found Viana too familiar and authoritarian.

On 10 March, Ena was warned that her husband had 'pulmonary flu', and the royal family immediately returned to Madrid. He suffered from high temperatures for several days, but on the 14th, he began to recover. While convalescing Alfonso practised gymnastics with his sons on the terrace and, during bad weather, in the throne room.

For several days, Ena mulled over the marquis of Viana's attitude regarding her eldest son. Angry that he had been humiliated in front of the English sailors, she decided to act. As she was sure the marquis was mainly responsible for the unpleasant treatment she had received for years, she summoned him to her private rooms, told him she was profoundly upset by his abominable conduct in having turned the king against her, and that she held him mainly to blame for her problems. When he tried to make excuses, she abruptly finished the interview, telling him it was not in her hands to punish him as he deserved: 'Only God can do so. Your punishment will have to wait another world'. He reportedly left in a state of shock, went home, and had a fatal heart attack. When she told this story to various people, who asked her if she felt at all responsible for his death, she merely shrugged her shoulders, but thought he had got his just deserts. For the rest of her days, she was convinced that they made Alfonso act against his true instincts and his true nature.

The truth was rather different. Viana was admittedly upset on arriving home, and on the night of 4 April, he had a stroke. The king was told the next day, went immediately to visit him, and found him sitting up in an armchair, able to converse albeit with difficulty. He received other visitors, including a nun who told him she had a premonition that he was going to die. Father Torres insisted he should make a confession, to which the invalid replied that he would do so the following day, but when the priest insisted, he did so at once. That night, he suffered a severe uremic attack, leaving him much weaker. Next morning, he was losing consciousness, when his family arrived, he did not know them, and that afternoon he passed away, aged fifty-seven. His death thoroughly upset the king.

Shortly afterwards, King Gustav V of Sweden paid an official visit, arriving by train in Madrid on 18 April and entering the city with King Alfonso in an open landau. He stayed at the palace, and after a family luncheon went to see the monastery of El Escorial. Next day, he visited the Prado Museum, and then left for Toledo and Andalusia. In Seville, he stayed at the palace of the dukes of Medinaceli. The following day, he visited the cathedral, the Hospital of Charity, and several antique shops, attended a *Fiesta Andaluza* and a grand party was held in his honour aboard the steamer *María Cristina,* moored on the Guadalquivir.

The next royals due to arrive were Ena's nephews from England, the prince of Wales and his brother, George, later duke of Kent. After a holiday in Biarritz, they came to visit the Feria of Seville, held annually in April. Established in 1846 as a major market for farmers and ranchers, it had become a popular public fiesta with singing, dancing and people on horseback throughout the week. In her memoirs, the *Infanta* Cristina noted that they had only a very distant relationship with the English royal family. Since 1922, when their uncle Leo died, Cristina and her sister, Beatriz, had spent a month in England with their mother. The only person they saw was their 'Guenguen' or grandmother, Princess Beatrice, who lived at Kensington Palace. So when the two British princes came to Seville, 'we had nothing to do with them. They went on their visits to amuse themselves in their own way.'

Bee also noticed that Ena had little affinity with the family when visiting England. It was only Queen Mary who invited her to tea although there was one lunch with King George V, who thoroughly disliked Alfonso. He always said that the days he spent in Madrid for the wedding were among the worst in his life. Over the years, he had become more embittered, and never returned the official visit his Spanish cousins had made to him. During her years of exile, Bee always found George V ready to support her, while Ali always treated him as a friend. When he learned of the British princes' imminent visit to Seville, he helped in the arrangements for their journey prior to their arrival at Madrid on 22 April where a large group from the British colony cheered them at the station with the king and queen waiting on the platform. Several days of receptions, banquets, visits to the races, and famous landmarks followed very successfully, although the king's English was poor, and he soon tired of talking to his wife's nephews.

In 1927, Alfonso celebrated his silver jubilee, twenty-five years since his coming of age and assuming the role of king. Fiestas, bullfights, illuminations, and various festivities were staged. The *infantes* came from Sanlúcar to take part in the ceremonies. On 17 May, a reception took place in the throne room, with Ali in the uniform of a flight commander, while his wife wore a dress of gold lamé, a Russian diamond diadem, and the sashes of various decorations.

In June, the king visited London, pleasantly surprised to find George V and his sons waiting on the platform to receive him, grateful for the good memories they had of their time in Spain. Although his visit was private, he was invited to lunch at Buckingham Palace. He returned by sea from Southampton to Santander on the *Reina María Cristina*.

When King Ferdinand of Romania died on 20 July 1927, Bee left for Bucharest and stayed with Missy for several weeks because Ali was in Santander, playing polo. That October, the king and queen went to Barcelona. In November, the queen was in Paris and London.

Many Russians who had escaped from the revolution were now living in Paris. By 1927, their situation was perilous, with many out of work or in poorly-paid jobs. Some but by no means all of them supported Grand Duke Kirill's claim to the Russian throne. The dowager empress, now living in Denmark, was publicly unwilling to accept that Misha and Nicholas were dead. Most of the imperial family refused to recognise Kyrill, as in accepting the provisional government he had broken his oath of loyalty to Nicholas. Nevertheless, Ducky asked her sisters to make works of art to sell to raise funds for the struggling refugees.

In March 1928, an exhibition opened in Rue Ranelagh, at the home of Madam Leon Nozal showcasing the items Ducky had collected to sell. All three sisters' work was highly praised. Missy displayed Romanian landscapes in oils, while Ducky showed her medallions, flower paintings, and seascapes. The *Infanta* Eugenia and the duchess of Rochefoucauld attended the opening, as did many ladies who eagerly purchased items. The society journalist 'Monte Cristo' wrote in *Blanco y Negro* that the most important exhibits were *Infanta* Beatrice's paintings, calling the watercolours 'a marvel of delicacy—orchids, roses, and other flowers appear deliciously grouped and are perfectly drawn and coloured'. Her religious pictures were also praised, as were 'the inspired enamels in the Russian style of lacquer on wood, the Flight into Egypt, The Three Wise Men, the Vision of Saint Peter, Saint Isabelle and two Madonnas, [which] reveal the distinguished princess's marked artistic temperament'. In conclusion, she mentioned that the *infanta*'s works had been so admired that copies were been requested: 'What a pity that they could not be exhibited in Madrid!'

Another exhibition was planned for 1930 but never took place. Bee liked painting flowers, carving wood sculptures, and embroidering tapestries in silver and gold, but was reluctant to work in enamels. In St-Briac, Ducky met Paul Grandhome, an expert in enamels, who completed Bee's works of flowers and saints.

The very influential duke of Alba was dining with friends and discussing Ali's latest project, as he had ceded some land to the nation for a university complex to be built in parkland near Madrid. Despite a ten-month national appeal, it proved hard to raise funds for the project, so Ali and Bee were invited to a dinner at which it was suggested by the marquis of Villavieja that Ali should go to the US and raise funds. They were both very enthusiastic about the idea.

Villavieja was the guiding light and organiser of the journey. For some years, he had wanted Ali to visit the US because he thought that he was the kind of royal person who would immediately impress the Americans as a representative of Spain. His friends told him he was crazy, due to costs and also because the king would never agree. He soon realised that his majesty was not against the idea. Villavieja had to battle with the scheming courtiers who would not believe he could arrange it without their help. As Ali and Bee had to dress in style (Queen Marie having told her sister that the Americans noticed such things), they spent a week in

Paris where Bee could order dresses from Callot Sœurs. Ever practical, she decided not to take her maid, Alice, but would look after her clothes and luggage herself. As it was winter, she obtained two new fur coats to travel with. From Paris, they left for England on 30 October. One week later, they left Waterloo Station for Southampton, where the liner *Majestic* was moored, and sailed for New York next day.

Much to Bee's delight, they had been assigned the luxurious royal suite, which apart from the cabins and sitting room also had a greenhouse, its large windows covered with flowers. Passing Governor's Island just outside New York, they received a twenty-one-gun salute. Although the visit was unofficial, a crowd awaited them on the quayside, led by an intimate friend of the marquis, their host, Percy R. Pyne. Next to him were Gen. Cornelius Vanderbilt and his wife, in whose home on Fifth Avenue the *infantes* and their entourage were to stay. Mrs Vanderbilt arrived at the pier breathless; the gun salute gave her a terrible fright as she had forgotten that the department of state had decided at the last minute to give the visit 'official' status.

A press conference was called. When the journalists heard Ali speak, they were surprised by his perfect English accent, and impressed when he told them how much he admired American aviation and especially Charles Lindbergh, who had crossed the Atlantic alone in *Spirit of St. Louis*. He spoke of aviation with great authority, and the reporters were captivated with this prince who had been a pilot for twenty years and undertaken military service.

That night, the newspapers reported the arrival of these illustrious personages, keen to obtain in-depth knowledge of American life in all its aspects. Percy R. Pyne showed them schools, hospitals, Colombia University and Wall Street, where the President of the National City Bank, Mr Mitchell, showed them how they bought and sold stocks and shares. On the day they arrived in New York, Mrs Vanderbilt took them to the theatre. At all meals, they were seated at a table for eighteen, so the *infantes* could ask questions. Everywhere they went they were offered sherry, until Ali told them they only drank water. At the Vanderbilt palace, a dinner for seventy was held followed by an enormous reception for 300. Mr Pyne, the generous host, had a home on Long Island, where the cosy atmosphere of the rooms reminded them of an English country house.

They left for Philadelphia, on 21 November, as guests of Mr and Mrs Joseph E. Widener at Lynnewood Hall, Elkins Park. Ali and Bee were most impressed with their gardens and art collection, comprising paintings by Rembrandt, Raphael, Van Dyck, El Greco, Turner, and Renoir. During the dinner, the Wideners gave in their honour, Villavieja received a telegram from the Spanish ambassador, Sr Padilla, advising him that President

Coolidge would receive their royal highnesses next day at 12 p.m. It was agreed that at 12.30 a.m., Ali, Bee, and their party would leave the dance, without changing their clothes, and go to Philadelphia station for the 1 a.m. train to Washington, arriving in the capital at 9 a.m. where Padilla, the Spanish ambassador, and embassy staff awaited them for their reception at the White House.

From Washington, they went to Wilmington, staying with the Dupont family, who took them to a football game between Princeton University and the navy, won by the latter in a fiercely-disputed contest leaving three players injured. After a short visit to Boston, they returned to the Vanderbilts' home in New York for the major event of their visit, a gala function at the Metropolitan Opera House, including a benefit performance of Verdi's *La Traviata* for the City University of Madrid. It was packed to capacity despite prices being higher than usual because the Spanish soprano Lucrecia Bori was going to sing. Although she lived outside Spain, she was keen to support the university project. After a performance at the Miramar Palace for Queen Maria Cristina, Alfonso spoke to her for a long time and he asked her how much a night at the Metropolitan Opera would raise. Without batting an eyelid, she replied: 'taking into account the presence of the *infantes*, the income would be thirty to forty thousand dollars'. Alfonso XIII excitedly exclaimed to Villavieja, 'When are you going, Manolo?' 'Sir,' he replied, 'the passages are booked for the 6th November.'

After the concert, Mrs Graham Fair Vanderbilt invited the majority of those attending to supper at her home. Ali, Villavieja and others made a night of it, but Bee and Mrs Vanderbilt retired to rest at a sensible time. As she left, Bori explained that she was not tired, but that 'she wishes to prolong her enjoyment alone'. The king later awarded her the medal of Alfonso XII.

After the official fundraising part of the trip, Percy R. Pyne took Ali and Bee to Montreal to see Niagara Falls, Buffalo, and Detroit. Then they stayed in Washington with Ambassador Padilla and his family. As many of their journeys were made at night, a special railway carriage with comfortable beds was hired to take them to the various cities. In Montreal, where they spent two days, they were guests of the general manager of the Bank of Montreal and Lady Williams-Taylor. They visited Macdonald College, saw an ice hockey match, and attended a reception. As 2 December was a Sunday, they attended sung Mass in the Roman Catholic Cathedral of St James. After lunch they went to visit the Royal Victoria Hospital, which Bee considered extraordinarily modern and among the best she had seen. Later they toured the main streets of the city, leaving for Detroit at 10 p.m. in heavy snow. When they arrived, the weather had changed to hail and thick fog. At 3 p.m., Henry Ford's son was waiting for them at the station with their hosts Mr and Mrs Roy Chapin, with whom they were to stay. The *infantes* were most interested in getting to know Mr Ford and his famous factories, and he gave them an 'interesting tour of the Rouge workshops'.

During the Ford visit, Bee told a journalist that they hoped they could 'do as much in Spain! You here are our inspiration. I feel, like my sister, Queen Marie of Romania, that I have always lived here in this country. You make us feel that you like us, and it moves our hearts how much you like and respect our country.' The reporter called her:

... a tall, thin woman who really does not look as if she could have an eighteen-year-old son. She has lightly waved dark hair, large blue eyes and a fair skin with an upturned nose and a captivating smile. The Princess appears friendlier when she smiles. She was dressed simply, in a beige suit and matching hat, and wore a diamond brooch, under a fur coat.

When it was suggested that she did lacked her sister Queen Marie's interest in clothes, she retorted, 'Clothes? There are so many more interesting things!' With that she returned to occupy herself with the machinery and the cast-iron:

It was evident that it was her smile, the captivating dimple in her cheeks, and her knowledge of engineering and her interest in big factories that won the attention and respect of Mr Ford. From four o'clock until after six, she and the Prince pondered over and admired what they saw on the long tour through the enormous workshops in the various buildings. It is surprising that a Spanish Princess should be able to distinguish a spark plug from a piston! Her Highness did. And Prince Álvaro of Orleans showed that he was a son worthy of his mother. He looked around the furnaces, he looked behind, above and around the motors and was as pleased as she was when at the end of the assembly line a Ford car appeared as if by magic.

In these workshops they built 9,400 cars a day, but with orders for 400,000 from countries all over the world, Mr Ford was keen to increase production. When he himself drove the car in which the *infantes* and their son toured around the factory, the vehicle suddenly lost speed, and there was a loud grinding of metal on changing gear. A deep groan was heard from Prince Álvaro: 'How badly this man drives!'

When they arrived at their hosts home at 447 Lake Shore Drive, it was late and they had to change quickly for dinner with 100 guests, followed

by a reception for 800. They rested quietly next morning. In the afternoon
they visited the city, yacht club, and zoo, returning to board their railway
carriage and arrived in Niagara at 8 p.m. to view the falls illuminated
by large spotlights. At 9 a.m., they were all ready to see the falls again.
On travelling from Niagara Falls to Buffalo, they stopped to visit Welland
Airfield. Villavieja explained:

> It was the first time that I had reason to be nervous and also angry. The
> *Infante* insisted on testing new aircraft, the weather was stormy with a
> gusting wind and low clouds; before we could stop him, the *Infante* was
> in the air at hundreds of metres altitude. As our time was limited and
> he had numerous new machines to try out, the *Infanta* soon decided to
> do it as well and she asked her son Álvaro to prepare another aircraft. 'I
> have to help my husband,' said the bold princess, 'but I never wear my
> pearls when I fly, so please look after them Pomposa'—and she gave my
> daughter her string of pearls. For more than a hour, the *Infantes* and
> Prince Álvaro were flying very high overhead, while I was on the verge of
> a heart attack. It was the first time that I was nervous and I admit that I
> was frightened. I was thinking of the terrible consequences which could
> result from this crazy 'escapade'. In the end they landed safe and sound,
> while I felt exhausted.

Back in New York, they could not accept every invitation offered. Ali
wanted to visit the military academy at West Point, and was very well
received by the staff and the cadets. They wanted to hear about his
experiences in Morocco, and especially the details of air operations at
Alhucemas. Their final dinner, at the home of the Percy R. Pyne's mother,
was attended by all involved in the visit, as well as Mrs Vanderbilt and Sr
Algara, the cousin of Villavieja. At the meal, Ali spoke of the advances in
aviation in the US. He related how the previous day, while everyone else
was out shopping, he had accepted an invitation from the pilot, Edward
M. Haight, of the Air Mail Service to fly with him from Hadley Field in
New Jersey to Philadelphia at 3 p.m. and return to Newark Airfield after
three hours of flying. After dinner, they left for the *Majestic* and went
aboard, where the *infanta* showed them around her cabin. Mrs Vanderbilt
eulogised over her French fur coat, much admired in New York. The
infanta gave it to her in gratitude for the wonderful hospitality they had
received at her home.

After a good six-day Atlantic crossing, they disembarked at Cherbourg
on 13 December 1928. Villavieja admitted that nobody, not even him,
ever thought they would return with $50,000 for the University City of
Madrid, and he feared this success might upset those who had intrigued

against the visit. He therefore begged Bee to be the one to give Lucrecia Bori's cheque to the king, as it was due to the *infantes* that the money had been raised.

They returned for Christmas with many presents purchased in New York that they could never have found in Spain. When people asked Bee what the visit was like, she replied with a smile: 'My husband flew from one airport to another and I from one marvellous entertainment to another'. Ali recalled all the interesting people he had met, especially Henry Ford, who years later became his employer and friend. Of his meeting at the Carlton Hotel with Colonel Lindbergh on 30 November, he said: 'The conversation between the two aviators, which was scheduled to last half an hour, went on twice as long'. The young pilot, enjoyed meeting Ali as he had been flying for more than eighteen years and who continued doing so through good times and bad. While in America, Ali flew in various aircraft, travelling several hundred miles from New York: 'As for Lindbergh, he was amazed at the unaffectedness and the profound knowledge of aviation of the Spanish prince'.

In Madrid, on 23 December, the *infantes* attended a dinner offered in their honour by the court. Bee sat between the prince of Asturias and *Infante* Don Fernando, and she was surprised to see how thin the heir to the throne was, as she had not seen him for several weeks.

On 3 February 1929, at another family dinner, Alfonso and Ena talked about King Christian X and Queen Alexandrine of Denmark who were to make an official visit to Madrid the following Wednesday. Not knowing them at all, they asked Bee for information, and she replied that she was Alexandrine's second cousin, both being great-granddaughters of Nicholas I. She had to think back to her childhood, when they lived at Château Fabron in Nice and the two princesses and her brother came to visit them. Frederick Francis wished to marry her, but she detested his mother, Grand Duchess Anastasia Mikhailovna, who interfered in everything.

It seemed tactful to appoint the Marchioness de la Romana as lady-in-waiting to Alexandrine. She was descended from a gentleman who left Denmark to help in Spain's independence struggles. On 5 February, a Red Cross benefit was held at the Zarzuela Theatre. There they met the entire royal family, from Queen María Cristina to fifteen-year-old Don Gonzalo. Maria Cristina asked Bee to take care of the Danes so that they would have good memories of Spain. Despite her seventy years, Doña María Cristina paid attention to every small detail.

That night, after the dinner, *Infantas* Cristina and Beatriz stayed up until 1 a.m. watching a film. They then walked their grandmother, Maria Cristina, to her room. She showed them how to make their formal greetings to the Danes, and reminded them that they must be ready next morning at exactly 10:30 a.m. for King Christian and Queen Alexandrine of Denmark's arrival. They would be on the upper part of the staircase, she would go forward and then then they had to bow to the floor. The *infantas* kissed their granny, went up to their room, and were about to undress when the telephone rang ordering them to come at once, as the queen mother had just died. Cristina said:

> We were frozen. The poor thing grabbed the telephone for help and had no time to say anything! She died instantly from a heart attack. It was . an enormous shock for us and poor Papa was destroyed. He adored his mother as he owed her everything. The mourning imposed would be unimaginable nowadays.

Years later, I got to know Dr Petinto, who was on duty that night at the palace. He explained that Martina, the lady's maid to the old queen, told him that on undressing, she had said to her: 'How tired I am!' She laid on her bed and a little later, on seeing the expression of pain on her face, the maid called the king, who came at once: 'A little later, I came running; but the Queen had died. I then learned from Martina that she had had pain in her arms for some days, but was looking forward to her first granddaughter's wedding and without doubt did not want to alarm'.

This granddaughter, *Infanta* Isabel Alfonsa de Borbón y Borbón, was a daughter of Mercedes, princess of Asturias, and Don Carlos of Borbón Dos Sicilias. As the princess of Asturias died the day after her daughter's birth, María Cristina had taken great care of her upbringing. Isabel was due to marry her cousin, Count Jan Kanty Zamoyski. Once the romance was official, Maria Cristina had started collecting gifts to give her granddaughter on her wedding but she had intended to add some beautiful jewels at the last minute. Not wanting the wedding to be postponed, Alfonso XIII fixed it for 9 March.

Ena herself broke news of the death of Maria Cristina to Ali and Bee, as they now had to go to El Escorial to meet the royal train from Irún carrying the Danes. Before leaving, they decided to go via the palace, where they found the king closeted in his office and Ali spoke briefly with his cousin.

On arriving at El Escorial station, the duke of Fernan Nuñez told them he had already given the Danish king and queen the sad news at Arévalo. The *infantes* went to greet the sovereigns, Bee wearing a black dress, coat, and a hat with a mourning ribbon and black veil, Ali in his aviator's uniform. When they arrived, King Christian in uniform immediately descended from the train. Queen Alexandrina, in a black overcoat with a fur collar, left the train with Bee at her side and the marchioness de la

Romana. The prime minister welcomed the Danish monarch and presented some ministers waiting at the station, the king replied in French and then reviewed the regiment, followed by Ali who was some metres behind in accordance with protocol. They went directly to the palace by car, where Queen Cristina lay in the Chapel Royal on a catafalque adorned with bunches of violets, her favourite flower.

The rest of the Spanish family and the government had been attending a mass celebrated by Cardinal Segura. The Danish king and queen prayed for a few brief moments at the start of the next Mass that was beginning. Ena greeted the Danish king and queen and invited them to join them for a private lunch. She advised them to visit the Prado Museum and the Gallery of Modern Art, with which Bee was very familiar. After lunch, presided over by Alfonso XIII, they toured the palace, walking through its gardens and visiting the royal armoury.

The Dowager Empress Marie of Russia had died in Denmark on 13 October 1928. Bee's sisters were keen to know what had happened to her jewels, which she kept under her bed, as she was so worried about their safety. They had not been seen recently. Bee was reluctant to ask, but the plain-speaking Queen Alexandrine brought it up. The box of jewels was sealed by Grand Duchess Xenia, the empress's daughter, and taken to Buckingham Palace, where Queen Mary apparently chose and paid for those she liked most. The rest were sold, with proceeds divided between Xenia, Olga, and little George, the son of Grand Duke Michael, who died in a car accident in 1931. Bee passed this information to Ducky and also told her that the imperial crown, the sceptre, and the other coronation objects, had all been left in Moscow—shadows of glorious days that would never return.

The death of Queen María Cristina was so unexpected that nobody could realise she had gone. As king, her own son could no longer ask her what to do, although he did not always follow her wise advice. In the twenty years of his reign before the dictatorship of Primo de Rivera in 1923, Alfonso XIII had thirty governments, which gave the monarchy little stability. Now he felt like an orphan, became very depressed, and acted more like a child. He would go out in his car when he had time to El Escorial to pray before his mother's remains in the *pudridero*, the 'rotting place' or first burial point for any royal corpses arriving at the Escorial after the person's death, located in a special area of the royal vault. All corpses remained there fifty years for 'rotting' before being buried in their final coffins in the main royal vault.

The death of her mother-in-law also affected Ena deeply. After the First World War, Ena felt liberated. On arriving in Spain, Maria Cristina had not helped or guided Ena, who referred to her as 'her cross' in the first years of marriage when, young and in love, she had been easy prey to mould. Queen Cristina had willingly accepted Alfonso's marriage to Ena at the beginning and liked her when she arrived in Spain. Over the years, the differences in characters between them did not make it easy for them to live together under the same roof, especially after the war broke out in 1914 and their allegiances sharply differed. Things became easier between them after the First World War and they became closer. The old regent hung on in the palace as a distant and exemplary sovereign. Maria Cristina had also listened to the rumours about Bee and Ena, believing them and becoming convinced that Bee sought to become usurp Alfonso's place in Ena's affections. She wanted Ali and Bee sent into exile, and only Ena remained loyal to them.

Ena had long dreamed of making changes in the palace when the moment arrived, but did not know where to begin. Her daughter, Cristina, described one innovation. Ena liked a cigarette before dessert, so she ordered the Ansorena Company to make individual ashtrays for her meals. In this way, the meal times were longer and the gentlemen could continue to smoke with the ladies in agreeable sessions around the dinner table. Previously guests' meals had been rushed as the king, no matter who he was talking to, ate quickly to go to the small smoking room that led from the dining room. Ena also arranged that on Sundays, all members of the royal family who were in Madrid would eat together without their entourages.

Cristina remembered those days of mourning for her grandmother:

We did not go anywhere, and we dressed in black from head to foot. We did not even go to the concerts as we used to do with Mama and which we enjoyed so much. I remember that it was six in the afternoon, time for the German class, which was skipped.

Mourning was so serious that I remember something that was like a scene from Turkey. The only distraction was to take a walk in the Campo de Moro, and I, who have always had a lot of energy, had to get a breath of fresh air somehow. I ran and jumped over all the low bushes I could find. Obviously, I was not wearing black clothing underneath and Papa was very angry. He said to Mama, 'Ena, how do these girls carry out their mourning? Why do they not wear black underwear?' And Mama answered him saying, 'Alfonso, for God's sake—let's not exaggerate! Or do you think that we even have to wear black nightshirts and corsets?' Mama, always with her English common sense!

At the beginning of March, cousin Bela married Count Zamoyski. Papa did not want to postpone the wedding, and so as not to spoil it, lifted mourning for the day and we all went dressed up."

Isabel and Jan's marriage was celebrated on 9 March. The bride wanted Cardinal Ilundáin to marry her because he was a friend, but the king wanted Cardinal Segura, as primate of Spain, to officiate. On the eve of the wedding, the duchess of Guise came from Larache, the numerous family of the groom, who lived in Cannes, arrived from Madrid. The *Infanta* Isabel Alfonsa stayed at the palace in the duke of Genoa's rooms. The presents were displayed in one of the palace rooms, and they were magnificent, above all the jewels the bride received from her mother, the princess of Asturias and from her grandmother, Queen María Cristina. The king gave the groom a Hispano-Suiza motorcar so he could go on his honeymoon in comfort.

The ceremony took place at 11 a.m. in the palace chapel, adorned with white lilies, irises, calla lilies, and carnations. The king, in admiral's uniform, gave the bride away. Because of mourning, she wore no jewels. Her dress was of white silk with a lace cape, while the groom wore the uniform of the Real Maestranza of Seville. He was escorted by the queen, in court dress adorned by a white mantilla. The *Infante* Don Carlos, father of the bride, followed, giving his arm to his aunt the Countess Zamoyski, mother of the groom. The prince of Asturias was paired with the *Infanta* Doña Luisa; the *Infante* Don Jaime with the princess of Saxony; Don Pedro of Orleans-Braganza with the *Infanta* Isabel; Ali, brother of the bride, with the little Princess Beatriz; Luis Alfonso of Bavaria with the little Princess María Cristina; and Don José Eugenio with his sister, Mercedes of Bavaria. The *Infante* Don Fernando came with his wife, the duchess of Talavera, Ali with his mother, the *Infanta* Eulalia; Prince Rainier of Borbón Two Sicilies with Bee. They were followed by other couples and ended with the three princes of Orleans. After taking the family photographs, which would become the last memento of the monarchy, the newly-wed couple left for Villamanrique, where their honeymoon was to begin. Then from the next day, *Infanta* María Cristina noted, 'and for almost six months, we all looked like ink bottles! Thankfully in the garden, we had tennis and we played among the family, because we were not even allowed to mount a horse.'

Bee knew this was the right time for her sister, Queen Marie, and her daughter, Princess Ileana, to come to Spain. She thought the prince of Asturias, whom she especially liked, could fall in love with her niece who was well-educated, and an excellent nurse.

Princess María Cristina of Salm-Salm and her younger daughter, Cecilia, arrived in Madrid on 19 March. She came to give her condolences to the king, and to collect some mementos that had belonged to her godmother and aunt, Queen María Cristina, although the latter had died intestate. The princess loved visiting Madrid, where she spent some time during the war. She had lost her husband, Prince Emanuel of Salm-Salm, at the Battle of Pinsk on 19 August 1916, leaving her with three daughters and a son, Nicholas. At the age of ten, on the death of his grandfather in 1923, Nicholas inherited the title and castles of Salm-Salm. The two elder daughters were married and the attractive, blonde, blue-eyed eighteen-year-old Cecilia, was inclined to be rather timid in society. She and the prince of the Asturias, who was four years older than her, seemed to like each other, and often saw each other during the week. It was hoped that they might marry.

Meanwhile, Missy and her daughter, Ileana, were at St Briac, spending a few days with Ducky. From there they went to Paris where they took the *Sud Express*, reaching Madrid on the morning of 27 March, accompanied by Prince Alvaro of Orleans, who came to spend his holidays with them. They went to the palace by car, Queen Marie in the first vehicle, accompanied by the king. On arriving at the palace, Ena told them that as they were in mourning this Holy Week, the royals did not have to attend public chapel nor wash the feet of the poor.

As soon as they arrived, the queen of Romania wanted to visit the Prado Museum with her sister. They spent over two hours going around the galleries. After a private lunch with the king and queen, Bee took her sister shopping in the city. At dinner, the king sat between Queen Marie and the princess of Salm-Salm with Prince Álvaro of Orleans on her right. The queen was on the right of the prince of Asturias, sitting next to Ileana, resplendent, tall with dark hair and blue eyes, looking older than her twenty years. Very likeable, she spoke perfect English because she had studied in England. Then came the Romanian minister, Prince Bibesco, who had a lively conversation with Bee. They spent Holy Thursday and Good Friday at the Casa del Campo and watched the processions passing in front of the palace. On Saturday, they took tea at the Pardo Palace, home of the prince of Asturias. As well as Queen Marie and her daughter, Ileana, the king and queen attended with their children, the *infantes*, and Princess Salm-Salm and Cecilia who were thinking of staying a few weeks more.

The queen, her daughters and her guests left early to drive to Ávila. As it was a fine day, a meal was served in the open air, and they arrived late in Madrid. Easter Sunday Mass was celebrated in the palace chapel, followed by a brilliant parade by the halberdiers who guarded the Royal Alcázar. The next day they then went to the *infantes'* estate at Castillejo, in the Province of Cuenca, where they lunched and spent the day contemplating 'the replanting of trees which so notably changed the ghostly look of the place'.

Toledo was left until the last day. They started out at 10:30 a.m., went straight to the cathedral, and visited its treasury and the Virgen del Sagrario.

Above left: Baby Bee, youngest daughter of the duke and duchess of Edinburgh, *c.* 1890.

Above right: Queen Victoria and Ena, daughter of Beatrice, princess Henry of Battenberg, 1897.

Below: The duke and duchess of Edinburgh with their children, and in back row, Prince Ernest Louis of Hesse and the Rhine, Prince Max of Baden, and Prince George of Wales, later King George V, *c.* 1891.

Above left: The duke of Edinburgh, now duke of Saxe-Coburg Gotha, and his daughters Sandra, Bee, Missy, and Ducky, 1894.

Above right: Ena, Alexander, and Leopold of Battenberg, *c.* 1895.

Below: Michael, Bee, Grand Duchess Olga, and her first husband, Duke Peter of Oldenburg, *c.* 1902.

Above: Bee and her sisters, painted by Kaulbach.

Below left: Friedrich von Kaulbach and his unfinished portrait of Bee and her sisters.

Below right: Ena, at the time of her betrothal, 1905.

'Uncle Bertie presents his nieces to the King of Spain', 1905. (*drawn by Bee*)

'Ena dances state quadrille at court ball with "Spanish Ambassador" "Caliban"', 1905. (*drawn by Bee*)

Bee, 1908.

Above left: King Alfonso XIII and Ali.

Above right: King Alfonso XIII and Queen Ena, *c.* 1906.

'Bee and Ena meet under very different circumstances but the friendship is unabated', 1906. (*drawn by Bee*)

'Here endeth second book of adventures of Bee and Ena', 1907. (*drawn by Bee*)

Above left: Ali in cadet uniform.

Above right: Bee and Ali, *ABC Magazine*, at the time of their betrothal.

Below: 'Ena and Alfonso think it is time for Bee to marry', 1907. (*drawn by Bee*)

Above left: Bee and her eldest son, Alvaro, *c.* 1910.

Above right: Prince Leopold of Battenberg, 1911.

Above left: Ali in airman's uniform.

Above right: Bee and her sons, 1914.

The family at the baptism of Alvaro at Coburg, 1910.

The court at Santander, including Ena, Bee, King Alfonso XIII, and *Infante* Ali, 1915.

Above left: Ena and Bee, 1915.

Above right: Ena and her children, 1918.

Bee and King Alfonso XIII.

Bee and Ali at the Vatican on a visit to Pope Pius XI, 1925.

Above left: Bee and Queen Marie of Romania at the time of the latter's coronation, 1922.

Above right: Queen Ena, 1922.

Bee, Ali, and their sons on horseback at Esher, *c.* 1922.

King Alfonso XIII, *Infante* Alonso, and their sons and nephews, all of whose names began with the latter 'A', 1927.

Bee, Ali, Henry Ford (centre), the marquis of Villavieja (left), and Don Alvaro in Detroit, 1928.

Queen Ena and her daughters.

Above left: Bee in nursing uniform, 1939.

Above right: Bee and Padre Federico Gonzalez Cornejo, 1955.

Above left: Queen Ena and Juan Carlos, prince of Asturias.

Above right: Bee and Ali at a gala function.

Above: Queen Ena
with Ataúlfo at
Lausanne, *c.* 1953.

Right: Ali and Bee's golden
wedding at Langenburg
in 1959. Family group
includes Queen Marie
(Mignon) of Yugoslavia
(front, left), 1959.

Bee, Ali, and Marina, duchess of Kent, El Botanico, Sanlùcar, 1963.

Ali, 1974.

At Santo Tomé, they were captivated by the beauty of the painting of El Greco's *Burial of the Count of Orgaz*. At 1:30 p.m., the prince of Asturias took them to lunch, then they went to visit the Palace of Aranjuez and the Casita del Príncipe, or the Little House of the Prince, a small pavilion in the park of the palace of Aranjuez, a lovely neoclassical little building used by the royal family in past times. A portrait displayed here of Fernando VII, who was decrepit and exceptionally ugly in his last years, caused much hilarity among the youngsters. That evening they attended the opening of the new Romanian Legation, in a small palace in Serrano Street. Prince and Princess Bibesco, daughter of the former British Prime Minister Herbert Asquith, were the diplomats in Spain at this time. Queen Marie presided, with Gen. Primo de Rivera on her right and British Ambassador Sir George Grahame on her left. At the other table were Princess Ileana and Prince Bibesco.

On 2 April, they left for Extremadura. The king and queen bid them farewell in their private rooms, and the prince of Asturias came from El Pardo to say goodbye and accompanied them until the Puerta Incógnita, a hidden side door used by members of the Spanish royal family to leave the royal palace of Madrid incognito. From there they went to Guadalupe to see the monastery, and the ruins at Italica. In mid-afternoon, they arrived for lunch at the estate of the marquis of the Romana.

Next day, they visited the cathedral in Seville, and climbed the Giralda; then went to see the air base at Tablada. Ileana asked if it was possible to see Seville from the air. The officers were delighted and her wish was immediately fulfilled. Next was the Art Gallery and the Hospital of Charity, with many works by Murillo, one of Missy's favourite artists. She was given private invitations to the Casa de Pilatos, the Palace de las Dueñas, and the Alcázar, with its gardens and patio of orange trees. In the morning, they visited the Ibero-American Exhibition held in Seville between May 1929 and June 1930 where the queen bought several items, and in the afternoon they walked around the Barrio of Santa Cruz. Another day they went to the picturesque town of Arcos de la Frontera, where the valley was dominated by the palace of the duke of Osuna, rebuilt by the Englishman Mr Hutton Riddell and his wife who invited them to tea.

The queen commented to Ducky:

What an ideal town Tetuán is! Among all these charms one figure stood out that dazzled us. You already know that I am an incorrigible romantic, but in truth, in an atmosphere like this, where we seem transported to a story in the Thousand and One Nights, we were presented to a person who seems to come out of an old romance.

He is the Commander in Chief of the Regulares, Lieutenant Colonel José Enrique Varela, a proud and charming man with his Moroccan uniform, an exceedingly brave and brilliant officer and has been awarded two Laurel Crosses, which makes him the most highly decorated soldier in Spain.

Ileana and our good Irene (a widow and not so young) were in love with him at first sight. Among other attentions he gave us a great Moroccan tea in a perfectly adorned room where we sat on multi-coloured cushions, which were, thanks to God, comfortable and high. Varela began by offering us a silver washbasin and he himself poured the rose water over our hands. The tea was really good, with a great quantity of sweet things, and while we took it there were a number of dances and Moroccan entertainments that were both amusing and interesting. What memories I will always keep of those days!

Many years later, during the Civil War and a few days after Missy died, Ali received a letter from her, which said: 'I hope that you have good news of General Varela, and may luck accompany him in this war'.

Before returning to Sanlúcar, they passed through Jerez, visiting the *bodegas* and lunching at Malabrigo, the winery of the count and countess of Villamiranda, friends of the *infantes*. They went to Cádiz for a few days, visiting the Museum of Painting, the cathedral and its treasures. Later they went to the town hall, where the mayor received them. They sailed up the Guadalquivir River aboard the *Torpedo 18* and on return went to Sanlúcar de Barrameda, staying again in the Montpensier Palace, where Bee had arranged everything for her sister. Missy so enjoyed Andalusian life that she delayed her departure.

They flew in a Junkers plane to Granada to see the Alhambra, and then flew back to Seville for the third day of the Feria, staying at the home of the marchioness of Yanduri. From Sanlúcar, the party went to Cordoba in various cars, and they liked Spain more with every day that passed. News came from Ena that Princess Salm-Salm and Cecilia had left on 17 April aboard the *Sud Express*, and she and the prince of Asturias went to the station to say goodbye.

There had been some decorations for the family during this visit. Don Jaime sponsored Prince Álvaro for the Order of Calatrava, and Bee received the insignia of a lady of the Real Maestranza of Seville.

Before leaving Sanlucar, the town which Bee 'had taken deeply to her heart', Missy wanted to do something for the residents. They visited the school canteens where food was given daily to 500 poor children, the young ladies of the locality distributing it personally. Missy ensured cakes from the best shops in town were given out too. They also visited the dining rooms for nursing mothers founded by Bee; and the hospital, where they handed out cakes and sweets. In the afternoon, they went around the fishermen's area, visited the fish auction and the agricultural community of La Algaba, where they received an enthusiastic welcome.

Leaving Andalusia, they spent two days in Madrid. On 30 April, they arrived in Barcelona, and stayed at the Hotel Ritz. At 11 a.m. on 1 May, the count and countess of Ruiseñada and the count of Montseny came to take Missy and Bee on an excursion to Montserrat, where they were captivated by the light and beauty of the landscape. They visited the church, the museum, and library, and went to to Barcelona for dinner. Next morning, they visited the Municipal Museum, saw the Spanish village, and went shopping for antiques.

For Princess Ileana, the visit to Barcelona was very important as there she met her future husband, Archduke Anton of Austria, prince of Tuscany. A tall, good-looking man of twenty-two years and an aviator, he was the son of Archduke Leopold Salvator and the *Infanta* Blanca of Spain from the Carlist branch of the family. They lunched together at Torre Luisa, the house of the count of Güell, and then took the express train to France.

According to Missy, of all her children, Ileana was the best suited to be a queen. Anton had gaps in his artistic and literary education, but she acknowledged he was an expert engineer, electrician, and pilot: 'big, solid, confident, he has no money other than that which he has earned with his own hands'. Ileana said: 'We like to fly and we have many things in common'. They were married on 26 July 1931 at the Sinaia Palace.

Writing to her cousins, Queen Ena apologised for not spending as much time as she would have liked with them while they were in Spain, because she had had to fit in other events. Princess Salm-Salm and her daughter had extended their visit until the end of the month. The king was inclined more towards the marriage of the prince of Asturias to Princess Cecilia, daughter of his first cousin.

In the spring of 1929, the queen took Ileana to visit Bee and Ali in Spain again. This time the prince of Asturias fell in love with Ileana and declared he would marry her. The Spanish court was delighted, for at twenty-one the Romanian princess was an outgoing personality with dark hair, brilliant blue eyes, slim and athletic build. Her early experiences in the First World War with death and hunger had given her a feeling of duty and a desire to dedicate herself to the common good. She immediately fell for the prince and his personal charm. Missy was somewhat concerned. The prince was an invalid and a haemophiliac, but the main argument against such a marriage would not be a sickly husband, but King Alfonso XIII himself, with his habit of forcing himself on every woman and then declaring they were to blame. No pretty daughter-in-law or wife of his invalid son was safe from him. Even now, at fifty-three, Queen Marie found the king of Spain difficult to manage. One had to be so careful with him, she warned. Neither age nor position would stop him, and it would be almost impossible for a young woman not to have to deal with him.

On the other hand, according to Cavalry Col. Gabriel de Benito Ibáñez de Aldecoa, a great friend of the prince of Asturias, he had recommended to the prince that, when the *Sud Express* passed through Vitoria, he should take flowers and sweets for his cousin, Cecilia of Salm-Salm. Seeing her again, the prince felt in love and declared himself. The young princess replied that she would think about it and, a little after leaving Spain, she said she was very sorry 'but I am not strong enough to assume such a high position'.

Recently a good friend came to see us and I told him about Cecilia. He had not known about this possible romance, but thought for a while and said, 'Perhaps the Republic would not have been proclaimed had the Prince been married, although I doubt it, because Alfonso XIII adored his first-born, and I do not believe that he would have abdicated. After all, he had been born King.'

15

Bitter Awakening

The death of the queen regent was as great a misfortune for the king as the prince of Asturias's worsening illness, exacerbating the king's chronic depression.

The last splendour of the dictatorship was seen at the international exhibitions. The first was at Seville, held in the María Luisa Park, opened on Ascension Day, and displayed the culture of Latin America. The second one in Barcelona, showing Spain at the pinnacle of European culture, was inaugurated on 21 May, a grandiose work that crowned the mountain of Montjuïc. Primo de Rivera was delighted. On his saint's day in Jerez, an equestrian statue by Mariano Benlliure, paid for by public subscription, was unveiled in the Plaza de Arenal, the people of Jerez paid for the house in which he was born to open its doors to the public, and celebrations took place.

'We should not forget,' wrote Ali, 'that many officers close to the King came from the artillery and that two weeks after the death of the Regent, and against the will of many of their supporters, the Artillery Corps was disbanded.'

On 21 October, the king and queen left for Seville to visit the exhibition, during its last days. The king awarded Primo de Rivera the collar of the Order of Isabella the Catholic and told the dictator he wanted to see his house in Jerez and admire the statue. Primo de Rivera then asked the royal family to honour him by lunching at his new house. On 26 October, the sovereigns, accompanied by their daughters, the *Infantes* Don Carlos and Doña Luisa and their children, and the *infantes* of Orleans, went to Jerez in a horse-drawn carriage and visited the Gonzalez Byass *Bodegas* after lunching at the general's house. 'The meal turned out very well,' wrote María Primo de Rivera to a friend, 'and the King and Queen were very pleased and they visited all parts of the house. As for the little *Infantas*, they seemed to be quite content chatting happily with their Orleans cousins.'

This time also marked the 'double engagement', which the *Infanta* Maria Cristina made: 'We were going to marry Beatriz to Álvaro and me to Alonso. We arranged for it to happen when we were sixteen or eighteen years old'. For the princes of Orleans, these were their first girlfriends, and they were happy though soon had to abandon their romance for their education. Both boys wanted to study engineering at polytechnic but their education at Winchester did not give them adequate qualifications, and they needed another year of study to catch up, for which they went to Zurich. Being in Switzerland meant they could see the snow and go skiing.

During December 1929, the king received tendentious information about the dictatorship. His mother's advice, which he never listened to during her life, was finally remembered after her death and he gradually distanced himself from the dictator. Primo de Rivera saw this, and asked the captains-general for their advice without asking the sovereign's consent first. It proved a serious error by the general. According to Eduardo Aunós, 'the replies were disheartening', and Primo de Rivera presented his resignation to the king. On 31 January, he went to the palace to bid farewell to the royal family. Don Alfonso and the prince of Asturias both embraced him. When the worried queen asked him what he planned to do, he replied that before anything else, he needed to rest.

Primo de Rivera died in Paris on 16 March 1930. Ali felt his passing deeply. According to what he told me, he saw him before he went to Paris and he found him 'so old that it hurt to see him like that'. Bee told me that she planned to go to the Paseo de la Virgen del Puerto, where his cortege had to pass, to pay her respects. In the garden was an arbour where she waited with the *infant* Don Jaime, the duchess of Talavera, wife of the Infante Don Fernando, who was presiding over the cortege in place of the king, and María Ángeles Tornos Sáenz de Santa María, who told me the *infantes* were very pessimistic about the outcome after the end of the dictatorship.

When I published the general's biography, which was awarded a prize by the town council of Jerez, I sent one of the first copies to Ali and he immediately sent me a handwritten reply (23 March 1974). It was a year before his death:

I have received your very interesting book about General Primo de Rivera, for which I thank you very much. As you know, I liked and admired him very much. He was always very good to me—a real friend. He was my colonel in Morocco the first time I was there as a simple officer in the San Fernando Regiment.

What a great patriot and head of government he was! It seems incredible that he did so much good for Spain in little less than six years. He ended the war in Morocco and, at the same time, managed to achieve excellent relations with France. He opened a great number of schools, the National Tourism Circuit, with good roads, tarred or paved with small concrete paving blocks. He got rid of corrupt local party bosses in many towns. I could go on writing for a long time listing everything he did for the Fatherland while not damaging the Nation's finances by overspending and my admiration for him has no limits.

What followed next was the *'dictablanda'* (bland dictatorship), as Berenguer's government was called. It did no more than undo what the dictatorship had done by drafting new laws to create a government that would come to exercise a shift in power.

The *infantes* of Orleans had been living in Spain for more than four years, but Bee often spoke of the surprising number of times that people believed they lived abroad. And for the queen, journalists would constantly mention inaugurations and parties attended by her, accompanied by her daughters, rarely mentioning that she had visited the Red Cross's San José or Santa Adela Hospitals, or a tuberculosis or cancer sanatorium. She was unfailingly brave and affectionate towards patients, often witnessing operations. But her own children, especially her first born, caused her suffering. It was always hard for her to see her 'Alfonsito', her favourite child, so ill, and she always blamed herself as she sat by his bedside. The king rarely visited, and it annoyed him when any supporter of the prince commented in his presence that the heir had a very dull life, away from the court. The heir lived on the El Pardo estate and Bee visited him regularly, something for which the queen was deeply grateful, writing repeatedly to her cousin: 'I know from experience what an angel you are when you enter the room of a sick person'.

Bee went before teatime, taking sweets and magazines which they discussed together. As she had lived so close to her children, she told little stories and jokes, and would leave when his friends from the tertulia (conversational group) were arriving to join him in the evening. As she was confident her sons would come to Spain for Christmas, she suggested they could go to Sanlúcar, taking the little *infantas* with them. They were excited about staying in the old Montpensier palace. The queen was enchanted with the idea, but they thought it would be better if Ali himself was to make the invitation.

Bee went to London for Christmas shopping, accompanied by her lady's maid, Señora Ruata, and spent over a week in England. Ambassador Merry del Val, now marquis, and his wife gave a lunch in her honour and invited the representatives of the US and Japan, thus erasing 'past oversights'. On returning to Madrid on 16 December, she heard of the unsuccessful revolt in Jaca, and Ali who informed her that he had had to leave for Paris because the *Infante* Don Antonio had had a heart attack. Fortunately, his father's condition had improved, but then Ali had to deal with some rebellious aviators. To protest the current political situation, they had intended to fly to the palace in Madrid. They could not land there because when they arrived they saw young boys playing in the Plaza de Oriente in front of the palace. So they gave up, and left for Portugal where they landed. Ali returned to Madrid to try and mitigate the crime of his companions in arms. Those who had rebelled included two commanders, Ramón Franco of the infantry, Ignacio Hidalgo de Cisneros in the Service Corps, and also six infantry captains.

With holidays approaching, the younger family members returned to Madrid. Juan de Borbón arrived from San Fernando where he was studying at the Naval College, and Álvaro returned from Zurich, very pleased at being invited to a party at the Spanish consulate. Bee had invited her niece, Grand Duchess Kira of Russia, so that she could get to know Spain and the *infantes* who lived in Madrid, Alfonso de Borbón, son of the princess of Asturias, and the two brothers, Luis Alfonso and José Eugenio of Bavaria. The Queen's Saint's Day was on 23 December, and at a banquet that evening, Alfonso XIII sat at table between his two daughters. Kira's neighbours at table were the prime minister, Gen. Berenguer, who spoke French and liked music, and the *Infante* Don José Eugenio, a great music lover but very shy and very young. Kira enjoyed seeing the Palacio de Oriente as the Madrileños called it, full of beauty and art.

Ali, an early riser, phoned Paris on Christmas Day to find out how his father was. His manservant replied that the gentleman had spent a good night and had just awakened. Ali told him to tell his father that they were all meeting in Madrid and that they all wished him a Merry Christmas. Only a few minutes had passed when the telephone rang and the servant sadly told him, 'His Highness has died smoking his cigar.' Much affected by the death of his Uncle Antonio, the king went to give his condolences to his cousin, then accompanied him to the station to catch the train. On arriving in Paris, Ali went directly to the Spanish Church in Rue de la Pompe, where his father's remains lay in the funeral chapel, then to see his mother, the *Infanta* Eulalia, who was serene but much affected. 'Death is always sad,' she used to say, 'but to die at Christmas leaves a bad memory for all.' The body was taken to the Monastery of El Escorial, and buried in the pudridero on 29 December at 8 a.m. at a ceremony attended by the king and Ali and Bee and their sons.

Friends and colleagues of Ali came to give condolences at Calle Quintana. While there, they told of their preoccupation with rumours about the dissolution of the Aviation Corps, which the king had created during the dictatorship (by the Royal Decree of 23 March 1926), six months after a successful operation at Alhucemas in which the aviators had distinguished themselves. The Aviation Corps was disbanded on 9 January 1931, and the wearing of their much-loved bottle green uniform was prohibited.

Pilar of Bavaria, Ali's first cousin, thought that the old military men were protecting their own in Spain, and belittling the air force. It was the same in England before aviation became a corps with its own leaders; in Spain, there was much envy and a lack of understanding of the new weapon of war. The old officers were upset that the government had taken control of a loyal, powerful, and mobile force with its own radio stations and aerodromes, which could rapidly dominate a revolutionary movement in any part of the Peninsula. Ali went to the burial in Guadalajara of his friend, Capt. Félix Martínez Ramírez, who had died in service. Representing the king was Capt. Gallarza and Ali was able to chat with him, and was worried about what he said in respect of the king's attitude.

Seriously depressed since his mother's death, the king was totally disenchanted with politics. Bee had already warned Gen. Kindelán of this when she said that, as a gentleman, he should ask for an audience with the king. *Infanta* María Cristina noted in her memoirs that her aunt and uncle had asked her to spend Christmas 1930 with them, and she caught pneumonia. Alonso never introduced her as his girlfriend, always as his cousin. Was it because he was ashamed of her, she asked him. No, he replied: 'It is because I am so young, that if I say you are my girlfriend, they will make fun of me'.

On 13 January 1931, the queen invited Bee to accompany her to the tuberculosis sanatorium at Valdelatas. They visited it together and discussed new extensions. On returning, Ena told her cousin of her worries, and especially about the changes in her husband, who seemed increasingly withdrawn and even distant. The young princesses returned to work at the Red Cross hospital, which they really enjoyed as they were with girls of their own age.

Princess Beatrice of Battenberg fell ill with severe flu in England on 28 January. Generally in good health, she was due to celebrate her seventy-fourth birthday on 14 April. The queen therefore left Madrid for London at once, arriving two days later. On seeing her, the patient began to recover and they passed the days of her long convalescence together. In view of this, the imminent student revolts at home, and the resignation of Gen. Berenguer's government, the queen decided to return to Spain, declaring that her place was now at the side of her husband.

Alfonso XIII decided to leave the formation of a new government to Sánchez Guerra, but in vain. Hoping to succeed, he had gone to the Model Prison, where they held important politicians such as Niceto Alaclá-Zamora, who refused to form a monarchical government. On 17 February, the queen returned by the 8:05 train. When she saw the platforms full of people who cheered her fervently, she was so surprised that when she went over to her Orleans cousins to hug them, she asked them in English, 'What's happening?' The crowd followed the cars climbing the hill of San Vicente and found themselves with the king who had just arrived at the palace, amid cries of 'Long Live the Monarchy!' and 'Death to the Republic!' Despite the cold weather, the king and queen went out on the central balcony and had the consolation of seeing the Plaza de Oriente full of people. It would be the last time.

Admiral Aznar's government was trying to prepare for elections, but the politicians thought they should begin with the election of members of Congress and not, as per tradition, with the town councils. On 11 March, the *Infanta* María Cristina was urgently operated on for appendicitis at the Red Cross Hospital where she worked as a nurse, much to the surprise of the old courtiers. Years later, remembering the episode, she would say, 'I was important for less than a week, they sent me flowers, sweets and books and everyone came to see me at home.' The king went to see her three times but suddenly on 13 March, 'he had to go to London' which seemed incompatible with imminent elections. It was said that he wanted to visit the princess of Battenberg, whom he did not bother to speak to for long periods of time when she was in Madrid. He returned from Paris eleven days later.

Holy Week 1931 began on 29 March with public chapel, which they celebrated as it was Palm Sunday. Ali and Bee's family did not attend celebrations at the palace because of mourning for his father, but they mixed in with people in the galleries.

Rumours of the two young princesses' engagements continued and *La Época* reported (23 March 1931) that Señor Mudarra, secretary to Ali and Bee, had sent a letter denying a false report that 'Prince Don Álvaro de Orleans was to be proclaimed as an *Infante*'. Actually, the Orleans brothers were to be found in Spain where they had been for several days. They had passed their quarterly examinations, went about elegantly dressed in grey flannel suits and woollen ties, accompanied by their girlfriends, the young princesses, sometimes to the theatre or cinema, with boxes or stalls always reserved for the royal family. Early every morning they went to the Cuatro

Vientos aerodrome to fly. Lecea, a companion and friend of Ali, gave them lessons during the holidays, and the *Infante* Don Juan asked the king to let him travel from Madrid to Seville by aeroplane on his return to Cadiz.

As flying was an obsession, the prince of Asturias, who loved hunting, wanted to do so on board an aeroplane. The expedition was fixed for 11 April, but his brother, Juan, as well as his Orleans cousins could not accompany him, and he only had bustards to attack. However, the recoil of the Mauser left him with severe bruising and some loss of blood which kept him prostrate in bed for some days while they were there.

The day of the parliamentary elections was 12 April, which many monarchist politicians did not consider important. The royal family did not leave the palace. In the morning, they heard Mass in the tapestry room as usual and the queen rode on horseback through the Casa de Campo. At 2 p.m., the *infantes* gathered with their parents in the daily dining room for a simple meal of soup, eggs, rice with meat, and a pastry for dessert with a cup of coffee and a liqueur afterwards. After lunch, the king spoke by telephone to the prime minister, Admiral Aznar, who told him that all was well and there had been no incidents. The polling stations closed at 4 p.m. Bee went to see Ena, finding her with Lady Irene, marchioness of Carisbrooke, the wife of Alexander of Battenberg, convalescing after an operation at the Red Cross Hospital. Ena told Bee of the good impressions that Admiral Aznar had passed on to the king. They took tea together and made plans for the following summer.

At 7 p.m., Alfonso XIII returned to the Palacio de Oriente and while having tea he called his dentist, Don Floristán Aguilar, an intelligent and loyal man with numerous friends, to check on the election results. Viscount Aguilar, a title given to him by the king in 1929, came to the palace. Accompanied by him, the king telephoned the minister of the interior, the marquis of Hoyos, and then Gen. Mola, who replied it would be premature to give any information on the election. Dressed in a dinner jacket, the king went to meet family members in Madrid who were traditionally invited to dine every Sunday. The queen went to the gathering, also to ask for any election details.

When they discussed the situation, the king did not foresee any serious repercussions, although the elections had been called completely unexpectedly. Yet the queen was frightened, without knowing why despite encouragement from Bee. At 9.30 p.m., the usual Sunday dinner at the palace was attended by the king and queen and their children, *Infante* Don Ferdinand of Bavaria and his wife, with two of their children, Fernando and Maria Luisa, plus Ali and Bee.

The grave illness of the Infanta Isabel, and confused news about the elections, weighed heavily upon the guests. After dinner, served by servants in knee-length trousers and white silk stockings and jackets trimmed with gold braid, there was a cinema show. Although they only watched half of the film, at midnight they decided to stop and continue another day. After taking leave of their guests, the king and queen retired to the king's study, where Aguilar was awaiting them.

The *infantes* of Orleans returned home but did not find it quiet on leaving the Palace de Oriente. They talked to anyone they knew on the way home. Ali learned that on returning to his estate in Guadalajara the night before, the count of Romanones, minister of state, had told journalists that 'the elections had been lost', leaving the news to be broadcast on the radio. The night of 12–13 April was completely quiet, as the Monarchists had gone to bed peacefully while the Republicans, now united, planned to form a provisional republican government next day. In the morning, Ali went to the palace to hear the news, but did not know that Gen. Dámaso Berenguer had sent a note to all captains-general ordering the army to guarantee the safety of the nation, avoiding and preventing all disturbances.

The names of the elected members of parliament were announced early that afternoon: Monarchists, 22,000, and Anti-Monarchists only 5,000. The latter only represented Madrid, Barcelona, Seville, and Valencia, but they were considered more important than the rest. The council of ministers was to meet at 5:30 p.m. A journalist asked President Aznar bluntly if he could confirm that there was a crisis. Undeterred, Aznar replied: 'What more do you want, that I tell you that people went to bed as Monarchists, and woke up as Republicans?' Entering the parliament chamber, he encountered two ministers, La Cierva and Bugallal, who intended to abandon the king before the approaching crisis. Proclaiming a new cabinet, or a state of war, would demonstrate more firmness they thought. They left the chamber with no solutions other than the knowledge that La Cierva was assumed capable of assuming power and governing normally.

At dinner, the queen's sad expression and silence contrasted with the king's lighthearted banter. After eating, they went to another room to view the rest of the previous night's film. Meanwhile the telephone never ceased ringing. The king had ordered that it should be answered by thanking the caller and saying that, despite the adverse election results, it would not affect the regime. Before retiring, he quietly gave instructions that the film should continue during the following day's session, 14 April.

Very early in the morning, the count of Romanones called Viscount Aguilar—the king's dentist—as he knew that nobody was as close to the king as Aguilar who was received at any hour in the royal chamber. What the celebrated politician wanted him to tell the king was so important that Aguilar asked him to write it down. 'Thus,' according to Rafael Borrás, 'using his dentist as intermediary, the Count of Romanones said simply and plainly to Alfonso XIII that he should pack his bags and go because of 'the events of this morning'—which he did not explain further to the king. Bee, who had visited the prince of Asturias as he had suffered a haemorrhage the previous night, then went to the queen's rooms. Very pessimistic about information the king had received from the politicians, she had asked her cousin bluntly not to leave them, and Bee and Ali had stayed for lunch at the palace. The ministers left, while a furious La Cierva repeatedly exclaimed: 'They have left me alone, completely alone!'

The marquis of Cavalcanti, who had just arrived, approached the minister and said to him, 'Now we are two, I will not permit this to happen.' Immediately, the murmur of voices ceased before the presence of the king who appeared in the chamber: 'Sir, Sir, listen to General Cavalcanti'. Cavalcanti appeared and, standing to attention, declared that the army, or a great part of it, remained loyal to the monarchy, and he was willing 'to go out into the streets to suffocate the revolutionary disturbances'. 'Thank you, Pepe, thank you very much. It is useless,' the king said shaking his head.

Years later, Gen. Cavalcanti was sent for some months to the Fortress of Guadalupe. My father visited him from San Sebastian, and heard from his own lips, 'I arrived too late, Romanones had convinced the King that he should leave. There had been intrigue and treachery.'

Just before 3 p.m., they told the king that the count of Romanones had arrived at the palace. Immediately, Alfonso XIII rose from the table and went to his study. Bee, who had been seated next to the king, looked with sadness at her husband: the name of Romanones was ominous for the couple. But Ali continued talking to the queen concealing his worries. 'It was a splendid day, we thought little of revolution when we went down through the palace gardens at around half-past four in the afternoon, on our way home,' he wrote. On entering, the doorman said to us 'Highness, your adjutant Don César Sáenz de Santa María has telephoned to ask you to phone him from the hall or on my telephone as soon as you arrive home.' On telephoning, Ali's adjutant told him that his barber, who lived in the Puerta del Sol, had told him that revolt against the monarchy had begun in Spain, and red flags were flying on the ministry of the interior. Ali and Bee returned to the palace by car. Once there, everything was confusion, nobody knew anything and all had an opinion. They went to the private rooms of the king and queen. On seeing his cousin, the king announced: 'They have thrown me out and they want me to go before sunset!' Ali, standing to attention, replied, 'And I shall accompany you!'

Bee's sentiments were the same as Ali's. On entering the king's study, Bee said her to husband in English, 'Ali, you are big and strong, run home, take your revolvers, go with him and look after him, in case he needs you.' Faced with the danger in which the king found himself, in her loyalty to the nation and the Spanish royal family, she had seemingly forgotten her years of exile for being a Protestant and the later unjust exile of more than eight years. Deeply moved by Bee's generous gesture, the king asked her quietly not to leave Aunt Isabel alone as she was very unwell, and to tell her not to worry about money. Bee asked him to stay calm, assured him she would stay with Isabel, and did not intend to say anything until she knew everyone was safe. Cars were prepared to drive them away in secret.

Alfonso XIII went to the rooms where the haemophiliac prince of Asturias lay after suffering several haemorrhages in the last few days. He was surrounded by his friends, Darío López, his companion since childhood; the marquis of Vega de Anzo 'as cultured, as intelligent and faithful'; Col. Gabriel de Benito, who was always there to serve him; Jaime Almodóvar, who on hearing the news, ran to the palace; Espinosa de los Monteros; Dr Elósegui who always tried to calm his pains; and the duke of Lécera. When the king arrrived, everyone else left the room while father and son talked alone for a few brief moments, where they may have discussed abdication. All the royal family wanted to bid farewell to the king. Prince Ferdinand of Bavaria and his two sons came in informal clothes; it was 6 p.m. and they were waiting impatiently for the tickets to catch the *Sud Express* that night.

Ali wrote some brief notes in English about the journey from Madrid to Cartagena which his grandson, Prince Alonso of Orleans, was good enough to give me. It is a very informal document in which Ali's tribulations in wishing to protect his king and cousin on his flight from Spain are vividly reflected:

At 18.45 on the 14-4-31 we left the Palace via the Puerta Incognita and the Puerta del Moro.

1st car. Alfonso and I driven by Salvear in the Duesenberg.

2nd car. Admiral Rivera (who we waited on) and Luis Unión (Duke of Miranda).

3rd car. Pablito (Martín Alonso), Gallarza and Urquiano (three adjutants of the King).

4th car. Paco (Moreno) (the King's man servant) with luggage.

5th car. Luggage

Plus one car of civil guards who, from loyalty, joined us when we left.

The departure was very sad and moving. All those working on the estate and the gardens gathered round. We tried to stop the shouts of

'Long Live the King!' as they could be heard by the crowds outside. Alfonso, melancholic and quiet.

Many Grandees, etc. went down with us from the room. We waited fifteen minutes because the cars were late. Maps forgotten, Alfonso ordered me to his rooms to look for them.

At last we left. The first difficulty was on arriving at the gate, which was closed. They had to call the gatekeeper. I am afraid that this could ruin the journey. The crowds could come. One thing worried me, if there are disturbances on the road, when should I fire my revolver? If I am too quick, it could cause a disaster and not be of any use. So during the entire journey I thought on all the possible eventualities in order to organise myself to take the most correct action possible.

At the first bend on the Cuesta del Vega we saw some groups of people but they were quiet. Only Alfonso, Luis Unión and Paco knew where we were going (Cartagena). We had the fastest car. We left. I was feeling bad for leaving Bee, Ataúlfo, Ena and the children behind. But the bitterness is against the King, who has to, in some way, leave the country. Alfonso is quiet and firm despite the terrible tension. Puerta de Toledo, red flags and shouts. Thank God there is no trouble. I hope that we pass unnoticed. Telephone calls. We stop further on. I wonder if there are wires across the road, but say nothing so as not to worry the driver. I think about the narrow bridge at Aranjuez. I hope that there will be no nonsense there. We cross Aranjuez. Empty. Many cars are going in the opposite direction. We arrive OK at Ocaña. I have to remember to burn Alfonso's books and maps.

I hope that everything will continue like this. These villages in La Mancha are spread out, but the streets are very narrow. I hope that they are not blocked by a car or a lorry. After Ocaña, a stop on the road. The column closes up. Everyone is OK. They tell us where we are going; the Arsenal at Cartagena. We decide that the King's car should not stop in the villages. We refuel on the road with cans from another car, which were filled in villages thus avoiding the 'column effect'. We had no time to paint number plates on the cars as we planned to do on leaving. They will see and will think that these are people from the Palace, or Palace cars in the service of the Revolution. In some villages there is an incredible silence. In others, very loud shouting of 'Long Live the Republic!' Further on a large group applauds us shouting, 'They are the Republicans!'

The car runs like clockwork: Salvear drives magnificently. Alfonso is apparently incapable of showing tiredness. Incredibly, we take some food at one of our four stops. I ask myself how we are going to cross Albacete. Some villages near Murcia are deserted, some people know about the journey and cry, 'Long Live the King!'

We cross through Murcia without incident. I ask myself what we should say at Cartagena. Everything goes well until the entrance of the 'Arsenal' There is a crowd, being held back by Infantry, and they are crying 'Long Live the Republic!'. We pass through and arrive at the arsenal. The sailors and Naval officers present arms. The worst is over. I think of putting the revolver back into its holster and give thanks to God.

Luis Miranda, the Admiral, Urquiano and the others had been magnificent throughout the entire journey. Serenos said little. The officers bid farewell. The Civil Guard sergeant kissed the King's hand. The launch arrived; time and time again, the cries of 'Long Live the King!' were repeated. Now Alfonso was safe. He asked me how Bee, Ataúlfo, Ena and the boys would be.

One last ovation, and Alfonso shouted 'Long Live Spain!' The officers responded, 'Viva!' (Long Live!). The cruiser Príncipe Alfonso is in the port. Alfonso, Luis, Rivera, Paco and I went aboard. Rivera will accompany Alfonso until Marseilles. On board, the King is saluted by numerous officers. They came to say goodbye to him. The sun was setting when we left silently.

It reminds me of past days in the Alcázares. I know every inch, every corner of this land. At six in the morning of the 15th [he puts 14th] I went to bed. I slept well, until ten o'clock, when they woke me. How will Bee be? We walked the decks all day. The weather is beautiful. No news. Why is there no news on the radio? After lunch, the radio informed us that Juan is safe in Gibraltar. How is Bee? I thought about it constantly. I said to Luis that Alfonso had to prepare himself to be interviewed by the journalists. Alfonso prepared messages to the Army and the Navy. Luis and I underlined the importance of these messages. The declaration to the press would be his first *communiqué* since his leaving. He prepared one—it was almost a manifesto. The King decided not to submit it without first consulting with some expert from the press and also with some political personality in Paris. That morning at dawn, the Republican flag was hoisted. Anyway, we will disembark at 4.30. Luis has informed Quiñones. He is a good man for this dreadful voyage. Always calm.' (*The signatures of the King and the Duke of Miranda support this story*).

Alfonso XIII, who loved driving cars and who was the terror of the queen and his assistants, was not going to drive 'the magnificent automobile capable of covering one hundred and eighty kilometres in an hour' that spring night. According to Melchor Almagro San Martín, 'it did less than half that, despite the good state of the roads, which were little used at night and in the early morning' contrary to what we have read written by Ali in his own hand. The road from Madrid to Cartagena gave the king a final memory of his fatherland, according to the poet Luis de Tapia:

It's sad crossing Spain now
When all the country is in flower!
When, with fruitful aromas all the flowers flourish
Except the fleurs-de-lis!

The marquis of Magaz and Gen. Zubillaga impatiently waited for the travellers, who had been delayed, and they arrived at 4:30 a.m., two hours late. On stepping down from the car, Alfonso XIII asked anxiously whether a state of war had been declared. Magaz, who was vice-president during the dictatorship, and remained faithful to the king, told him that everything was quiet.

In the archives of Lt-Gen. Kindelán, there is an account by Ali:

On arriving on board the *Príncipe Alfonso*, the King was received with all correctness. The Commander gave his cabin to his Majesty. We ate with him. We carried no flag, as, on sailing nobody knew what the Republican flag was like and the Commander did not dare hoist the old flag and much less the flag of Castile on the stern.'

We leave the illustrious travellers resting for a few hours aboard the *Príncipe Alfonso* until the first light of morning, and we return to Madrid where we have left Bee and Ataúlfo helping the Royal Family prepare their luggage.

'At the Palace, nobody has deserted their post; however, the mysterious spirit of the unseen gives it a look of abandonment,' noted Almagro San Martín.

At the end of my childhood, the news that the Royal Family spent the night at the mercy of a shouting mob which surrounded the Palace impacted upon my imagination and I have been able to question many people who lived through the long night of the 14th /15th of April in the Royal Palace.

Among them, Don Manuel de las Casas who, together with his family, lived in the Palace and advised the King on his personal finances. He was the son of a civil servant who had guarded the hearse carrying the body of the young King Alfonso XII to the Escorial.

Confidentially, he told me the following:
The King, before passing the Prince of Asturias' rooms to say goodbye,

passed through the administration office. He spoke to Don Luis de Asúa in the small office, and I heard him say, 'Everyone has to be paid for all of the month of April and, if possible, find them a position. This is something which I am most concerned about.' When I was leaving, he took me by the arm and said to me bluntly, 'Manuel, your wife is French and I have here this envelope with a million pesetas for you to put in her current account.'

'Sir,' I replied in alarm, 'the account is in my name.'

'Well, see you pay my debts, beginning with the poorest. I believe that you will be able to do it.'

'Sir, I will do what you order, but it is so much money and without a receipt.'

'Ay, Manuel, now I am beginning to get to know people!' he replied as way of farewell.

'I was paying the debts for months and at the end of the year they asked me to send the King what remained.' Then his wife interrupted, 'He wrote a cheque for all that was left in the account; including the fourteen thousand pesetas savings which we had.'

Juanita las Casas lived in Anglet during the summer. She and her daughters helped pack many items which were later returned to the royal family. I also knew Dr Petinto, who signed Queen María Cristina's death certificate, and other friends such as the wife and elder daughter of Albert Searle who was appointed by Edward VII to protect his niece, and who lived in the palace and who had to leave. They told me that the shouting of the crowds was insupportable and that they screamed against Queen Ena more than against the king.

They left Spain the following morning, Anita Berenguer told me: 'That night there were people in the Alcázar, but as it is so big it seemed deserted compared with the days of Public Chapel and Fiestas; we were helping to pack things all night'.

The *Infanta* Beatriz, in her bedroom on the second floor, continued packing suitcases with winter, spring, and autumn clothes. The cases were filling up and she called her younger brothers' teacher who was good with his hands, and asked him to close them. After doing so, 'Doña Beatriz took a medal from around her neck and gave it to me,' noted Luis Rodriguez Pascual. The royal bedchamber is on Calle Bailén, or more accurately has a terrace on the street, and as the queen feared, an intruder could enter her private rooms while she guarded her jewels, the *Infanta* María Cristina had asked her mother to sleep next to her.

That night, they watched in horror as Republicans climbed up the front of the palace and put the red flag on top: 'Through the windows we heard cries of "Death to the King! Death to the King! We want the head of a child!"' It was frightful, Cristina said, to see 'those women like crazy things.' They were terrified, aware that anything could happen. It was not long since all the Russian imperial family, her mother's first cousins, had been assassinated. Not wishing to forget anything, the queen went in and out of her room. The queen asked the marchioness of Santa Cruz, who loved animals, 'Casilda, you know that I have five dogs and I cannot take them to England. May I leave them with you?' The lady-in-waiting immediately replied, 'Madam, I would be delighted I will take Pink (the Queen's favourite) and another small one today, and tomorrow I will take the other three.'

The *Infanta* Maria Cristina continued:

> The maids left very early for the Station del Norte with the luggage and were attacked and almost did not get there. They then called the Palace and said, 'The Queen and the *Infantes* should not go to the station, as it will be too dangerous.' It was decided that we should go by car to El Escorial. The leaving was terrible with poor Alfonso being carried in their arms. Everyone was crying and we were leaving our home where we had always lived, believing that we were never going to see it again.

The queen wanted to say goodbye to all the staff before leaving, a personal act in which she showed her good-heartedness in listening to the old servants who plaintively cried, 'Oh, what are we going to do?' The last farewell was to be in the garden. On embracing the marchioness of Valdeiglesias, the queen said: 'Concha, don't leave my Red Cross, see that it continues'. Seeing that Ena's nerves were at their limit, Bee, 'who during these critical days had passed so many tests of loyalty and devotion, was the first to start to leave accompanied by her son Ataúlfo', commented the marquis of Castel Bravo.

Bee was particularly annoyed with the Spanish custom of sympathising with the loser, with many people saying to her, 'Are you not afraid now that you are alone?' She cut them off, saying, 'What more can they do to kill me!' 'There were various farewells,' María Ángeles Tornos recalled, but perhaps the most spontaneous was at Galapagar. The queen sat on a rock to smoke a cigarette, surrounded by many young people who had come to say goodbye to the little princesses, among others José Antonio, Primo de Rivera's eldest son, and his two sisters. It was something she never forgot.

As the time for the train to leave was nearing, they entered the station at El Escorial where Admiral Aznar, the count and countess of Romanones, and the British ambassador, Sir George Graham, were waiting. The ambassador approached Ena and asked if he could do anything. She replied: 'It's too late'.

Gen. Sanjurjo, who commanded the Civil Guard, wanted to accompany the royal family to the French Frontier. Impossible though it seemed, wrote the *Infanta* María Cristina, they sent the royal train with an immense crown on both sides, to cross Spain. In Ávila, the carriage overheated and they had to change to a normal carriage, which greatly annoyed the queen.

Bee was still worrying about the train leaving and chose to go along the platform, followed by her son, to look for the carriage waiting for them. After returning to the station waiting room where the courtiers were still talking, she found the count de Romanones, downcast and sad, alone on a bench. He had evidently not felt happy about the welcome he had received from those present, and moved away from the countess, who was much esteemed by Madrid society. Without hesitation, passing near to the politician, Bee cried out as if hard of hearing, the short phrase, 'Count, you are always seeing people off!' Romanones lifted his head and looked fixedly at her until she disappeared from view. My good friend, Agustín Santo Floro, the count's son, told me that in later years his father felt guilty about what he had done to Ali and Bee.

Meanwhile Ali, accompanying his cousin, was still steaming towards a French port, at 12 p.m. on 15 April 1931:

They had not taken off the scarves covering their mouths. At first, when the King passed (The King, Luis Miranda and I were in mufti), the sailors stood to attention but by the afternoon they no longer did so. The King and I spent most of the day pacing the decks far from the others. There were many hours of interminable conversation. I remember part of one conversation, and although the words are not accurate, as I cannot remember them well, the sense was as follows:

King: Ali, do you think that it was possible to have done something else?

Me: Don't torment yourself uselessly, you did what you thought was the best for the country in the circumstances. Later you may see it differently, but decisions cannot be taken using more than the data available at the time. You cannot see the future.

King: What happens to me is just a detail; I think of Spain. What does Luis think? Let's go and ask him (I go look for Luis and tell him that the King should prepare himself for the assault by journalists. We go to meet the King and after talking for a while the King goes to his cabin and prepares some declarations which result in being so important that in the end it is decided that nobody will say anything to the press. Not the King, nor Luis, nor I, until we have consulted with experts on the press and politics in Paris. Will advise Quiñones by radio. I return to walking with the King).

King: Who should I consult with in France?

I: When there is a revolution, not only the King and his family have to abandon the country but also generals, ministers, bishops, etc.... Some have a bad time. I can assure you of this as I have seen various exiled kings in Switzerland.

King: At least in Marseilles we will have more news of what is happening and what has happened to the rest of the family. Poor Aunt Isabel, she is so ill!

Now evening, the King directed some kindly phrases to me thanking me for having left Bee and Ataúlfo to accompany him. I dared to ask him three favours:

1. That he is kind to Ena in this common misfortune and that there is no discord. It should not be forgotten that Ena's nerves have suffered greatly.

2. That they live together in a house, no matter how modest it is and not in a hotel.

3. That every effort should be made towards the Restoration. If a King stops practising the art of reigning he loses the ability to reign. I begged the King strongly that he dedicate at least two hours, five days a week more or less on average to meet people capable of being ministers. For example, that he appoint a gentleman to monitor all new measures taken with taxation and to prepare amendments to laws, to be made when the monarchy returns.

The King promised to comply with the first point and as for the second he said he did not know what to do, as right now there was no other option but to stay in a hotel. As for the last point, he did not believe that there were enough people of significance within his reach, but he thought it a good idea.

Some people may think that it strange that it was possible to converse so much and about such varied topics. In order to test this it is necessary to be ten hours without a break in a confined space with nothing to do except talk. Besides, one will rack one's brains trying to think about the more or less near, and immediate, future.

The officers were in an uncomfortable position and for the first time the King was on a warship without being able to give orders and more or less a prisoner. The King was continually expressing his faith that God would always protect Spain.

A little after midnight, the commander of the *Principe Alfonso* advised the King through Luís Miranda that as he would probably have to hoist the Republican flag in the morning, he was sure that His Majesty would prefer to disembark before he did so.

The King agreed, and at approximately half-past four in the morning, the commander told the King that the tender was waiting. Admiral Rivera said that he would accompany his Majesty to the shore.

A little before arriving at their destination, the King, who had already said goodbye to the officers, went to take leave of the commander. The King asked the commander to give him, as a reminder, a small pennant of Castile like that used on the tender.

The commander said; 'I can't because I would have to charge you'. The King took out his wallet and said to the commander dryly, 'I am willing to pay you for it'. The latter went pale with anger and said; 'I am going to bring it to your Majesty right away'. He returned in a few moments with three of them, giving one to the King, one to Luis and another to me. With emotion in his voice, the King thanked him, and shook his hand firmly.

We were in the Bay of Marseilles, and the lights of the city could be seen in the distance. We boarded the tender, the King, Admiral Rivera, Luis Miranda, Paco Moreno, and I. The tender was started up and we moved away into the night. No one spoke, not a single word.

We were separating ourselves from Spain. After what seemed to me like a quarter of an hour, we came alongside a ship whose lifeboats carried the name *Tritón*.

I found it very strange not to see any lookout on board and I made sure that my pistol was ready in my gabardine pocket. We climbed a very rough wooden ladder in the following order: first Luis with a small electric torch which the King had lent him, then the King, with me behind and last of all, Paco. Some sailors from the cruiser helped Paco bring up some four or five suitcases and the tender left immediately leaving us in the dark.

We were on a ship tied up to a quay. We did not see any one on board the Tritón. In the same order, we reached land via a narrow gangplank without guardrails. Once on dry land we saw by the light of some lampposts that we were in a large coal yard. I did not like it, as Marseilles is full of undesirables.

I saw a man, one of those rogues who is always idle. I called him over and said (in French), 'Here are fifty francs, get me a taxi and I will give you a hundred more. If you can, bring two taxis but don't waste any time.'

He went off like a greyhound and soon arrived with a taxi. I got in with the King and I admit that I left Luis and Paco to luck. I was in a great hurry to see the King in a place of safety. I said to the taxi driver, Hotel de Noailles'.

Suddenly, we arrived at an iron gate and a customs officer stopped us saying in French, 'Customs. Passports.'

I called out with authority 'This is the King of Spain!' He saluted and let us pass, saying, 'Pardon Sir!'

In the taxi I said to the King, 'Be careful with the journalists.'

All was clear when we arrived at the hotel. I jumped from the taxi, closing the door. I said to the doorman, 'As fast as you can, give me any room which is not on the ground floor, I'll be right back'. I ran to the taxi, which already had three newspapermen at its side. The King and I quickly left the taxi and entered the lift with the doorman. The doorman recognised the King. He put us in a room with adjoining bedrooms and, for fear of the newspapermen, advised me to lock the door. I explained to the doorman that the Duke of Miranda would soon be arriving and I asked him to pay the taxi and order us breakfast. I was at peace at last: the King was safe. After breakfast there was nothing to do as the suitcases had not arrived. There was a telephone on the table and the following conversation followed:

I: What do you think? Should we 'phone Madrid to see what is happening?

King: What a stupid idea; there will be no communication.

I: It costs nothing to try. I rang my home in Madrid and in less than ten minutes the King was talking to my wife who had refused to leave so as not to leave the *Infanta* Isabel alone, now that the rest of the family had left. She gave us details of the leaving of the Queen which had been complicated by the arrival of Ramón Franco; of how he gave the bad news to the *Infanta* Isabel; etc., etc. If you want details, the *Infanta* can give them and said that she hoped to leave with the *Infanta* Isabel within a few days and I said that I would go to Hendaya to meet them if the French did not put up any difficulties. The King thanked her for having stayed with his aunt.

Luis and Paco arrived a little later and the King went to change. Around half an hour later everyone began to arrive: the military governor, the naval governor, the prefect, the mayor, etc. All were exceedingly friendly.

The journey to Paris was arranged and as there are so many witnesses to the event, among them Jimmy Alba and Pepe Quiñones de León, who met the train before his arrival in Paris, I shall write no more as others will do it better.

The first thing the exiled king asked on landing on foreign soil in Marseilles was if in any part of Spain there had been a reaction by Monarchists, which he saw as inevitable. According to those present, Admiral Rivera and the duke of Miranda, he was visibly disappointed to hear them say no. He occupied rooms 102 to 105 on the first floor of the Hotel de Noailles. Ali immediately went out to buy English and American newspapers, and those hot off the press in Marseilles. They now had enough to read until catching the *Côte d'Azur Express* at 12:10 p.m., arriving in Paris at 11 p.m. that night.

María Ángeles Tornos reported years later:

> On entering the mansion in Calle Quintana I noticed that there was no
> guard in the porter's lodge. I went up to the *Infanta* Beatrice's flat and I
> found her in excellent humour, having had spoken to her husband and
> the King, who were now in Marseilles and were to leave for Paris at
> midday.
>
> I was now thinking of telling the *Infanta* Isabel what had happened,
> but as it was still very early and, according to Maria Cuevas, she was still
> snoozing, I waited, intending to try to speak to the Hotel Meurice.
>
> She, who was the Princess of Asturias, was now seated in her
> wheelchair, but as Bee was no saint in her devotion, she received her
> brusquely. They had spent more than three days without seeing their
> families and they missed them. On glancing around and seeing Ataúlfo
> kiss her hand, she smiled, because he is her godson and she loves him
> dearly.
>
> Princess Bee tells plainly what had happened and that the King and his
> cousin were now outside Spain, as were Ena and her sons, and on their
> way to Paris. Lovingly, Ataúlfo, who was just seventeen years old, cried
> out, 'Mama and I have remained here to be with you until you are better.'
> The old *Infanta* lifted her head, which was resting upon her breast, and
> cried, 'The King! The King!' He was the centre of her life. Bee told her
> that they would remain...

There was great silence among 'the backbone of the institution' as the
family often called Isabel. It was difficult to comprehend that the throne
had fallen. Hours later she perhaps remembered that when newly married
she remained in the Paris embassy awaiting the arrival of her mother,
Isabel II, and her brothers. Because an *infanta* of Spain should always be
near the king, she thought it best to call Bee and she rushed to ask her to
prepare the journey to France.

Isabel's maids, Juanita and Margot Bertrán de Lis, who felt like family,
as their grandmother, Isabel Fernandina, was a sister of King Francisco de
Asís, wanted to convince her to stay until she was better. 'You don't think
that,' Isabel replied. After a day of anxious waiting, the procession of the
Good Shepherd passed in front of the palace. Isabel ordered them to put
on her mantilla for her. They gave her a veil that had adorned the Holy
Thursday altar in the royal chapel, and took her on to the balcony where
she prayed as the procession passed.

Then Isabel asked the private secretary, Francisco Coello de Portugal,
to prepare an estate car from Public Works to carry a bed. It was fixed for
the night of 19 April. First they had to save the *Infanta* Isabel's magnificent

jewels. Bee mentioned that hers had been sent via the Romanian Legation, but Isabel wanted to take her own personally: 'There is an argument between the two *Infantas* and in the end the elder says that she wants to see the jewels. Bee arranges them on top of the bedspread, Doña Isabel looks out her favourites and suddenly indicates with a sign that they should be put away'. Bee did so rapidly as she knew she had to follow orders.

María Ángeles ordered a small hatbox from her dressmaker in which to put the Mellerio Diadem which Isabel II had made in Paris by the eponymous jeweller in 1868 for the wedding of her elder daughter to Neapolitan Count Girgenti. The diadem was of diamonds mounted in platinum, 45 mm high, simulating sea shells with seven large pearls in the form of a pear attached and twelve important diamonds which were hung from above in an original rococo design. Matching the diadem was a fantastic collar of pearls, later dismantled by Alfonso XIII.

On receiving the hatbox, María Ángeles bought truffles from the Patisserie Prat in Calle Arenal. She put the diadem and the collar at the bottom of the box and on top one or two layers of chocolates separated by golden paper. The *Infanta* Isabel's other diadem, of a floral design in emeralds and diamonds, was concealed by sewing it into a hat, which was at first to be worn by Margot Bertrán de Lis but as she was so nervous, María Ángeles decided to cover it with another, much simpler hat, that belonged to the infanta and add more tulle, and put in a handbag.

Sunday was quiet, and late in the afternoon, a Red Cross ambulance collected Isabel from the interior patio of the house. Bee, accompanied by the nurse Ángeles Santos and by Maria Cuevas, went in the ambulance. They were followed in another car by Prince Ataúlfo, next to María Ángeles Tornos, and Margot Bertrán de Lis, who cried incessantly at having been separated from her sister. They took small items of luggage and went to El Escorial and were never searched.

Coello de Portugal, and another functionary, went directly to the station with the baggage. On arriving at the Real Sitio, two riflemen boarded the wagon put aside for the nurse and asked Coello how much money the *infanta* carried. 'Sufficient to live,' replied the secretary. María Ángeles, who was on the platform, asked Ataúlfo to get on the train and told his mother to lean out of the window, as she was trying to accommodate the *Infanta* Isabel who felt exhausted. The train was about to leave when Bee appeared with a smile. María Ángeles curtsied without thinking, and as she was very tall, the hatbox wrapped in paper from the Patisserie Prat landed in the hands of the princess. She continued smiling while her lady's maid said to her, 'These are the truffles that you like so much!' Quickly Ataúlfo grabbed the heavy hatbox and exclaimed 'Oh great!' They told me this little anecdote many times.

By morning, they were in Hendaya where the *Infante* Don Fernando of Bavaria and his wife, the duchess of Talavera, were waiting for them, and helped them transfer the invalid to the French train. They were still 800 km from Paris, and it was Bee's forty-seventh birthday. Isabel had not forgotten. With tear-filled eyes, she gave Bee a jewel because the memory of the Bourbons was still alive within her. None of the royal family was waiting for them at the station and the *Infanta* Isabel Francisca made her last trip around Paris in a taxi. They arrived at the pension Villa Saint-Michel at 17, Rue de l'Àssomption, Auteuil, run by Mother Dolores Lóriga, who was Spanish, and where the *Infanta* Eulalia occupied a room which went out onto the garden and a bedroom with a bathroom. *Infanta* Isabel had more servants as she had a lady's maid. The *infantes* of Orleans stayed temporarily at the villa, as Bee was rather pessimistic about the invalid's state.

The king had gone to London with *Infante* Don Juan to try and secure his admittance to the naval college. Queen Victoria Eugenia appeared next day with her four sons. The invalid had been tired by the visit, although she maintained some lucidity and seemed to have recognised them. The following day, she felt fatigued and was growing worse, and on 23 April, her heart was slowly stopping. They called for Father Julián, a Spanish missionary, who gave her the last rites. Her sister, Eulalia, had already read the prayers for the dying. At 3 p.m., Isabel Francisca of Borbón, who had twice been princess of Asturias, died in Paris. Far from her fatherland and her king, she had only survived leaving Spain by five days.

Ali immediately telegraphed King Alfonso at Claridge's Hotel, London, informing him of the death of his aunt and godmother. Deeply moved, the king asked him to 'look after everything and represent [him] at the burial and the funeral'. The news spread rapidly around Paris and numerous Spaniards came to pray before her remains at the Villa St-Michel, where she was dressed in a Franciscan habit. On 25 April, an entourage of seven automobiles took her coffin to the cemetery of Père Lachaise. Later her remains were transferred to the cemetery of Montmartre until May 1991 when they were interred in the parish church at La Granja de San Ildefonso in front of the tombs of Philip V and Elisabeth Farnese, the first Spanish Borbóns.

According to the *Infanta* Eulalia:

Ali and Bee are in the apartment of the Marquis of Villavieja, 240 Rue de Rivoli, and the Marquis has gone to his brother's house in Avenue Victor Hugo. My grandchildren (Álvaro and Alonso) are coming for a few days at Pentecost. The two 'fiancés' went to Fontainebleau to spend the holidays with the little princesses.

Nobody in the family has made plans for the summer although I will go for a few weeks to Knokke in Belgium to breathe the North Sea air before my annual visit to Paz in Nymphenburg.

I cannot get used to the idea of not being able to cross the frontier because it does not seem credible that 'those who signify nothing in politics' are, as Spanish citizens, stopped from going to our fatherland. It has to be an *error in comprehension.*

Apart from being received with honour in Paris by the French and Spanish aristocracy, the queen and the *infantas* went riding and playing tennis at Fontainebleau. The erstwhile sovereign, who did not like the countryside, was always in Paris where he had a suite at the Hotel Meurice, giving rise to certain encounters with ladies that greatly concerned the queen, who still hoped for a reconciliation.

The death of *Infanta* Isabel helped the king, as he was heir of his godmother, who took her jewels from Spain. Apart from the Mellerio Diadem, they did not take long to disappear. Alfonso XIII reputedly had more than 41,000,000 pesetas, in addition to other assets confiscated by the republic. Despite this, he did not agree to the wedding of the *Infanta* Beatriz with Álvaro. The king did not want his daughter to marry without a dowry and said that, for the moment, he could not give a *centime*. Ali and Bee made him see that they would happily accept Beatriz with nothing, that they had never spoken of money, and that he could give whatever he wanted when he could, but to no avail. Eulalia had 'comported herself splendidly', offering to sell her jewels to provide dowries for her two future granddaughters.

Ali was particularly preoccupied with his estates in Andalusia as his father had recently died and some were not in his name. He summoned his administrator, García, to Paris:

> You do not know how grateful I am to you, my friend Delgado, for your moral support and advice. García has an unbreakable faith in your knowledge and good sense and for this reason I will be bothering you should there be any doubt. Do not take it badly as it is the *Infanta* and I who are at fault.
>
> I continue being one of those millions of decorative men of little use who are called 'without work'.
>
> It is not what I want. On the contrary, I continue looking for work and I hope to find it even if it is in Patagonia.

Suddenly Ali became sentimental, writing that nobody could imagine how much he and his family missed the good times they spent in Sanlúcar, 'and how we pray to God that there comes a day when we can return and be among those who have shown us so much love.'

The *infantes* stayed in Zurich, in their sons' house near the university. Bee, who was used to castles and palaces, found it quite small, but the princes were happy as they were well liked and had many friends. Suddenly the ex-king of Spain decided to fix a date in the spring for Beatriz's wedding. Álvaro, who was very independent, was annoyed to be treated thus; the date, the 25th, was the day before his exams. He went to Rome and asked to meet Alfonso XIII, who said: 'I have decided on the date of your wedding'. Álvaro asked how could he do so without telling him.

'Because I am the King.'

'If you do not take account of me, I break the engagement,' was Álvaro's retort. The monarch seemingly did not take him seriously. As they were inseparable, Álvaro told Alonso about his visit to the king and all that was said. Alonso felt his brother was right and as he had no wish to lose his liberty too, and although they still loved their fiancées, it was more as sisters. Alonso, like his older brother, voiced his discontent, and the enchanting, pretty princesses were left alone, 'all dressed up and without fiancés' thanks to their father.

16

Forced Exile

Ali, now forty-seven years old, found himself retired and unemployed. Too old to test new aircraft, the commercial companies did not accept older pilots, he tried to remain positive in front of his sons but Bee was worried.

A Christmas card from Henry Ford and his family, whom they had known in Detroit, changed his luck. Ali had always had the highest admiration for Ford as a person and dedicated worker, so he sent a telegram thanking him for his card and added that he would like to be part of his workforce; any job would suit. He did not have to wait long for a reply as Ford asked him to start work immediately at his factory at Asnières, on the outskirts of Paris. With the name of Mr Orleans, modest as ever, Ali took a position as a 'cleaning man' for which he received 6Fr 50c an hour. His first job was hosing down the tarpaulins that covered the tractors kept in the open air until they were sold. As he carried out his work conscientiously, he was later given various jobs until he became a company salesman:

> I went all over France when travelling salesman were considered a scourge. I never imagined how horrible life is until I was appointed a salesman in the provinces! This is the lowest form of sales and especially if you are selling trucks. I passed from selling tractors, then trucks and finally the aristocrat of sales—the sale of automobiles—but even so I continued having bad spells.
>
> Once a colleague and I were ordered to go to Lyons, France's second city at the time. As Ford had excess stocks from previous years, we were to sell these older models at twenty per cent discount to prepare for the selling of more modern models. My friend chose the even numbers of a

certain street and I the odd numbers. You go from one house to the next and in the first place the servants are disagreeable, stopping you from talking to or bothering their masters, so you turn about and try to speak to someone else, even the cook, and this goes on day after day. In the end you're tired and very down.

The company management soon recognised Ali's linguistic skills. His English and French were perfect, he could do comical accents, and his German and Spanish were extraordinary. According to his granddaughter, Beatrice, his Italian was fluent, and 'he could be very funny when he played the part of a sailor or a peasant from these countries'. One day they asked him to accompany a Mr Smith in Paris. They spent the day together and he left him at his hotel, unaware that he was dealing with the managing director of Ford in Dagenham, England. A little later, Ali was transferred to an important position in England where he got to know Sir Percival Perry, who called him to his office to tell him how pleased the firm was with his work. He would no longer have to clock in, he could lunch with management and come to Perry's office when he thought it appropriate. During those four years, Ali, who neither smoked nor drank, saved a few pounds (two an hour) to go flying. His daily expenses were small. He only bought newspapers that he read avidly as he was always looking for news of Spain.

Bee settled down in her new home and decided to have open house during term time for her sons' friends, who came and went as they wished. Among these friends were two very likeable and generous Brazilian boys, who loved to be with the princes of Orleans, despite having everything that money could buy: magnificent cars, beautiful girls, travel, and expensive restaurants. Joaquim (Baby) and Alfredo Monteiro de Carvalho, from Rio de Janeiro, were missing their family, and deeply grateful to Bee for welcoming them into her home. They wanted her to visit Brazil, which she did twenty years later in 1953, on what would be her last transatlantic trip. Another frequent visitor was Robert Sulzer, son of a Swiss arms manufacturer who was good fun, polite, and rich. As a native of the country, he helped them greatly with the country's bureaucracy and showed them the cheapest places to go skiing.

Other friends, with a mutual love of music, included the brothers Paolo and Gerardo Parodi-Delfino, who were fluent in German, English, and French. In the long Swiss winter evenings, Bee played the piano with Gerardo. She enjoyed hearing him sing the *lieder* of her childhood. The brothers played harmonica and sang yodels. Ataúlfo never had formal lessons on the piano, but had such a good ear that he could play any song that was popular. Bee supplied snacks, liked making them various dishes and sometimes she would run the kitchen herself when trying out a new recipe.

Sometimes Paolo and Gerardo's sisters, Marina ('Mimosa') and Elena Parodi-Delfino, who were studying at the university, also came to these soirées. One day, Gerardo invited his friend Álvaro to come and spend a few days with him in Rome. They went via Florence where they met Gerardo's other sister, Carla, in the Piazzale Michelangelo, and she drove them to Rome. Twenty years old, very pretty with an independent and cheerful character, and a good sportswoman, she made a great impression on Álvaro. Having finished her studies at university, she was on a three-year nursing course at the San Giuseppe Centre on the Via Trionfale. With three female friends, she planned to open a clinic for treating the minor ailments of the poor.

During the journey, they talked of winter sports, and of going to large resorts and expensive hotels to ski. Álvaro told them that that winter they had thought of going to Mürren, a small town in the district of Interlaken, in the Canton of Bern, at 1,600 metres altitude, well connected with Lauterbrunnen with a station and funicular. Little known and unspoilt, it had excellent sporting facilities. Despite the bad road between Florence and Rome, the journey flew by. On arriving at Rome, they headed for the zoological gardens as the Parodi-Delfino home was nearby. Dona Beatriz de Orléans-Borbón y Parodi-Delfino of Orleans y Borbón described the house to me:

> It was an old convent with an adjoining pretty villa from the 1700s, and which my grandfather Leopoldo had bought from some nuns. The nuns remained in a house whose orchard adjoined our garden: all that needed to be done was to build a wall to screen it from the top of the villa. We enjoyed an Italian garden, a tennis court and a stable with eight beautiful stalls, and an ample garage with cars.

Once settled into their rooms, the boys and Carla were served dinner, by two servants in tails! Then it was time to get to know the rest of the family. Álvaro immediately got on well with Leopoldo, his friends' beloved father. The Parodi-Delfino family belonged to the upper middle class of Milan and Genoa and had founded several businesses. There were six siblings who obtained engineering degrees at the Polytechnic Institute in Zurich. The third brother, Leopoldo, stood out among the brothers for his care for those who worked in his factories. He founded chemical companies, and Marsala wines in Sicily. In association with Bombrini of Genoa, he created BPD (Bombrini-Parodi-Delfino) in the town of Colleferro, 100 kilometres south of Rome. He also built houses for employees and workers, a church, community centres, schools and sports grounds—this grew into a small town with its own railway line in the 1920s.

The industries of the North of Italy, such as Agnelli's Fiat factory, began to do the same thing. My grandfather travelled constantly to Germany to keep up to date with the latest advances, and he brought German technicians with him to train the Italians. Besides Italian, my Uncle Leopold also spoke French, English and German and wanted his five children to speak the four languages.

My Grandfather got to know my grandmother Lucia (Lucy) Henny (who was born in Batavia), when she had a puncture, at the side of a road in Switzerland. In those times, the beginning of the 20th century, it was difficult to find anyone who knew how to change a wheel. Leopoldo, who was passing by, did not hesitate to help and left the car perfectly shod.

Though Lucia was fifteen years younger than Leopoldo, and of a different faith, they enjoyed a happy marriage and had five children. Their three eldest were very close.

At the end of 1931, the three Orleans brothers headed to Mürren, to enjoy the British Ski Club, run by Mr Arnold Lunn. They immediately passed the Club Test and in January 1932 were chosen as part of the slalom team. Ali and Bee followed them to Mürren so they could keep an eye on their boys, and get to know Mr Lunn who had ambitions to turn the mountain resort into a famous place for international competitions. They both enjoyed the place with its breathtaking view of the Jungfrau and modern installations. Bee wrote to Lunn (23 February 1932):

Many thanks for your letter which I should have answered some time ago, but I have had a series of terrible migraines and all my family was skiing at Engelberg, so I have had to wait to dictate this letter to Ali.

We are very grateful and the boys are delighted because you have given Álvaro and Alfonso the Golden Ks [a much-coveted award made to gifted skiers at the Kandahar Ski Club, see below] but I wish to point out the following:

Álvaro did very well in the Parsenn and Grindelwald races. Alonso fell in the Parsenn Derby and hurt his knee in such a way that he could not finish the Grindelwald race. Ataúlfo did very well in the Parsenn Dienst and won a bronze medal.

We all consider that Álvaro is completely qualified for the Golden K and he will write to thank you. Alonso is able to gain the Golden K but, because he fell, he is tormented by thinking of getting it and we leave it to you to decide when he should do it. Ataúlfo is rapidly getting better and we think that he will soon be able to get the Golden K if he continues progressing as he has until now.

I think that I have given you my opinion on the book about King Alfonso and its author. It has been written to obtain money, a thing which is pardonable in these so very hard times, but it has no historic or literary value, nor is it accurate in its details.

We are delighted with the prospect of your visit to St Anton. If you do not go there, perhaps you can visit us in this little house where we will try if possible to make you comfortable.

My husband is very pleased that you want his photograph and he will send you one and hopes that it does not matter if he is in uniform; but he has no other.

Arnold Lunn, son of Sir Henry, was a journalist, a famous alpinist and a great ski instructor. He was married to Lady Mabel, a sister of Earl Iddesleigh, also a friend of Bee. In 1933, a year after meeting the princes, Arnold converted to Catholicism, and Bee asked to be his godmother. When talking of Arnold, she used to say that he had such persuasive ability that he could sway even the most reluctant. She confided in a letter to Arnold that she was worried that her three sons, faced with their quarterly exams, were forgetting their religious obligations, and asked him to ensure that they went to confession and communion: 'They have promised to do so but I will be completely sure that they will go if you get them to, as they always do what you say'. He soon became their mentor and best friend, as well as a great admirer of Bee. Bee was often alone while Ali worked at Ford, and Arnold tried to be a father figure. In 1932, the three Orleans boys, as a group, carried off the Golden K in skiing events, proving they were capable of everything in the sport, 'and more courageously than many'.

Years later, Álvaro remembered that, during those years he 'did not have the money for proper clothing' for skiing. All three were given the full equipment to participate in races and a photograph was taken, still in the Club House at Mürren, inscribed: 'The white trousers were donated by courtesy of the Duke of Aosta, who took exceptional care that his skiing relations did not wear grey flannel rags like sacks'. Amedeo of Savoy, duke of Aosta, was their second cousin. He had just married Princess Anne of Orleans, and the duke and duchess of Aosta were very popular in Italy. Both were grandchildren of the *Infanta* Isabel, elder daughter of the duke and duchess of Montpensier and thus cousins of Ali's family. Amedeo was an athlete and he loved seeing the trio excel at skiing.

Despite difficulties caused by Madrid republicans, Álvaro and Alonso were allowed to represent Spain in the FIS (International Ski Federation) meetings at St Moritz in 1934 and Mürren in 1935, and won the first prize at the Racing Club. In 1933, Álvaro finished third, at the Centre of International Studies at St Moritz. Their most memorable competition was in the Parsenn Dienst in 1933, one of the most prestigious events in the racing calendar and one of the longest. It was 11 km (7 miles) long and at 24 degrees, almost vertical; 6.505 feet high. The princes took part as a team. Twelve teams of three skiers from all the Alpine countries entered the competition. The Orleans brothers entered for the first time as members of the Kandahar Ski Club, an exclusive organisation for skiing set up in Mürren, in Switzerland, where the three Orleans boys often went.

Álvaro modestly recorded that they were lucky because, except for the high-ranking professional team Fraser-Prager-Fopp, all the others had at least one member injured, so the Kandahar Team came second. Yet they were too honourable to ask about the times as the results had already been given: 'Ataúlfo had to be very courageous during the descent, as it was so long, his eyes froze on contact with his glasses. However, he won the junior classification which was a great achievement'. Lunn said he thought it was the only time a family had produced a trio in a skiing competition, adding that the achievement was not luck but 'because of their courage and determination'.

Álvaro continued to ski until his eighties, and spent part of each winter in Gstaad and Megève. He never forgot Mürren, and one day he went to the club house he had helped to build before the war in Spain. In a letter (14 February 1933), he thanked Mr Lunn, for letting them join the Alpine Club which was reserved for British subjects or those educated in Great Britain. Their miserable Winchester days had counted for something at least. Five days after Team Orleans covered itself in glory, Bee wrote to Mr Lunn (9 March 1933) on hearing of his conversion to Catholicism:

We have returned to Zurich. Ali has now flown to London. Pardon me for not having replied to your letter before but we were travelling. First let me congratulate you on having been 'received'.

I did not understand exactly what you were telling me in your P.S. until a friend's cook read the great news in a Swiss R.C. newspaper.

Very often great events are reported thus through humble means. Please pardon me. I have joked with you about it very often, but believe me I am delighted for you and I hope that you will be happy, but not a bigot.

I have received all sorts of exciting information about the cruise and now I have begun to believe that it will happen. When do you and Lady Mabel embark? I will meet you somewhere near the end of the trip, preferably Milan. Please let me know when you go to Venice. About

Peter [the Lunns' only son], I have tried to find out but I have not found out anything. It would be best if he comes to us and looks around on his own. He could be here with us until the 1st October, when we leave the house. Perhaps we could even remain until the 1st November and we would be delighted to have him until then. We have lots of space and he could come and go without bothering anyone. It could be a great saving for him in the beginning (as now I do not allow my servants to receive tips).

A few weeks after his conversion to the Catholic faith, Bee told Lunn she felt rather contrite as she had done nothing but 'tease' him. She felt 'like an ordinary person who has interfered between a couple on their honeymoon and who insists in demonstrating that the bride has a wart on her chin. So, wishing to prove the sincerity of my contrition I am going to sculpt an Annunciation for you.'

In the summer of 1933, Mabel and Arnold Lunn and Ali and Bee cruised around the Greek Islands, which they always fondly remembered. Greece was then a republic, but the ship's crew showed Bee as much deference as did the tourists. Instinctively Bee came and went first in everything. One day in Sparta, she noticed this and, turning towards Arnold, commented on how pleasant they were towards her. 'It seems to be some kind of favouritism!' Arnold, who was very sincere, replied, 'Yes, ma'am. It seems to be and it is.' After that, she changed her conduct in order not to come first all the time.

Bee felt a true affection for Arnold's son, Peter, seeing him as 'a good person for this house because he fits in with the ways of the mother and sons. He speaks non-stop of skiing with the boys and is a great critic, talking books with me as well as dissenting on religion'.

In the spring of 1933, the prince of Asturias, semi-forgotten in a sanatorium at Leysin near Lausanne, informed his parents he was in love with a young Cuban lady, Edelmira Sampredo y Robato, slightly older than him, and living in the same convalescent home. To obtain the permission to marry that he wanted, they obliged him to renounce his rights to the throne of Spain, citing his incapacity and his wish for a morganatic marriage. He signed the renunciation of his rights on 11 June 1933. Ten days later, the wedding was celebrated in the church at Ouchy in the presence of Queen Victoria Eugenia and his sisters, *Infantas* Beatriz and Cristina. Cristina wrote:

In 1934, our brother Alfonso had come to know some girls in Switzerland, where he had been in a sanatorium getting better. He said that he was to marry. He had to renounce his rights as Prince of Asturias.

And immediately Jaime, who understood the situation clearly, also renounced his rights, and then, as is natural, Juan had to give up his career in the Navy and come to study at Leuven.

Alfonso's first wife, Edelmira, was a very good person and always comported herself very well. As we now know, Alfonso had had a knock or something, and was paralysed from the waist down and needed a male nurse to bathe him and everything. The poor man was too ashamed to tell her everything before and 'la Puchunga', as we called her, found herself in this unenviable situation. For this reason, the marriage did not last. But poor Edelmira was always very loving, When she was able to come to Paris, we saw her, and later—much later—when she heard that Mama was so ill, and she took much interest in her. So much so that when Mama died, we sent a her a ring as a memento.

For Ena and Bee, so tied to family tradition, Alfonso's wedding was a real trauma. Bee went to visit him in Lausanne on repeated occasions but later, on seeing him getting better, spaced out her visits more. Ena found it easier than Bee to put the past behind her, Bee 'always had to face the facts'.

In November, Bee wrote to Lunn that she was sorry not to be able to attend the Kandahar Ski Club dinner, as she could not leave Zurich:

> I would have liked our affairs to work out better and to be able to have the boys in the new house to spend all the month of December there before leaving for England, but I see that I will not be able to do it. When I was planning this I was still under the influence of Greece. Since then, the storms of Helvetia and the honest desires of the descendants of William Tell have reduced my vitality and limited me to being an elderly lady who fights with her cook and scolds her maid for not cleaning the rooms properly. However, I hope that Ali will be able to enjoy the food.

In different letters, Bee commented that Henry Ford was 'a tough manager and my husband is a great worker without a duro (five cents) and I see him very little these days.'

Among the crowned heads who helped the *infantes* after leaving Spain were King Alexander of Yugoslavia and his wife, Marie (daughter of Missy), who invited them to spend the summer in Milocer. In 1934, they shut up the house which pleased Bee as she could take her servants, Alice and Carmelo, to Yugoslavia with them, as maid, chauffeur and valet. Yet tragedy was about to strike.

Alfonso XIII spent his annual holiday at the Austrian town of Pörtschach, where he was accompanied by his children, Beatriz, Cristina, and Gonzalo, who was studying at Leuven, having just completed his agricultural engineering course. Lake Wörth nearby was perfect for excursions by car, and one day Beatriz asked Gonzalo to accompany her in the king's Porsche, which she drove. Swerving to avoid a cyclist, they hit a crash barrier. With the cyclist's help, Baron Newman managed to get the Porsche free and they returned home in the car. That night, Gonzalo, who had seemed uninjured, complained of a blow in the stomach and cried out in pain. They called the local doctor, who apparently did not know what had happened but suggested it could be an internal haemorrhage. Gonzalo was a haemophiliac. They telephoned Queen Ena but she arrived too late. He died the following morning, 13 August 1934. The news caused deep sorrow among all social classes in Spain as Gonzalo had been much admired during his short life and Beatriz was grief-stricken.

In November, George, duke of Kent, married Princess Marina of Greece. Ali and Bee attended the wedding in London, accompanied by Ataúlfo. Ducky and Kirill were also there as he was the uncle of Marina, and Kira was one of the bridesmaids. Their son, Vladimir, was responsible for holding the crowns during the Orthodox ceremony. Bee noted her sister's happiness on returning to Windsor and Buckingham Palace after so long away from court. She was shown particular affection by King George V, perhaps as the deaths of the tsar and his family had been perpetually on his conscience. Now old and ailing, he wanted to help his unfortunate cousins who had neither country, nor money to live on, and lived modestly in France.

The marriage of Kirill and Ducky had been crumbling since her discovery that he had been unfaithful to her for some years. She had attended the wedding in Coburg of Princess Sibylla to Crown Prince Gustav Adolf of Sweden, on 20 October 1932, without her husband. Significantly, Kirill had attended the funeral of the dowager Russian empress who died in Denmark in 1928, on his own. When Vladimir came of age on 30 August 1933, a party was held at their home in Normandy at which Grand Duke Dmitri Pavlovich gave a banquet.

After the wedding, Ali and Bee spent a few days as guests of Baron Howard de Walden and his wife, Lady Margarita, at Seaford House, in Belgrave Square. At this time, the de Walden's third daughter, Pip, who had just 'come out', began to pay attention to Ataúlfo, or 'Touffles' as he was known to the family. She no longer saw him as the boy with whom she had played at Brownsea Island, but as a charming young man. Pip's girl cousins remembered him as 'not good-looking', with a round face and chubby cheeks, but the women liked him for his sweet manners, amusing conversation, and talents as a pianist and dancer.

The next family event was the wedding of *Infanta* Beatriz, on 14 January 1935, to a Roman aristocrat, Alessandro Torlonia, the 5th prince di Civitella-Cesi. Over 4,000 Spaniards arrived in Rome bringing presents for the bride, including orange blossom for her bouquet. Queen Ena did not attend the ceremony as she was in England, having bought a house in London. Yet it was a joy for Álvaro to see his 'former fiancée' and cousin, Beatriz, happily married.

That year, Álvaro finished his engineering studies with very good results. At twenty-three years old, he was thinking of seeking work in England. However, he did not want to leave Zurich where he was friends with Gerardo Parodi-Delfino, and he was in love with Gerardo's older sister, Carla, a very accomplished young woman and great sportswoman, whom he had seen skiing at Sestriere, near Turin. She was also a fine horse-rider and had won prizes for show jumping. Like her father, she loved horses and went foxhunting twice a week.

The Parodi-Delfino family bought a 12-metre yacht in England and Carla and her father went to collect it. They sailed through the Bay of Biscay, down the coast of Portugal, stopped off at Gibraltar and Mallorca, and arrived at the port of Anzio, south of Rome. Álvaro joined them and they visited the Brijuni Islands, in the Adriatic Sea. The family often spent summer there staying at Tegetthoff castle, now a hotel. It was an idyllic life, as on the island it was only possible to travel by horse or bicycle, cars being prohibited. The stay on the island left Álvaro with warm happy memories as he headed to his destiny in England.

Álvaro often told his children how hard it was to find cheap lodgings in England, how he sometimes had to share a room, if not the bed, and had to work the same hours as the labourers. Life in England was much more expensive than in Switzerland. Ali was having the same issues. He wrote to Bee to tell her that the long stay in the Grosvenor Hotel, near Victoria Station, had been too expensive for his modest income, now that matters in Spain had deteriorated. Bee tried to find a cheaper home for herself at the same time as selling-off family mementos. Ali wrote to her:

When I am with you, seeing you, it is always for such short time, and I am not brave enough to tell you about these sordid and painful matters of money. You tell me that all day seems like a nightmare; the same happens to me when writing. Our problem is that we have to live two lives and we only have time for one. On top of everything, with all the encumbrances (family), the problems of princes, and with no servants to help us with the work, we have our own daily problems of life.

Bee decided to move to leave their Zurich home at Zollikerstrasse 93 to go to England. She did not complain to her husband, but in a letter to Arnold, 'her spiritual godson', she gave free rein to her unhappiness:

It is sad to leave our house here and I feel old and alone because all the birds have now flown. Forgive these scribbles; I am overwhelmed by work. I am writing these days with cramp in my hand (stupid comment, as if in the foot it would not cause annoyance). Álvaro and Alonso have arrived safely at Sestriere, I do not think that they have had much luck because they say that there are many foreigners who do not know how to drive.

Paolo, Carla, and Gerardo were waiting at Sestrière for Álvaro and Alonso. All five enjoyed magnificent Christmas holidays there, but for one of them it would be their last. Bee was very apprehensive about the coming year of 1936, which would be disastrous for her. Meanwhile, Ali wrote to her: 'I can see light again. I think 1936, as I have said to you before, will be a year of great events'. He finished: 'From the bottom of my heart, I give thanks, to God, because in his wisdom he has given me such a woman, such a friend, such a mother for my sons, and such a lover for me'.

Ducky was thinking of spending Christmas with her daughter, Maria, in Amorbach as she was expecting a baby. Kirill and Vladimir went to Paris and the latter enrolled at university, but on 8 December, he went down with whooping cough. Ducky, alarmed, had a chill but did not want to postpone her journey. She left St Briac on 19 December to see Vladimir, then went to visit Maria who gave birth to a girl they called Mechtilde. Mother and daughter were together in the Palace of Amorbach when they learned of the illness and death of King George V on 20 January 1936.

In Romania, Missy remembered how she and George had been childhood sweethearts. Ducky only recalled how affectionate he had been to her a year ago at the Kent wedding. Bee could not forget how good he had been towards her, offering her King's Cottage in Kew while the Spanish republic was settling down, so she would not have to look for a house. She wrote to Gen. Franco, who as sub-secretary of war presided over the Spanish commission, assuring him she would be careful: 'you will remember that when you attended the burial of King George and I had the pleasure of seeing you in London, I did not make a single gesture nor to say a word that could have caused you the slightest discomfort in front of the Spanish Delegation'.

Despite the sadness of the occasion, there were happy days for the couple who settled into King's Cottage turning it into home. Yet Bee was preoccupied with her sister's health.

'Poor Ducky!' exclaimed Ali, 'What a tragic life! Kirill and Kira seem unable to help her. I am in complete agreement with you about how difficult it is for them to help her, or for anyone who wants to do so, as she unleashes her anger against all.' Her chill did not improve and her doctors said she had no will to live. In February, a stroke left her paralysed on one side and unable to speak coherently. Kira went to look after her and when the doctors said she was getting worse, Kirill and Vladimir went to her side, as did her three sisters who sat by her bed in turns. 'She knew that we were there and the first day gave a murmur of gratitude for each of us,' Bee wrote: 'At the head of the bed my sister entrusted me to attend and care for Vladimir like a son, and I promised to do so. While we took turns sitting with her and holding her hand, Kirill came near and she shuddered when he touched her, so he was left exiled by the door jam, not daring to enter her room'. Early on 1 March her pulse began to fail and Missy, Sandra, and Bee began the long vigil, 'praying to God to take her rather than let her suffer prolonged agony.' Fifteen minutes after midnight, she passed away. 'She brought tragedy with her,' wrote Queen Marie of Romania: 'her eyes were always tragic, even as a girl. We loved her very much, there was something very powerful in her. She was our conscience'. On 5 March, she was laid in the Glockenberg mausoleum at Coburg, and the funeral was held next day in rain and snow.

Elections in Spain on 16 February 1936 brought to power the Popular Front, formed by socialists, republicans, communists, anarchists, and the Catalan and Basque separatists. Manuel Azaña became president and the divided right had to abandon power. The government of the Popular Front began an orgy of revolution. The *infantes* of Orleans were horrified, and a worried Ali asked his administrator, César Sáenz de Santa María, a special favour: 'To burn all the daily records which were kept in Sanlúcar'.

Since childhood, Ali had written a daily record of what he saw and heard and made an impression on him. In the circle in which he lived in Spain his experiences could generate enormous interest, as he wrote with great realism. His cousin, Alfonso XIII, was very annoyed when he saw Ali absenting himself for a few moments to add to his notes, his disappearances making him so angry that he called the news that Ali wrote in his diary 'Ali's *cabronadas*' ('infamous consensual acts against one's own honour'). They were surely accurate commentaries on what happened at court.

During the Republic, Ali could have made a fortune by publishing his diary instead of working at Fords, and Bee would not have had to sell her valuable mementos. But he remained faithful to the monarchy and, fearful of the contents of his notebooks, wanted them burnt. Years later, María Ángeles Tornos said that they went to Sanlúcar and in a corner of the palace, the *auto de fé* began. As the diaries were written in notebooks with oil-cloth covers made specially for Ali, it took several days to destroy them all.

In mid-June, the Sáenz de Santa María family met Ali and Bee in France and accompanied them to Cap Ferrat, where they were guests, as they had been the previous year, of the Monteiro de Carvalho family in their Villa 'les Bugas'.

In February 1936, a leftist front, a coalition, the 'Frente Popular', had won the general elections, causing alarm among the right political parties and the wealthy classes. Confrontation between radicals from the left and the right increased during the next few months, generating great unrest among the population. A *coup d'etat* by the generals aimed against the Republic's new government was expected at any time. The Republic was threatened from all sides, and some generals such as Franco, Mola, and Varela were conspiring in readiness for an assault on the government. The upper classes and some wealthy people such as Juan March were financing the rebel generals behind the back of the legal government. In July 1936, the right-wing politician José Calvo Sotelo was assassinated in Madrid, a catalyst for the generals to proceed with their *coup* against the Republic on 17 July. That afternoon, the garrison of Melilla-occupied Madrid, and next day the army in Africa received Gen. Franco, who had come from the Canaries. Queipo de Llano took control of Seville, and Gen. Varela took control of Cádiz while Emilio Mola, helped by the Requetes (the Carlist Red Berets), applied himself to the conquest of Madrid where the Falangist movement had failed. Ali immediately returned from Bucharest to London, to be with his wife, and wanted to enter Spain with their sons. Meanwhile Alfonso XIII was on summer holiday in Czechoslovakia, while Ena was living at Fontainebleau. Varela was jailed on 17 June in the Castle of Santa Bárbera but liberated the following day by Gen. López Pinto and took command, pacifying the Provinces of Cádiz and Seville. Later he liberated the Alcázar of Toledo.

Ali's fears about his diary were justified as Sanlúcar was soon in Nationalist hands, Castillejo and the mansion at Calle Quintana were in the Red Zone. Ali headed for Spain, entering Navarre through the customs post at Dancharinea on 2 August 1936, in Memel Mitjans's car. In Pamplona, they told him that Gen. Mola was in Burgos, so he passed through Vitoria and arrived there, going to the captain-general to offer his services:

One can imagine the joy with which I travelled to Pamplona and Vitoria, finding myself once again in Spain and each moment nearer the front. One may also understand the sadness with which I made the return journey after the Chief of Mola's High Command (Commander of the High Command, Don Hilario Etayo Esparza) told me that, 'not wishing to give a Monarchist character to the Movement' he begged me to return over the frontier immediately. Nor did he want to accept the services of my sons.

Before returning, he wrote to Mola notifying him of what had happened, and again from the Grosvenor Hotel, London, SW1 (3 August):

I wrote you two letters in order to ask you not to blame Memel Mitjans nor put any difficulties in his way for having taken me to Burgos in his car last Sunday. I do not doubt that you will be in agreement that the least every courtier can do is to present himself to defend his fatherland when it is in danger and, as I am also a soldier, it is also a sacred duty.

You know me well enough to know that I never disobey orders and for this reason I left when your Chief of High Command told me that he wanted me to return over the frontier immediately. He promised to give me orders if I, or my sons, could be useful in any way. I am sorry not to be able to see you to embrace you, which I do through this letter.

Ali had an office at the Grosvenor Hotel, to assist students and young people in England to enter Nationalist Spain. The chief general of the Northern Army replied (Burgos, 8 August 1936):

I have received your letter of the 3rd inst., and you can be sure that I have not been annoyed in any way by your friend Mr Mitjans.

I am deeply sorry not to be able at this time to use your valuable services, but I will not hide from you the obstacles that exist in the present circumstances. Anyway, I hope that the difficulties will disappear little by little and I have hope that the day will arrive when you can return to this land.

Our operations go well, although we appear to be stationary. We are waiting for the columns that are coming from the south under Franco. They are already in Badajoz and Mérida and are moving closer to put pressure on, and to enter Madrid. I include a sketch so that you can understand without difficulty, the part that we control.

The days passed without bringing Ali himself permission to enter Spain to serve his Fatherland and on 19 August he wrote to Franco, who was fighting in the south:

I am writing you in case you have not heard that on the 2nd of this month, I presented myself at the Captaincy in Burgos.

I asked to see Mola but I did not manage to do so. I saw your Chief of High Command (Etayo) who was very friendly but said that I should return across the frontier as quickly as possible.

I said to him that I was looking for no more than to fight for Spain, which I could do unnoticed from some aerodrome. There was no way in which I could convince him.

Nor was I able to obtain permission for my sons who are twenty-six, twenty-four and twenty three years old, to come and fight. If they think it would be difficult for me to pass unnoticed, it should be easy for them.

I leave my address so that you can ask me to be of some service, inside or outside of Spain. I see many important people in various countries and I make all the propaganda that I can, but I want you to know that I am always thinking of you and of those fighting under your orders, not only for Spain but also for European civilisation which is menaced by the red wave.

If I can serve in any way, wherever it is, it goes without saying that I am always at your orders.

May God help you and give us victory soon!

Later (27 September), he wrote to a friend from London:

We are living in the hope that we will soon join Franco's army. What joy we had when San Sebastián was taken! (13 September).

I hope that you have had news of your family, as I understand what suffering it is thinking of them. Thanks to God we have no family in the power of the Communists, but we do have people like Señora de Ruata, the Santa Marías, etc., and the brothers and mother of Carmelo who for us are like family.

Besides, one should not forget that they killed many of our near relations in the Russian Revolution. You may imagine the emotion with which we follow the news and with what anger we feel being here without being able to take part in the fight.

We have read with joy in today's newspapers, as you can imagine, that the heroes of the Alcázar have been saved. These boys, and above all the women with them, who refused to surrender, will pass into history as did those at the siege of Saragossa. While people of such courage exist, Spain can be confident of a future as noble and brilliant as in its golden age, when we were the major world power, not only in arms but also culturally. I am told that we will find everything the same as we left it. The affection will perhaps be the same, but we have all changed.

Early in October, Ali learned from García, who was in Sanlúcar, that Gen. Kindelán had been chief of Nationalist Aviation from 1 August and was in Burgos. Ali was relieved as he feared that like his brother (Ultano), he was in Madrid with his family.

With the confidence and friendship between Kindelán and Ali, the latter asked if it was possible to have news of family friends the 'Santa Marias' as 'it would remove a terrible worry. We do not dare to make inquiries through the Embassies, for fear of drawing them to the attention of the Reds. Since they left France for Madrid, in the first days of July, we have had no news of them at all.'

He then explained to his old friend:

I confess that I do not really understand Mola's attitude, as this fight is
not the Monarchy against the Republic, but of order against anarchy
and communism.

My offer did not have, nor does it have today, any party political
significance but the common desire of every descent person to fight for
his Fatherland when it is in danger, and to fulfil as an officer the duty
of putting oneself under the orders of the military chiefs who combat
a poison, brought from abroad, which threatens to destroy the Nation.
I have no greater desire than to serve the Fatherland, with my sons at
the front and my wife caring for the wounded, without any party
preferences.

As a pilot, you already know I would get on well with our 'year' from
Cuatro Vientos.

Franco still did not reply. That autumn, Bee's great preoccupation was with
those who were in the Red Zone and in danger of being detained and of
going to prison. It inspired her to begin her work on prisoner exchanges, a
slow and thankless task that Ena also threw herself into. Both cousins put
their hearts and souls into providing this service for distraught families
and were a great comfort to people though they received little credit.

In Madrid, there were many friends of the *infantes* caught in the
rebellion. Ultano Kindelán, brother of the general, and his two sons were
detained; the *infanta*'s bridesmaid, Doña Belén Ruata, went to Huesca;
the Santa Marías had disappeared; the duke and duchess of Santa Cristina
were in prison; and Luis Rodríguez Pascual, the *infantes*' teacher, had
taken refuge in an embassy. José Antonio, and Miguel Primo de Rivera
and his wife, Margot, his aunt, María, now eighty years old, and his niece,
Carmen, were all prisoners in Alicante. Then there were the brothers
Rafael and Valeriano Weyler, Afriquita Carvajal, the Dávilas. Liberation
was slow as there was no agreement in Salamanca.

A terrible event would change the lives of Prince Álvaro and Carla.
The former had advised his friends Paolo and Gerardo Parodi-Delfino to
become pilots, as aviation was the weapon of the future. They followed
his advice, and one day in October, Paolo was about to go flying when
Gerardo arrived, told him he did not know what had happened to the
engine, and that he was going to test it. Paolo insisted on accompanying
Gerardo. At first all went smoothly, but moments later the aircraft dived
and crashed into the ground. Cardinal Gasparri, driving past in his car,
saw the aircraft fall, and pronounced the words of the 'Last Unction' over
the brothers.

The deaths of both young men were deeply felt in Rome, where the funerals were held in the Church of Santa Teresa. Paolo left a wife, a three-year-old son, and a daughter a few months old, while Gerardo was unmarried. Lucy was disconsolate but found comfort from the words of a Catholic Cardinal, even though she was a Protestant. In her grief, she was consoled by studying Catholic dogma, converting two years later.

Meanwhile, Ali travelled to Finland and on returning to London, wrote to his friend Kindelán:

> You know all about my life intimately and know that I am not driven by personal ambition. My past is proof of this for those who know me less. Today, I have a well-paid position with Ford, which gives me authority throughout its vast organisation in Europe. I say this because there may be people who believe that I wish to return in the hope of regaining a more comfortable life in Spain. All I want is to serve my Fatherland in these critical times, returning abroad if God wills, once victory is achieved and the situation normalised, and my presence is no longer useful. We live in perpetual anguish, thinking of the terrible times our friends are having, and we suffer even more from not being able to take part more actively in the triumph of a Holy cause.
>
> I hope that Franco's reply permits my sons and me, to go to the front soon.

Franco's command needed to prepare for the offensive to conquer Madrid that autumn. While they had the aircraft, it was difficult to find pilots, most of whom were based in Madrid and Barcelona. Álvaro, now twenty-six, had completed his engineering course with honours and held Spanish and English pilot's licences. Alonso, twenty-five, had become a pilot at Cuatro Vientos at only eighteen, and just lacked a year to complete his engineering studies. Both princes entered Spain via Portugal and joined the Movement on 3 November 1936. As he still needed to pass more exams Alonso entered as a gentleman legionnaire at Tablada, Seville, as a second lieutenant being sent first as an observer on Romeo Ro. 37 aircraft.

In Alonso's service record, it was noted that on 18 November 1936, his Romeo aircraft dropped out of formation at the same latitude as Monasterio, and broke up on entering combat, having been shot down. The charred remains of the aircraft were found along with those of this officer, and also of an Italian NCO. According to Álvaro's version, they left Talavera as they had been ordered to escort a Savoia 81 with important passengers. They used the Romeo although it was not the best suited. On arriving at the Sierra there were many clouds, the Savoia went into them and they descended so as not to lose sight of it. At that moment, his brother, who was on his left, bought it. He always knew that he would die if he went up with an NCO.

The aircraft in which Alonso was killed was a Romeo Ro. 37bis, piloted by an Italian sergeant, Aniello Fazzi. After the accident various controversies arose, and some Red radio stations said it had been shot down. Officially they left the airport at Tablada in Seville for Talavera de la Reina. The aircraft crashed into a mountain near Ventas de Culebrín, near Monasterio, in the south of the Province of Badajoz.

Álvaro told Arnold Lunn that he and Alonso went to Spain together. Alonso had a strange feeling about his imminent death during his journey to the Peninsula and did not talk much, but Álvaro knew what he felt. The day he died, he put his watch and his money and other small things in a packet and closed it up very carefully, took off after Álvaro, and for a time they flew together. Álvaro waved to him but he did not respond, instead giving him 'a rare and strange look'. He was not piloting, but observing, in terrible weather, with dense cloud and rain. Alonso's aircraft disappeared in the cloud and moments later crashed against the side of the mountain.

17

Living the War

To Prince Álvaro fell the unhappy duty of sending telegrams with the news of Alonso's death to his mother in London and his father, in Detroit working for Ford. In his sadness, he thought of Carla, who had just gone through this with her dear brothers and was in Rome. Once she was told, Carla immediately left for London to be with Bee.

A telephone bill for the house in Kew showed that on 18 and 19 November, Bee made several phone calls. She then went to stay at the Grosvenor hotel with Carla, where friends came with their condolences. Years later, Carla told her eldest daughter, Geri, that the *infanta*, in her intense grief, could not stop saying that Ataúlfo would take the place of his dead brother in the war. Some friends protested, saying she had fulfilled her duty to the Fatherland, to which she responded sharply that they did not want her to have one son a hero, and the other a deserter.

Whenever she suffered from depression, Bee found it impossible to pick up a pen. She excused herself to Arnold Lunn for not having written before, because of her low spirits: 'I have spent four months without breathing fresh air and I have been far from well all this time. I have become so old lately that you will hardly be able to recognise me'. Although it was a great effort for her to write at the time, she managed to contact her husband's great friend Kindelán and ask him for help:

From the bottom of my heart I thank you for your loving words of comfort in our horrible sorrow. Alonso went with immense happiness to fight for his country and died in flight in combat formation. He wanted to give all his effort for the Holy Cause and it was God's will that he gave his life. I bow before the immense pain of all those who are suffering martyrdom. I pray that God protects and shelters yours and that your son, Alfredo, soon gets better from his serious wounds. On hearing of the death of his brother, my other son, Ataúlfo, does not want to postpone his leaving for Spain and, as he is not yet a pilot, asks to come as a soldier. He will leave as soon as possible. They tell us here that there they lack cars and he will bring one which he will put at the disposal of the authorities.

On hearing of Alonso's death, Arnold Lunn wrote in November:

Because you and yours symbolise for me the model family with your courage, happiness and charm, I feel a sensation of almost physical amputation on thinking that this unity has been overshadowed, but not destroyed, by death.

I feel as if Alonso has been very near, awakening in new places. Because he has died for faith, this faith which seemed so remote when the snows were calling him, to go to Mass, this inexhaustible faith which is hidden in the Spanish soul and moves in the national culture, which Alonso has helped to save.

Álvaro headed straight to London to comfort his mother. Ali had arrived in Quebec on 6 November after a bad crossing, went to Detroit and reached Washington on 14 November so he did not know about Alonso's death until the 19th. He set sail on 2 December aboard the *Queen Mary*, arriving on 7 December at Southampton where Bee was waiting for him, accompanied by the duke and duchess of Kent, Regent Paul of Yugoslavia, and his wife, Olga.

Carla and Álvaro were devastated by Alonso's death and her brothers' fatal crash. Having been in love for some time, they decided to marry. Bee, who felt great affection and gratitude to Carla for being there to support her, helped the young couple. She arranged for Carla to serve as a nurse in the war so they could spend their months as an engaged couple there together, promised her she would arrange everything, and they would stay at the home of some friends, the Pérez Taberneros, whose estate (where Franco had been elected as supreme commander) was near Salamanca Airport and the Matacán airbase.

Ali was less pleased by the imminent wedding of Álvaro and Carla as he had hoped for a real princess for his first-born, but gave his consent on seeing his son so much in love. They also asked for the approval of King Alfonso XIII, who gave it immediately, announcing that if the wedding was to be celebrated in Rome, he and the queen would like to be witnesses.

From the Grosvenor Hotel, Bee replied to Arnold Lunn on the 'Day of the Kings' (Epiphany, 6 January 1937):

> Your lovely letter was a great comfort to me. I do not mean this to sound trite. I want to say to you that your words warmed my heart and I have re-read your letter when I have found my pain unsupportable.
>
> Happy Mürren! We spent the best days of our lives there—a time which will never return! My brother-in-law, Grand Duke Kirill, his daughter, the Grand Duchess Kira, and his young son, the Grand Duke Vladimir, are to go to Edelweiss on the 15th of this month. Can you look after Vladimir? He is also my son, because I promised my sister on her deathbed to look after him. He has a sweet nature and is incredibly trusting. He very much wants to learn to ski, please take him under your wing.
>
> Thank you once again. You helped me in the darkest hour of my life.

Missy invited the whole family to Bucharest to help them through their grief. They spent two weeks with her travelling around the country, returning later to London. On Christmas Eve, they went to dine with Ena and Cristina and attended Midnight Mass. They met up with them again, in complete privacy, to end the tragic year 'sad but united'.

Ali's job was due to take him to Portugal and as Bee was still feeling depressed, he decided to take her with him to see her sons in Spain. They embarked on 7 January 1937 on the steamer *Usaramo*, reaching Lisbon after a bad five-day crossing. The Spanish consul arranged for them to have 'safe-conduct' passes to enter Spain via Badajoz and they arrived in Salamanca two days later, staying at the Kindeláns' home, in the requisitioned Monterrey Palace. On 15 January, Ali was received by Franco and his brother, Nicolás, and they all agreed on propaganda for the war. Álvaro joined his parents, and Ataúlfo arrived later. On 17 January, Bee went to Seville to pray at Alonso's tomb, where a Mass was celebrated. On 20 January, they returned by car to the Hotel Aviz in Lisbon and three days later embarked on the *Almanzora*, arriving in London on the 26th. Bee remained at Kew while her husband inspected Ford factories in Belgium, Holland, and Denmark. The duke and duchess of Kent and Queen Marie of Yugoslavia visited them frequently, and Queen Mary went to tea with them on 11 February.

The matter of prisoner exchanges deeply preoccupied Bee. British embassy staff, based in Valencia with the Republican government, found the Nationalists hard to cooperate with. One thing that annoyed Bee greatly, and made arranging exchanges difficult, was that during the first winter of the war the Nationalists had been ordered to shoot all foreign combatants they captured. In March 1937, during the battle to conquer Guadalajara at Brihuega, 497 Italians fell prisoner and were exchanged for other foreigners from the International Brigades, leading to the cancellation of the order to shoot on 1 April 1937. Bee was very persistent, and often wrote to the military authorities in Salamanca about exchanges or went there personally to see if there was any news. She was very grateful to the Romanian Legation in Madrid which saved so many people, among them the Saenz de Santa Marías who were refugees there, and Missy herself obtained passports for Bee's friends so that 'the administrator of her property in Spain could leave Madrid with his wife', although he 'held a commission as an infantry commander'.

On 14 March, Bee received a telegram from Bucharest saying Queen Marie was ill with suspected leukaemia. She left immediately to join her, they spent two happy weeks together and said a sad farewell two weeks later. Nobody foresaw that they would never see each other again.

In Spain, a date was set for the taking of Bilbao, though as in all wars, things did not work out as planned. On 3 June on a short flight from Vitoria to Burgos, Gen. Mola's aeroplane crashed in bad weather. Ali was very upset by the death of Mola, an old comrade at the military academy, and who he was confident would reintegrate him into the army. He could not understand why he had chosen to fly such a short distance 'when only the height of La Brújula separated the two cities which were joined by a road which he remembered as very flat'.

Ali and Bee decided they must return to Spain where their sons were fighting for the country and where they had so many friends. They arrived in Salamanca on 24 April. Ali went to see the *generalissimo* and his brother, Nicolás, who received him next day, and the Francos invited them to a meal. Bee visited Ávila and went as far as el Cerro de los Ángeles on the Madrid front. On 4 May, they visited San Sebastian and went for lunch to the home of the Rich's, friends from their first stay in London. They had to return Salamanca, because the *generalissimo* wanted to speak to Ali, and two days later they left for Sanlúcar. On 25 May, they were in London where Ena invited them to lunch as she wanted to know if the exchanges were working. The British business secretary, Mr Leche, had been helping Ena and Bee. The diplomat had also dealt with the case of Martina Álvarez de Toledo, duchess of Santa Cristina, who had been a prisoner in the Ventas Prison since October. Ena desperately wanted to save Martina, the youngest of her ladies-in-waiting who was only thirty-six. The poor lady was alone and separated from her four children, who had been sent to San Sebastian, and her husband, who was imprisoned at Alcalá de Henares as he was a captain in the artillery. All Mr Leche could find out was that Martina's fate was uncertain, having been condemned to three years forced labour. Ali and Bee, who had known Martina as a girl, were also upset about her fate.

While in London, the *infantes* also saw Marina and George of Kent. 'All are interested in the news from Spain', Ali wrote. Ena had befriended the family of the British prime minister, Neville Chamberlain, and spoke to them about the situation in Spain. In London, the duke of Alba, who represented the Nationalists, managed to get the prime minister to listen. The queen convinced Chamberlain that without British intervention, the Spanish navy would fall into the hands of the Spanish Reds and they would sell it to Russia.

Faced with silence on the matter of prisoner exchanges, Ena decided to seek help personally from the president of the National Red Cross. She knew Fernando Suárez de Tangil y Angulo, as he had been mayor of Madrid during the dictatorship. After the republic was established, he continued in politics as a deputy for the Monarchists. Gen. Mola appointed him president of the Red Cross, and he enjoyed Franco's trust. She wrote to him from Palazzo Torlonia, Via Bocca de Leone, Rome (4 July 1937):

Despite customarily not involving myself in political questions, I am writing to you today about a humanitarian matter, which is of interest to all Spaniards. I have discovered from confidential English reports that the lives of hundreds of women and children, refugees imprisoned in cities still under the control of the Reds, can be saved. This can be done if the Spanish Red Cross can arrange a free handover, by means of the English representative in Valencia, of some women and children, such as those in Seville, who are not prisoners but have families on the other side.

I know from my work in removing people from the Red Zone, that an exchange of the kind that I propose will have very good results if done as soon as possible.

I know one of the representatives of the British Embassy in Valencia [the British *chargé d'affaires* John Hurleston Leche], and I know that his heart is with us and he is willing to do everything humanly possible; but he is naturally prevented from doing more about this matter because of the few facilities existing to get anyone out just now if it is not by exchanging them.

As a worthy President of the Spanish Red Cross, I know that you will use your influence to do everything possible in regard to this sad matter, on which the fate and lives of so many friends depend.

The *infantes* went to Paris in June, accompanied by Carla so *Infanta* Eulalia could see her new granddaughter, and she made such a good impression that Bee was more than satisfied. Accompanied by Alice, Bee's maid, and their faithful chauffeur, Carmelo, they arrived in Rome on 8 July, where Ena and her children were waiting for them at the station. They visited the Torlonias, dined with the Parodis, and lunched with Alfonso XIII next day.

The wedding of Prince Álvaro de Orleans to Carla Parodi-Delfino was celebrated in Rome, in the church of San Roberto Bellarmino on 10 July, with the former king and queen of Spain as witnesses. The bridegroom wore the simple green uniform of the Legion, while most of the gentlemen wore morning dress. Duke Amadeo of Aosta wore white and Ultano Kindelán, a friend of the groom, wore Spanish Air Force uniform. Carla wore a beautiful dress and diadem belonging to the *Infanta* Eulalia, who was still living in Paris, and who commented gracefully that she was not present 'because it was difficult to fit me in!' Bee wore a simple but elegant dress, while Ena wore a broad-rimmed hat and a floral dress. The morning ceremony was followed by a brilliant lunch. Yet it was a sad wedding, in wartime and in a period of mourning. The newly-weds went to the Vatican to receive the blessing of Pope Pius XI, who asked them of news of Spain.

After the wedding, Ali and Bee returned to London and Bee continued working on the exchange of Spaniards persecuted by both sides. A letter from Valencia, where the Republican government was based, came from Mr Leche (30 June 1937) thanking the princess for the food she sent via the embassy for the Scottish Ambulance Unit:

This will bring happiness to many people. I have sent a list of the people who particularly want you to help. Timoteo Stuart and his mother (the Dowager Duchess of Peñaranda, Carmen Viana) are in Valencia and will be evacuated within a few days. I was hoping that they would send me provisions in quantity, but Your Highness has been the only one who has responded. The suffering in Madrid from the shortage of food is terrible. I do what I can but it is just a drop in the ocean. May I ask you Your Highness to use your influence in Salamanca that they be more open to negotiation and flexible on the matter of exchanges? After three months of hard work I have the people here in the palm of my hand and they will agree to any exchange that I want and they constantly ask me to arrange them. Irujo and Giral (Republican Ministers) only wish to avoid suffering, but in nine cases out of ten Salamanca does not allow them, apparently because of Vallellano. It is most distressing for me!

However, I have dealt with the exchange of Don Francisco de Borbón y de Castelvi (the retired Lieutenant General) and his wife, and the Primo de Rivera family. As for the former, he embarked yesterday on HMS *Delhi* for Palma and I hope to send off the others next Monday.

With luck, I also hope to send off Marilú and Maribel Larios who were captured at Brunete, where they were nurses.

I am also happy to be able to say that the sentence to which Martina, Duchess of Santa Cristina was condemned has been annulled and she will be in the Embassy in a few days.

To this typewritten letter, he added a postscript by hand to say that the exchange of the Primo de Rivera family had foundered 'because, at the last moment, instead of the Primos, they asked for a man that Valencia ought to give, despite the terms approved over a month ago'.

Faced with these difficulties, Bee decided to go to Salamanca to speak personally to those who carried out the exchanges. Ali was still obsessed with returning to Spain to fight, despite the *generalissimo* considering his work abroad much more important for the National Cause; in London, he was working on facilitating the delivery of Ford trucks, and on propaganda. Bee replied to Mr Leche from King's Cottage (5 September 1937) that she hoped to be in Salamanca in about three weeks and then to do everything possible to make the prisoner exchanges that he mentioned:

As you say, it is in Salamanca that we find the main opposition to [them], in part because of the difficulties in choosing between victims and also because one always receives the same answer when talking to Franco himself (it seems that Franco has explained the matter personally to you)—it is scored out and he adds to it. On our side, nobody is unjustly imprisoned and, if they have committed no offence they are free; if they have committed a crime, they cannot be exchanged. However, it may be that I might be able to manage to achieve some small success, which would give me great pleasure because, in this way, I may be able to demonstrate my gratitude for the marvellous work which you have done in helping so many of our unfortunate friends.

Immediately after the death of Alonso, his younger brother, Ataúlfo, volunteered to join the ranks. At this time, the Condor Legion was being organised, and Ataúlfo was required to act as an interpreter for the Germans, while Bee took charge of raising funds on behalf of Spain. One of her best friends was Margarita van Raalte. She and her husband, Baron Howard de Walden, who were very rich and generous with donations, were among the first to contribute.

Their third daughter, Pip, now aged twenty, was with Ataúlfo at the wedding of the duke of Kent. She was in love with him and wanted to go to Spain as a nurse: 'In the middle of March 1937, Ataúlfo asked me for a photograph, I jumped up and danced with joy at the thought of going to

Spain and I began to learn Spanish'. She longed to be of use, but felt stupid. She wrote in her diary: 'It is going to be difficult travelling there, but I think that I am capable of doing it'. Her Spanish progressed rapidly as did the first-aid course, which she attended assiduously. In June, she wrote that she had just received letters from Ataúlfo, when he arrived unexpectedly in London on the 23rd: 'He telephoned me and we lunched together at San Marco, and spent the afternoon buying gramophone records and chatting. Nothing has changed and I like him as much as I always have'. Six days later, she went to Croydon to see him off as he was returning again to the front. Her interest in the Nationalist cause was revived and her notions of what was happening came almost exclusively from Bee, 'who really knew what she was talking about: I simply adore her and I admire her greatly for her courage in everything'.

On 6 July, Pip gained her nursing qualification with very good grades. Ali was passing through London and while they dined together, Pip told Bee of her firm intention to go to Spain and asked for her help. Her nursing qualification and her progress in Spanish assured Bee that Pip was serious and could be useful to the Nationalist cause. The big step forward in Pip's plans came when Bee replied to a letter from Margot Howard de Walden, telling her that in September, she was thinking of going to Spain and proposed that her daughter accompanied her. Pip's childlike joy was completely understandable, now that she was not only travelling to Spain to help, but would also be near Ataúlfo. 'Princess Bee is truly a saint,' she wrote on 8 August, 'It is going to be so nice to go with her.'

On 18 September, she accompanied the *infanta* to Portsmouth to meet Ena, who gave them various errands relating to her friends and to whom it seemed so good that a young woman from such an aristocratic family should go to help the Nationalists. She was interviewed at the Foreign Office by William H. Montagu-Pollock who provided her with a passport for the journey. The *infanta* also received her passport, under her maiden name of 'Princess Beatrice of Saxe-Coburg-Gotha'.

On 21 September 1937, they started their journey in a limousine, carrying several hatboxes containing medicines, clinical equipment, and surgical instruments, driven by Carmelo Herrero, the *infantes'* chauffeur who had just married Alice Wallington, Bee's maid. They were received at Dover by the station master, and shown to a private compartment in the passenger area. On arriving in Paris, they visited the Universal Exhibition. Curiously, they went to visit the very large German pavilion and the English, which they found bad, but not the Spanish pavilion, featuring Pablo Picasso's painting *Guernica*. Bee had never liked his work.

They followed the route along France's beautiful roads until arriving at Biarritz where Sir Henry Chilton, the British ambassador to Republican

Spain, had been transferred. He presented them to his French colleague who put no difficulties in their way to crossing the frontier at Hendaya. They also went to the Villa Nacho-Enea for their safe-conduct passes. Here the family of the marquis of Caviedes, a strong monarchist, immediately recognised Bee, giving her two nationalist flags, which on passing customs, Carmelo proudly fitted on both sides of the car.

The people of Irun had been burned-out by the Red miners and it affected this little party deeply to see so many houses destroyed by fire. On the other hand, 20 km further on, in San Sebastian, 'they found the beautiful tourist resort bathed in the sun as if it was holiday time'. They stayed at the Hotel de Londres, facing the Bay of La Concha, and next day they found that little or nothing was lacking behind the Nationalist lines. There were many soldiers in the cafés and bars; some, wounded, had crutches and others 'aeroplanes' for broken arms.

Carmelo was told to go by coastal road to Bilbao, which had been captured in July, early in the morning. Bee, who had great confidence in her chauffeur, followed his instructions. When they arrived at Bilbao, destroyed bridges revealed signs of war, though it was still a bustling city. The Hotel Torrontegui welcomed them. Life there had not changed; its food was excellent and they often recalled the luxury of its cotton sheets.

Bee wanted to pass through Santander, which had been liberated on 22 August, 'because Ena liked the city very much and felt at home there, and wanted to know how it was'. The people of Santander worked hard to tidy up the city. She introduced herself and asked the military governor to let her visit the Magdalena Palace, which had been given to the king and queen many years before. Surviving the republic, it had been converted into a summer university. Some portraits of the sovereigns had been kept, but the English furniture and comfortable cotton upholstered sofas, which Ena liked so much, had disappeared. The guide who accompanied them told them succinctly, 'They took them.' The queen, very annoyed to hear this, wrote to her cousin: 'It is terribly sad to think that nothing remains in the house and that the Reds have destroyed everything'.

The hotel where they stayed was next to the beach and they were well looked after, but the city had suffered from food shortages over thirteen months of occupation and several people had been killed. These were the last days of the northern front, where the Condor Legion had been fighting for the liberation of Asturias, and so Prince Ataúlfo could be spared to meet his mother—they had not seen each other for three months. According to Pip in her diary, he was much thinner, and tanned, 'hopelessly attractive'. At the airport, he showed her the enormous Junkers in which he could only fly as an 'observer' because of defective eyesight. He would never become a pilot despite his desire to take his brother's place in everything.

Although it was a diversion, Bee was very interested in visiting Santillana del Mar where the *Infanta* Paz, her husband's aunt, had an attractive medieval house. Bee was able to deal with the chatelaine and was satisfied that the mansion had not suffered too much damage. The sleepy village with its cobbled streets remained peaceful, ox carts still went around slowly, while the women sewed in the doorways of their homes, emblazoned with coats of arms. They returned to the more protected roads, arriving finally at Burgos. Bee took Pip to visit the cathedral, and they visited Valladolid which was dealing with constant troop manoeuvres, arriving at Salamanca at sunset. For Bee, the aim of the journey was to speak to Gen. Kindelán and to get Franco to let her husband continue his military career. Ford were insisting that he return again to work in Detroit, which he did not want to do at this time.

Although I have no sources, Bee allegedly had a discussion with *Generalissimo* Franco about the exchange of people who were to be found as prisoners in the Red Zone, and she asked him to let Ali enter Spain. Franco was surprised by her resolute attitude as, having lost a son, and having two others fighting in the air force, she still fervently wanted her husband to join up as a pilot. He assured her he would speak to Kindelán, who had helped in Franco's election as head of state and was appointed *generalissimo* of all the armed forces. Franco's accession to power came on 1 October. Bee and Pip witnessed the joy in Salamanca; from the Grand Hotel, they watched the procession of various regiments, as well as the brilliant comportment of the troops of *Regulares* under the command of Spanish officers and 'the Moroccans, who wore capes of magnificent and varied colours, and were on Arab horses with golden trimmings'.

Prince Álvaro was destined for the new Matacán air base, constructed between October and November the previous year. Pip was delighted to inspect the Savoia-Marchetti trimotor bombers that Álvaro and the Italian volunteers piloted. They left Salamanca on 4 October. Three days later, after crossing the mountains of Extremadura, they arrived at Sanlúcar de Barrameda, where they learned that Ali was to rejoin the military and could fight for Spain. He wrote to Franco (2 August 1937, The King's Cottage, Kew, Surrey):

One year ago today I presented myself at the Captaincy General of Burgos. I was so sure that I would be able to take part immediately that I carried in my arms my flying overalls, balaclava, goggles and pistol. Nobody knew what was going to happen. So when Mola (may he rest in peace) decided that my presence could be a distraction for the use of elements of a Republican tendency, and that I should return abroad, I, as a military man, obeyed immediately. I returned in February and May, to beg you to allow me to fight at the side of my two sons, covering the loss of Alonso.

You know that I have never asked for favours and many times I have suffered from being treated in an arbitrary manner and stopped from serving in campaigns (I have still not taken in my not having fought in 1921 and 1924) and it is not possible to throw in my face that I have been favoured with rapid promotion in Africa for the campaigns of 1911, 1913, and 1925.

Dynastically speaking, I am of no importance at all, as I am the least of the Royal Family. Since 1931, I have constructed a new life for myself. I have no ambition other than to serve the Fatherland and not to walk through the world as a dishonoured man after the final victory.

In giving to my children, I have given what constitutes my future. If God gives them life, they may carry their heads high, as they have fought as decent people. I cannot believe that you wish me to walk in shame before everyone, as a professional soldier who did not go to the International War, which put his Country in danger.

More than two months passed until the *generalissimo* relented and let Ali enter Spain as an infantry commander in the air force. The news reached him when he was working in Germany, and he wrote to his 'Dear Kindelán':

You can understand my happiness on receiving the telegram from the *Infanta*, telling me that the Generalissimo had returned me to active service and that I should cancel my journey to America.

I left Groningen for Amsterdam like a rocket, and from there came here by aeroplane, arriving yesterday. In the afternoon I saw my boss at Ford (The President of the Administrative Board of Ford Europe) with whom I left for Detroit on the 16th and gave the sad news that they had to find someone else to occupy my position. The good gentleman, whom I like greatly, confessed to me that I was giving him serious difficulties but he understood perfectly my position and joy in serving my country.

He also told me that it had been his hope that I would occupy his position when he retired in three years, and he hoped that I would have enough time for the hand-over to my assistant and that he would like my opinion on various matters. My natural desire is to take the first train, aeroplane, whatever form of transport, so as to arrive in Salamanca as soon as possible. You can imagine my hurry, when you realize that I have longed for this for over fourteen months!

I went to see the doctor today. He gave me an anti-typhoid injection, and will give me another on Wednesday and another on Saturday. He told me that I should not travel until two days after the last dose unless I go by sea and can be relaxed.

Along with this letter, I am sending one to Bee in Sanlúcar along with a copy of this one. She wrote to me that she will come to meet me at San Sebastian or Salamanca. I will arrive via Biarritz if I can. What happiness to be able to stand in front of the Chief of Aviation and say, 'At your orders, General!' You, who have also suffered the bitterness of exile, do not know what it is like to be in Spain, among friends, during wartime— as a civilian. Going to an aerodrome as a tourist. The shame of it!

There was an emotional meeting between Bee and Ali at San Sebastián on the evening of 19 October. She was at Salamanca to complete certain formalities regarding prisoner exchanges, as the Nationalists were making the deals more difficult. She had managed to get Kindelán's son liberated from Red Madrid, and he was being evacuated via Marseilles. Ali wrote that he had spoken to Ena who was taking a great deal of interest: 'The *Infanta* explained everything to the Foreign Office, as you will recall, and also talked to Ambassador Chilton. The Queen told me that she was certain that he had already arrived at Marseilles and she asked me to telegraph you'.

Three days later, Ali put on his uniform. The *infantes* were only in Salamanca for a short time, but Bee found time to paint a small picture showing a young man with a red handkerchief by the River Tormes, and the slim tower of the new cathedral could be seen in the background. Its bells rang out ecstatically at the taking of Gijón, the principal port of Asturias, and with its conquest the war in the North ended. Later the Navarre and Italian divisions were moved to the Madrid front because Franco was obsessed with entering the capital. Kindelán was very grateful to the *infantes* for the return of his son, who told them what he suffered in Red Madrid. People there, much less important than he, were still incarcerated or had been killed. María Ángeles and her husband, César Sáenz de Santa María, were also finally found, to everyone's joy.

The *infantes* left for Sanlúcar, where they were received by a group of German pilots whom Ataúlfo wished to look after. Pip, who was working in the hospital in Jerez, also came to join them. 'Princess Bee seemed genuinely delighted to have me back again and I was awfully pleased to see her as I adore her and have missed her a lot,' she wrote in her diary on 29 October.

On 4 November, to his delight, Ali was appointed commander of the air force, 'raised to Lieutenant Colonel', and was moved to the Hotel Cristina in Seville. He spent the day at Tablada, studying the new bombers that had come from Italy.

Bee had Alonso's mortal remains transferred from Seville to Sanlúcar de Barrameda on 18 November, the first anniversary of his death. His mother wanted him to rest in the church of the Franciscan Fathers, under a tombstone without any inscription, only the three *fleur-de-lis*, symbol of the Orleans family. Two days later, she left for England to collect her mail and give reports of those liberated from the Red Zone. She returned a month later loaded with medicines and surgical supplies which she handed over to the Military Medical Corps at Burgos.

She then moved to the Ventosilla Palace, near Aranda de Duero, where Ali was in charge of the 1st Air Force Brigade. It formerly belonged to the dukes of Santoña, and its new owners, the Velasco-Nesprals, had created a model farm on the estate. Bee was delighted with the house, and invited Pip to spend Christmas with them there. Pip arrived in her new car (a present from her father) on 23 December, and met the Kindelán family on her journey who gave her the bad news that Álvaro of Orleans had crashed. His wife, Carla Parodi-Delfino, was almost hysterical, and Pip had to calm her. Ultano and another member of his family returned from the flight and they said that they had seen Álvaro descend, but he had been able to land:

> We were all scared stiff and everyone was trying to get news. At last, after about an hour, Álvaro himself rang from Soria. What had actually happened to Alvaro was that his right-hand engine had blown up, and, as on those machines you can't stop the engine in flight, he had got into a spin with smoke billowing all over the machine so that he thought it was on fire. But he let down his slots and got her out of the spin and then, finding she was not burning, very slowly came homewards on two engines.

Bee was waiting for them with her husband and Ataúlfo. Despite the thick fog, they arrived at eight. She had a Christmas tree on the table, Pip noted, adding that it was 'a lovely house' and they joined all the family for Christmas dinner. Next day they went to Mass at a small church and, although it was Christmas, Álvaro and Carla had to go to Burgos as he was on duty at the aerodrome that afternoon and night. After Christmas, Ali took Ataúlfo back to the Condor Legion at El Burgo de Osma where they were stationed, 58 km from Aranda. On New Year's Day 1938, Pip drove there and took Ataúlfo to lunch.

On 8 January 1938, Col. Rey d'Harcourt had to surrender to the Republicans. Ena, who always talked of 'our poor Country', told Bee (London, 19 January) that the English newspapers had 'been hateful when talking of the victory of the Reds in Teruel. It has been a heavy blow for our prestige abroad'. She had received Bee's letter from San Sebastian, and was overjoyed to know that her furniture from Magdalena had been recovered.

A month later Ena wrote (Rome, 12 February 1938) that the birth of Juan's baby son had been a great joy:

> ... because he is such a sweet baby, he has a small head, a delicious face and is blond. I came three weeks ago because María's waters broke early. Queen Elena is so sweet and she has lent me a small apartment in the Quirinal because there was no room in Baby's house (the *Infanta* Beatriz). I saw the King at the baptism (I was godmother). But now it seems that they do not wish to see me! You are the only person to whom I can talk about everything of Spain, within Spain, and about the Spanish...

The boy born during the Battle of Teruel would become her favourite grandson, and at the age of thirty-seven king of all Spaniards as Juan Carlos I.

Ali wrote to Kindelán (10 November 1938) that he wanted to be an active pilot: 'Not just because I like it but because in these anti-monarchist times which prevail in the world, I want to demonstrate that those of us "from good families" take on the "bull" as happily as the rest'. At the time he was fifty-two, yet still the first to arrive at the aerodrome to inspect his aircraft before flying: 'One day the order arrived that Ali's group did not have to be at the aerodrome until 9.00. On learning this, he was so pleased to think that he could stay in bed until 7.30 that according to Pip Scott-Ellis in her diary 'he jumped around the room as if he was doing gymnastic exercises'.

Returning from Sanlúcar, where she had spent ten days planting trees and plants, Bee's life took on a more warlike aspect, as she dedicated herself more to the soldiers, and those who suffered most because of the war, the children and the old. She and Ena were frustrated by the delay in the exchange of the Primo de Riveras, who had been in prison since the shooting of their son, José Antonio, on 20 September 1936, one of the prisoners, the general's sister, being over eighty years old. Bee continued working for prisoner exchanges, as noted in her archives: 'Ultano Kindelán and his son, 3rd April 1937'; 'Manolo G. 3rd August 1938'; 'The Molina family, saved. Many thanks'. In 1938, one of Bee's friends was released and left Madrid for Rome. She had been in the same cell as Franco's niece and was the daughter of Pilar Franco Bahamonde, the *generalissimo*'s only sister: 'The Republicans, or Loyalists as some call them, wanted to complete the exchange of prisoners, but Franco's policies of state did not allow this. For this reason, many prisoners, including his niece, would never forgive him'.

Bee was tired of her lack of success in completing the exchanges. She received protests and complaints from families, who did not understand what was happening. At the beginning of the year, she began to actively occupy herself with the 'Assistance for the Fronts and Hospitals' (*Delegación Nacional de Asistencia a Frentes y Hospitales*) which followed the conquering troops and entered the towns and villages they had ransacked with medicines and food. The organisation had been founded by María Rosa Urraca Pastor, a schoolteacher and fervent traditionalist. From the beginning, it had been so successful on the Northern Front that the *generalissimo* officially named her as a leader of the national delegation. Its emblem was a cross, signifying sacrifice, half yellow and half red, the colours of the Spanish flag, surrounded by a green laurel branch, the symbol of victory. Later on, they mainly used a white cross with two green branches, the symbol of the Medical Corps.

Bee arrived in Salamanca, left for Sanlúcar on 27 January 1938, and on 4 February she went to Cintruénigo, in Navarre. On arriving, she met Col. R., sent by her nephew, King Carol II of Romania, asking for news. Immediately, she wrote to Missy (Cintruénigo, 5 February):

I send you a letter from Gibraltar, which I hope will reach you. On returning almost exhausted from a long trip, I met a gentleman sent by Carol. As I have to return again, I am putting down a few lines so that you have some news. Álvaro and his wife are going to Rome because they have ten days leave.

Their arrival was a sad one because of a dreadful explosion in the arms factory (the biggest in Italy) belonging to Álvaro's father-in-law. All their engineer friends have died. It is very sad for Álvaro who is exhausted by incessant flying and he had to be at his father-in-law's side because of the disaster. He cannot rest. Ataúlfo is at an aerodrome near us, which is a consolation.

The weather continues to be very cold and we were almost frozen when we arrived at Salamanca. Today the sun is glorious which cheers one up. In Sanlúcar, all the new trees and things that I have planted have been frozen. Ataúlfo was desperate because he is a fantastic gardener. The garden means as much to him as the nightclubs do to other young men: it is his excitement and his relaxation. Everything seems to go terribly slowly, but the situation is good and I believe that everything will get moving as it did last year in Asturias.

On 8 February, they were visited by Kindelán, his wife, Lolita, and the chief of the Condor Legion. They visited again on the Thursday and celebrated the taking of Malaga with a tea. Bee, accompanied by María Ángeles, returned from San Sebastian, where they had been for four days collecting medicines and provisions. On another day, they went to Zaragoza to pray to the Virgin of Pilar, and spent a week in Sanlúcar.

Bee began her work in the first days of the Nationalist offensive on Teruel, which was conquered on 22 February 1938. The city was destroyed and almost all its inhabitants had fled. She was there the following day, thoroughly saddened because two days earlier, Carlos Haya 'who had rescued those in the sanctuary of the Virgin of la Cabeza had been shot down in enemy territory'.

Pip received a letter from her saying that 'she had not been able to see them because Prince Ali did not allow it'. Until then, she lived a nomadic life following her husband and living in 'pilots' houses'. When the legion's aircraft were at the aerodrome near Épila, they moved there, where the bombers were kept. The village was built on the side of a hill and most of the houses were subterranean or excavated out of the hillside. There was an enchanting palace, the Hilar, that belonged to the House of Alba, 'requisitioned by the Air Force'. Of 'Arabic' origin, it had several bedrooms but only two bathrooms and three toilets.

The *infantes* lived there for most of the war with Álvaro and Carla because he was in the legion's air force. Because the Red counteroffensive was considered imminent, the Nationalist pilots were obliged to fly a great deal. Alvaro was annoyed that the bells of the neighbouring convent would wake him regularly at 6 a.m. each day and he repeatedly asked the nuns not to ring them, but, faithful to their customs, they took no notice until one day he strafed the bells with his machine gun and they fell silent.

Bee enjoyed acting as hostess at the Hijar Palace where she welcomed several pilots. The Condor Legion had remained in Zaragoza and Ataúlfo, with the German pilots, came regularly to visit his mother. Sometimes they went to Zaragoza, 30 km away, to buy food, now that 'the teas they gave were real meals'. Accompanied by Carla, she worked hard in the kitchen, cutting bread and preparing sandwiches, *empanadillas* (small pies), supervising tortillas, croquettes, and apple tarts: 'When the pilots left, Ataúlfo would play the piano very loudly but very well'. Pip also recalled how Bee, who had her own bathroom, would let the ladies use it, while that of Álvaro and Carla was used by the male guests.

Spring had begun well, after the horrible winter. On 22 March, the siege of Huesca came to an end, and Barcelona began to suffer intense bombing. Next day, the nationalists arrived at the River Segre and established a bridgehead at Serós, 27 km from Lérida. The fierce fighting cost the life of the commander of Mola's Castilian Regiment, the young Alfonso de

Borbón y Pintó, a brilliant cavalry officer who distinguished himself on the Northern Front and then later at Teruel.

It was decided that Bee should follow the troops into Lérida with all the gifts, medicines, and food because the shield of the city was emblazoned with the three *fleurs-de-lis*, and as it was the first Catalonian city to be liberated. On 1 April, they announced that the Navarre Brigades had achieved their objective but, faced with ferocious defence, it would be the army's Moroccan troops that would enter on the 3rd. That day, they collected their baggage in Zaragoza, the expedition went in several lorries and Bee took the ambulance, driven by Carmelo, filled with supplies. They took the Barcelona road as it was in better condition, despite holes and pitting caused by the bombs. Finally, the city of Lérida appeared in the distance. Lérida had once been a stronghold, isolated with its old cathedral on its highest point. The modern city was on the right bank of the River Segre, the weather was very cold and the wind gusted until one's eyes watered.

The change from the Navarre Brigades to troops of *Regulares* was decided by the commanders at the last minute. The commander was annoyed at being told that the head of 'Fronts and Hospitals' was a princess. After learning that Bee was sleeping in the ambulance and that she and her team had been working hard, the commander decided to visit them and she received them warmly. They had friends in common, including Gen. Varela, and they both liked horses.

Pip noted in her diary that it was difficult to be able to help her but he did his best:

> She has been having a terrible time in Lérida for the last few weeks. The Relief Fund has set itself up in a huge asylum there in the middle of the town. They have the Reds fifty yards away shooting explosive bullets up all the streets, no doctors nor help of any sort and about four hundred old freaks to look after. The filth was evidently terrible, as these wretched old people had been completely deserted for ten days. Princess Bee and her helpers removed the mess. The place was full of corpses. There were dead people sitting at tables or lying on the stairs, as the Reds shot a lot of people before leaving. There is no one to take away the corpses and bury them, no food, no doctors, nor organisation of any sort except Princess Bee and the Relief Fund. She just had to act as doctor and do whatever she thought best with the few things she happened to have with her, and no light, no water and everything filthy. However, now I think she has cleaned it all up a lot.

In that inhospitable environment, Bee received a visit from her good friend from Zurich days, Arnold Lunn, who was working as a journalist, and according to Pip, had come to Spain to record the 'Red Horrors'. In the newspaper *The Universe*, he dedicated the following article to Bee:

> I visited Lérida a few days after it was liberated and went up to the castle where the Moroccans were stationed. I looked over the parapet and saw that below, the earth had been moved towards the river. On the opposite bank was the enemy, who remained silent; but, in my honour, the Moroccans fired and they responded with a great mishmash of shooting which produced broad smiles among the Moroccans.

A lady, English by birth and Spanish by marriage, who organised aid after the taking of the city, described her experiences in Lérida to me:

> Many of them were prostrate in bed and some in such bad condition that when we wanted to undress them, the skin was so joined to the clothing that we did atrocious damage to them.
>
> The only priest who had survived came out of his hiding place and set up a small altar and celebrated Mass aided by an eighteen-year-old altar boy. We all felt edified by his reverence and devotion. The following day a woman entered the hall while we served food and on seeing the altar boy let out a cry of terror. 'That boy,' she exclaimed 'threatened to kill me and he boasted of having killed two priests!'
>
> The devoted altar boy was detained while he protested, saying that some older men had tricked him. The following day two of his fellow countrymen to whom we gave food, were identified as the men who had buried people alive during the Red occupation.

Bee returned from her stay in Lérida tired but content with the work done, and with experience for more such work in future. At Épila, she found the palace full of people, as it was Holy Week. On 15 April, the arrival of Nationalist troops at Vinaroz, on the Mediterranean, was celebrated with joy. The Republican Zone was divided in two, Catalonia and the Centre-Levante-South, so there was a great fiesta that Easter Sunday in many cities. Five days later, the Navarre Brigades arrived, through the Valle de Arán, at the French border. Franco then decided to attack Valencia, the headquarters of the Republican government, the Nationalist forces faced heavy resistance, lengthening the war substantially. For this, he was much criticised by Kindelán, Solchaga, and other military men who had favoured continuing with the invasion of Catalonia.

Arnold Lunn, Bee's 'spiritual godson' was in Épila for Easter and he had fond memories of his stay there. Thanks to her, Lunn was received by

Franco. As a conservative Roman Catholic, he was carrying on a brilliant campaign in England on behalf of the Nationalists. On his way from Biarritz to Lourdes, he wrote to her about his impressions of his interview with the *generalissimo*:

> He asked me if I was not impressed with the good order which existed behind the lines. He also assured me that the English, when they returned to Spain after the war would find excellent golf courses and good salmon fishing.
>
> That which most impressed me about the Generalissimo was the contrast between his steely tenacity, his bravery, and his calm and kind welcome, which was from the English point of view, more like that of a Benedictine Abbot than that of a Fascist Generalissimo. An English general told me that, in his opinion, General Franco was the most outstanding military genius of his time.

Sir Arnold Lunn remained a friend of the *infantes*, and many years later (1 July 1973), he wrote to Álvaro remembering his stay at Épila:

> I remember that I was greatly impressed by the stoic courage of the *Infanta*, of whom I was very fond. During the days that I spent there with her, various members of her family were flying. The only time that she showed her emotions was on an occasion when the *Infante* and Ataúlfo were flying over enemy territory while we were taking tea. On hearing that the flight was returning, I made for the window. Then the *Infanta* exclaimed, 'For God's sake do not count them!' She could not have shown more fear, thinking that one or another of the pilots was missing.

May had passed uneventfully because the Republicans in the Tremp sector only attacked from time to time. A great offensive was being prepared and it was rumoured the target would be Valencia or Barcelona. Suddenly the Galician Army Corps began to attack, advancing towards the coast. Its commander was the defender of Oviedo, Gen. Antonio Aranda Mata, who was two years younger than Ali and had had a brilliant military career. The *infanta* had met him and knew he would help her. She still vividly recalled the entry into Lérida, where the authorities had fled before the arrival of the Moroccan troops, and she therefore asked her friend Casilda Ampuero for an additional team, with a strong desire to work, to come from Vascongadas. Among the nurses, Gloria Ozalla stood out for her kindness (she died aged 100 while I was writing this biography). She told me they arrived on the afternoon of 13 July, following behind the troops at Castellón de la Plana, less than 3 km from the sea:

As there had hardly been any fighting, the people received us with joy. It was the first (provincial) capital city of the Kingdom of Valencia to be liberated. The *Infanta* arrived by car on the 14th, and we all gave out the food, which we had with us. There were some wounded in the hospital who had preferred to remain. We carried out a general cleaning of all the centres, assisted by the young people of the town who, thanks to the vegetables and the fish, were well nourished.

On asking her what the *infanta* did, she replied:

She did everything with everyone, the old and the young, because she was interested and she listened to their complaints with great patience. We finished our work early and we went to swim at the beach at Grao which was then more or less unspoilt. It was the 19th June! Spring was over.

Pilarón and her husband Juan Antonio Ansaldo had been to eat with the *Infantes*. The couple were good friends of the *Infantes* and they often sent Bee, a heavy smoker, the cigarettes she needed.

A short time afterwards, I was at the Mola Hospital in San Sebastian and met a Commander in the Air Force.... On seeing his medal, the Royal and Military Order of Saint Ferdinand, I asked him, 'Are you Commander García-Morato?' 'No', he replied, 'I am Ansaldo *el fracasado'*. (Ansaldo the failure.) It was pathetic, as I did not know how to reply while I accompanied him to reception. The following day I went to the Equipo Carulla to receive sessions of short wave therapy as I had suffered from severe back pain since the Teruel campaign during which I had flown for many hours. While I received the treatment, I was told how he came from the Aragon front and that the *Infanta* Beatrice of Orleans who, according to him knew more than many doctors, had advised him that he should go to San Sebastian to be cured.

As the treatment was to last a few months, I took the opportunity to listen to some of his curious anecdotes. He was a Monarchist and felt a real admiration for the *Infante*. Regarding the *Infanta*, he told us about her quiet work on the exchange of prisoners and of her expeditions to the front where she arrived by car or ambulance accompanied by her faithful chauffeur Carmelo, to deliver everything from medicines to babies' feeding bottles and from condensed milk to Bovril.

Various letters from this time from Ena to Bee have been kept, notably one (London, 24 July 1938), about the death of Queen Maria of Romania who had died six days earlier:

My heart simply suffers for you since I heard that Missy had died. I know how much you loved your two older sisters who have been taken from you in two years. They leave such a terrible void in your life, my poor dear, the two were such magnificent women, each in their own way, and they loved you so much. I understand too well what you are suffering, isolated as you are from your family.

Poor Missy suffered because she felt that she was not getting better in Dresden, and with a great effort decided to return home. The long journey to Romania must have hastened her end as she died the day after she arrived. It is too, too, sad! I am thinking about you with such loving sympathy and I wish so much to be able to be with you during these hard times of suffering; this new sorrow is just too cruel.

I had the luck to dine with the Howard de Waldens, and their daughter, who has returned to Spain, and with Consuelo Montemar. You can imagine what a pleasure it was to have a long and interesting chat with them about you and how heroic and marvellous you are.

I saw Doña Sol a few days ago in the lobby at Claridge's. Her lack of manners was incredible. She was sitting between her brother (the Duke of Alba) and Rosario (the Duchess of Híjar) reading a paper. When she saw me she, she looked at me in such a way, and opened the paper again without attempting to get up. Bless her little heart!

On 7 July, Pip went home to recover after having been ill in Épila with paratyphoid for four weeks. Carla also had it and needed to go and convalesce in Rome. During the spring, both had been cared for by Bee at Épila. Once in London, Pip wanted to return to Spain as the Battle of the Ebro had erupted during her absence. Accompanied by Consuelo Montemar, she returned by sea to Gibraltar and arrived at Sanlúcar on 25 August. The following day, accompanied by Bee, she left for Épila. After seven hours by car, she wrote:

We have a room belonging to a lieutenant colonel who luckily is away for one night. He is a tidy man, thank goodness, so all his possessions do not get in our way and the room is clean. It is already midnight and we are being called at four o'clock tomorrow morning, so won't get much sleep tonight. It was very hot (yesterday) and we both sweated all the way. We talked and sang and enjoyed ourselves, at least I did. We had two bottles of iced coffee in thermoses to slake our thirst, but it had frozen stiff so we had to scrape and scoop it out with a knitting needle and a nail file. It was most refreshing.

Saturday 27th August, We arrived at Salamanca at half-past ten and we went to Air Force Headquarters to ask for Prince Ali. Then, at the aerodrome, we motored down to the end and collected Prince Ali from his plane. He was deaf and half silly from exhaustion. He is now a colonel and is working hard organising a new brigade.

That night, they slept in the Monterrey Palace. Bee continued to Épila with Pip, Carla, and Consuelo, while Ataúlfo and other friends went to Torremolinos to enjoy the pilots' holidays. There they received the news by radio that the prince of Asturias had died in Florida in a car accident. Ali and Bee were deeply affected. Ena wrote from 34, Dorchester Terrace (20 September 1938):

> It was such a comfort to receive your lovely letter last night. I was wanting to know about you because you loved my dear son so much and you can understand better than anyone what his death means for me. I know that I cannot wish that he had lived, poor thing, because his life was only suffering, But that he had to die in this horrible way so alone and far away with no one who loved him or tried to help and comfort him at the end, the idea breaks my heart and makes my pain even more on hearing it.
>
> I love all my sons equally, but without a doubt there was a special bond of love and understanding between Alfonsito and me, in part because of his health and how he suffered. It is terribly hard having lost my two darling sons in the same tragic way and without doubt I am going to spend dark days of suffering and loneliness. There is not a soul in London, and you know how our English relations are. What a difference it would have been if you had been here! We both know the agony which I am once again called upon to go through. We both love our children who we have together seen growing up in the happiness of days gone by. Unfortunately, in the last year of Alfonsito's life, I had not written him very often and now I am tortured by the idea of his thinking that I did not love him more. If my poor son had returned with me two years ago when I went to America, he would have been spared so much unhappiness, and me as well!
>
> I am too sad to write more, but I am very grateful for your words and your understanding.
>
> I miss you more than I can say. Please thank Ali for his dear letter, which has crossed with others.

Re-reading this letter suggested that Ena was crying out for her cousin, Bee, to come so that they could be together, as she felt so alone in her deep sorrow. Did Bee fully understand? All we know is that she then continued at Épila with her husband and sons, working for the war, which was becoming interminable. The initial advance of the republicans was a surprise, but then they failed in the taking of Gandesa and Bot. The fighting, which lasted 115 days, was very bloody for both sides. The battle of the Ebro was undoubtedly the most important of the war.

At an international level, that autumn, Hitler seemed to want war in Europe, though this did not break out for another year. Bee suspected that after months of fighting, there would be a pause. She was pleased with the work of the last few months and made much of how the loyal Carmelo had helped her. She thought that the best way to replay him was to take him to London so that he could get to know his son who had been born in April. She was also thinking of Alice who, uncomplaining and faithful, continued looking after the house at Kew Gardens.

At the Comandancia in Saragossa, she asked for a passport for Carmelo who was of military age and serving in the air force. They were so close to the frontier that going by car was an easy drive and they crossed France embarking for Newhaven at Dieppe on 26 November. They arrived safely at Kew where Carmelo was happily reunited with his wife and son.

Bee very much enjoyed spending some days with Ena, purchased items for the front and also decorations for the Christmas tree. Ena was in mourning for her son so received few visitors, but she felt that Bee should meet her friends the Chamberlains, so she invited them to tea. Twenty days in England passed in a flash. Carmelo was really overjoyed with his son, and with Alice, neither suspecting the long separation about to follow. Again they crossed France and entered Spain at Irun *en route* to San Sebastian, where, at the home of the Richs, many packages were awaiting them for collection, including overcoats and medicines for the soldiers.

'The *Infanta* was passing through,' explained Lusita Rich years later, 'On the other hand the *Infante* used to visit us often during the war. On finding the Hotel de Londres full, he only had to call us to ask for a bed. He used to say, amusingly, "As I get up at six and I shower with cold water, I don't expect to bother you in the bathroom." He used to breakfast on an enormous cup of coffee with milk and toast, but he never dined with us.'

Although the car was full of packages, Bee wanted to go to Burgos to talk to Gen. Kindelán and give him a message from her cousin, the queen.

Ena was a friend of Neville Chamberlain, his wife, and sister who always supported the Nationalists. After Chamberlain's meeting with Hitler in Munich, Bee had had tea with them and she found them so pessimistic that they advised the war in Spain should end before the Second World War began. On 23 December, the Nationalist offensive against Catalonia began, breaking the front in four places. Bee had arrived the night before at Épila and as usual prepared an English-style Christmas with a tree, turkey, plum pudding, champagne, and sweets, while the table was decorated with holly and pine:

On 28 December at lunch, we were given rissoles made with cotton wool... and for a time nobody noticed. Princess Bee was laboriously trying to cut hers with a knife while Carla was chewing happily. When we all realised,' recounts Pip, 'we started to laugh and Carla kept on chewing and asking what the joke was. She nearly swallowed it, cotton wool and all.

They saw the old year out together and toasted the arrival of the new, 1939. It was called the Year of Victory and, for many, it would be that of peace.

18

And Peace Came

By the first quarter of 1939, hostilities were almost over. Bee, who had much relief work to do, asked Pip to come and help. On 14 January, Tarragona was taken by the forces of Gen. Solchaga who commanded the Navarre Brigades. In the cathedral, the first Mass for two and a half years was celebrated. Reus, which also offered no resistance, fell the next day. Miles of exhausted troops passed through the city marching an average of 30 km a day for three days. 'Unluckily the fun of a frantically pleased population waving flags and making whoopee was missing as the Catalans are Reds,' wrote Pip, 'so don't look on us as heroic liberators.'

Bee's provisions were taken out of her hands and distributed by local religious associations, much to her chagrin. Pip commented in her diary that Bee 'goes crazy when I have no real work, which makes one feel even more guilty for leaving her.' At midday on 26 January 1939, Bee learned that Barcelona was now under the Nationalists and that the association had two lorries ready to enter the city. They had to make a long detour because of roads being blown up, but they were there early on Friday morning. Ali, who had had flu for over a week, was recovering and he accompanied Bee the next day. They went to Barcelona and he returned to Lérida to sleep, but she remained as there was much to be done. Pip wrote in her diary:

Barcelona is a lovely big spacious town and quite unharmed though very dirty. The port is a shambles due to bombing from the air. The streets were crowded with people showing considerable enthusiasm. Everyone shouting and cheering, and all the girls were parading up the street with flags.

The troops marching through were surrounded by cheering crowds, yet as soon as one was out of the main streets, where all the fun was going on, the people looked surly and as though there had never been a war.

They had assigned the *infanta* to the enormous dilapidated Civil Hospital. The wards were dirty and full of wounded, desperate, and unable to leave:

> After attending Sunday Mass, the *Infanta* received Mercedes Mila who was the Head of the National Nursing Corps and they argued because the former wanted Consuelo Montemar to be in the same team as her friend Pip; but as Mercedes Mila did not like this solution, she left very annoyed.

Bee and Consuelo lived in a small flat belonging to a very elegant Catalan couple. They were in charge of a pavilion with 200 wounded, and worked unceasingly. At night, the roads were unsafe and traffic was heavy during the day as many people came to Barcelona to see their relations.

Pip, who was living in Monzón, entered the city and gave Bee three dozen eggs, ham, cheese, sugar, cocoa, and meat. She passed it all it to her hostess who was delighted, then went with the Diplomatic Corps on a tour of inspection of the checas, the infamous Communist torture chambers. On returning she was quite sick, and disgusted by what she had seen. On 10 February, she and Consuelo returned to Épila noticing how quickly the Catalans had returned to work and how, little by little, the goods the shopkeepers had hidden began to appear in the shops. People were buying all kinds of items which they had been deprived of for so long.

Azaña, former president of the Republic, crossed the frontier and entered France on 6 February. That same month, Pope Pius XI died and the election of Cardinal Pacelli improved relations with the Holy See. In Barcelona, the atmosphere changed with the arrival of a new era, now that the Nationalists had reached the French frontier at Le Perthus. At the end of February, the French and British governments acknowledged the Nationalist government. For the *infantes*, who had worked so hard for the cause, it was true satisfaction. However, the war continued in the central sector where in Extremadura the Republicans maintained hostilities. On 6 March, the Republic's navy fled to Bizerte in Tunisia. Gen. Miaja continued in Madrid as head of the Republican forces; it would cost him dearly to be defeated and to hand over the capital city. A final offensive started in Extremadura which was quickly held by the air force. Ali headed to Talavera following the offensive, and Bee joined him, impatient for the order to march on Madrid. Grateful for the work that she had done, she had promised Pip that she should be with them to enter the capital.

Early in March, Carla and Álvaro returned to Italy as Carla was pregnant and needed rest. Bee wrote a long letter to Ena who replied (19 March 1939), reflecting the dreams and hopes the royal family, now living in Rome, had for their restoration:

A million thanks for your dear letter which Álvaro has brought me. It was a real joy to hear from you again. You were always in my thoughts during the great events which have been taking place in Spain. It was a consolation for me being here with my children during the exciting events we have lived through.

I am so pleased to hear that Carla is expecting, because I know the great joy that it will be for you. Without doubt, it is a satisfaction to know that the family continues. I see my grandchildren often. They are very sweet and great fun. María (Countess of Barcelona) had a good confinement, and left the clinic today and has returned to her flat.

I had a long private conversation with Álvaro. Juan will not obey any order, except those from X. (Franco). When the moment comes, the call will come from Burgos. I fervently hope that A(lfonso XIII) will be the first to be told of the discussions which they have, and there will thus be no upsets. He will remain to one side, but he wants to receive the news first, and I know he is openly waiting for it. It is a small detail, but his Spanish friends ask this, as it will be better for all if it is done this way. You may pass this on. God willing, the new offensive will be short and quick. Poor and unhappy Madrid! One wonders what will be found after the recent fighting between the Communists and the Anarchists. Álvaro has told me everything, about your splendid work in Barcelona and how you were exhausted afterwards. You really are a great woman and I only hope that they show you the gratitude that you truly merit.

Luisa, Nino and Esperanza have been here for six weeks. I cannot see them doing any kind of manual work. Poor darlings! they have always been a bore, they are at the limit now! [The *Infante* don Carlos ('Nino'), his wife Princess Luisa of Orleans, and their only unmarried daughter Princess Esperanza de Borbón, who had returned to Seville at the end of the war with very little to do and finding Luisa's country property, the palace of Villamanrique, in poor condition. Being short of money, they rented a house in the centre of Seville. Don Carlos, a staunch Catholic and Doña Luisa were rather stiff and never very lively company. Esperanza later married Prince Pedro of Orleans-Bragance].

The new German game is really very worrying, and one has to ask oneself how long other countries will put up with Hitler's system of annexing that which takes his fancy. Chamberlain's speech is ugly and I fear that his anger against Hitler will explode into a war sooner or later. Selfishly, one longs to return to Spain before the storm clouds of war break. It is so terrible not belonging anywhere at this time and not knowing where to go!

A good number of foreign princes came to the Pope's coronation. We saw various members of the Spanish mission but naturally Raimundo Fernández-Cuesta did not ask for an audience nor signed the books, although I believe that A(lfonso XIII) and he talked on the Vatican terrace while they were waiting on the acts of coronation.

My thoughts and Prayers are with you and with yours in the next weeks in which I hope that there is an end to all the cruel worries that Ali and the boys have borne for so long.

The *Infanta* Cristina wrote in her *Memoirs* that once the war was finished, papá (Alfonso XIII) organised a Te Deum to thank God that peace had returned to the Spain of his heart and soul. They attended, full of emotion and hope: 'During the war, every time they took a city, Franco sent a telegram to Papá telling him about it. Madrid was taken in March 1939 and Papá waited for the telegram which never came. "The Gallego (Franco) has been playing with me!" he said to us. He then knew that he would never return to Spain again.'

Bee had chosen the town of Valdemoro, 27 km from Madrid on the Cádiz road, for her meeting with Pip. It had a railway station, but above all it was controlled by the Civil Guard and an orphanage was located there. There was also a large property called Juncarejo, with plenty of space for Bee to arrange the numerous lorries filled with supplies. As Bee always got up very early, she left that morning before 8 a.m. to Leganés where they had storage areas close to the capital.

Ali sent Álvaro a telegram (28 March 1939) to say mama was entering Madrid with the first air force troops, ahead of the army. At 10:30 a.m., they heard that Madrid had fallen, and some legionnaires told them they had entered the Real Sitio in Aranjuez at 9 a.m. Bee arrived back from her stores, her car loaded with provisions, including condensed milk, Bovril, biscuits, chocolate, and tinned meat, but no luggage.

Pip noted:

We went to the aerodrome, where I filled up with petrol, while she contacted the Air Force captain whose convoy of lorries we were to join. We set off again in the highest of spirits, the *Infanta* in front in an open grey aviation car, a grey convertible, with the captain and a lieutenant, then we four bringing up the rear. We were in high spirits and arrived at the other side of the Madrid suburb of Carabanchel singing and laughing. Then, to our horror, we found the road barred and no cars allowed to pass. The captain got down and produced papers, rang up on the telephone and argued a lot about his column of lorries which had to pass, but it was all to no avail, and we had to turn back. We were told all roads were barred, as the troops of the occupation had not yet entered. Evidently Madrid gave in even before our forces were ready to enter. We returned to Carabanchel where we drew up on the side of the road to wait. The lorries of the aviators turned up and joined us too. The soldiers gave us some cold fried fish and a little bread; the officers, a bottle of wine and a sausage. Finally, the *Infanta* and the Captain went to see if they could get a special pass. Soon after they had gone, there was suddenly wild activity. The order had come that the column could pass. Frantic action immediately ensued and all the lorries started to leave, everyone was leaping into their cars, but I said that we had to wait for the *Infanta*. Her chauffeur leapt into the road pale with agitation saying that we must not move until she came, so they calmed down again and after touring the cars we sat down to wait. I produced my last bottle of sherry, and passed it down the line to cheer them up. We passed it from hand to hand drinking out of the bottle for lack of a glass. It seemed an eternity but at last the car arrived. The captain said that he could not pass us all and everyone had to abandon cars and go in the lorries with the troops. However, finally the *Infanta* and I were allowed to take our cars. At last we set off and this time after a slight argument, passed the guards and were on our way. There were many pauses and much running up and down by the fat Captain before it was all fixed. We entered Madrid passing through the famous University City along a road built up ten or twelve feet high on either side like a trench. The view of Madrid from there was a wasteland. Not a house standing, one mass of ruins. It was a ruined mess. From there were enormous numbers of cars and lorries and troops and we had to crawl along. The people of Madrid were pouring out, shouting and jumping on the running board, begging for food, cigarettes, anything. The *Infanta*'s car, which I followed, broke down and I had to push it for most of the way. What with that and the heat, my car boiled over and cracked the radiator pouring steam in all directions. The fortifications of Madrid were unbelievable. Line after line of barricades of brick with loopholes all along for machine guns. It would have been totally impossible to take Madrid except by completely destroying it and with great losses. The enthusiasm was unbelievable. A thing I shall never forget in my life. Flags and shawls and sheets hanging from every window and the streets were full of people shouting themselves hoarse, waving and saluting. We drove all the way in through a delirious crowd. As we had to crawl along they leant in at the windows and patted on the backs, shook hands, laughed, cried, anything and everything. All the time the aviators were flying over low, zooming over the rooftops. We followed the *Infanta* a long way. She stopped from time to time and the captain leapt out to requisition a car. Finally, as she was taking him to Air Force Headquarters, we parted company as Consuelo and Rosario both wanted to find their relations. We arranged to meet them at the Romanian Legation later. That was our first call as Rosario's brother had been hidden there. We were told that Rosario's brother, Ignacio, had fainted in the street and would be back soon. When he turned up it was terrifying to see how pleased he was. Rosario gasped out his name and they clung to each other crying with joy. We made him sit down and gave him a cigarette, otherwise he would have passed out. He was pale and trembling with tears streaming down his face. We were all so touched we were gulping like mad. I have gone through so many emotions today for other people that I am limp as a leaf. Then, Consuelo and I went in a little car belonging to the legation to see her family. I accompanied her for moral support. Her father (the Duke of Montemar) and Juan were living together in a room in a 'pension' and were delighted to see her. We gave them cigarettes and promised to bring more and food tomorrow.

They found Bee at the Romanian embassy talking to Helfant, the Romanian commercial *attaché*. He was highly regarded in the diplomatic community for his work on behalf of prisoners. In 1936, he managed to convince the anarchist Melchor García Rodríguez to return to his old position as inspector general of prisons. Because of his work, the *sacas* and *paseos* at Paracuellos, or violent revenge attacks both Republicans and Nationals launched on their enemies throughout Spain, came to an end (*sacas* involved taking people out of prisons and shooting them mercilessly somewhere, while *paseos* was the same proceeding, but taking people out of their own houses for 'a stroll'). In agreement with the International Committee of the Red Cross, Rodriguez managed to have prisoners considered as prisoners of war.

On 18 November 1936, the shooting began again as well as the *sacas* at San Antón and Polier. Melchor Rodríguez wanted to resign but Henry Helfant convinced him not to do so, arguing that it was his obligation to help overcome these crimes, and Helfant helped to save many lives. Knowing of the noble actions of the Romanian business *attaché*, the *infantes* gratefully sent a telegram to their cousin, King Carol II, at Bucharest (Madrid, 28 March 1939):

Having entered Madrid on the first day, we were proud and happy to see the splendid work of the Romanian Legation in saving thousands of lives. Stop. Those who were saved have asked us to request that the Commercial *Attaché*, Helfant, continue at his post in Madrid in recognition of his outstanding service.

King Carol replied (20 April 1939), sending his best wishes for Bee's birthday, adding that he hoped 'the matter of Helfant will be arranged very soon according to your wishes'.

Bee also paid a visit to the Orleans Palace at Sanlucar, built by the old duke of Montpensier. She initially found it locked up, in disarray and with the façade badly damaged by bombs. On coming back in the afternoon, she found the old caretakers who had been looking for her, as a battalion of *Regulares* had occupied the building and the patio was filled with domestic animals. The entrance was guarded by machine guns that the Reds had abandoned in haste and the electricity was not connected properly, so she decided to return the following day. There were trenches in the garden and the palace exterior was badly damaged. Bee entered her home while the younger ones went for lunch at the Legation.

Pip described in her diary:

All round the Orleans Palace was full of shell holes and its enormous windows and glass galleries were smashed, giving it a very dishevelled and forlorn look, especially from the patio. It is very, very spoilt from outside as the stone balustrades and everything are broken and twisted and marked by shrapnel. We were shown all round by the two old porters who had managed to stay on. The bottom floor is ruined, due to military occupation.

The *Infanta*'s room, all decorated in cream silk, with 'B's embroidered all over the walls and furniture covers, was a mess, with one torn armchair and a chipped bedstead. However, the upper floor, which is the most important part, is almost untouched. We had to go round with torches as the electricity does not work properly and all the windows are sandbagged, which has saved it enormously. It must have been one of the most beautiful palaces in Europe, and I hope will be again one day. It was strange going all around it just as in the dark.

The furniture is almost all still there, stacked away in some of the rooms, and there are still some of the pictures, although most of them have gone and all the tapestries are missing. The worst part is the outside, which is utterly ruined and will take a colossal amount of work to repair. There are two rooms with shell holes in them, but luckily not the best rooms.

The staircase is a dream of beauty and unharmed except for two or three shell holes way up in the domed ceiling. I should love to see it all properly, as some of the rooms are wonderful. One entirely made of china, walls, ceiling and everything. It sounds awful but is actually very pretty, the whole room papered with exquisitely hand-embroidered silk. When we finally left the palace, the *Infanta* went to tea with her erstwhile lady-in-waiting, Belén Ruata, who had been wounded in an air attack in June 1937 and had not left the Red Zone since. She is now very old. After tea, the *Infanta* went to bed as she was feeling very ill again.

Meanwhile, on entering Madrid, Ali went straight to the royal palace and prepared a report to send by telegram to King Alfonso XIII (29 March 1939):

Visited palace Wednesday. Stop. Façade Campo Moro badly damaged. Stop. Interior looted. Lacks almost all the paintings, tapestries and carpets and most furniture. Stop. I saw intact your portrait by Sorolla, Ena by Sotomayor, Sito (Alfonsito) by Laszlo. Stop. Servants Juanito and Lucio did all possible to save some things. Stop. Genoa (apartments of the Duke of Genoa) very bad, sala de armas (hall of arms) bad, hall of columns moderate, Gasparini good, throne room good, la cámera good, banqueting hall very good, daily dining room good. Your rooms, Ena's, your mother's good but looted. I will finally move to the Madrid Brigade and continue keeping busy.

That same day, Ali attended one of the saddest acts in his long military career when Franco demanded the 'unconditional surrender' of the Republican Air Force. Gen. Kindelán had had the confidence to put Ali, and his brigade, in charge of receiving the surrender, at Barajas aerodrome outside Madrid. Two officers had flown to Burgos days before to try and change the terms of surrender. The negotiations failed because the Republican Air Force did not wish to surrender thus. Fernando Medina Martinez, a Republican pilot, recorded what happened:

On the 23rd March we received the order to hand ourselves in at Barajas. Our chiefs said this was essential so that they would recognise our position as combatants. We took off from San Clemente in nine 'Katiuskas' with another six from Tarazona, landing in the early hours at Barajas. Twelve 'Chatos' and some twenty 'Natachas' also landed. We formed up in front of the aircraft and an officer inspected us. We had not yet broken ranks when three 'Messers', one of which was Richthofen

(Colonel Baron Wolfram Richthofen, forty three years old, Chief of the High Command of the Condor Legion, and cousin of the famous Red Baron) inspected the aircraft, Kindelán and Don Alfonso of Orleans exchanged some, not exactly friendly words, with Joaquín Calvo, leader of the Republican fighters. They ordered us to line up and take off our flying gear including the jackets. We protested, but to no avail and all the equipment was shared out among them.

The following day we were taken to Porlier as Kindelán had said that 'as there were so many in Madrid, it would be easier for our families to visit us in that prison than in Alcala de Henares.' where they wanted to take us at first.

From that moment, Ali always tried to help his old comrades who had fallen into disgrace, helping their families or looking for work for them when they left prison, now they had lost their careers. As for Bee, 'she did what she could as times were very difficult and, for many, she continued being a foreigner and did not understand Spanish ways'. Years later, she confessed in a letter (Palace of Sanlúcar de Barrameda, 22 December 1960):

At first, after the war, I worked a lot at the Aviation Board of Our Lady of Loreto, as President, organising charitable events, etc. They got rid of me in complete silence, naming another President and nobody remembers us any more these days.

According to what María Ángeles Sáenz de Santa María told me, what annoyed the *infanta* most was that they treated her and her family as foreigners. Apart from the loss of her son, Alonso, at the beginning of the war, her husband was one of the first volunteers, though he was rejected and waited fourteen months before he was able to join up, and in the end, he flew innumerable hours. Prince Álvaro was also a pilot; he took part in three aerial combats, flew 264 hours on 138 missions of war, forty of them under anti-aircraft fire. As for Prince Ataúlfo, who could not be a pilot because of defective vision, he entered as a translator in the Condor Legion and took part in many actions, taking part in 354 missions, sometimes as observer, flying a total of 643 hours, and reaching the grade of honorary lieutenant.

Bee was very eager to find out how Castillejo, her estate at Riba de Saelices, was faring. Early in the morning of 30 March, the *infanta*, Consuelo, and Pip left in a car driven by Carmelo, and though the estate was next to the main road from Madrid to Valencia, Carmelo preferred to go via Guadalajara to avoid the heavy traffic. Back to Pip's diary:

From Guadalajara to Tarancón (about 100 kilometres) we saw no troops of ours at all and round about forty thousand Reds. In no other country in the world could one do that; three women and one chauffeur drive alone through an army in flight without mishap. All along the road, some going one way, some the other, in groups of twos and threes or tens and twelves. They all looked dead tired, pale and exhausted but quite cheerful. Lots were limping and hardly able to walk. All carrying their rugs and packages on their backs, but no arms at all. I think that they were glad to be able to go back to their villages at last, because most of them have no idea what the war was about anyhow. In Saelices, we went directly to Carmelo's house accompanied by the Guards and followed by the entire population. As so far no troops had entered the village, they were all wildly excited to see Carmelo. At first they did not recognise the *Infanta* and asked Carmelo rather diffidently who he was driving, not sure whether to arrest him for driving for Reds or fête him for bringing Whites. Then they began to recognise the *Infanta*.

Carmelo's mother has rheumatism and is unable to move, so could not come to the locked door to let him in when he called. However, he got in by the back and she nearly had hysterics as she thought it was her son Justin, who had disappeared. The *Infanta* went in too and relations of Carmelo's poured in. They all had fits and their shrieks and wails echoed out into the street where we were waiting. Then we left Carmelo and went with the Mayor to see Castillejo. He had appointed himself Mayor, and I think he is very Red, and a thief. The *Infanta* was horrified as her estate was well known for its miles of beautiful woods and now not one tree was there ... it has all been cut recently, as they flew over six months ago and it was still all right. The house too is ruined. Filthy, with no furniture, no doors, no windows, everything broken and the bare rooms filled with straw. The garden the same. The only thing there were her American mules. It was tragic, and she was almost in tears. Amongst the mules, she found an old white one who was twenty-one years old when she left eight years ago. It was pathetic. She stood a long time looking at it in the old and dirty stable and then said in English, 'Poor old dear, you are about the only person I know that is left here now'. It must have been a lovely house and estate, but it is now a ruin.

The Mayor had offered for us to sleep in his house, as the estate was impossible, but Carmelo said he was a Red, and on no account was the *Infanta* to sleep there, so we slept in his house.

Carmelo had been in service with the *Infantes* for over twenty years. He joined the palace, aged fifteen, as a bootblack, and his natural inventiveness and interest in study, converted him into a very competent mechanic. We lunched on chickpeas with black pudding there, and about seven they gave us cocoa and biscuits, and so as to go to bed early.

His mother is a dear old lady. We all sat around the fire while she and her relations told us the usual stories of what had gone on in the village. If people could see the *Infanta*, Consuelo and myself all sitting down to lunch together round the kitchen fire in the little cottage with no embarrassment at all, they would not run down royalty in the way they do. Carmelo's mother had been terribly brave as she had hidden a certain amount of linen from Castillejo and had buried what she could save of the silver in her back yard. If it had been discovered. She would have been shot. So I finished the war by digging for buried treasure, in the rain and by the light of a candle.

The whole village stood outside the house all evening wanting to see the *Infanta*, but Carmelo, as Prime Minister, would allow no one in, as he said, until they were sane and justice had been done she could shake hands with no one as they had all been stealing her things and cutting her trees.

Friday morning we got up at 5.45 at Carmelo's house in Salices. It was cold and almost dark but as we had gone to bed early at least we were not tired. After a nice hot cup of cocoa we set off back to Madrid. Carmelo had filled my car with petrol and it must have been filthy because it almost at once began to run badly, until after about half an hour I had to stop as it would go no further.

It was pouring with rain and poor Carmelo had to get soaked clearing the petrol pump and the carburettor, which were cluttered up with dirt. It took nearly three quarters of an hour and we had only gone a few kilometres when it started again and we finished the journey very slowly in jerks forcing the car on in every way I could think of. By the time I got back I was a nervous wreck and I don't know how I did not kill anyone, as I did not know if the car was going to shoot forward or stop. The rest of the day and all Saturday we went with the *Infanta* from place to place in the usual tiring and boring way. Canteens, hospitals, emergency stations, etc. I do not know how she stands it.

I met Miss (Fernanda) Jacobsen (she to whom the *Infanta* had sent food to Valencia in the Red zone), Head of the Scottish Ambulance, which has been very Red indeed. The *Infanta* wanted to see her about whether she would go on with her relief work amongst the population or not. She (Jacobsen) had two porridge canteens, but one was removed by Auxilio Social (the Falangist relief organisation). She had a dreadful discussion with Prince Ali as to whether she was a Red or not.

On Sunday, Consuelo and I got up at five in the morning and set off at
six, picking up the *Infanta*'s agent at Cuenca. We collected the *Infanta*'s
secretary and headed towards Cuenca. We stopped in Saelices where we
forced the Mayor to give us copies of all the papers about where all the
things from Castillejo had gone. It was a dismal day. We found neither
the very valuable books nor the silver and jewellery which was supposed
to be there, and to finish with, the agent, who had come to look for a
Red brother, found he had been shot three days ago. So we arrived at
the *Infanta*'s at nine in the evening tired, depressed and hungry. There
we found Ataúlfo, who had got two days leave. He was pretty gloomy.
He stayed for dinner to our great relief. Today we spent a good deal of
it going from place to place as usual. We lunched in one of the canteens,
where we were joined by various women. All afternoon I spent driving
about with Ataúlfo and Helfant's daughter.

The Prince said that nothing would induce him to come back here
again and that he did not want to go to Castillejo. He snapped at
everything anyone said. The poor *Infanta* was quite upset. She ended
by trying to cheer him and all of us by saying we must all try and go to
Sanlúcar together. Ataúlfo did not answer, so she asked him if he wanted
to. He said of course he was going as soon as he got a chance, but he
did not know or care if it was all the same to us. Definitely surly. Poor
old Ataúlfo, he is so upset to see his beloved Madrid the way it is and,
like everyone else, was having a nervous reaction, now the war is over.
When we said goodbye, the *Infanta* begged him to be careful flying and
not to think the danger was over because there was no more war. How
right she was! Today the best pilot in Spain, Morato, was killed doing
an exhibition flight. The second best, Ibarra too and five or six others.
Everyone is terribly upset about Morato, as he was a brilliant man as
well as a brilliant pilot and the one person people counted on to deal
with the future of the Spanish Air Force. Apart from that, he was a great
friend of Prince Ali's, and his poor wife, whom I have met from time to
time, a great friend of the *Infanta*'s so everyone is miserable about it.
After bidding goodbye to Ataúlfo, the *Infanta* and I went about twelve
to Barajas to see the canteen and get Prince Ali to start inquiries about
Carmelo's brother Santos, who has also disappeared. It was pelting
with rain, cold and very windy. We first sat in Escario's (Ramón Escario
Nuñez who was ADC to Ali, and had joined the Air Force from the
Infantry) and then Prince Ali's offices waiting about, admiring the rain
swept field. Escario was frantically telephoning, not letting any machines
leave for Barajas, but three had already gone, one of which smashed and
another still missing.

Prince Ali, the *Infanta* and I lunched in a little alcove off the kitchen where there was just room for the table, a chair for the *Infanta* and a high stool for me. Prince Ali ate standing up in a corner. Then we went to pack. We spent the afternoon trying to find wine, glasses, cups, chorizo, corkscrews and tin openers for the Barajas canteen. We found all except the wine, and took it there. Finally, about seven, I collected my luggage and all the food stores and I moved into our new house. It is a wonderful palace, very comfortable, big, and with all luxuries as it was the Turkish Legation.

After dinner, Prince Ali and Escario, who is living here too, went to see Morato lying in state so the *Infanta* and I stayed talking by the fire. We talked a lot of hospitals, as I have decided that I want to do the English end of providing orthopaedic instruments and plastic surgery for the war cripples. It would be very interesting.

Thursday, 6th April. We can't all go on being so depressed and miserable, and as no one seems to be going to cheer us up I have decided I have to do it. Someone must or we will all die of depression. So I am trying to organise an amusing Easter: after all it is the first Easter of peace since 1936 and we ought to celebrate it as we have not yet had time to celebrate the end of the war. We have got paints from Helfant's daughter, with which to paint the eggs for breakfast; we are going to try and locate the peach brandy and try and get Ataúlfo to come. He swore he would on no account return to Madrid. Tonight we tried to ring him up, but could not get through as the telephones are in dreadful disorder...

In May, Pip was awarded the Military Cross with red decoration for valour at the Escatrón front. Bee was delighted as she had always believed in the young Englishwoman's eagerness to serve. Pip had not seen her mother for a year, but now the war was over Margot Howard de Walden came to Spain with her son John. The meeting was to take place in the Gran Hotel, with a Pip 'disinfected and deloused' before seeing her mother and her brother John. On 23 May 1938:

We started out early on our journey to Épila, leaving about seven o'clock. We made record time and arrived at Zaragoza at 12.45, and Épila in time for lunch. It was grand to see Mama again. She and my brother John were sitting with Princess Bee and Prince Ali in the little garden, when we pranced in absolutely filthy. As they had not expected us until the next day, they were all very surprised. I was rather ashamed of my dirty uniform stained from head to toe, no make-up and my hair long and untidy, but Mama did not seem to mind a bit.

Pip gracefully told them what she did and Margot complained to the *infanta* about the horrors Pip was experiencing. She replied: 'I promised you dear Margot, that I would care for her as if she were my own daughter and, if I had a daughter, without any doubt, she would be at the front'. Now, the war happily over, Bee wrote her friend Margot about the character of Pip's work:

> In Madrid, we found the population in deplorable conditions, with scenes of starvation. We have had to make visits separately because there is so much work [from twenty to thirty visits to homes without lifts]. Pip has cared for these people, she has given them injections and brought them food. At night she typed reports for the hospitals absolutely alone and in perfect Spanish. Where there is no doctor to turn to, she makes the diagnosis herself. She took cancer patients to the oncological hospital, those with TB to the sanatorium—she never made a mistake. Her intelligence and patience have been amazing. She did all this alone, and without a single day off. Now she is known over the length and breadth of Spain,. she is never nervous or impatient.
>
> I want you to know all this because in organised England, perhaps you have never seen her going ahead with a job of work without help as she has done in Madrid.

Maria Ángeles and her husband returned from Castillejo with Bee's Easter presents. They were a part of her favourite belongings which she (Maria Ángeles) managed to save: a precious and old Spanish bedspread embroidered in yellow and red, really divine, and really a valuable museum piece; Bee's pistol with her initials and crown engraved on it, very light and pretty; and some vacuum flasks. Santa María had a mountain of things to tell of his two-day stay at Castillejo. Some fourteen people had been jailed for robbery, and many of Bee's belongings were reappearing. The estate was operating well and had produced a good harvest. In fact, it seems as if, at last, all was ending well. Bee's joy on seeing her things again was endless and we all laughed at Santa María's stories about her receiving them and her persecution of the criminals.

Bee planned to give a dinner on 13 April for the German and Italian pilots who had to return home, but the general of the division forbade any partying until the grand victory parade in Madrid. It was disappointing as they had everything prepared: the band, the meal, two cooks, waiters, and everything, brought specially from Bilbao. That morning, Bee, annoyed about only knowing of the cancellation at the last minute, went with her lady-in-waiting, María Ángeles Tornos Sáenz de Santa María, to visit the new flat they were to take at number 47 Calle José Abascal.

It was large and spacious, but rather dark. During the war, the building had been the Norwegian embassy, housing many refugees and saving lives.

On 14 April, Bee, Consuelo and Pip left for Valdemoro, followed by an empty lorry. They had to collect what still remained in the store there. They asked for the help of six soldiers to carry the sacks of sugar, the boxes of tinned meat, and the condensed milk which they loaded on to the lorry. Pip noted:

We dropped the milk in at the emergency station store, where the *Infanta* was presented, to her disgust, with a paper informing her that she had been elected President of the Emergency Stations, which means still more work, and to her delight she was also given some onions and oranges. We ate onions all the way back in the car. The *Infanta* suddenly suggested we should go to Seville for the march past the day after tomorrow. I said we would if she came too. But she said she would not go, excusing herself by saying she was too tired and ill to travel, which she is. So we said we would stay with her. God knows I would love to go and have fun in Seville!

Bee then had a letter from Ena (Rome, 11 April 1939), foretelling the start of the Second World War:

I wrote this letter thinking that Álvaro was returning to Spain on the 20th March, I have only added a few words. It seems to be too good to be true that the war in Spain has finished. If only the situation in Europe was not so dark, one could have a light heart. Thanks to God, Spain has a sane and good man like Franco who will help poor Spain to get through these times. But I still tremble when I think that our poor country, which has suffered so terribly, could become involved in an inevitable European War. I return to London on the 19th with a heart filled with premonitions, wondering when I will see my children again. Ali's telegram giving us news of how he found the palace interested us greatly.

I wonder if anything remains of your home. Firstly, have you been able to get a good idea of Madrid? It has been incredible how quickly Madrid has surrendered. I could not believe my eyes when I read in the newspapers that each city surrendered without a fight. Tomorrow we have a Te Deum of thanksgiving for the end of the war, in the Church of Jesus, where Baby married, and to which we are all going. I saw Álvaro two nights ago at a family meal at the Torlonia's house and he told me that he is much better and that he will soon leave and he will be able to give you this letter.

I only want you to know how much I think of you and how much I want us to be able to be together and to talk about these long years of anguish.

Ali, very pleased with his new post in charge of the 2nd Aviation Brigade, wrote to Bee (26 May 1939):

Aranda has asked after you: he was a lieutenant colonel with Jordana in Morocco. Yagüe and Camilo Alonso have been comrades of mine. Solchaga and Carlos Martinez Campos are naturally closer friends, as is Valiño. As you can see I am in good company.

In Pip's diary, hospital visits are confused with social events. For example, on 20 April, Bee's fifty-fifth birthday, they went to a cocktail party that Perico Chicote gave for Frentes y Hospitales. Two days later, they went to the Carmelite Convent of Cerro de los Ángeles where they had no food or water, and so they delivered some. The Mother Superior showed them around. It was completely ruined, with what remained of the convent surrounded by trenches and barbed-wire entanglements. They found two very small rooms, one the chapel, the other a bedroom with just room for their eight beds. As they were not allowed mattresses and could find no straw, they slept on cork mats.

On 14 May, a grand victory parade of the air force occurred at Barajas. Bee and Consuelo went to Barajas at 5:45 a.m. to serve breakfast to the soldiers. The grand parade was celebrated the same day in brilliant sunshine and the airport, all newly painted and elegant, looked at its best, decorated with flags and flowers. The Moroccan Guard surrounded the platform where the *generalissimo* was to review the troops, arriving at 11:45 a.m. Pip reported:

We all saluted while they played the National Anthem. He drove round inspecting the machines which were lined up about six deep in front of the buildings as far as one could see. Hundreds of them. Then we took up our positions on the first floor balcony to serve drinks to Franco and the Generals. He made a speech and, then we handed round drinks while they all talked until the march past began. Franco is a weeny little man the size and shape of a tennis ball and looked too funny beside huge lanky Kindelán and even taller lankier Queipo de Llano. The march past, which we saw beautifully, was the same as they usually are. The Germans' goose-step made us laugh, the Italians were very few and the Spanish held their own well. Prince Ali marched at the head of his men looking splendid.

On 24 May 1939, Franco ordered the disbanding of Frentes y Hospitales, an organisation akin to Carlist ideas that aimed to provide clothing, laundry, and hospital services during the war. Now the fighting was over, he maintained that it was no longer needed. Moreover there were many Carlists among the 40,000 girls who worked for it, and he wanted to strip the Carlist organisations of any real power. Once it ceased to exist, it had to hand over everything to Auxilio Social, a humanitarian organisation created in 1936 to serve the ideas of Franco's new regime. It ostensibly aimed to provide social relief, but was a means of easy propaganda for the unique political party of the new regime, which was Falange Española y de las JONS. A strong Catholic institution, it was under the command of Falange and initially followed the model set up by the Nazi Winterhilfswerk. After the 1940s, it became the main social relief institution in Spain. Falange Española Tradicionallista y de las Juntas de Ofensiva Nacional Sindicalista was the unique legal political party during Franco's regime, created in 1937 as a blend of incomprensible ideas mixing the ideals of Jose Antonio Primo de Rivera and Italian fascism. In Madrid, people were reassessing their lives. Some decided to move from their homes with sad memories, others returned to empty ruined houses to try and recover what they had lost, some even writing 'reclaimed' leaving their names on pieces of furniture and objects which were either theirs, or someone else's that they rather liked. That summer, there was much romance among those who had lived in embassies, those who had suffered imprisonment and those behind the lines. Many girls wanted to get married, among them Pip Scott-Ellis, who had been deeply in love with Prince Ataúlfo for more than five years. During the war, she had always tried to help him although each time he rejected her.

Pip always tried to please Bee, and mentioned her frequently in her diary. She wrote (23 April) that all evening, both of them had been playing the fool imitating people they knew: 'Our conversation became more and more ridiculous, the *Infanta* is really incredibly funny'. Pip knew that Bee liked her and thought she would not oppose the wedding, though she remembered that her mother had written her about Bee's last visit to London in December 1938: 'She says that Princess Bee likes me very much, but Prince Ali has his sights set on royalty and that Ataúlfo is not in love with me because he knows me too well, although likes me better than anyone else'.

Although some people warned her that it was useless to hope, Pip remained optimistic. Ali and Bee knew that Ataulfo was gay, and would not have allowed such a marriage to take place. Ali was very fond of her; he had recently taken her up in a Savoia-Marchetti 79 bomber and had let her pilot it for ten minutes. Ataúlfo left for Germany with the Condor

Legion. She re-read her diary and found that Ataúlfo had taken her to visit
Calle Quintana:

> We forced the padlock and began to explore. It was in a terrible state and
> I am sorry that Ataúlfo saw it, as he adored the house and wanted to tidy
> it up. Although the windows were broken, the doors were in a good state
> and the parquet flooring, although covered with mud, had not been torn
> up. The two rooms where the bombs had fallen had disappeared. Now
> there is only one room with a bath and a shower that float in the middle
> of the room. While Ataúlfo wants to do it up and live there, the *Infanta*
> says that she wants to sell it.

On another occasion, Ataúlfo, on seeing Pip unwell, said he would stay to
keep her company without going to a 'Review', 'but the *Infanta* wanted
me to go, so I went.' Her last day in Madrid was 31 May. She went with
the *infanta* to dine at the Hotel Ritz, and dressed as best she could. There
were twenty present, and Bee gave the girls handbags as presents.

Ataúlfo's departure with the Condor Legion to Germany made her
think, and Pip realised it was time to leave for England. She sailed from
Gibraltar on 5 June 1939 and was in her home at Seaford four days later.
One of her first tasks was to inform Ena of the situation in Spain. She
told of how Red the Falange was, and that Serrano Suñer was ambitious,
egotistical, and not to be trusted.

When she could, the *Infanta* Beatrice left for Sanlúcar hoping to rest,
accompanied on the flight there by Ultano Kindelán and his fiancée,
Doreen. They arrived at Jerez and then went by car to Sanlúcar. A long
letter, which she typed in English to Álvaro, described the summer
immediately after the end of the war:

> We are here with the old life and working hard. Everything is very difficult
> and one has to force oneself to work [hard] to keep the fires in the house
> lit. Little brother (Ataúlfo) is now busy with Castillejo, because Santa
> (César Sáenz de Santa María) cannot cope alone, especially because he
> has no car. Naturally things at Castillejo are very complicated because
> everything was destroyed and we have little money to start again.
> Ataúlfo really should work a little, like me who has worked hard all
> my life in the *fincas* [written in Spanish] and I am becoming old (having
> completed fifty-five years) and I find things here in Sanlúcar, as much as I
> can handle, especially now that we have to look after the house and keep
> up its maintenance.

Many friends continued visiting them and were received affectionately.

Among those spending summer at the palace were María Ángeles Tornos and her husband, Gen. Sáenz de Santa María, old friends who had had to live in Red Madrid. María Ángeles remained Bee's only lady-in-waiting.

Pip returned to Santander on 19 July, because she did not really like England. Ataúlfo appeared in London 'very handsome, brown and healthy', according to Pip who confessed in her diary: 'In the first place he is not in love with me. In the second place, he has no money so he cannot marry anyone. And finally, he has promised his mother to marry a princess'. But together again in Sanlúcar, they spent their time arranging the garden

Bee was overjoyed at the birth in Rome on 25 August of her first granddaughter, Gerarda, who was baptised by Cardinal Gaspari at Altipiani di Arcinazzo. She wrote to her son of her disappointment at being unable to attend the ceremony, and longed to see the child: 'Tell Carla from me that she should be proud of her ancestry. Gerarda must be a record for her age. I hope to be able to go to Rome later. It seems that we will be here all winter'. Turning to events elsewhere, she expressed her grave worries about those who had disappeared in Finland: 'I have many friends there from times past and God knows what will happen to them'.

This naturally referred to the Second World War. Horrified by the new conflict, Pip drove across Spain and France, arriving in London on 9 September 1939. An exhausted Spain remained neutral. 'Grandmother is in San Sebastian and wants us to go and see her; but I cannot leave here just now,' wrote Ena referring to Ali's mother, Eulalia. At the beginning of September, *Infanta* Eulalia, fleeing from the war, arrived in San Sebastián. She settled herself in the home of the countess of Pedroso, a small but comfortable flat in the centre of the town that the countess shared with her daughter, María Luisa.

It was like living through 1914 again. Veterans of the last war rushed to enlist as volunteers to fight again in Germany, France, and England. Born in England and educated in Germany, Bee had known many young pilots from Ataulfo's Condor Legion during the conflict in Spain who perished. She was deeply preoccupied by the international situation, though she did not mention it in a letter to Alvaro in which she wrote:

I think that El Botánico will be very pretty with the beautiful flowers that Ataúlfo has planted. He really is a slave driver (and feels lent upon) by all the ladies invited there, who come in teams to marry him. Naturally, he feels furious, and treats me all the time as if I were 'gaga' and that (according to him) I have never seen a garden in my life. I gently reminded him that if there is a Botánico it is all due to the sweat of my brow, but this does not impress him very much.

Bee was going to end the year with these thoughts although, at the bottom of her heart, she was hoping to live in Sanlúcar and to improve the lives of her neighbours. Nobody suspected that war would devastate Europe again.

19

Confined to Sanlúcar

In the summer of 1939, peace descended on Spain. It left Bee without a project, or any community work, but she had an idea very dear to her heart, a maternity home for the women of Sanlúcar:

> First time mothers are generally looked after until the moment of birth by their family, and from then on receive further support from the family. But in the case of those who have two or three children, they are frequently consumed by their daily chores and they forget to care for themselves and when the birth arrives they find themselves in bad condition and then it is too late to save them.

She found an experienced doctor, Ramón Otaolaurruchi, a skilled obstetrician. He was enthusiastic about Bee's plans but had some doubts as to whether they were realistic. They began with £100 and the support of another renowned obstetrician, Don Jacinto Ovin—but almost no doctors. Bee had qualified as a nurse at the age of eighteen and was always interested in children and nursing mothers. She continued her education in Lucerne. Meanwhile, there were over twenty estate workers at the palace, the Torre Breva Estate, and the Botánico, tending fruit and vegetables; two gardeners; five caring for the poultry, chickens, ducks, and geese; a miller; a plumber; a groom; a carpenter and his assistant. Economies would be called for.

Sanlucar society looked to her for entertainment as well. She started holding what became her famous 'teas' for the ladies of the town. In order to attend, each lady had to have a hat, which few possessed, so they were passed from one to another, hence their comment, 'Now the hat dance has begun'. Bee spotted the same headgear time and again so she decided to give the ladies of Sanlúcar the privilege to come dressed in traditional Flamenco style instead. But nobody dared invite Ali and Bee to their own home except for the rather eccentric couple, Manolo Ruiz de Somavía and his wife, Pilita Mergelina. Society was amazed when Ali and Bee accepted the invitation. Manolo and Pilita trained their maid to announce their illustrious visitors and dressed her up in a lace apron and cap on the day. Pilita laid out lunch in a shady spot in the garden and put the Spanish flag on the collar of their dog. When told the *infantes* had arrived, the girl became nervous and remembering only the nicknames used for the *infantes* in the town, cried out: 'Don Labaro (Mr Gardener), Don Trufo (Mr Truffle), and Miss *Infanta*!' At the announcement, the dog began to run dragging the flag behind it, a donkey took fright and fled in terror, and the farm overseer was worried because the pigs had gone into a neighbour's corral. Ali then seated himself in cane chair which collapsed under him leaving him sprawling on the ground. On leaving, he was greatly amused by the consternation of his hosts, and he exclaimed: 'The next time—I will bring a carpenter—but with a flag.'

In the spring of 1940, Germany began its occupation of Europe. On 10 May, the troops of the Third Reich invaded Holland, Belgium, and Luxembourg, and entered France. A month later, they were at the gates of Paris, obliging the French government to seek an armistice. Ali was worried about the arrival of the Germans at the Spanish frontier, as his mother now lived in Irún, on the French border.

Bee's nephew, King Carol of Romania, also gave them grounds for concern. He had banished his wife, Queen Helen, from the country, installed his mistress, Elena Lupescu, in the palace, and aligned himself with the Nazis. Eventually his government sent him into exile. In his diary, Ali noted how, on 18 September 1940, he had to go to Sitges and meet Carol, who had arrived in Spain incognito and installed himself in the Hotel Terramar with Elena. He was allowed to bring nine wagonloads of paintings, furniture, and jewels from Romania.

On the morning of 20 September, Ali, accompanied by Ultano Kindelán, went to Madrid to see if he could guarantee residency in Spain for Carol. At the Ministry of Foreign Affairs, Ali obtained full assurances that he could live in Spain. Returning to Sanlúcar, he telephoned him to give him the good news, inviting him to come and stay in Sanlucar with himself and Bee, on condition that he came alone.

Three weeks later, Carol arrived in Seville and next day went to hear Mass at Tablada. Ali commented in English in his diary: 'I took tea with Carol and told him that no lady could replace his wife'. On 7 November,

Carol left for Madrid visiting the count of Mayalde, the mayor of the city, and the Minister of Foreign Affairs. Without a word of thanks to Ali, he then left Spain. In his diary, Ali only noted in English: '4th March 1941. Carol escaped to Portugal'. His lover, Elena Lupescu, completely dominated him. After many years in America, they married in Brazil and later went to live in Portugal.

Having abdicated in favour of his son, Juan, on 15 January 1941, Alfonso XIII died in Rome on 28 February at the Grand Hotel, from heart disease. Ena visited him and the doctor present remembered him saying, 'Ena, it's over!' He was surrounded by all his children except the *Infanta* Maria Cristina, who was in Turin awaiting the birth of a daughter. She wrote to the Ali and Bee to thank them for their condolences:

> I know how disappointed you will be for my not being able to come and share with all my heart our great sorrow. Poor Papa, he was a great personality and the best of fathers. I miss him very much and find it difficult to accept that he has gone forever, as it was all so quick. It was tragic not to be able to go to Rome and to be with him at the end, to receive his last words and a goodbye kiss.

The funeral took place in the Church of Santa Maria degli Angeli e dei Martiri in the presence of the Spanish royal family and the king and queen of Italy, while Alvaro represented his parents. The former king was buried in the Church of Santa Maria in Monserrato degli Spagnoli, the Spanish national church in Rome. On 2 March 1941, the funeral mass for his soul was celebrated in Seville Cathedral. The *Infantes* Don Carlos and Don Alfonso presided over the ceremony.

Bee's maternity home was now open. It looked after the poor of Sanlúcar, Chipiona, the Campo de Jerez, Campo de Rota, and Trebujena, performed some 7,000 interventions and oversaw 6,000 births. Bee insisted that one of her major priorities was to solve the problem of medical help for the middle classes and ensure that it was affordable. One case which shocked Bee greatly, and which she always remembered, was that of Manuela Rey Cámara who lived and worked in her Torre Breva mansion with her husband and son. Pregnant again, Manuela went to the home for her confinement, but died giving birth to twins, called Domingo and Teresa. Bee was saddened as she had been really fond of her, and she sought a wet nurse who kept the twins for a year. For eight years, until the twins received their First Communion, and without missing a single day, she sent someone with 5 litres of milk every morning from the Botánico to Torre Breva.

The home was housed in the old palace in Sanlucar, purchased by Bee for a million pesetas, apparently from her sale of jewellery inherited from her mother. Her friends had been invited to contribute furniture, and she set up a *bodega* to make the local Manzanilla wine to help finance the running costs. There were sixty beds, all looked after by consultant obstetricians, assistants, and nurses. Bee was in charge of collecting those about to give birth in her car, which had to be deloused every fifteen days. All expenses were paid by the *infantes*, with the help of income from an annual fair and donations from friends. In El Botánico, there was a dairy and chicken farm, the production of which was destined for the home. When Bee died, Ali continued her work, apart from the annual fair, replaced by a raffle for charity. It is no surprise to learn that the *infantes* were loved by the local adults and children alike. The children especially loved that they ensured toys were traditionally left in their shoes on the first days of every year, the 'Reyes' (three kings) festival. As for the adults, they wanted to work on the estate of El Botánico where they received their daily wages from the profits made by the bodega. Half the profits were shared equally among all the workers.

Bee really was the soul of the home. I owe Lolita Bustillo, Encarnita's sister, for giving me so much information about Sanlúcar:

One of the oldest nurses was Pastora Díaz who was from Seville and entered service at the Gota de Leche (Drop of Milk) when she was sixteen. The *Infanta* did not put people so young in the delivery area but she watched them and the older ones, and when they were of an appropriate age, they passed to the Maternity Home and she, herself, taught them with great patience. When Bee died, the Medal of Merit which she had been given was given as a present to Pastora who wore it always until the day of her death, in 2003.

Pastora remembered that at the Maternity Home all the staff called her Doña Beatriz when they joined the team. The expectant mothers arrived hungry and covered with lice, so before taking them to the delivery room, the first thing they did was to put them in a bath so that the newborn babies did not catch infections. The *Infanta*, Consuelo and the girls put on bonnets and aprons, above all the bonnets so that they did not catch lice, and they practically put themselves into the baths with the women because the women were frightened and refused to bathe. Later, clean and dry, they passed to the gynaecologist's office.

At the time of the grape harvest things were complicated because, in order to cut the grapes, they wore trousers under their skirts and the poor women were only able to stop work at the last minute. When the girls, among whom Pastora was to be found, heard a cart approaching, and recognised it by the clatter on the cobbles, they immediately called for Doña Beatrice. It was she who cut the trouser legs with scissors, because the babies' heads were sometimes almost out. Some did not arrive at the delivery room and if they had not been born on the cart, they emerged at the door of the Maternity Home. Later, the *Infanta* would tell them off lovingly saying to them why did they go to cut grapes in their condition. The women replied, 'Señorita *Infanta*, hunger is very bad!'

Curiously it was the *Infanta*, together with the administrator, who helped organise the grape harvest, by being present at the breakfast of bread, lard, and coffee with milk. At lunch there was a good stew of bacon, black pudding, chorizo, and beef. Before eating they were served a jug of wine. At night, there was steak with potatoes, or fish, and pudding, oranges, melon or grapes. A wine skin of 500 litres was produced. The cook, María Muñoz, took great pains in giving food to thirty people. Some went to their homes, but most slept on straw mattresses.

Ali was assigned to duties in Seville, but travelled back 70 miles every night to Sanlúcar. In his official car, he brought leftovers from the barracks for the home. One day he went to Malaga where he exchanged precious rose seedlings at Tablada Airport for sugar needed at the maternity home. Bee started breeding chickens so there were fresh eggs for the home, with enough left over to sell. She also brought in a machine to make butter every day, as there was none in the town.

The dairy was run by five cowmen, and a delivery man to distribute the milk. *Infanta* Eulalia commented kindly that her daughter-in-law had dedicated herself to rural matters as she liked organising things and did it so well: 'Besides, the butter factory gives the children something that goes with the bread, which is good for them. Things, which no doubt, were forbidden during her childhood!'

In the second winter of the post-war period, the ravages of hunger were more noticeable among the poor, and Bee worked hard to obtain provisions. On 29 March, she left for Rome where she had just a six-day holiday, spending time with Alvaro, Carla, and their daughter. Carla was expecting another child and Bee promised to go to the baptism.

Ena was still living in Rome, at the home of her daughter, *Infanta* Beatriz, who was married to Prince Alessandro Torlonia. The cousins were able to meet again, going for walks around the city like two tourists. Ena's position was precarious, as she had a house in London but Italy had been at war with Britain since 9 June 1940. Mussolini and the Germans wanted her to leave as she was Queen Victoria's granddaughter and a fervent supporter of the Allies. Nor was the *Duce*'s government happy to have Juan, Alfonso XIII's successor, in Rome. He too was unable to live in Spain. There, he was represented by Don Juan Vigón, Franco's aviation minister. During the monarchy, Vigón had been the *infantes*' tutor and an aide to Alfonso XIII. In the Civil War, he was head of the high command of the Navarre Brigades, enjoyed great prestige in the army and had the confidence of many who thought he could bring Juan as king under the name of Juan III.

Meanwhile, at the end of January 1941, Ali's disreputable brother, Luis, had installed himself in Sanlúcar. In 1930, he had married the princess of Broglie, the widow of Prince Amedée of Broglie, who was thirty-one years older than him, spent all her money and was thrown out of Italy, penniless. He believed he could obtain funds from Torre Breva, a trust set up by the old duke of Montpensier in England for the benefit of Ali and Luis, who owned it jointly, in order to prevent the latter from spending and squandering more of the family's fortune. Ali and Bee spent several months trying to cajole Luis into reforming himself. Bee said:

> García Muñoz saved the estates during the revolution and the Republic, often at great personal danger, and we found them in rather better condition than other owners found theirs. I tried to reason with Luis to live in Sanlúcar quietly and take a good look at Torre Breva and what its income could be; but he replied, 'Bee, you are stupid: if I know exactly what a mediocre income we have, how can I make people believe that I have millions and take money off them. He caused such scandal in Paris that he was banished again. We tried to get him to return to Spain, but he argued that he was too ill to travel and he remained under German protection, although our Embassy, the Consulate, and my mother-in-law made it impossible for him to return. We sent him what money we could from his share in Torre Breva, despite restrictions and the complete lack of communication with France. The balance of the payment was in his name in a bank in Sanlúcar.

At the end of September, he left, dependent on alcohol and drugs, and randomly giving money to strangers in the street. Ali said that he could not live with them 'because we lived like poor people, because we had no liveried servants nor luxuries'.

That summer, Carla had given birth to a son in Rome, calling him Alonso. His circulation was poor and he was 'a blue baby' as any effort made him turn that colour; otherwise, he was a lovely child, blond, with brown eyes. Bee went for a few days to Rome to see him.

In the autumn, *Infanta* Eulalia obtained a diplomatic passport for Bee so she could go and visit her family in Germany. She left for Berlin on 20 November, returning three weeks later. Everyone in Germany looked sad, talked little, and seemed strained, and Bee returned very worried about them. Those living in Italy took refuge in Switzerland or Spain. Carla and her two children came to stay in Sanlúcar.

In April 1942, Ali received a telegram from Ferdinand, the aged ex-tsar of Bulgaria. Since his abdication in 1918, he had lived in Coburg, surrounded by memories of his old splendour. He said that Sandra (Alexandra of Saxe-Coburg and Gotha) had died suddenly on the 16th, and wanted to prepare Bee for the bad news as he was very fond of her. The death of her last remaining sister was a hard blow for Bee. Sandra had married a man fifteen years older than herself when she was only seventeen. She and Bee were very different in their tastes and in their focus on life. Sandra was said to be jealous of Bee because her mother bent over backwards for her. In fact, the duchess had often been bored by Sandra's company. During the First World War, Sandra, encouraged by a lady-in-waiting, had had an affair with a doctor, much to the duchess's anger. Bee wanted to travel to Coburg and be with her nieces and nephews and their children, but that was impossible. Later she was able to invite them to Sanlúcar.

In May 1942, Franco invited the *Infanta* Eulalia to stay at the Hotel Ritz in Madrid, putting two diplomats at her disposal in turns and a car with chauffeur. She enjoyed inviting Ali to lunch with her and to go around Toledo, Ávila, and other nearby places. Although she admired Ali for his intelligence and elegance, she sometimes treated him as if he were a little boy. Ali, who had a great sense of humour, would say to his close friends, 'It seems that Mama thinks that I am running in!'

Now chief of the Strait of Gibraltar, Ali was busy in the winter of 1942. The Germans, Italians, and British frequently asked him for news of aircraft that had disappeared, and of the pilots' fate, a thankless task he undertook very well. In April, he fell ill with typhus in Sanlúcar, and Bee cared for him unremittingly. For the first time she felt he might actually die in his bed and not in a flying accident, as she had always thought he would. On 21 April, after fifteen days' rest, he was able to go out for the first time. His natural strength had helped him through his illness.

On 22 June 1941, the Second World War reached a critical stage with the start of the German attack on the Soviet Union. In Spain, it was believed that Hitler would be victorious, although some were firmly convinced of an Allied victory, among them the *infantes*, who always tried to appear neutral. Ali was worried as Franco had made no pronouncement on any change during the war. He had written to his nephew, Juan, who was in Switzerland with his wife and sons. Juan took some time to answer and his reply was rather thankless. Ena wrote to Bee (Lausanne, 30 March 1943):

I feel sadness and am depressed by the news from Spain. It concerns us, although I am cheered that the people are beginning to become more prosperous. I know that Juan has written to Ali that he wishes that his letter were different from the previous one, which made him so sad. You will understand that I cannot bother Juan all the time and be checking if he has written to one person or another. But I deeply deplore that he has not written to Ali for such a long time and has done so in such a brusque manner. As for Sotomayor, his not having let Ali know that he was Juan's representative since October is unreasonable, and this was aggravated when he informed my chamberlain, Fernando Mora, of his new position. Fernando asked him to let him communicate the fact to the *Infante*, so he has no excuse for not having done so.

As for the matter of El Escorial, he was not to blame. I came here with Franco's verbal permission, telling us that an official Mass would be celebrated in Madrid and all provincial capitals, this year for poor Alfonso, and then at the last moment, he cancelled everything that he had promised (when Perico (Sotomayor) was already here) and organised this absurd funeral *for all the Kings of Spain* at El Escorial [In Spanish].

If people had not been so blind, they would have seen what F(ranco) was up to at El Escorial: the end of the Monarchy, erasing all personal sentiment towards the memory of Alfonso and leave it lost in the past. Because of this, Perico has resigned from his political position and Juan has accepted this and is quite content because he is too stupid and timid, and it is an echo of times past forged by Vigón and now by his ambitious and little son-in-law (Alfonso Hoyos) whom everyone dislikes. The real annoyance is that there is a lack of a bond in Spain that all will follow unconditionally. Calvo Sotelo, Honorio Maura, and the Reds would have known who to choose to get rid of in the future. Juan has now organised a group of seven people among them Paquito Eliseda (who I like and trust) and with whom you should be in contact and who should tell you of the decisions taken and of the work done. Another is Ventosa. But what is now needed is a head for the group to harmonise the bloc: this person has to be found.

The Captains General mean to block it completely. F(ranco) has been clever enough to keep them quiet, by paying them and not losing his position or risking some pro-monarchy action. Naturally, the only sure and reasonable thing would be that Juan returns before the end of the war, but nothing can be done until F moves from where he is. As you say, 'he has taken great pleasure from the honours and power and is not disposed to lose them.'

Juan has written a brilliant letter to him, which you will certainly see sooner or later. This, at least (we hear), will make him change his speech in the Cortes, provided that he does not proclaim himself Regent, as was his intention. Only God knows.

If the Allies win the war, which seems the most likely, then I expect that the days of Franco and his precious Falange will be numbered. I cannot see England and America supporting or accepting Franco and his totalitarian state. All the more reason for Juan to return before they can lift a finger, because they will have a *fait accompli*, and they will, without doubt, accept him and the Spanish Monarchy, which is after all, as old and traditional as the British Monarchy.

After speaking of her family, Ena ended with a postscript sending Ali her love, and telling him how much she wanted to come and see them all. This letter reveals the intrigue now surrounding her son, who they were calling Juan III. With Ena by this side, Juan showed energy and willpower. But when he left to live in Portugal, he did not. Many visited him there from Spain, playing a double game, professing royal allegiance in front of the king while blindly obeying Franco.

Carla, expecting her third child, planned to return to Seville for her confinement. Due at the end of April, at 11 p.m. on the 25th, it seemed imminent. Acording to Pip's diary:

> We left at half past twelve. The *Infante* driving the car along the bad Jerez road rushed to take Carla to the Red Cross, but on their reaching Seville and entering the clinic, the pains ceased. The *Infanta* then advised her daughter-in-law to take a horse drawn coach and go for a long ride. It was just what the doctor ordered: a day later, at four in the morning, on the 27th April 1943, while the Ferias were on, Carla gave birth to a beautiful girl who was named Beatrice after her grandmother.

The child was baptised in Sanlúcar on 20 May in the parish church of the Virgen de la O. Her godfather was her uncle, Ataúlfo, and her godmother was the countess of Barcelona who, unable to enter Spain, sent her mother, *Infanta* Luisa, as her representative. Luisa carried the babe in her arms, and almost lost her balance as the little girl weighed as much as she did. Born during the April Feria, Beatriz de Orleans would be the most Andalusian of the *infantes*, enjoying Sanlúcar which she called '*mi pueblo*' (my town) and learned to dance sevillanas at a very early age and at the express wish of her grandmother, 'when it was still not fashionable to do so and was even considered somewhat common'.

In September 1942, the mansion in Calle Quintana was sold for 900,000 pesetas, a low price bearing in mind that it was located in an aristocractic neighbourhood and next to the upmarket Calle Princesa. Ali, who put the money into the *bodegas*, had made an excellent investment.

Juan, waiting in vain for a reply to his letter to Franco, named Ali his representative in Spain on 8 March 1943. Ali travelled to Lausanne, and in his diary he noted laconically:

26 May. I went to see Franco and in the afternoon I was with Perico Sotomayor (who it is understood went to visit the Generalissimo to announce to him that he was to be the King's representative).

27 May. I saw Vigón and Muñoz Grandes.

28 May. I went by plane from Madrid to Barcelona, where I caught the plane to Zurich and from there to Lausanne where I stayed at the Hotel Royal (room number 218).

29 May. I go to Juan's office and he received me along with Juan Tornos. I look at the signature book, letter from Kindelán. Lunch at Les Rocailles (the villa of the Count and Countess of Barcelona). After lunch I have a long walk with Ena. Dinner at the hotel.

30 May. Saint Ferdinand's day. Les Rocailles. Mass. Lunch at the Golf. Walk with Ena until dinner at Les Rocailles.

31 May. Nicky of Romania phones me.

1 June. I see Roby Sutter, Nicky. Lunch at Les Rocailles.

2 June. I see Pepito Gandara. Lunch at Les Rocailles. Confession. Eugenio Vegas. I see Espinosa de los Monteros.

3 June. I go to eat with Ena and Crista. I see Bulnes at Les Rocailles. I go to Zurich and sleep there.

4 June. I leave Zurich by air. Arrive Barcelona, I see Ventosa.

5 June. An agent of Ford travels with me to Madrid. Bee in Madrid. I see Juanito, and Rodezno. I see Vigón. I see Kindelán.

6 June. Lunch at Santos, the Santa María's home. I see Caraquino. Ortega Monday 7th June. I see Vigón and Padilla. Telephone E (Ena?).

8 June. I see Joaquín Gallarza. I see Franco. Dinner at the home of the Duke and Duchess of Montellano.

9 June. I see Kindelán, I see Jordana. Lunch with Beatriz. I see Varela, Kindelán, Tornos, Paco B.

In Seville, he visited Cardinal Segura.

20 June by car to Jerez and Seville. I see Barrón (Sub secretary of Air). I am in bed five days with (a temperature of) 39.5. I have my head bandaged but I go out.

A letter from Ena to Bee (Lausanne, 1 June 1943), after Ali's visit, revealed her interest in Spain.

A thousand thanks for your dear letter, which Ali brought me. I am enchanted to see him again, he is so well and has not changed in the least except for a few grey hairs. He and Juan have long chats every day and according to all appearances, get on splendidly and agree on everything.

It was really necessary for them to meet and to get up to date on so many things, as it is impossible to do so by letter under the present circumstances, although now, after putting everything into order even this will be easier. You can imagine how very content I am that Ali should have been able to come. We have taken great walks together in the afternoon and we have exchanged opinions.

F[ranco] must understand that the critical moment has arrived when he has to give way for the return of the Monarchy. If not, he will be responsible for whatever happens in Spain when this war ends. If England and America are the victors, it is certain that neither he nor his regime will be tolerated by them. For this reason Juan should return and install himself before the war ends as, if these ignorant and adulatory Americans are the victors, they will interfere by protecting the old Red leaders so that they can return to exercise power in Spain, and I do not know what that will mean, and I prefer not to think on it. The blindness of F. [Franco] and those surrounding him is truly incredible.... Ali says that your new little granddaughter is very sweet and pretty. I am so content that you now have two babies with you. Besides, Italy at this time is not a healthy place for children. It is really sad to think of all the beautiful cities that have been destroyed by aviation.

Ten days later, Ena again wrote to her cousin (Lausanne, 11 June 1943) about Franco's reply to Juan's letter of 8 March 1943. Her opinion of the general whom Alfonso XIII had honoured by promoting him in the army as a young man and also standing as a groomsman at his marriage to Carmen Polo in 1923, was interesting:

By the time you receive this, you will have a copy of the charming epistle from Franco to Juan, which will be in Ali's possession. You can see from the date that it was written and completed before the latter went to see him and even before he came. He sent it with his usual bad intentions, after Ali left and knowing that Juan would receive it after Ali left Lausanne. I interpret from this that Franco made no mention of this letter to Ali at either the first or the second interview at El Pardo. I hope that the said letter causes him as much annoyance as us. I should like it made known from the contents of the letter that the supposed monarchical sentiments of Franco have disappeared forever. Nothing will open your eyes more than what is contained in this letter. I really would like to hear your opinion and that of Ali after reading it. I have great faith in Ali, his arguments are so good and solid, and I hope that events help him in his arduous work of convincing these so slow people to act before it is too late. I fear that it will not be possible to do anything with this vain and obstinate F. I can imagine your state of nerves when Ali is facing up to the lions in this den.

Please give him my dearest love and tell him that I often think of him and the chats we had together. It is so sad that we are separated by such great distances during these critical months and weeks. But at least we have confidence in him, to which can be added our personal affection and admiration.

I visited the *Infanta* Eulalia at the end of July that year, congratulated her on the high position and admiration that Ali enjoyed, and was very surprised by her response. 'He is too much for this position,' she said to me, 'With his education, and his savoir faire he should not be the representative of anyone. Perhaps they should make him Regent if the Restoration is to come, something which I very much doubt, because Franco finds his present position to his taste and it is even more so to those who surround him.'

As we walked down the narrow staircase of her house, Eulalia told me a secret.

When I was young and my brother King Alfonso XII was alive, a minister pointed out at a lunch that he was going to build in the Guindalera area and that it would be advisable for the younger members of the family to buy some land. I think we paid one thousand five hundred pesetas, and now they offer me a million and a half. My grandson Ataúlfo is going to be in charge of building me a little villa at the entrance to Irún. In this way, when I die, the box will not have to jump about in this narrow staircase.

In November 1943, a letter from Juan ended up in Franco's hands, discussing Juan's project of organising a rupture with Franco. There were whispers that Ali was involved. Ali wrote: 'I had not advised breaking with Franco, and Franco knew this'. Ali went to Madrid. to meet Franco who confirmed, 'It was only for him [Franco] to decide the moment of the Restoration.'

At the end of the Christmas holidays, the *infantes* learned of the death from flu' of Lola Kindelán, on 14 January 1944, and left for Madrid to join the general and his family. It was a blow for Bee, as Lola had been one of her first friends in Spain, and the couple were always at their side, during the good and bad days. During the war, the Kindeláns opened their home in Salamanca to them and she consoled her in her darkest hours. They were always pleased to see them in Zaragoza, Épila, or Madrid. The burial on 16 January reunited many aviators, some of whom had now left the service but had not hesitated to show their feelings towards Gen. Kindelán.

Count Jordana died at San Sebastian on 3 August 1944 and was replaced by José Félix de Lequerica, the Spanish ambassador to Vichy.

This foretold a change in the pro-German outlook of Spain, apparent in Franco's speeches, a view supported by Gen. Vigón, the minister of aviation, who was convinced Germany could not lose the war. However, Juan maintained that the triumph of Nazism would be 'a catastrophe for the Catholic and Latin world'. The Allied troops, who had landed in Italy the previous summer, had just entered Rome. Despite the German fortifications, they had also invaded Normandy, occupied much of France, and reached Paris in August.

A letter from Ena to Bee showed how bad matters were becoming for those who had put their hopes in a Restoration coming soon:

> I often think of you and Ali now that I know from Juan the very difficult time you are having. It seems that there is real persecution by F of those who dare call themselves monarchists. I also find it very sad to think that confidence has been put in a certain individual who it was believed (from their record) to be capable of achieving it. Fighting against these things is really disheartening or a hopeless labour. It does not surprise me that you feel miserable. I feel the same as you and would wish that we could chat about these things.
>
> Very few people want to risk the future and they live in the present. I always have found them terribly parochial, without any interest in what happens outside Spain. Besides, F has the extraordinary mentality of dictators: 'After me comes the flood'. It is supposed to be patriotic. It seems really bad to remain switched off until the inevitable fall comes and throws the nations into chaos and ruin as one by one, all do the same.
>
> The memory of the past in these last two days (15th and 16th April 1944) revive in me what happened three years ago and still fills me with melancholy. In my two small hotel rooms, I am not able to stop recalling everything which we had to abandon, perhaps forever, and having to learn to live a new life.

Sanlúcar was considered paradise by Ali and Bee's two oldest grandchildren. Álvaro escaped from Italy and came to live there as well. Bee continued celebrating Christmas with the same excitement as before, still putting up the Nativity and the Christmas tree.

On 2 February 1946, Juan moved to his family to Portugal. Ali wrote (Sanlúcar, 29 January 1946) that Franco would send all the undesirable monarchists he could to Portugal: 'It is indispensible that good and efficient Monarchists defend the King, not only against Franco and his minions, but also against opportunist Monarchists'.

Ali apparently told his intimates that someone had hindered relations with Franco, telling him jokes and stories about the king and his entourage.

He was too discreet to say who it was but it turned out to be the minister of aviation, Don Juan Vigón Suero-Díaz, who had been the *infantes'* tutor and was considered by all a true monarchist.

Juan de Borbón's manifesto was dated 19 March 1945, six weeks before the war in Europe ended with Nazi defeat. In Spain, there were no violent changes. Gen. Vigón had revealed the game he was playing. He did not want Ali to continue being the king's representative, so he confined him to Sanlúcar, thus cutting off his military career at a stroke. They invented a story that Ali belonged to the Freemasons. Franco hated freemasonry.

Franco also believed that Ali wanted to tour Europe, to counteract the work done by some ministers for the good of the economy. He therefore ordered the minister of the interior not to give him an exit visa on his passport, and to withdraw his diplomatic passport. The minister countered that perhaps these reasons were untrue, as Ali was not going to announce them with a fanfare so that the police could find out. 'The *Infante* has always been loyal and was very committed to our Army, to which he belonged, so what you have told me seems very strange.' Franco replied, 'In that case, I will study the matter again.' Not until 1953 was Ali allowed to travel abroad again, to visit Brazil, invited by his old Swiss friends. Until then he was confined to Sanlucar, and had to ask for permission to move anywhere. In a letter to his friend, Eduardo Gonzalez-Gallarza (Seville, 1 April 1945), he explained how surprised he was by his dismissal:

> When I notified the Duke of Alba, Ramón Carranza and Rafael Medina (the Duke of Medinaceli) of the order issued by the King (the count of Barcelona) that I should resign my positions, I received a letter from the Minister of Aviation (Lieutenant General Don Juan Vigón) asking me for explanations about this point. As it was not a military matter, he asked if he could see a copy of my letter to Franco (As it was not a military matter I replied as you can see in the attached copy of my letter to the generalísimo.) In this I had explained to Franco that I felt my position as representative of His Majesty the King, for whose army I had been accepted by Franco, was incompatible with the command I performed in Seville. For this reason, and with deep feelings, as well as my love for his honourable career at arms, I put at the *Generalissimo*'s disposition my present command, hoping he would soon return to carry out his service 'to the greater interest of my country and faithful to the principals of our glorious crusade which I always felt would culminate in the restoration of the Monarchy.

On 7 July 1945, Ali explained that he had read in the press of his dismissal from the RAE *(Región Aérea del Estrecho/*Strait of Gibraltar Air Region), and about a thoroughly inaccurate letter from the *generalissimo:*

It seems to me an injustice if it is considered incompatible for me to be Chief of a Region at the same time as being the King's Representative, as you are making it difficult for me to act as Representative by confining me to Sanlúcar. Confining a person is a punishment, and when one punishes, the punished is usually charged with an offence and allowed to defend themselves. I know that the latter point seems antiquated to those who profess the new totalitarian faith, but I do not follow it. I believe in our old laws (of Carlos III), which permit even bringing ones grievance before the King.

I swear to God and promise the King to constantly follow his banner. I comply with my oath and promise. I have told the King of my grievance. Despite being almost sixty years old, I have not been cured of talking with brutal clarity. I always did and it has cost me what it has cost me. I did so with King Alfonso XIII, and I do, and will always do, with King Juan III.

As part of the restrictions on his movement from Sanlúcar, Ali was required to surrender his diplomatic passport. The palace was under surveillance, with names taken of those who entered and when they left. Some Spaniards ignored the intimidation, especially the Orleans family, the Borbones of Seville, and many ex-kings and princes who were friends or relations.

During the war, Pip had worked as a chief nurse with the Polish troops, reaching the rank of colonel, but in France, as in Scotland, where she managed a hospital, her nostalgia for Spain followed her. 'I know that this is my country but it does not seem to be,' she would say, 'I feel as if I were in exile and cannot return home.' In the spring of 1943, she returned to Sanlúcar and attended the Feria of Seville. She was destined for the British consulate in Barcelona, where her duties included helping and facilitating the passage of pilots shot down in France. They passed through Spain on route to Portugal and then returned to England. In Barcelona, she came to know José Luis de Vilallonga, son of the baron and baroness of Segur, a good writer, and according to some, 'a handsome and dissolute playboy'. She fell madly in love with him although the *infantes* did not approve of her marrying him. Seeing that she was standing her ground and because her parents could not come to the wedding, the *infantes* offered the Montpensier Palace for the ceremony.

In his *Memorias*, Vilallonga noted that the Orleans family were very interested in his marrying Pip, and insinuated to various people the utter falsehood that his future wife was a daughter of Ali through a fraternal relationship with Margot van Raalte. Pip was born in London on 15 November 1916, daughter of Lord and Lady Howard de Walden. At the end of 1915, Lord Howard was at the Gallipoli front and lived with his wife in Egypt, until May 1916 when they returned to England. Ali never left Spain during 1915 or the first six months of 1916, leaving for Switzerland with all his family on 25 July that year.

Pip was delighted to marry in Sanlúcar, and the *infantes* arranged the ceremony for the end of summer, so she had time to reflect on her dubious choice. Vilallonga was pleased to marry a rich heiress from a great family and mix with the international jet set, and inclined thereafter to comment on his pleasure in marrying money and escaping from Spain. The Roman Catholic wedding was on 20 September 1945 in Sanlúcar with Ali as godfather, and a reception in the palace. The bride and groom spent the night in a hotel in Cadiz and then they left for Portugal, staying at the Palace Hotel in Estoril. It proved a miserable marriage, Vilalonga constantly humiliating Pip with his infidelities and spending her money. In his *Memorias*, he confessed that because he 'made a miserable and humiliated woman of her for the rest of her days', he '[repented] infinitely for having made such a good and loyal woman suffer so much for having had the horrible stupidity to fall in love with [him]'. The marriage had a disastrous effect on her friendship with Ali and Bee. Pip dropped all contact with them as she was incapable of admitting that they were right. They had two children, John and Carmen Susana Beatriz, divorced in 1973, and Pip died in Los Angeles in 1983. She deserved better.

Not content with having Ali confined, a few months later, Gen. Vigón attacked him again, thus ending his military career. Ali recounted all in a rather reserved letter (3 December 1945) to his successor to his post as general chief of the Aviation Region of the Straight:

> The Minister of Aviation knew that I had toothache and that I wanted to see my dentist Dr Schermant in Madrid, who was soon to leave for the United States. Without my asking, he (Schermant) telephoned Vigón to authorise me to go to Madrid where I arrived on the 30th November 1945 at half past ten at night. Naturally my first action was to present myself to the Minister on the 1st December 1945 and I made a summary of our interview which began at a quarter past twelve.
>
> The Minister asked me how my teeth were. I explained to him my fears of a general infection because of an operation I had had some time ago on my mouth. We sat down and he said to me that I should understand that he had authorised me to come exclusively for the dentist. That my confinement in Sanlúcar was specifically to prevent certain activities of mine and that, besides, he knew what people I would see. I replied that I came to visit the dentist but I would also see my lawyers, Don Cirilo Tornos and Don Joaquín de Satrústegui, and General Kindelán,

the joint executor, with me, of my father (may he rest in peace) regarding the complicated matters of my brother who died recently. I did not think to hide those I wished to see as I have always done things openly. For example, I was to see General Kindelán that afternoon at six. The Minister said to me that he would not authorise me to see Kindelán nor Tornos, nor Satrústegui nor anyone who had monarchist activities. And that I should leave right now for Sanlúcar. And *moreover, that I should leave right now without any lunch.*

I explained to him that I have a certain love for my teeth, that Dr Schermant is going to the United States and if I can I will go to see him this afternoon at half past four and I will leave that night. I will not see anyone who has anything to do with the Monarchy as he has ordered. We have politically opposed ideas. Militarily I obey, but I consider, as I wrote to him in the summer, that he should charge me with being a monarchist and dismiss me from the Air Force, because I would certainly continue with the same ideas and with the same activities. At this he fired me.

Privately, he opened his heart to Gen. Kindelán, telling him how the visit to Gen. Vigón ended: 'In the end he told me that my family had always been in opposition'. I asked him, 'What family?' He replied 'Orleans.' I drew myself up and said to him, 'Will you allow me to retire?' I left without waiting for his reply. Vigón is not someone to argue about the Orleans family with. After consulting with Kindelán by telephone, I telegraphed Vigón: 'I beg Your Excellency's permission to authorise my going to Madrid for some private matters.' I received a telegram from Vigón: 'Minister of Aviation to General of Orleans Division. You should stay at the residence which you have been assigned'. Fortunately there was a change of minister and Gen. Vigón left the Aviation Ministry. On 25 July 1945, Kindelán wrote to Ali: 'I have written to Gallarza asking him to allow Your Excellency full liberty of movement, stating that you are not confined'.

Gallarza, a good friend of Ali, was appointed the new minister of aviation. He had spent the first ten months of the war in Red Madrid and had such bad memories that he was supporting Franco. However, he knew Ali's attitude very well.

Ena wrote to her cousin (15 October 1945) as she knew exactly what Ali's confinement meant for the monarchical cause:

The letter which you sent me from Seville never arrived.

It really is shameful that Ali continues being confined to Sanlúcar. I understand your desperation too well. One can see clearly that Ali's work was good because Franco fears his influence. It must be so tiring having to write everything down. I am pleased to hear that the general who now occupies his old position is a friend and lets him go to Jerez or Seville if it is necessary.

Despite the annoyance it causes that all those who should help are so weak, I have a feeling, according to the latest news, that the next few months will be decisive. Juan remains firm in his attitude towards Franco. If he had to return, Franco should leave first and it is not a question where Franco dictates the terms. If he had been enough of a patriot to leave two years earlier, then things would have been different.

Logically, Ali's confinement in Sanlúcar impeded the continual journeys he should have made as the king's representative. From April 1945 to March 1946, Gen. Kindelán continued his work with great zeal and success, but after Don Juan arrived in Portugal in February they confined Kindelán to the Canary Islands. With true phlegm, Alfredo Kindelán bore his new punishment for being a monarchist. He was always annoyed that he, the supreme chief of national aviation during the war, was punished, first through dismissal as captain-general of Catalonia in 1943, two years later while on holiday, from the Superior Army School and, a year later, deported for seven months to La Palma, the Canary Islands. During this time, Ali wrote long letters to his old comrade, keeping him up to date with the sad situation that the Monarchist party found itself in.

In the summer of 1946, Alice arrived from Kew with her son, Alonso, to visit. Disembarking at Lisbon, they arrived on the *Lusitania Express* in Madrid, where Carmelo was waiting for them. They spent some days in the *infantes'* home in the capital, then arrived in Sanlúcar, where Bee was delighted to see them again. Alonso, the delight of his father, was seven, very alert, well-mannered and soon spoke Spanish with an Andalusian accent. Alice's arrival caused gossip in the town though it was soon realized that she was the *infanta*'s lady-in-waiting, while Carmela the housekeeper remained there. Carmela was unpopular in Sanlúcar, perhaps because she had come from Madrid where her family served the king and queen faithfully. Alice was reserved and a very hard worker; the palace had so many wardrobes and chests to tidy that the days flew past.

Ali had military chauffeurs while he was on active service, so he had not used Carmelo's services so much. But Bee very much enjoyed it when Carmelo drove, and remembering past times used to say, 'Ay! What damage the war did us, you lost your brother and I lost my son.'

After the end of the war, various nephews and nieces of Bee travelled to Sanlúcar, especially Sandra's daughters and grandchildren. One important guest was Grand Duke Vladimir Kirillovich, pretender to the Russian throne, who had to flee Germany in 1945 when the Soviets arrived. At that time, Spain offered him true peace as it was the only European nation that did not recognise the Union of Soviet Socialist Republics and he was completely safe. At first he was happy in the company of his uncle and aunt, attending the Andalusian fiestas that so charmed him, and playing bridge. He attended the wedding in Seville on 12 October 1947 of the only daughter of the duke of Alba to Luis Martínez de Irujo, son of the duke of Sotomayor. Ali was a witness to the ceremony, and met up with many of his old friends. They could not believe how he was not full of bitterness. Bee could not attend because she was unwell, but her children enjoyed themselves greatly.

It was said that at the fiesta, Grand Duke Vladimir received much attention and many encouraged him to go to Madrid, where his supporters from different countries would be able to visit him more easily in the capital. The life he enjoyed in Sanlúcar was rather sad for a good looking, cultivated young man of twenty-six years. Bee liked him very much, and was sorry to see him go as she knew his generous and timid character that did not really bode well for him to fight hard for his position in life. Soon after arriving in Madrid, he met Princess Leonida Bagration-Mukhranski, whose brother had just married the daughter of Prince Ferdinand of Bavaria in San Sebastian. She was three years older than him and a widow, her husband having died in a German concentration camp, leaving her with a small daughter. Vladimir fell madly in love with this elegant, intelligent, and lively character.

Bee entreated them to think carefully about getting married. She disliked the Georgians, as the Bagrations had a bad reputation in Spain at that time. Leonida's pretentious and ambitious brother Irakly had just married the poor *Infanta* Mercedes Baviera whom it was said he treated badly, and Bee could not put up with Leonida, there being many unpleasant rumours about her and her past. Nevertheless, the grand duke was determined to make her his wife. As they were both Russian Orthodox, a civil wedding in Lausanne on 13 August 1948 was followed next day by the pope's blessing in a simple ceremony. Bee broke with them and never spoke again of her nephew because his wedding upset her greatly, while letters from Ena also showed that other European royal families disapproved of the match.

Time passed without any great advance in Ali's situation. The new minister of aviation, Eduardo González Gallarza, a close friend, had written to him to say how he wanted to say, 'I wish this situation to end. I consider aeronautic activity is for Your Highness, as it is for me, as almost a reason for living.' Ali went three times a week to Jerez, where he flew his aeroplane and could enjoy living among the clouds for a while; it was his recreation, his dream of youth. Although he did not like to criticise, he had such a bad time being confined to Sanlúcar that in one letter to Bee, written as usual in English (9 February 1946), on a visit to his dentist in Madrid, he vented his anger: 'All the world is indignant over Vigón's being appointed for two "cargos" (positions) in the High Command and the Superior School. They think that Franco is rewarding Judas a little too much'. He was awaiting the return from the Canary Islands of Gen. Alfredo Kindelán, his faithful friend who had spent several months confined to Garachico on the island of La Palma on Franco's orders. Once they allowed Kindelán to return to the peninsula, the first thing he did was to write to Ali to announce his return. He said he had decided with his daughter, Lolita, to take the boat, arriving in Cadiz on 14 October. Ali had telegraphed him to say he would be on the quayside with his car.

They lunched at the palace at Sanlúcar and that night, father and daughter took the express for Madrid. On his arrival in the capital, he was much honoured and, from Estoril, the 'King' appointed him organiser of the political activities for the Restoration without consulting Ali, something that upset him considerably. On 25 October 1946, he wrote to Juan to resign his position. Ali did not feel envious; he and Kindelán had a sincere mutual friendship that the intrigues of Estoril were not going to poison. Those at court tried to draw up a letter in which the king severely criticised Ali for having failed as his representative because of his desire to follow his military career. It was apparently drafted by Vegas Latapie, 'The more I read the notes and letters of Don Alfonso, the more unspeakable I find his actions.'

Ali was deeply wounded by his words. Juan signed the letter (11 November 1946) accepting Ali's resignation, and it was sent to Gen. Kindelán with a copy for Ali. After reading it, a worried Kindelán kept the original in his archive in an envelope, wax-sealed with the royal seal of the Borbóns, and addressed to Ali. It remained unopened during the sixteen years from its writing to the death of Kindelán, and it took Ultano (one of the general's sons) another fourteen years to open the envelope. Kindelán thus ensured that Ali never knew of its existence (it is reproduced in full in Alfredo Kindelán's *La verdad de mis relaciones con Franco* (*The Truth About My Relationship With Franco*), published in 1981, six years after Ali's death and King Juan Carlos I's accession).

On 11 December 1946, during the Christmas holidays, Don Juan wrote his uncle a 'more friendly' letter according to Vegas who smoothed over some passages in the letter in which Juan accepted his resignation, which had however been accepted and was irreversible. Ali's reply accepting his decision greatly pleased the king, who wrote to Gen. Kindelán (31 December) of its 'cordial and affectionate terms'.

Unfortunately, the Orleans-Borbón archive in Sanlúcar does not have the correspondence between the prince who would have been Juan III and his uncle, Don Alfonso. As Kindelán had retained the first letter, Ali suspected nothing. The general called his great friend Ali 'a very sensitive man, but at the same time, highly disciplined and truly respectful of royal authority'. Neither Ali nor Gen. Kindelán obtained permission to go to Estoril on the occasion of the First Communion of Juan's son, the prince of Asturias, though many other Spaniards attended. Kindelán apparently informed Ali that the court at Estoril had won the game: 'The King has declared that our way of thinking and acting is not adequate nor is it in present circumstances'.

The war over, Carla and Álvaro returned to Italy, where Don Leopoldo Parodi-Delfino died in 1945 and the prince took charge of his father-in-law's businesses. The *infantes'* grandchildren only went to Sanlúcar for their summer holidays, which delighted Ali and Bee as they loved the children. They had the horses ready so that Geri and Beatriz could learn to ride and they listened carefully to Granny's advice. She also tried to find them 'amusing games and interesting places for picnics'. Frequently on returning from La Ballena, the house the *infantes* had on the beach, to the palace Ali would ask his wife in German: '*Aber was macht Fraülein Meyer hier?*' ('But what are you doing here Miss Smith?') To the younger generation, it seemed strange that someone like their grandmother who had dealt with and lived with the most important figures of the century would have not only stayed in a little town like Sanlúcar, but also have spent so much energy and love on Sanlúcar's people in helping them improve their economic situation. 'She was quite proud with important people,' related one of her granddaughters, 'but got carried away with simple people. She tried to remember the names of the nurses and their children, something which the poor ladies appreciated greatly because they felt recognised.'

Bee did not walk around the town much, but she liked visiting the Franciscan church in which Alonso was laid to rest, and also went on the days coinciding with fiestas, when Ali lunched there. She did not attend the banquet, but being an excellent cook she went to the monastery kitchen to 'lend a hand'.

On 1 March 1947, Álvaro and Carla had another son in Rome whom they called Álvaro Jaime, as his godfather was *Infante* Don Jaime, second son of Alfonso XIII. He inherited the intelligence and the restless spirit of the Orleans family. His first communion was in the chapel of the Virgin at the Franciscan monastery, whose decoration his grandmother Bee entrusted to Miguel Castro, an Andalusian painter. She ordered him to paint a Byzantine virgin whose face resembled that of Geri, on a background of gold, and she also appeared in the painting, dressed in a Franciscan habit.

The summer of 1947 passed uneventfully, to the unhappiness of true monarchists who saw Franco had kept himself in power although the United Nations had withdrawn their ambassadors from Madrid on 13 December 1946. Juan was planning to attend the regattas at Cowes aboard *Saltillo* when he was informed that Gen. Franco wished to meet him near the Basque Coast. The ship docked at Arcachon on 20 August, and the meeting was held five days later at a simple lunch on board the Azor. Years later, Peru Galíndez, who owned the boat sailed by the king, told us how the latter, accompanied by his brother, *Infante* Don Jaime, docked:

> The weather was magnificent and we were six miles from San Sebastian, and on seeing us arriving the *Generalissimo* raised his arms in welcome. The three of us boarded the yacht, but when the King went ahead, Franco who had thought on embracing him, was somewhat put off by the corpulence of the Pretender.

Mercedes Maiz de Galíndez interrupted him, 'Peru, tell them what you feel.' 'At that moment,' recalled Mercedes, 'I noted that it was as if two currents had collided and I realised that a terrible dislike had arisen in Franco towards the successor of Alfonso XIII'.

In December 1951, when I published the biography of Queen Mercedes, I did not know *Infanta* Beatriz, although María Ángeles Tornos had talked to me about her with true devotion and love. Through her, the *infantes* provided me with numerous photographs and before Christmas, I sent them one of the first copies. At the end of January, Bee wrote me a long letter thanking me for the biography of Queen Mercedes, which had interested her greatly, and saying she hoped to get to know me soon.

On her first visit to Madrid, we were invited by María Ángeles and César to lunch with the *infantes* at their home at Velázquez 14. I remember being rather intimidated, but when the bell rang and Jacinta, the maid, opened the door and on seeing the *infantes*, I made a small curtsey while they familiarly shook my hand and asked after my family. I almost recovered my aplomb. However, on meeting Doña Beatrice, I remained a bit shy when she hugged me and said she had liked my book. Ali, whom I knew from wartime, immediately addressed me, informally as *tú* and introduced me to his mother the *Infanta* Eulalia. From then on, when I went to Madrid to see my dentist, Dr Schermant, María Ángeles contacted us and, as we stayed nearby, invited us to dine often with the *infantes* at her home where the cook, Teodora, took pains to please them.

The atmosphere that surrounded Bee in the summer was of past joys, with Antonio Lucas Moreno playing the piano in the afternoons at the palace. She wanted her guests to enjoy themselves. 'Chimpún' was a place where people went to dance, and Doña Carla and her sister, Mimosa, used to go there. One night when Carla was not present, Bee asked Manolo Somavía, husband of Pilita Mergelina, to look after Mimosa. Manolo, who had been a merchant sailor, was very amusing and very happy to be able to show Mimosa the joy and rejoicing of Sanlúcar during the fiestas. He took her all over the town in a horse-drawn carriage, returning to the palace at 5 a.m. Later that morning, the rumour spread that the *infanta* had ordered him to call. He went to see her with some trepidation, but was surprised when all Bee wanted to do was to thank him, as Mimosa had had such a good time.

María Ángeles, a born monarchist, enjoyed presenting people to 'her *Infantes*'. On hearing that my husband was going to Egypt at the end of the year and that we would embark at Gibraltar, she told the *infanta* who invited us to Sanlúcar to taste the grapes and spend a week in the old palace of the duke of Montpensier. Unfortunately, we had to postpone our leaving as my nine-year-old son was ill with chicken pox. We arrived in Sanlúcar on 2 January 1953, and it was easy to find the palace in the upper part of the town. On seeing two cars with Madrid number plates, he let us into the garden, stopping us in the covered gateway.

We immediately spotted Ali, who despite the cold was wearing short trousers, knee-high woollen stockings, short-sleeved shirt and a thick gold chain around his neck. María Ángeles and her husband, Gen. Sáenz de Santa María, accompanied him. After a few moments, we went to the office of the duke of Montpensier, where Bee was waiting for us to take tea. We sat at a round table; I was on Don Alfonso's left, and the dowager duchess of Montemar, a silent and sad looking lady, was on his right. Suddenly Bee asked me, 'Ana María, how do you take your tea?' Stammering, I said, 'I don't señora,' before she quickly interrupted me: 'We are not in the Pardo here, our guests come first'. Then she told us of the times they had been there, and how they served Señora Franco first. She told us she was still astonished that in European courts it was customary to do otherwise. We chatted for a while and soon she got up. Despite María Ángeles wanting to accompany us to our rooms, she dissuaded her, saying, 'It is a real pleasure for me to show her the rooms of Queen Mercedes.' We went up to the second floor and entered a room with a curtained bed, to the right of which was a door opening onto a bathroom where, in the centre, shone a high bronze brazier: 'It has been lit for two days, but it should be hotter!' She asked us if we were tired or if we wished to dress and dine with them. We replied we would be delighted to follow palace custom.

We went down at 8:30 p.m. for an aperitif and enjoyed a delicious dinner. Bee wore a long dress of black velvet with a V-neck and a necklace with a fine chain and a large pearl. Ali wore a dinner jacket, which was most elegant after the clothes he was wearing when we first met him. My son ate earlier at a small table with María Ángeles and Consuelo Osorio de Moscoso, the daughter of the duchess of Montemar, who was kind enough to accompany him at all meals. When our son went to bed, in the room of the *Infanta* Cristina, Bee called her housekeeper, Carmela Louro, asking her which bedroom he was in and that he be watched in case he awoke. 'I have been so frightened by stories of ghosts in the palaces of Europe,' she explained.

Next day we breakfasted in our room but on other days we went down to the grand dining room (now the town council chamber) at 8:45 a.m. It was a pleasure to see so many things displayed on the English-style table— eggs, ham, porridge, fruit—and then continental breakfast with toast, sponge cakes, rolls, honey, jam, and homemade butter. On Sundays, they added chocolate with churros. They told me that in summer, a tame stork passed by the dining room window at breakfast time, and the servants told the *infantes*, 'Look out for the rolls!'

As Ali was not flying that day, he took us by car to Torre Breva, a magnificent estate the duke of Montpensier had bought as a hunting estate and then converted into a farm by planting selected vines whose grapes they sold. In 1943, Bee, having sold the carriages and the mansion at Calle Quintana, decided to create the Bodegas Orleans-Borbón in partnership with Barbadillo's *bodega*, designing labels for the bottles and taking an interest in the business as the Manzanilla was among the best. In the afternoon, we visited the town, its churches, white streets and beach. After dinner, we played bridge with the *infantes*. Bee and I had a winning streak.

The following morning, as it was raining and cold, María Ángeles suggested we could go to the maternity home, where Bee went each morning. We found her chatting with some women in a small office. They were all talking at the same time, despite the deep voice of Doña Beatrice calling out, 'I am not leaving, tell me slowly.' She had infinite patience with these women who sometimes did not know how to clearly express what they wanted. María Ángeles accompanied us to the bedrooms and then through the nursery where there were various new-born babies. We went to enter the treatment rooms and operating theatre where we were surprised by the *infanta*, accompanied by Consuelo Osorio de Moscoso, who ran the clinic and whose benchmark was cleanliness and order. Inside the simple building, the main luxury was the instruments, kept in cupboards, and donated by the Americans from the base at Rota. Imported from the US, they were the most modern available. Later on, Bee wanted the ladies of Sanlúcar to pay some symbolic amount for consultations, to avoid having to go the Jerez or Seville for treatment. She tried the nurses' food on a daily basis. Knowing that some women arrived exhausted, to give birth, she created 'The Drop of Milk' (*La Gota de Leche*), a dining room where for two months before giving birth and six months after they gave them food every day, as well as milk for the baby if necessary.

That same day we visited *El Botánico,* the beautiful estate bought by Montpensier. Bee and her son Ataúlfo had built a small and comfortable mansion there, and constructed a marvellous garden. Having lived under many skies, she was happy to have a house built to her liking, and most satisfied at how the work was progressing, while Ali enjoyed living in the old palace with its long corridors and cold patios where the sun never shone.

We had to embark at Gibraltar for Naples on the eve of *Reyes* (Epiphany) at night and decided to do so after tea, but Ali thought the weather was bad and that we could bump into fog, so after a long time sitting around the table, we went to the palace chapel where a beautiful statue of St Anthony (now on the main altar of the Capuchins) patron of the duke of Montpensier, dominates the High Altar. We went downstairs with the Sáenz de Santa Marías to take communion.

We then bade farewell to Bee in the office of the Montpensier. On seeing me, she hugged me affectionately. She was accompanied by her niece, Princess Dolly, daughter of Princess Sandra. The poor thing had lived for a year and a half in a horrible Allied 'holding' camp and they say that she had forgotten how to laugh. Meanwhile, my son, who followed Ali about like a puppy dog, kept running to where he was. Apart from the attraction exercised by older people, it was fascinating how children responded to the prince, and dogs and cats loved him too. He evidently used to photograph his guests as they were leaving.

At the end of March, we received a letter with a photograph, 'The Last of the Guests at the Montpensier Palace', in which María Ángeles and Consuelo Montemar could be seen next to us. He wrote:

I enclose a photo taken when we had the pleasure of having you here last January. We are sure that you will be spending some very interesting days during the present negotiations. If the English remove their troops from Egypt, our situation in Morocco will become complicated.

He was always thinking of Spain, almost half a century after fighting in Africa as a simple lieutenant and then as a pilot. His letter told us that within a few days they would be leaving for Brazil with their son, Ataúlfo, and staying there until the middle of May. After being confined to Sanlúcar for ten years, they dreamed of travelling and seeing new worlds.

20

La Señorita Infanta

Travelling to America was very tiring for Bee. She no longer wanted to see the world, and was happy to return to Sanlúcar, where she had spent ten years anxiously wanting to escape, returning before her husband and son. She returned happy but feeling her years: she would be seventy next spring. In the routine life she led, with many hours at the maternity home, she had lost the notion of time. And now she had to leave the Montpensier palace and move everything necessary to El Botánico. What worried her most was having to dismiss the staff. Some had worked in the palace for thirty or forty years, thought themselves secure, believing their children would succeed them. Another worry was the duke of Montpensier's immense library, untouched since it was created. She asked María Ángeles to find a suitable person in Madrid who knew the subject, and the task fell to the antiquarian librarian Julian Barbazán.

Early the 1950s, she called him to ask if he was interested, telling him 'the library was sick'. If he could come by train, she would send a chauffeur to meet him. Barbazán asked Bee for their telephone number, and he would make enquiries about train times next day: 'She gave me the number and thus began my suspicions and doubts. This of the library being sick, was it a joke at my expense? What I did first was to examine the telephone directory and the number really was that of the *Infante* Don Alfonso de Orleans'. He booked a seat, rang Sanlúcar de Barrameda next day to confirm, and recognized the voice as that of the person who had phoned him before.

In due course, he reached El Botánico, the *infantes'* summer palace, slightly daunted, as he had 'never socialised with *infantes*, princes or kings and dreaded making a fool of himself.' 'Don't worry,' was the reply, 'the *Infantes* are very down to earth and understanding. If you belong to the aristocracy they will not pardon any incorrectness; but if you are not, you do not need to bother—you'll see.' We arrived at the palace, the chauffeur introduced me to the *infanta* and she introduced me to the ladies with her, her niece, Princess Alexandra ('Dolly'), and the duchess of Montemar, very naturally—as if we had known each other for years. 'How was the journey? Do you need anything?' 'No Señora,' I replied. 'Did you get up early?' She asked. 'I got up at eight.' 'Good, I waited to have breakfast with you. Carmela, accompany the gentleman to his room,' she ordered the housekeeper. On entering the room I was stunned and did no more than rub my eyes and pinch myself, as I felt I was dreaming. The birds awoke me with their singing, especially the goldfinches, of which there were hundreds as the palace was in the centre of a great park, and I prepared for breakfast. Although I did not know where to find the dining room, I recognised it immediately and the *infanta* was waiting for me. 'Pass me the marmalade—help yourself to butter—pass me the fruit bowl,' and so forth, as if we had known each other for years. We were fully occupied when I heard the characteristic sound of an aircraft and on hearing it, she said, 'That is my husband flying.' 'I assume Your Highness knows this from the way in which he flies.' She smiled quietly and they continued with the job in hand.

She explained that most of the books were stained, and wanted this dealt with before they were all damaged. The library was in the main palace, built by the duke of Montpensier and *Infanta* María Luisa, and they agreed a plan of work. Breakfast was at 8:30 a.m., with an aperitif at 1 p.m., lunch at 2 p.m., tea at 6p.m., and dinner served three hours later. Andres, one of the palace chauffeurs, was to help him lift and carry. As this was my first day, and in order to meet the *infante*, I went to take the aperitif, but did not return (to work). 'They have spoken very highly of you,' he said. 'Pay no attention, Your Highness, they are all liars,' I replied.

He asked me what had happened to his books, and I replied it was the same as what happens to many people who lack oxygen. The magnificent artistically-wrought iron library consisted of two parts: the lower with a depth of about 80 centimetres, with doors of the same material, and the upper, which reached the ceiling, to a height of some 4 metres or more, had glass doors that should be but were never ever opened. Humidity from the sea or the rivers gets everywhere, no matter how hermetically sealed they are. The French paper made in the nineteenth century used abundant chlorine causing decomposition and stains, or *rousseurs* (foxing). The books only needed to be moved regularly, thus merely requiring a transfer of all 80,000 volumes in the library. I set to work enthusiastically, trying to hunt down and analyse the small creatures produced by the humidity, as their excreta was damaging the books.

Over the dinner table, the *infanta* said to me 'Tell me, Barbazán, as an antiquarian librarian, you buy books don't you?' 'I do indeed,' I replied. 'Well, there are lots in the library that you could choose,' she continued. 'Yes, but that supposes that I would select the best.' 'I would imagine so, as you do not look stupid,' she said. He assumed it was a very elegant way of paying for his work, very well remunerated with the attention they lavished on him, without prejudice to the money from the sale going to the maternity home financed by the *infanta*. He selected some 1,500 volumes, and on informing her of the value, her reply was that if he was not mistaken, it seemed excessive. He assured her if so, it would be the first time that he had made an incorrect valuation. He continued with his work, so happily that he wanted to prolong it as long as possible.

One day Ali went to his grandfather's palace to see how it was going, and at the same time to tell Barbazán that that afternoon they were going round the estate by car. Without appreciating the fact that royalty did not like to be disobeyed, he explained apologetically that he wanted to finish what he was doing. Good-natured as ever, Ali postponed the excursion until the following day. He drove the car and the librarian sat beside him, while an invited couple occupied the main seats, from where one could see children playing nearby. When they identified the royal badge, they lined up by the road saluting in a most amusing military manner. Being present at the salute really moved Barbazán, but Ali assured him that it was nothing in particular, as they were friends of his.

The ever-likeable Don Alfonso of Orleans was inclined to put on weight, and worked hard to keep in shape. In the evenings, he did not appear at dinner and at midday, after lunch, he took a lawnmower and worked with it for at least an hour. On one occasion Barbazán offered to lend a hand, but immediately tried to push it, found it weighed about about 50 kg, and had to hand it straight back to him.

At the end of the war, he was appointed chief of aviation for the Straight, which coincided with the time when they were semi-isolated from the rest of the world. Petrol being short, he ordered the confiscation of cars used for the transport of personal to the aerodrome at Tablada, giving an example by travelling daily the 8 km to and from the city to Tablada on shanks' pony. He had many North American friends, and there was rarely a day when one did not accompany him to eat. His private secretary, Don Ángel Louro Viana, showed the librarian a silver cup on which the most illustrious aviators in the world had engraved their signatures, accompanied by a sympathetic dedication.

As for the books, after Barbazán had been there twelve days, those books selected were put to one side and the rest stored after light treatment. Bee told him he would be leaving the next day, and she had already ordered his ticket. It was agreed Barbazán had to visit Prince Ataúlfo, to get his agreement for the sale. They met at the Ritz for lunch. Ataúlfo immediately gave his consent. Later Barbazán said that the days spent in the Botánico in Sanlúcar were among the happiest of his life.

One day in April 1953, Bee was listening to the radio, when it was announced that King Carol II of Romania had died in Portugal. The lack of details and news affected her deeply and she asked Ignacio Muguiro, who was in Estoril at the time, to send her reports as strange rumours were spreading. Yet it was Don Juan, count of Barcelona, who wrote to her (Giralda, Estoril, 8 May 1953), showing the great love he felt for her and for Ali, when speaking of his banishment. Gen. Kindelán was quite right keeping that dangerous and unjust missive in his archive:

It should have occurred to me some time ago that you would be interested in knowing something about the death of your nephew Carol. But the truth is that it passed me by completely and it has only fallen on me on account of my speaking about the matter the other day with Ignacio Muguiro, who began to ask me things so as to be able to tell you and it was then that I said that I would write you. I'm not able to say much about what happened to Carol before his death. You well know that we had very cool relations with him and La Lupescu, but some friends in common and the lady herself, when I went to see her on the day of his death, have assured me that Carol never had any previous symptom of the attack that finished him. Carol and Lupescu were reading in their sitting room after having said goodbye to some guests who had come to eat when suddenly he felt really bad with a sharp pain in his left side. This first attack passed relatively quickly. However the lady telephoned the doctor to come as soon as possible. The second attack was not long in coming and he died at half past twelve at night without the doctor having time to give him an injection.

We received the news at home at seven in the morning in a call from Urderiano to my secretary and I visited the home of the deceased around ten, coinciding with the King of Italy. The lady was distraught, but was able to converse with us for a few minutes.

The burial took place three days later. The Portuguese government was represented at the burial by the Minister of Foreign Affairs and all the Ambassadors accredited to Lisbon attended. The procession took place here in Estoril with a cavalcade of motorcycles from the Republican Guard in dress uniform and some eighty cars with which we went to Lisbon. Carol has been provisionally allocated a place in the Pantheon of the Braganzas next to Queen Amelia. The only strange thing that happened during all the funeral ceremonies was that a protestant priest, an Anglican, officiated when nobody in the family was Anglican.

I believe that there is no will, but all the fortune had already been in Lupescu's name for a long time. As for future plans, I know nothing, but some say that they are thinking of selling the house and going to live in Paris. This is all that I know about Carol and I hope that reading this letter does not bore you too much.

When I saw Nicholas at the funeral and after in my house he asked me permission to establish his residence in Spain for financial reasons. I have seen no reason for not allowing this and therefore I think that he will be living in Madrid or nearby. Joanna is not a bad woman and has no defect other than to be conceited when she has nothing to be conceited about. I said this so that she would not have any unpleasant troubles in Spain, but as for others, I do not think that a social boycott is warranted.

I suppose that Uncle Ali will be having a magnificent time in Brazil, a little change of atmosphere after not leaving Sanlúcar for so many years. For you, it must be a bit hard being so alone, but surely all your good friends will keep you company.

I should like to come and visit you again, but although it's late, you know that you will never be without our love. Tomorrow I leave for Rome to spend some days with Crista and I hope to see Álvaro again, as he was here on business only a few days ago.

I have great news on Mama: she is in London until the 12th and people are looking after her a lot. Her recuperation after the two tremendous operations is truly remarkable and when I saw her in February and found that she was better than five or six years ago.

Bee greatly appreciated the friendly letter from her nephew, replying to thank him (19 May 1953):

Carol was a very loving nephew and I loved him dearly. Clearly since he married Lupescu, I no longer saw him, as I did not wish to go to his house without his wife being there and it was impossible for me to receive her after all the horrors and wickedness she caused my sister, contributing in great part to her death. Despite this, Carol always sent me his regards when he could. He always seemed so strong, while Lupescu made him marry *in articulo mortis*. What strange things there are in life! I do not believe that poor Miguel and Sitta will gain anything out of legal action, but obviously they are obliged to do it. Lupescu will have put all Carol's assets into her name, and Miguel and his wife are suffering real hardship in living.

Nicholas has been living in Spain for almost three years and he often comes here to see me. For more than a year now, he has had a flat in Madrid just in front of us. Joanna (wife of Prince Nicholas of Romania), although she is not of the calibre of Lupescu nor has she done any international harm like her, comes from the same social and moral milieu and also caused a lot of trouble for my sister. She now supposes herself to be the first lady of Romania. Personally I do not see it. My two nephews make much of their mother pardoning them on her deathbed. What mother would not do this!

I hope that this letter arrives before you leave for London. How beautiful the coronation will be! I wish you a wonderful time, from one who always sees the worst of everything in England.

Your mother must be magnificent. She writes me very happy letters despite the great sadness the death of May caused to us both. Those who have seen her tell me that she is prettier than ever.

We are all here waiting on the agricultural situation. The year began very badly but improved in an extraordinary manner and God willing they will not lack bread or chickpeas. What worries me most is the depression in the wine business now that England is almost unable to buy. I am now involved in the horrible task of closing up the big house so that we can go to live in a tiny house in the orchard of the Botánico. It is impossible the way things are today, to continue to live in such an enormous rambling house.

Up until now I have very good news of Ali. They are rushing about, from here to there and always in an aircraft, something that he loves.

The correspondence between Ena and Bee continued, becoming even more intimate. Bee offered to help care for her after her 'two terrible operations', as her daughters Beatriz and María Cristina were doing so under a nurse's instructions. The queen explained to her cousin what the doctors had told her, writing in an undated letter:

In the autumn of 1916 I suffered a kind of peritonitis and a miscarriage when Alfonso made me go to La Granja in the very delicate condition in which I found myself, to help with a hunting party, and it snowed. It had fatal consequences for me as I suffered some damage to my intestines. I was filled with pain, with temperatures of forty degrees and I also had appendicitis and did not know it. The surgeon could hardly find my appendix. [Casilda Figueroa y Alonso Martínez, duchess of Pastrana, who looked after the queen, recorded with horror what the sovereign suffered.]

I have felt the death of Bertie [George VI, in February 1952] deeply. How very different everything will be. I have the sad feeling of not belonging to any country and have no connection with England, leaving me feeling small, and, as things are, I do not expect to ever return to my adopted country. And although I am happy in my little house here, I cannot feel Swiss!

She wrote again that year (October 15, 1952) from Villa Giralda, Estoril:

> I am so touched by the very loving letter that you have written me when
> you heard of the death of poor Jimmy (Duke of Alba) in Lausanne. It was
> terribly sad for me, when he came on his own to see me, as he did every
> year, but this time he was dying. He was up only two days before he died
> and he dined every night at my home. He went to Geneva on the 21st and
> he felt unwell and was breathing badly when he returned to the Royal
> Hotel. Three of the best doctors in Lausanne attended him and decided that
> he should be put into a clinic, and that his family should know the truth
> about how he was. Naturally, nobody thought that the end was so near,
> because he was in no hurry to tell his family to come as he liked me caring
> for him and living without any fuss. During those last two days of his life,
> I could only sit in his room for a long time during the day. He had a heart
> attack on the 24th September in the early morning and this precipitated
> his end. His right lung was now practically destroyed by the cancer and
> the other was not much better because of a deep scar caused previously
> by tuberculosis. I was with him all day, although he was unconscious and
> breathed his last at half past six in the afternoon with my crucifix in his
> hands. It is certainly a great loss for our cause and I personally feel the
> going of a loved and devoted friend who I had known since I was sixteen.'
> [Queen Victoria Eugenia opened her villa to install a funeral chapel in
> which a loyal servant of the monarchy could lie. He represented Spain in
> London successfully during the Civil and Second World Wars.]
>
> I am content being here these three weeks. Juan is always so loving
> and affectionate towards me and I should also say that María (countess
> of Barcelona) is also very kind towards me. The change is most agreeable
> because I spend most of the year alone, but I cannot live in this country
> with its so tropical climate as it saps my energy, and everything is poor
> in comparison with Spain; the language is really horrible, impossible to
> understand.
>
> I feel so much that you are not well. Look after yourself, because you
> are more necessary in your home than I. However, in recent years, I try to
> keep up my morale.

In October 1953, the *infantes* went to Irun to visit *Infanta* Eulalia and
passed through San Sebastian where, at the Miramar Palace, they got to
know Don Juan Carlos and Don Alfonsito. The queen was pleased that
her two grandsons had made such a good impression: 'My favourite
is Juanito, there is something in him that reminds me of my poor Sito:
his thin silhouette, his square shoulders and way of walking, besides he
has always been very loving towards me. His brother and sisters are too

Orleans for me, as much in looks as in character. I see Luisa and Fernando Montpensier in them'.

Ali found they were indifferent linguists. Juanito's English seemed poor, as he did not even understand simple phrases, nor speak at all. He said it would be a rarity at any family gathering, now all the royal families spoke English because *'Tú'* did not exist in that language. His advice was listened to because he was such a great polyglot, and gained much from years in exile. The prince of Asturias, who spoke Spanish and French fluently, also knew Italian and Portuguese through staying in both countries. The *infantes* were so keen for their grandchildren to know different languages, explained Bee, 'that we began, first with German and the Sanluqueño that we spoke with the servants, then English and Italian, with French coming in last'. They had also learned the Swiss dialect *Schweizerdeutsch* by ear and Italian through operatic librettos.

They say that there are places which influence their residents, and do so in a special package. On leaving the Montpensier Palace to live among the flowers and palm trees of the Botánico, Bee seemed happier and more confident, reflected in her letter to Ignacio Muguiro who guarded the king and queen in Estoril. Muguiro, a regular visitor to Sanlúcar, judged her as 'not only a very beautiful person, but also very amusing'. She confided in him:

Despite my mother-in-law insisting that no one comes to her ninetieth birthday, Ali, as he is a good son, has gone to Irún. I, with my seventy years, have allowed myself to take account of the capricious desires of my mother-in-law, and remained quietly here in our little house, nice and warm, so as not to run the risk of putting myself out as I did last year after a terrible journey through the snow.

Ali left me in charge of opening all letters and one can understand that I opened letters from him with much joy and enjoyed his charming humour. You are totally correct that I love reading what he says about family life.

I know that I am often very harsh with outsiders to the point of being proud of having the reputation of having a sharp tongue (an ability I acquired with difficulty in Spain where there is no defence but the tongue), but within the family I have always tried not to say more than pleasantries, even if it appears to be criticism. It seems a lie but Ataúlfo, whom I value so much, becomes like a devil if they say four disagreeable things among the family, and I can say that, treating it as one should, there is no better son nor one who cares better for his mother. There is no doubt that life is a very complicated thing and the older I become, one sees living is a profession and not a recreation.

It has been terribly cold here. There were heavy snowfalls which greatly alarmed the people as they had never seen anything like it before. The result is great misery and I am almost ashamed to live in a house which, although small, has central heating.

We have spent many sad months with the grave illness of our good administrator, García, who is neither living nor dying and, as there are no qualified nurses here, a great deal of work has fallen upon me. The loss of García would be a terrible thing for us as he does everything admirably and besides it is very sad to think that he has been killing himself for us for thirty years and it is now so difficult to save his life.

My principles of friendliness cease with doctors and, in my opinion, they are perfect sharks and hyenas who only think about showing off their theories and ruining one with their extravagant bills. [This was because of a Seville doctor the *Infanta* favoured].

I say nothing of politics because this is now understood, as you already know what I think.

Queen Victoria Eugenia very lovingly invited me to accompany her to Rome to Sandra's (Princess Sandra Torlonia) ball, but the same fear of a cold journey stopped me from accepting and I have stayed. God willing, I will be visiting her in May and also making the journey to Rome to see my children and grandchildren.

Our grandson Alonso seems to be getting better. God grant that the danger has passed. Ataúlfo, Carla and Álvaro, and their Monteiro friends have just spent some days at St. Moritz and seem really happy.

Princess Carla, duchess of Galliera, and her ten-year-old daughter Beatrice went to Irún to congratulate the *Infanta* Eulalia who was about to complete ninety years. She was euphoric as she had a very spacious new chalet, 'Villa Ataúlfo', and sent all her friends a photo of the little villa, which she loved and where she felt happy. Little Beatrice called her great grandmother 'Nonísima' and was very proud to have shown her how to roll up spaghetti. She remembered from her stay in Irún how one afternoon Doña Eulalia sent her mother and her to go for a walk, telling them she had to rest. Carla said to Beatrice that they had to pretend to go because it was probable that Bee wanted to see what the fashion was by snooping through their hats. They saw the Nonísima slowly climb the stairs and go into the guest bedroom.

The death of the *infantes'* administrator, Señor García, on 12 March 1954, changed the fortunes of Carmelo Herrero. He had worked loyally during Garcia's long illness until Torre Breva regained its rhythm and Ali decided he should take up the position of the late administrator. Every morning, Carmelo came to tell Bee of the plans and day-to-day events while she breakfasted, sometimes sharing the food with her old chauffeur, and they recalled times during the war. Bee thoughtfully decided to improve Carmelo's house in the Botánico, by adding a garage and two new bedrooms so Alice could enjoy an English cottage. She was as organised as ever, tidying the cupboards, preparing her delicious jams and cakes, and making butter together with Bee.

Wanting a new maid from among the staff, as Bee was greatly bothered by any changes in staff, she chose Victoria Torres Coronado. Forty years old, she was from Cádiz and had spent many years at the palace, being in the *infantes'* service for over thirty-five years. She had an agreeable and sweet character, married to a taxi driver and had a son, Francisco, for whom Ali had found a position as a sailor.

Bee's confessor, Padre Gonzalo, had returned to his native Cordoba. She wrote to him (11 March 1955):

I much appreciate your kind letter and your questions regarding my health. I am now much better although I still suffer from furunculosis on the neck and face, which is very painful and stops me from leading a normal life. The cold, humid weather does not help my complete recovery. Thanks to the Roter medicine, I am almost completed cured from my gastritis. I say this to recommend it as of interest to everyone. You already know how against medicines I am, so if I say this, it is a very good thing.

Here, the latest news from Seville concerning the Cardinal (Segura) is much talked of. Although it was seen coming, I, from our visit to Rome, had no doubt that it was going to happen. I am very sorry that it has come to this extreme. Although the Cardinal has behaved 'frankly' badly towards us from the moment that he saw that the *Infante* could not provide more financial advantage, I recall the good friendship which he showed us when my husband was sent to Seville, in not ceasing to visit us and in comforting us with all his ecclesiastical power. I suppose that in Córdoba it will be the news of the day....

Father, we are still missing you greatly here. When will you return? I have not ceased confessing myself on the first of every month in order to be at peace with my religious obligations, but I greatly miss your good advice. How are you keeping? Up the hill in the convent here the cold is terrible. Tomorrow, the twelfth, is the anniversary of our poor García. We are going to have a requiem Mass in the parish church and I have asked the Capuchin choir to sing.

Gen. Sáenz de Santa María died in May 1955, just before his seventieth birthday. It was a loss for Ali, as they were the same age, although César looked older. His great friendship dated back to the years in the academy in Toledo, when he was chosen by Ali to accompany him to Japan. His goodness, loyalty and work was priceless. During the Republic, he zealously occupied himself with the *infantes'* properties in Spain. Although María Ángeles continued to live in Madrid, she was to spend long periods of time with the *infantes* each summer and winter.

On 12 June 1955, Bee attended a celebration as godmother, the first Mass celebrated by the newly ordained priest Father Francisco González Cornejo. His godfather of honour was Manuel María González Gordon, marquis of Bonanza, an intimate friend of the infantes and who greatly praised the excellent qualities of the new priest. A short time later, Bee invited the new priest to tea. He arrived at the Montpensier Palace and his godmother told him in detail of the long process culminating in her conversion on 2 February 1928, when she placed her renunciation in the hands of Cardinal Ilundáin who was passing through Sanlúcar on a pastoral visit. Bee had in-depth knowledge of the Evangelists and was truly 'ecumenical', as she had begun studying Catholicism when she married.

The year 1955 ended happily when Spain was admitted as a member of the United Nations in a solemn ceremony on 14 December in New York. Ali was satisfied, expecting much from the power of America. Yet tragedy would soon follow. For Holy Week in 1956, María Ángeles went to Santander to spend Easter. She told me that on the evening of 29 March she took a telephone call at the Botánico, from Estoril. A voice told her between sobs that young Prince Alfonso, aged fifteen, had just died and would she inform the *infantes*. After returning from Mass, Don Juan Carlos and his brother, Don Alfonso, were cleaning a pistol in the study, when the elder fired a bullet that entered the forehead of his younger brother. Death was almost instantaneous while he held him in his arms.

After obtaining permission, Ali left for Estoril to assist at the solemn funeral masses. Ena also attended, and those who saw her all said she looked like a Mater Dolorosa. The death of Don Alfonsito was a terrible blow for her as she had already lost two sons in accidents. Yet again some blamed it on her change of religion. She felt more protected with Ali nearby because the inhabitants of Villa Giralda were so disconsolate that they could neither resign themselves to, nor find peace after, the dreadful event. Ali therefore promised to send Bee to Lausanne when she returned to Switzerland.

The queen was overjoyed to see her cousin, and cancelled all her appointments to be free for those days. She also ordered colourful lilies to adorn the upper part of the city, in the Avenue de l'Elysée, Vieille Fontaine, as it was called, which seemed somewhat isolated as nobody lived there. Just in front there was a sports ground where they skated in winter. 'A sandy path opened up in the midst of the garden filled with old trees,' explains Marino Gómez Santos, 'The villa looks as white as a palace in Seville. Between the foliage its iron gates were highlighted with *fleurs de lis*.'

At the entrance hung the painting by Juan Comba of the royal wedding in the church of the Jerónimos, showing the king and queen before the altar with their godparents, and surrounded by the court. Above a table next to a sofa, was a portrait of Alix, the last tsarina, at the height of her beauty. In another room, in two display cases, was the collection of green jade and quartz roses, bought together over the years in the living room of the Palacio de Oriente. On seeing the gemstones, Bee remembered what her cousin liked and searched for throughout Europe. They were fortunate with the weather, and sometimes they went on excursions with Ataúlfo as chauffeur, so the two cousins could enjoy more privacy. From there they went to Rome, stopping in cities such as Florence, which Bee liked so much, although she wanted to get together with her children and grandchildren. 'What joy I had on seeing them!' exclaimed the queen, 'We were all under my roof until the 29th.' Bee brought her a statue of the virgin as a memento. 'I know what you did for me and it is always on my bedside table to remind me of you,' wrote the queen on 31 August 1962.

In Rome, they found the grandchildren had grown greatly. As good students, they expected to do well in their exams and also wanted to go to Sanlúcar, which for them was the most amusing town and had the friendliest people. They suffered greatly when the summer of their dreams was cut short, as Carla preferred not to go to Spain that year. In July 1956, a little after the *infantes'* return from their travels and stay in Madrid, there was a crisis in the marriage of the duke and duchess of Galliera. Álvaro had fallen in love with an older Italian lady who had a glass eye. The upset lasted about a year or two, until the sheep returned to the flock.

A draft letter from Bee to her daughter-in-law, Carla, told of her great interest in her:

> Álvaro has just left and I think I should tell you I have found him very calm and wanting everything to be better. The bitterness seems to me to have gone. He has changed and I feel that if he is left alone for a while (to think) about his feelings, perhaps we may be happy again.
>
> I can assure you that he does not want to take any action relating to your children that could cause you unhappiness.

The reunited couple went to Spain to see the *infantes*, and Bee gave her daughter-in-law a beautiful Russian bracelet with a diamond interwoven with a pearl. The grandchildren were the happiest as they were finally allowed to return to Sanlúcar, which they had missed so much. Geri was eight and would paint postcards in the Egyptian room at the palace. Bee was taken by surprise by the artistic taste of her granddaughter and wanted to be her teacher.

Although ninety years old, *Infanta* Eulalia continued to lead an active life and went to France almost every day, buying newspapers, noodles, biscuits, and butter. She continued receiving people at audiences after teatime, naturally less often in winter, but there were always those who wished to meet the daughter of Isabel II. Just like her mother, Eulalia was very kind towards the servants and did not like showing her displeasure. One day on visiting her in the afternoon, I found her worried and she told my husband and me that her maid Honorata, on serving her lunch, had served the tortilla from the frying pan to the plate. Immediately she said to me, 'You get on so well with her, go see her and tell her what I am accustomed to.' I went to the kitchen and found the maid in tears. She told me she had done it to ensure it was hot. In France we had the good fortune to find a gadget to warm the plates, which really thrilled the *infanta*.

For her last two years, she was confined to a wheelchair after a fall, and could no longer run around. In January 1957, when my daughter was born, I took advantage of her birthday to congratulate her and give her the news. She sent me a telegram by return showing 'the joy she had felt knowing that the girl was called María de las Mercedes'.

That summer I went to see her regularly. Although she still had a clear head, she felt tired so I did not bring my baby daughter. At Christmas she replied to my good wishes by telegram. In February 1958, on reaching ninety-four, she did not reply and at the beginning of March the *infantes* and their grandson, Ataúlfo, went to Irún. It was the beginning of the end. She used to talk about death with naturalness, 'because sooner or later we have all to pass through it'. At the end of her life, the parish priest visited her and judged her very intelligent. She shared with him all that is human and all that is divine. As a good Christian she wished to receive the Sacraments and on 8 March she prepared herself to die well. The priest from Seville, Don Camilo Olivares, a great friend of the royal family, came to visit her in her rooms.

I will never forget the impressive scene on meeting her, I could hardly see the tiny face and the almost immobile hands. On the right, on a sofa, were her son, Ali, and Bee, both also now elderly. At the side of the patient was the venerable, 'intelligent' parish priest. When he paused in his prayers, the great lady painfully lifted a hand asking him to continue. The parish priest requested my help and it was strange: we began the prayers and intercessions in Castilian, and she responded in French, but if we changed to that language, she replied in Castilian. The *infantes* smiled and made gestures of admiration. With some annoyance, the intelligent priest turned towards me and said between his teeth 'Padre, have you seen anything like it? A leopard never changes its spots!'

Smiling, *Infanta* Eulalia closed her eyes forever. Although it was now almost springtime the snow covering Spain had come to El Escorial where, in the pudridero, her cousin and husband, Antonio de Orleans, had been awaiting her for more than twenty-seven years.

The following year, Bee was urged to cut down on her smoking. She did but could not stop completely, and in June 1956, she had pneumonia. That summer was especially interesting with the arrival of the *Infantita* Beatriz, as the common people called her. She found Sanlúcar much to her liking. Visiting the maternity home on various occasions, she was amazed by the work of her aunt.

The *infantes'* golden wedding was on 15 July 1959. As half a century before, everything had been very quick: three ceremonies on the same day and no photographic memories, they decided to accept the invitation of Prince Gottfried of Hohenlohe-Langenburg, who lent them his castle for the celebration. It was attended by the princes, Álvaro and Ataúlfo, but Carla said she could not go. Also absent were Beatrice and Álvaro, who regretted being unable to join their grandparents. However the eldest grandchildren, Geri and Alonso attended, as did María Ángeles Tornos and Ramón Escario who was Ali's last aide. Sitting next to them was Mignon, queen of Yugoslavia, who had come from England where she lived very simply in the country.

Since we returned from Egypt and went to Madrid, I frequently saw the *infantes* at María Ángeles' house. My biography of Queen Mercedes had been well received and gone into several editions. Juan Ignacio Luca de Tena based his play, *Where are you going Alfonso XII?*, on it, but Bee was unimpressed (Sanlúcar, 16 November 1958):

Many thanks for your most interesting letter which I was delighted to receive. As I am no mistress of the pen, I am not going to try to answer it in detail. God willing we will arrive in Madrid on the 22nd and it will be a very great pleasure to see you there and to talk about the film which I am sure will be magnificent and compensate for the disappointment that we had with the comedy in which the Duke of Montpensier was treated, unjustly in my opinion, as the villain of the piece.

When we met, I promised the infanta that as historical adviser to the film, I would try to do everything possible for it to approximate the truth, without making the duke of Montpensier appear ridiculous, as I also felt that there was no motive for this. Months later, when in Mallorca and hearing from María Ángeles that she had liked the film, I wrote her and sent some reviews. She replied by return of post (Sanlúcar, 3 June 1959), using a typewriter because her eyes were dimming:

> A thousand thanks for your letter. It was a great joy for me to receive it. For some time now I have wanted to write to tell you the immense impression the film *Where are you going Alfonso XII?* has made on us. I would not have believed it possible that a film would unleash such great enthusiasm among all social classes. Perhaps it was the part of Mercedes (played by Paquita Rico) and that of Queen Isabel (Lola Membrines) [*sic*], [Isabel II was actually played by Mercedes Vecino], the other ladies of the family were not so perfect, but the artist who did Alfonso XIII (Vincente Parra) played the part marvellously. You know what a big critic I am regards the theatre.
>
> I am awaiting the arrival of your promised book with great interest and thank you a thousand times in advance for your kindness in sending it to me.

Prince Juan Carlos completed his baccalaureate at the Miramar Palace, San Sebastian, followed by spells in different military academies, army, navy, air force, and at the University of Madrid. At twenty-three, he lived apart from his family, with his own house and under the strict vigilance of Franco and his party. Queen Frederica of Greece organised a cruise through the Greek Islands aboard the *Agamenon*, to which she invited all the royal families of Europe. The count and countess of Barcelona went with their children, Pilar and Juan Carlos, who were young when they first met the Greek prince and princesses, Constantine, Sophia, and Irene, who were about the same age. They saw each other again in June 1961 at the wedding of the duke of Kent to Katharine Worsley. The king and queen of Greece invited the Barcelona family to spend some days at Corfu with their children. They were related through Kaiser Wilhelm II, Queen Victoria's eldest grandchild and great-grandfather of Sophia. Juan Carlos was a grandson of Ena, youngest granddaughter of Queen Victoria of England.

Juan Carlos and Sophia's engagement was announced in Lausanne on 13 September 1961 at Ena's home, with the wedding arranged for 14 May 1962 in Athens. Ali decided to attend because of his great friendship with King Paul, as well as his relationship to Don Juan and Don Juanito, who had visited them at Sanlúcar when he was eighteen. Bee did not go to Athens as she felt tired, and the maternity home took more and more of her time.

When she returned to Sanlúcar, Beatriz gave her grandmother such a detailed description of the wedding in Athens that it seemed that the latter had been there:

Grosspapi—*(the Infante)*, Álvaro, Ataúlfo, Alonso, my brother, José, Uncle Ataúlfo's butler, and I, left Rome.

Before landing, Grandfather told us that Michael of Greece would meet us, and that we were not to laugh at his dazzling Bavarian uniform in sky blue and silver.

He took us to the Hotel Grande Bretagne. On our floor were Aunt Beatriz (Torlonia) and Aunt Crista (Marone) with their children. We went about half naked through the corridors because of the heat: the men in their underpants and we in our petticoats and all shoeless and delighted with the fitted carpets. There was a mixture of ages, and languages—they were most intrigued, and rather scandalised. Each group had an aide who occupied themselves with reminding us of the various events, and advising us in time. We also had a chauffeur-driven car with a crown on a red background as a number plate. The drivers drove like madmen through the chaotic Athens traffic sounding their horns and more than one cousin or aunt arrived at their destination pale and queasy.

The letter from Queen Victoria Eugenia (Vielle Fontaine, Lausanne, 17 May 1962) was the most interesting for its information and intimate comments. Bee liked to keep her missives, which was not one of the queen's customs. Now when she received them she insisted that they be destroyed, a precautionary measure that it seems she followed throughout her life:

This is the letter which I promised to write you on my return from Athens. It is useless to tell you how much I wanted you to be there as well, where Ali and I were the veterans, and because we were almost unable to get on with old Marina of Greece. I should say that everything went wonderfully and that we were all in excellent humour. The procession was splendid, only Juanito was rather pale because he was in pain all the time as the broad band of plaster which he had to wear since damaging the bone in his neck, caused a flesh wound.

They received very nice presents. The best jewels which Sophia received were the diamonds and the pearl diadem which I passed to Juan to give her, and a splendid collar of cabochon rubies and diamonds in two rows and a diamond diadem, both from Niarchos. *C'est beau la fortune!* I found Paul and Freddy's [Queen Frederica] present, four simple bracelets of gold chain with small cabochon rubies, sapphires, and emeralds, rather poor, but it is a fact that they had bought two boxes of cutlery in London for the couple and a great silver boat for Juanito.

Sophia did not receive any pearls from her parents, I think that they could have given her earrings or at least a chain of pretty cultivated pearls instead of the bracelets and the boat.

I sent them a brooch of the Order of Carlos III in diamonds.* [It seems that they did not appreciate the magnificent eighteenth-century present.] I am annoyed about the latter.

The two balls were a magnificent spectacle, as everyone went well dressed (except María, my daughter-in-law) and wore splendid jewels. During the days we were in Athens it was thirty-five or thirty-six degrees centigrade!

Everyone enjoyed lunching in the restaurants along the coast. Sitta, Tim and Catalina, Olaf (King of Norway), Ingrid (Queen of Denmark) and her three children, Juliana (Queen of the Netherlands) and Bernard with their three children and I were in Tino's old house, now the Royal Palace.

Olaf and I were neighbours, the two doors being on the lower floor. On Saturday morning there was a parade of 3,500 Spaniards in the garden. I persuaded Paul and Freddy to let the people shake their hands, and so they were perfectly happy and satisfied, which would not have been the case if they had passed them by as Freddy wanted.

Luca de Tena organised a party for all the Spaniards on Saturday night. We went down mixing with them and they were really emotional towards me. One poor middle-aged woman had brought a small package for me from La Granja; a box of those coffee with milk caramels wrapped in little papers which I am sure you remember.

Monday, the day of the wedding, was especially hot. All were dressed and ready at nine in the morning. The Catholic Church was beautifully decorated with red and yellow carnations and the singing was very good. Sophia was so sweet in her wedding dress, and her eight bridesmaids were enchanting dressed in pleated white chiffon with silver patterns. Each pair of bridesmaids wore a ribbon on their belts: one pink, another pale blue, light yellow and their headdresses were the same colour, matching the ribbon on the belt. Pilar and Alexandra of Kent were last and wore pale green: the two were very pretty that day. On leaving the church, the Marine Guard formed a sabre arch so that the newly-weds passed below it. This was arranged by the minister, Abárzuza who I knew when he was a young and elegant officer commanding a small and ridiculous boat called Mac-Mahón at San Sebastian. He seemed very pleased to see us all again; his wife, who is enchanting, is English.

After the wedding we returned to the palace where we were for twenty minutes and then we left again for the Orthodox Church. The sight on entering the church was lovely. Naturally having to stand for three quarters of an hour without moving was agony for my feet. At the end, when we returned to the palace, we had to stand once again for a long time because the photographers asked us to. We only sat during lunch in the garden which was beautifully arranged, and finished at half past three. Having had only a little cup of coffee at a quarter to nine in the morning, I was very empty. When lunch ended, we once again had a long wait in the garden until Sophie and Juanito appeared in their car to be showered with rose petals, which we all threw. By then all Sophie's family were drowning in tears. That night, so as not to be alone, Freddy and the young Tino again arranged for us all to go to a restaurant so that the young couples could dance. I was rather pleased to have been able to stay until the bitter end. I switched off the light in my room at fifteen minutes to two in the morning and my maid came to call me at half past six.

I am now resting a lot, because my feet and my ankles are terribly swollen because of tiredness and the heat. I am going to Sirmioni, on Lake Garda, to spend fifteen days, until the 23rd, to take inhalations of sulphate, which help victims of the symptoms of sinusitis like me. I returned again yesterday for the third time and they x-rayed my head. Professor Tallens has just called me to say that I have not improved much since the 27th March.

I almost always carry those little turquoise eggs which you gave me and which I have had made into a little bracelet.

Ali and his boys were in great form and seemed to have great fun.

Juan has said to me confidentially that Sophie will convert to Roman Catholicism at the end of the month in Corfu, they will then go to Rome where the Pope will receive them on the 4th June, and from there they will do a trip around the world in jet aircraft, which is one of the presents from Juan to Juanito. They will be away for two months.

Every year the Raffle of the Poor was held in aid of the maternity home. It was very simple, but the organisers exaggerated the prizes: 'magnificent soap, strong smelling perfume, etc.' The maternity home, in Almonte Street, near the sea, was paid for by the *infanta* in its first years, but the running costs increased so much that a grand fundraising fiesta was held in the summer. The maternity home improved year by year with the purchase of modern equipment, and when the Americans came to the base at Rota, they contributed milk, medicines, and clinical instruments. The admiral, officers, and some of their families attended the party in their dress uniforms and danced with the young women in their Andalusian dresses. For the young ladies, the fiesta was the best of the summer and they asked their families to let them stay until the finish: 'And it was the only day on which one saw so many and such beautiful automobiles in Sanlúcar. It was also the only day on which the mothers allowed their daughters to stay out all night and to return at dawn'.

The fiesta had two distinct names, *dèl Abanico* (of the fan) and the *El y Ella*

(His and Hers). Apart from the supper and the dance, the tickets provided a number in the raffle. To entertain them, they could count upon the celebrated presenters Bobby Deglané and José Luis Pécker. There was also an auction of fine objects given to Bee, who used to paint little pictures of flowers, which were a great success. When Ali went to the raffle, he would buy a bundle of tickets which he gave to the children. Those who could not open them would ask anyone else to do so, and if someone did so slowly Ali would say to them nervously, 'Hurry up, they're impatient'. Bee always received huge ovations.

She received many letters asking for help, and she tried to do so by contacting those who could give help or money. In this she relied upon the collaboration of Ali's secretary, Ángel Louro Viana, who had served him for many years. In the summer, before arranging the fiesta, she wrote to many people, and again afterwards to thank them. Writing to the marquis of Salvatierra two years before her death, she expressed her satisfaction and gratitude for a successful effort:

> I do not know how to thank you for the marvellous chickens which have been the success of the fiesta. A million thanks also in the name of all the poor women of Sanlúcar for your generosity. This way of roasting chickens is an extraordinary thing, giving them a completely different flavour. Everyone threw themselves on them like ogres and all the time I was thinking with satisfaction—they have not cost us anything! Thus a fiesta, which worried me greatly because of the bad times which we are going through, and because of events in other places such as Cádiz, El Puerto, Málaga, etc., has been a definitive success.

What was not known was up to what point the *infanta* had been the soul of the foundation, because neither she nor Consuelo Montemar spoke about it.

In the spring of 1960, Beatrice was in Rome studying for a bachelor's degree in arts. On achieving a good result, her very satisfied parents asked her what she would like and she surprised them by replying, 'What I would like most would be to be able to go to Sanlúcar to my grandparents.' That summer all the family went sailing to Greece but Alonso, who was studying for his forthcoming exams, and Geri who was working as a journalist. She had decided to enrol at Bryn Mawr College, considered the best North American university for ladies, and her father wrote to the Dupont de Nemours family of Delaware. They offered their home to Geri and she spent Christmas 1961 with them. By then she was studying and living in Bryn Mawr, in the outskirts of Philadelphia, where she met Harry Saint, a young man from New York who was studying nearby at Haveford College. Two years later, on 26 July 1963, they were married in a civil ceremony in Ellenville, New York.

In December 1963, I returned to be with the *Infanta* Beatrice at her home in Calle Abascal. She had asked me to bring my daughter, named after the unlucky queen, because she had not met her. Five-year-old Mercedes was lively and amusing, and she recited a Christmas poem for her, which she liked very much.

The *infantes* were very pleased with the arrival of the king and queen of Greece who had come to Madrid, as Princess Sophia was about to give birth. The Greek sovereigns came to eat with them that day. The *Infanta* Bee told me the baby's godparents would be Doña María, the countess of Barcelona, as paternal grandmother and Ali in the place of King Paul who, as maternal grandfather, had ceded this honour to Don Ali as great-uncle. On 20 December 1963, the *Infanta* Elena was born in the Clinica Loreto. From then on Ali, on writing to Doña María, headed his letters: 'My dear cousin, Queen and godmother'.

After staying in Madrid, Bee was very tired on returning to Sanlúcar, because she liked to go to concerts and the theatre in the capital, and hold audiences for people who wished to see her. At the Botánico she enjoyed the garden and the house; remembering the Montpensier Palace, she would say, 'It is much cosier here'. She still wrote to Geri in America, and seemed content, although she missed her family and especially her granny.

Beatrice was in love with Tommasso, son of Count and Countess Farini, a young aristocrat from Ravenna, and on 25 April 1964 they married at the Church of St Ines, Rome. Ali attended the ceremony, but Bee excused herself saying that as the honeymoon would be in Spain, she would wait for them in Sanlúcar. Although she tried to continue a normal life, Beatrice found her very old, so she decided to return quickly as she feared losing her. The following year she and her husband returned to spend the summer there and 'Granny said to us that she loved the visit because she had so little time left'. The couple returned at Christmas, as did the duke and duchess of Galliera, to find the Botánico decked out as usual. Presents were distributed to staff and toys to the children, while Bee still went down to the dining room for lunch and dinner despite the lack of a lift.

She received few guests, as they tired her, and the card games after lunch and walks around the garden were now shorter: 'Later she told me that she was thinking of not taking the grapes to celebrate the New Year of 1966 because she feared choking'. Her granddaughter returned in February, to find her walking about, but that month the doctors made her stop smoking again and she exclaimed, 'I cannot live without smoking!' She lit a new cigarette almost before finishing the previous one.

Now that Alice was old and lived in another house with her husband and her son, she had a new maid, Victoria. The ever loyal Carmelo had become the administrator of the estates, and every morning he told Bee of the previous day's happenings. Carmela, ever attentive, continued as housekeeper. María Ángeles was now living at the Botánico, as was Consuelo who continued working at the maternity home, and now she only told her the good news. Ali, remembering sadly the death of his grandmother Queen Isabel II in Paris, and how they were obliged to spend hours at her lying in state, did not wish their grandchildren to be there at the end, so that they kept their memories of the figure of the granny that they loved so much. Carla came from Italy and cared for her during the last two months and used to read to her as she could not see because of cataracts, which were never operated on. Not to harass her, Ali continued with his normal life, desolate at facing the idea of seeing the love of his life leave.

Bee, who had helped so many die, did not fear the moment. She only said to Carla in English, 'What a time it takes to die!' Father Gonzalo de Córdoba visited her every day. On 13 July 1966, he gave her the Last Sacraments, and she said, 'God will reward you'. They were her last words. They dressed her in a simple Franciscan habit while the bells of the churches of Sanlúcar tolled her death and the deeply moved old ladies said, 'The Señorita *Infanta* has now ceased suffering'.

Epilogue

Bee's death caused genuine grief in Sanlúcar and the funeral, in the church of the Capuchins, was well attended. The prince and princess of Spain came from Mallorca, Beatrice and her husband from Italy, and numerous members of the Borbón and Orleans royal houses families and many friends from Andalucía and from all over Spain. Ali informed them and all their friends abroad of the news. To the closest, he sent a commemorative card, which the *infanta* herself had made with the date left blank, printed in Spanish, with only a prayer in German, and a portrait of her as a nurse on duty at the maternity home. They had celebrated the 'His and Hers' fiesta for the last time in August and raffled a car. Bee had not made a will and her widower distributed her things among her intimates.

Beatrice cheered him up when he went to Rome for Christmas, accompanied by his son, Ataúlfo, and his butler, José, who was a great help in the house. Nearly a year later, on 23 November 1967, Beatrice had a baby boy in Bolonia, his first great-grandchild, named Gerardo. He stayed until after the baptism. The following year he went to the Canary Islands, where his grandson, Alonso, lived on a magnificent estate. The eldest son of the prince and princess of Orleans, he later became head of the house. He had married Doña Emilia Ferrara Pignatelli, daughter of the prince and princess of Strongoli, on 12 January 1966 in Naples. Their first son, Alfonso, was born on 2 January 1968 in Santa Cruz de Tenerife. Ali was overjoyed to see his favourite grandson again, whom they called 'the hero' from childhood, because of his bravery when faced with several operations on his heart. Two years later, they had another son, Álvaro.

The visits to Italy and the Canaries were a delight as Ali had always loved children, and now he had the pleasure of a new generation. In the 1960s, he used to go to London at the end of November to do his Christmas shopping, a custom he loved and continued, as all his staff and members of the household received a present from England. Ali was always accompanied by his son, Ataúlfo, and the faithful butler, José. I believe the last year he could go was 1968.

Matters in Spain had changed little. On the birth of their son, the prince and princess of Spain asked Ena to be the baby's godmother. She came to Madrid, as did Don Juan and Doña María, who attended the ceremony which was held at the Zarzuela Palace in the presence of *Generalissimo* Franco and his wife. They say that the queen was friendly towards the Caudillo and his wife, and at an opportune moment she said to him, 'General, you have the three to choose from here.'

The visit to Madrid greatly moved the old sovereign, who visited the Red Cross, with Dr Don Enrique García Ortiz, and they checked on recent improvements. She stayed at the Liria Palace, property of the dukes of Alba. Through her tears she saw the Oriente Palace, where she had lived for almost twenty-five years. On saying goodbye at the airport, she said simply, 'Now I can die in peace!' A year later, 15 April 1969, she died in Lausanne, on the thirty-sixth anniversary of her leaving Spain. It was a hard blow for Ali, as since his wife's death he was an assiduous correspondent.

When I arrived at the Botánico to prepare this book, I found various additional letters from Ena to Ali. It was a great friendship of more than seventy years that united them, and they were both united as much in their way of thinking as acting. They said he was not at the baptism of Prince Don Felipe so as not find himself with Gen. Franco, thus avoiding difficulties of protocol. In fact, he avoided fiestas as a letter to Col. Don Manuel de Montoro y Varela, head of the Military Stud at Jerez de la Frontera (Sanlúcar, 21 July 1971), showed:

I was born in 1886, when I am in uniform I not able walk [sic] with the assurance that all soldiers in uniform should. Nor can I spend much time standing firm and still, and when I say firm, it is the old meaning— without making the slightest movement during all of the Mass. For this reason I go to very few military acts where I have to go in uniform or in civilian clothes if there are official functions which tire me too much.

You will be thinking then how it is possible that I can fly, but it is like the Cavalry. I will say that, when I was young, all good people (outside of the Infantry, or country people) were horsemen—caballeros. The old people said, 'I cannot manage hard obstacles and can only walk a little; but on horseback I can spend all the time I want because the horse makes the effort'. In flight, it is the aircraft that makes the effort.

According to his granddaughter, Beatrice, he wanted to fly solo and die of a heart attack, among the clouds, looking at the sky. He was very annoyed when they advised him that he should always be accompanied and it was decreed that his old friend, Pepe Cotro Florido, should accompany him. 'I am eighty-six years old,' Ali wrote, explaining that during Christmas 1972 he could not celebrate as was his custom, but we leave him to tell the story on returning to Sanlúcar:

> The elderly acquire customs and are greatly tired by a sudden change in their long lives. I have spent the last quarter century here: good climate, pure air, doing lots of physical exercise, and I got up early and I went to bed early. The food was good, light and varied.
>
> On the 16th December 1972, I went into the Air Force Hospital in Madrid, for preparation for and to be operated on my prostate. Life was totally different as you can imagine. The air in Madrid is very dirty, they did many tests on me and give me many medicines. They looked after me magnificently and with a love that I will never forget. I was in hospital for forty-nine days: They operated on me on the 11th January 1973, removing my prostate.
>
> I returned to Sanlúcar on 2 February. Here life is completely different from the hospital, and I have to take great care not to tire myself too much until I have got used to the change in my old body.

His granddaughter, Beatrice, was the light of his life. An excellent nurse, she cared for him during the day, and slept at the house of María Ángeles, who accompanied them. Although he was of a different generation, his grandchildren always entertained him when they came to Sanlúcar every summer. Yet it was Beatrice with whom he especially enjoyed going on long walks along the beach at Chipiona and telling curious anecdotes about his long life. On starting to recall he would stop for a second and ask, 'Perhaps you already know?' 'Tell me again. I never tire listening to you!' she replied with great interest.

He recovered quickly from his operation. In October that year, when I went to Jerez to collect the prize from the town council for my biography of Primo de Rivera, he telephoned me at the Hotel Los Cisnes early the following day to congratulate me and to say he expected me for lunch the following day at the Botánico with María Luisa Beltrán de Lis and her children, and Maravillas and Pepe Domecq who would take me there. We arrived early in Sanlúcar, and they left me at the Botánico with Carmela while they went on an errand.

Chatting with Carmela was most amusing because she was very intelligent and discreet. She talked to me about everything at the Botánico, and about Bee, and warned me not to mention her to Ali because it made him sad. He appeared immediately, at 2 p.m., as punctual as ever. On seeing me, he immediately embraced me and said, 'I want you to know that in her last years, the Infanta said that your book and the film about my aunt, Queen Mercedes, brought her great pleasure.' Then María Luisa arrived with her children, and we went into the dining room. It was a most amusing lunch, with Ali raising his voice asking for news. That week they had visited Don Juan Carlos and Doña Sophia, 'the Prince and Princess of Spain' as they were then known, and they had visited Jerez where they had an extraordinary reception.

He told us how the princess had telephoned. She was the daughter of his great friend the late King Paul, and said that both of them wanted to go to the Botánico: 'As I am old, I asked if she wanted to organise a reception or a meal, but she replied, "No, Uncle Ali, the only thing we want is to be able to be with you and in slippers. Something which amused me as now I am not really up to parties." However, on returning to Jerez we thought he was in excellent form'.

As usual, at the beginning of the spring of 1974, he wrote me a long letter in a firm hand. That summer, María Ángeles, who went to Sanlúcar to spend her holidays there, told me she had found him thinner and tired. In a letter of 27 July 1974 to the chief of the Maestranza de Tablada, Col. Valle, he said the doctor set his timetable with lunch at 2 p.m., at 3:30 p.m., he had a siesta until 5:30 p.m. and then went for a walk: 'They do not let me out at night, nor let me invite friends to dinner, and I have to be in bed by 21.30. I am explaining all this so that you may see the difficulties that I have to see my friends. I have an incurable illness: born in 1886. It has been half a year since I last flew, but I prefer to wait a little more until it is less hot'.

That August, Spaniards were surprised by Gen. Franco's illness, and Prince Don Juan Carlos took interim power. The count of Barcelona was in Sanlúcar, visiting his uncle Ali. On hearing the news, Don Juan cancelled his planned cruise and returned to Estoril. It was a false alarm, and Franco resumed the reins of power.

Ali was always devoted to the Virgin of Regla, the patron saint of Chipiona, which he had visited when very young, accompanied by his grandmother, María Luisa Fernanda, the duchess of Montpensier, on 8 September, the day on which the saint is celebrated with a great festival. As a boy, he was surprised by the ancient image of the Virgin, which is very dark while the baby Jesus is white.

Years later, on 8 September, the day the landing at Alhucemas took place, Ali spent the day in the air calling upon the Virgin, feeling that her divine protection brought victory. When he was appointed general-in-chief of air force troops in the Straight, two aircraft accompanied the procession from above, throwing rose petals that increased the fervour of the people who came all over Andalusia to watch. Ali attended the fiesta for the last time, but did not walk in the procession. He remembered that twenty years earlier, accompanied by Bee, they were godparents at the coronation celebrated by Cardinal Segura. Now he was the only survivor.

In mid-September, Prince Don Ataúlfo did not go to Sanlúcar every week as usual. He was at a clinic in Malaga, where they could not determine the cause of his illness. His worried butler visited the marquis and marchioness of Salvatierra, who were intimates of the prince, and on changing to another health centre they diagnosed an inflammation of the pancreas. The Marchioness Pilar cared for him with the love of a mother, and Álvaro and Carla came from Italy. The latter felt great affection for her brother-in-law, and they were deeply concerned about the virulence of the illness. He died in Malaga in a most Christian manner on 8 October 1974.

For Ali, the loss of his youngest son was a shock from which he never recovered. His granddaughter, Beatrice, spent part of the winter in Sanlúcar. At Christmas, in mourning, he did not send any festive greetings. On his saint's day, I sent him an *ensaimada* as usual, and he thanked us, as friendly as ever, the following day: 'A thousand thanks. Excellent, immense, *ensaimada*. I am better. Kindest regards, Alfonso' (24 January 1975). He declined slowly, and the marquis of Salvatierra never stopped visiting him. Beatrice arrived at Easter and stayed, as did María Ángeles Tornos, who arrived in June, bringing forward her summer holidays. On hearing of his condition, the countess of Barcelona went to Sanlúcar to say farewell to her 'beloved Uncle Ali' who she had always admired. He no longer went downstairs to the ground floor, but remained in his room on the terrace. The Franciscan Fathers always made an effort to visit him. A profoundly religious man, he did not fear death, and in his pocket diary he had noted the anniversaries of his friends' passings. From Houston, Texas, where he was in hospital, his grandson, Alonso, telephoned him every afternoon at exactly 3 p.m. to speak to him and ask him about things. 'The hero', who was very ill, asked God for him to outlive his grandfather so as to avoid upsetting him.

He died on 7 September 1975, aged only thirty-four.

Álvaro had married Giovanna San Martino d'Agliè, daughter of the marquis and marchioness of San Germano (to whom this book owes much), on 24 May 1974 at Campiglione, and had a daughter named Pilar. Temperatures rose that August and the nights did not allow the necessary rest, so Ali was uncomfortable, but he later became calmer. Beatrice took advantage of the moment to go downstairs to the dining room for a cup of coffee. When she went up, she saw her grandfather was awake, having a heart attack, and took his hand. After a few minutes she thought the danger was over, but then a second attack started. She continued to hold his hand, but he did not squeeze it. It was 10:05 a.m. on 6 August 1975, about the hour when he used to take off in his aeroplane, this time he was flying into infinity.

Two months later, *Generalissimo* Franco became ill. On his death on the morning of 20 November 1975, the monarchy, in the person of King Juan Carlos I, was proclaimed.

Genealogical Tables

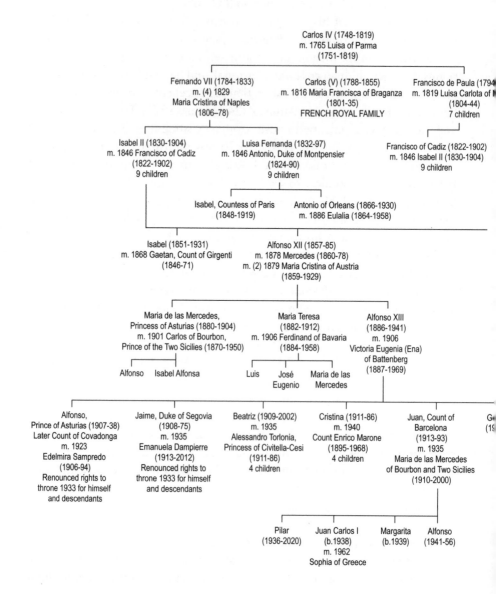

Carlos IV (1748-1819)
m. 1765 Luisa of Parma
(1751-1819)

Fernando VII (1784-1833)
m. (4) 1829
Maria Cristina of Naples
(1806–78)

Carlos (V) (1788-1855)
m. 1816 Maria Francisca of Braganza
(1801-35)
FRENCH ROYAL FAMILY

Francisco de Paula (1794)
m. 1819 Luisa Carlota of N
(1804-44)
7 children

Isabel II (1830-1904)
m. 1846 Francisco of Cadiz
(1822-1902)
9 children

Luisa Fernanda (1832-97)
m. 1846 Antonio, Duke of Montpensier
(1824-90)
9 children

Francisco of Cadiz (1822-1902)
m. 1846 Isabel II (1830-1904)
9 children

Isabel, Countess of Paris
(1848-1919)

Antonio of Orleans (1866-1930)
m. 1886 Eulalia (1864-1958)

Isabel (1851-1931)
m. 1868 Gaetan, Count of Girgenti
(1846-71)

Alfonso XII (1857-85)
m. 1878 Mercedes (1860-78)
m. (2) 1879 Maria Cristina of Austria
(1859-1929)

Maria de las Mercedes,
Princess of Asturias (1880-1904)
m. 1901 Carlos of Bourbon,
Prince of the Two Sicilies (1870-1950)

Maria Teresa
(1882-1912)
m. 1906 Ferdinand of Bavaria
(1884-1958)

Alfonso XIII
(1886-1941)
m. 1906
Victoria Eugenia (Ena)
of Battenberg
(1887-1969)

Alfonso   Isabel Alfonsa

Luis   José
Eugenio

Maria de las
Mercedes

Alfonso,
Prince of Asturias (1907-38)
Later Count of Covadonga
m. 1923
Edelmira Sampredo
(1906-94)
Renounced rights to
throne 1933 for himself
and descendants

Jaime, Duke of Segovia
(1908-75)
m. 1935
Emanuela Dampierre
(1913-2012)
Renounced rights to
throne 1933 for himself
and descendants

Beatriz (1909-2002)
m. 1935
Alessandro Torlonia,
Princess of Civitella-Cesi
(1911-86)
4 children

Cristina (1911-86)
m. 1940
Count Enrico Marone
(1895-1968)
4 children

Juan, Count of
Barcelona
(1913-93)
m. 1935
Maria de las Mercedes
of Bourbon and Two Sicilies
(1910-2000)

G
(19

Pilar
(1936-2020)

Juan Carlos I
(b.1938)
m. 1962
Sophia of Greece

Margarita
(b.1939)

Alfonso
(1941-56)

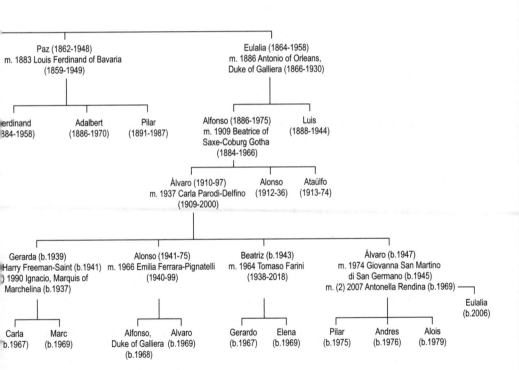

Paz (1862-1948)
m. 1883 Louis Ferdinand of Bavaria
(1859-1949)

Eulalia (1864-1958)
m. 1886 Antonio of Orleans,
Duke of Galliera (1866-1930)

erdinand
884-1958)

Adalbert
(1886-1970)

Pilar
(1891-1987)

Alfonso (1886-1975)
m. 1909 Beatrice of
Saxe-Coburg Gotha
(1884-1966)

Luis
(1888-1944)

Álvaro (1910-97)
m. 1937 Carla Parodi-Delfino
(1909-2000)

Alonso
(1912-36)

Ataúlfo
(1913-74)

Gerarda (b.1939)
Harry Freeman-Saint (b.1941)
) 1990 Ignacio, Marquis of
Marchelina (b.1937)

Alonso (1941-75)
m. 1966 Emilia Ferrara-Pignatelli
(1940-99)

Beatriz (b.1943)
m. 1964 Tomaso Farini
(1938-2018)

Álvaro (b.1947)
m. 1974 Giovanna San Martino
di San Germano (b.1945)
m. (2) 2007 Antonella Rendina (b.1969)

Eulalia
(b.2006)

Carla
b.1967)

Marc
(b.1969)

Alfonso,
Duke of Galliera
(b.1968)

Alvaro
(b.1969)

Gerardo
(b.1967)

Elena
(b.1969)

Pilar
(b.1975)

Andres
(b.1976)

Alois
(b.1979)

Bibliography

Archives

Orleans-Borbón Archive, Sanlúcar de Barrameda Archive of the State of Coburg
Archive of the Royal Palace, Madrid
Archive of Her Majesty the Queen, Windsor Castle Archive of the Royal Palace,
    Rumania
Archive of Don Antonio Maura, Fundación Maura, Madrid
Archive of the Duke and Duchess of Santa Cristina, Torrente, Valencia Archive of
    the Count de Romanones in the Royal Academy of History, Madrid Archive of
    Don Alonso Herrera Wallington, Madrid
Archive of the Count of Vallellano, Madrid
Archive of the Rodríguez Pacual family (1880–1942), Madrid
Archive of the Rich family (in the Orleans-Borbón Archive)
Archive of Don Cecilio Yusta, Madrid
National Library of Spain, Madrid
Central Universitary Library, Madrid
Archive of the author

I should like to express my gratitude to Dr Yuri Saveliev of St Petersburg, and to my
    young friends Don José Luis Sampedro Escolar and Don Ricardo Mateos Sáinz
    de Medrano, who have helped me for so many years, and had 900 letters in the
    Central State Archive, from Grand Duke Michael of Russia to his cousin, Princess
    Beatrice of Saxe-Coburg-Gotha, photocopied in Moscow and brought
    to Spain.

Newspapers and Magazines

ABC, Years 1903–1982, Madrid, National Library of Spain, microfilm 0178
ABC, Years 1906–1911, Madrid, Library of the Royal Palace, sig. VIII-M-Hueco
Blanco y Negro, 1924–1931
El año aristocrático, 1914–1916, Madrid.
El Nuevo Mundo, 1909, 1915, 1916
La Época, 1849–1936, Madrid, National Library of Spain, microf. 0005
La Época, Madrid, Library of the Royal Palace
La Ilustración Española y Americana, Madrid, 1870–1921
Royalty Digest

Books

Alcalá Galiano, Álvaro, Marquis of Castel Bravo, *The Fall of a Throne* (London, Thornton Butterworth, 1933)
Alexander, Grand Duke of Russia, *Once a Grand Duke* (London: Cassell, 1932)
Alfonso XIII, King, *Intimate Diary* (Madrid: Archive of the Royal Palace)
Alice, Grand Duchess of Hesse, *Letters* (London: John Murray, 1884)
Almagro San Martín, M., *Cronica de Alfonso XIII y su linaje* (Madrid, Ediciones Atlas, 1946); *Lapequeña historia. Cincuenta años de vida española (1880–1930)* (Madrid, Afrodisio Aguado, 1954); *Bajo los tres últimos Borbones* (Madrid, Afrodisio Aguado, 1950)
Anon, *The Imperial House of Russia* (Moscow, Perspective Moscow, 1992)
Ansón, Luis María, *Don Juan* (Barcelona, Plaza & Janes, 1994)
Aronson, T., *Grandmama of Europe: The Crowned Descendants of Queen Victoria* (London, Cassell, 1973); *Royal Vendetta: The Crown of Spain 1829–1965* (London: Oldbourne, 1966)
Ashdown, Dulcie M., *Victoria and the Coburgs* (London, Robert Hale, 1981)
Barbazán Beneit, Julián, *Recuerdos de un librero anticuario madrileño (1897–1969)* (Madrid: Sucesores de J. Sanchez Ocafla y Cia., 1970)
Baviera, Pilar, Princess, *Alfonso XIII. A Study of Monarchy* (London: John Murray, 1931)
Belgium, Princess Louise of, *Autour des Trones que j'ai vu tomber* (Paris: Albin Michel, 1921)
Bing, Edward J. (ed.), *The Letters of Tsar Nicholas and Empress Marie* (London: Ivor Nicholson and Watson, 1937)
Blasco Ibáñez, Vicente, *Alphose XIII demasqué* (Paris: Flammarion, 1924)
Borbón, Paz, *Infanta* Deespaña: *Through Four Revolutions, 1862–1933* (London: John Murray, 1933)
Buchanan, Sir G., *My Mission to Russia and other Diplomatic Memories*, 2 vols. (London: Cassell, 1923)

Buchanan, M., *The Dissolution of an Empire* (London: John Murray, 1932)

Bülow, Prince Von, *Memoires du Chancelier Prince de Bülow*, 3 vols. (Paris: Plon, 1930)

Cabezas, Octa Vio, *La cara intima de los Borbones* (Madrid: San Martín, 1979)

Carretero, J. M., *El caballero audaz,¿ Alfonso XIII fue buen rey? Historia de un reinado* (Madrid, 1934)

Casal, E., (Leon Boyd), *Fiestas aristocráticas (1913–1914)* (Madrid, M. Núñez Samper, 1914)

Cierva, Ricardo De La, *El veneno en la sangre* (Barcelona: Planeta, 1993)

Cortés-Cavanillas, J., *Alfonso XIII: vida, confesiones y muerte* (Barcelona, Juventud, 1966)

Crawford, R. and D., *Michael and Natasha: The Life and Love of Michael II, the Last of the Romanov Tsars* (New York, Alisa Drew Book Scribner, 1937)

Curtis Perry, John, and Constantine V. Plesharov, *The Flight of the Romanovs, A Family Saga* (Basic Books, 1999)

Diesbach, Ghislain De, *Les secrets du Gotha* (London: Chapman & Hall, 1967)

Domin, M. A., *Anastasia Mikhailovna Romanova Grande Duchesse de Russie* (Paris, Atlantica, 2002)

Eilers, Marlene A., *Queen Victoria's Descendants* (Falköping: Rosvall Royal Books, 1967)

Erskine, Mrs Steuart, *Twenty-nine Years of the Reign of King Alfonso XIII of Spain* (London: Hutchinson, 1931)

Escandón, Manuel, Marquis of Villavieja, *Life has been good* (London: Chatto & Windus, 1938)

Figueroa, Á. de, *Count de Romanones: Notas de una vida. Obras completas* (Madrid: Aguilar, 1934)

García Luapre, P., *Eulalia de Borbón Infanta de España. Lo que no dijo en sus memorias* (Madrid, Compañía Literaria, 1995); *Paz de Borbón, princesa de Baviera. Escritora y pacifista* (Madrid, Compañía Literaria, 2000)

García Rodríguez, J. C., *Las carreras de caballos de Sanlúcar de Barrameda* (1995)

Gómez Santos, M., *La reina Victoria Eugenia de cerca* (Madrid: E. M. E. S. A, 1969); *Las reinas de España,Id. Correspondencia / Epístolas 1905–1906* (Madrid: Biblioteca Nacional 7/171594)

Gould Lee, A., Helen, *Queen Mother of Roumania, Princess of Greece and Denmark* (London: Faber and Faber, 1956)

Graham, E., *The Queen of Spain: An Authorised Life-history from material supplied personally by Her Majesty to the Author in Audience at the Royal Palace at Madrid* (London, Hutchinson, 1929)

Greece, Prince Christopher of, *Le Monde et les Cours. Mémoires de S. A. R. le prince Christophe de Grece* (Paris: Plon, 1939)

Nicholas, Prince of, *My fifty years* (London, Hutchinson, 1926)

Hardinge, Sir A., *A Diplomatist in Europe* (1927)

Hijano, Ángeles, *Victoria Eugenia, una reina exiliada* (Madrid: Alderabán, 2000)

Hough, Richard (ed.), *Advice to a Grand Daughter, Letters from Queen Victoria to Princess Victoria of Hesse* (London, Heinemann, 1975)

Kindelán, A., *La verdad de mis relaciones con Franco* (Barcelona: Planeta, 1981); *Mis cuadernos de guerra* (Barcelona: Planeta, 1982)

Kirill, Grand Duke of Russia, *My Life in Russia's Service—Then and Now* (London: Selwyn & Blount, 1939)

Majolier, N., *Stepdaughter of Imperial Russia* (London: Stanley Paul, 1940)

Mallet, V., *Life with Queen Victoria: Marie Mallet's Letters from Court 1887–1901* (London: John Murray, 1968)

Mateos Sáinz De Medrano, R., *Los desconocidos infantes de España. Casa de Borbón* (Barcelona: Thassàlia, 1996); *Nobleza obliga: una historia íntima de la aristocracia española: los Alba, los Romanones, los Urquijo* (Madrid, La Esfera de los Libros, 2006)

Meer Lcha-marzo, f. Ernando de, Juan de Borbón, *Un hombre solo*, Valladolid: *Junta de Castilla y León* (2001)

Menéndez Prendes, P., *Boda y fiestas reales. Recuerdo histórico del casamiento de S. M. el rey Alfonso XIII con la egregia princesa Victoria Eugenia de Battenberg* (Madrid, s. n., 1906)

Moreno Luzón, J. (ed.), *Alfonso XIII: un politico en el trono* (Madrid, Marcial Pons, 2003)

Mossolov, A. A., *At the Court of the last Tsar* (London: Pilenko, 1935)

Noel, G., *Ena, Spain's English Queen* (London: Constable, 1984)

Nourry, P., *Juan Carlos:un rey paralos republicanos* (Barcelona, Planeta, 2004)

Olivares, Camilo, *Isabel Alfonsa de Borbón y Borbón: silencio y humildad de una infanta* (Sevilla: Real Maestraza de Caballeria, 2004)

Packard, J., *Victoria's Daughters* (New York: St Martin's Press, 1998)

Palélogue, M., *Aux portes du jugement dernier: Elizabeth Feodorowna, grande duchesse de Russie* (Paris, Plon, 1921)

Paley, Princess O., *Memories of Russia, 1916–1919* (London, 1924)

Petrie, Sir C., *King Alfonso XIII and his Age* (London, Chapman & Hall, 1963)

Polovtsov, Gen. Petr Aleksandrovich, *Glory and Downfall: Reminiscences of a Russian General Staff Officer (Memoirs)*

Poutiatine, Princess Olga, *Revue des deux mondes*

Preston, P., *Palomas de guerra: cinco mujeres marcadas por el enfrentamiento belico* (Barcelona, Plaza & Janes, 2001)

Pridham, Sir F., *Close of a Dynasty* (London, Allan Wingate, 1955)

Prieto Tuero, I., *Convulsiones de Espana: pequenos detalles de grandes sucesos*, 3 vols. (Mexico: Oasis, 1967)

Puga, M. T., *La vida y la época de Alfonso XIII* (Barcelona, Planeta, 1999)

Rayón, F., and José Luis Sampedro, *Las joyas de las reinas de Espana* (Barcelona, Planeta, 2004)

Romanov Y Grecia Dmitri, *Memoirs of Grand Duke Dmitri* (1919)

Romanov, Grand Duchess Maria of Russia, *Education of a Princess: A Memoir* (New York, Viking Press, 1930); *Una princesa en el destierro* (Barcelona: Juventud, 1942)

Romanovsky-Krassinsky, Princess, *Souvenirs de la Kschessinska* (Paris, Plon, 1959)

Romania, Princess Ileana of, *Memorias* (Barcelona, Imprenta Moderna, 1955)

Romania, Marie, Queen of, *The Story of my Life* (New York: Charles Scribner's Sons, 1934)

Sánchez Carmona, José Ramón, *El infante don Alfonso de Orleans* (Madrid: Instituto de Historia y Cultura Aeronauticas, 1991)

Scott-Ellis, P., *Diario de la guerra de España* (Barcelona, Plaza & Janes, 1996)

Seco Serrano, C., *Alfonso XIII* (Madrid, Arlanza, 2001); *Viñetas históricas,* introduction by Javier Tusell (Madrid, Espasa Calpe, 1983)

Sencourt, R., *King Alfonso XIII* (London, Faber and Faber, 1942)

Sullivan, M. J., *A Fatal Passion: The Story of Victoria Melita, the uncrowned last Empress of Russia* (New York, Random House, 1997)

Thorwald, J., *Sangre de reyes: El drama de la hemofilia en las casas reales de Europa* (Barcelona: Plaza & Janes, 1953)

Van der Kiste, J., *Princess Victoria Melita, Grand Duchess Cyril of Russia (1876–1936)* (Stroud, Sutton, 1991)

Van der Kiste, J., & Jordaan, B., *Dearest Affie: Alfred Duke of Edinburgh, Queen Victoria's second son* (Gloucester: Alan Sutton, 1984)

Van der Kiste, J., & Hall, C., *Once a Grand Duchess: Xenia, Sister of Nicholas II* (Stroud: Sutton, 2002)

Vorres, I., *The Last Grand Duchess: Her Imperial Highness Olga Alexandrovna* (Toronto, Key Porter, 2001)

Youssoupov, Prince Felix, *Avant L Exile (1887–1919)* (Paris: Plon, 1952)

Index

Adlerberg, Alexander, Count (1860–1915) 64

Ageo, Mila 47

Aguilar, Floristán (1872–1934) 203-5

Alacalá-Zamora, Niceto (1877–1949) 202

Alba, Jacobo, duke of (1878–1953) 182, 243, 301, 314

Albert of Prussia, Prince (1837–1906) 67

Albert Victor, duke of Clarence (1864–92) 25, 29

Albert, prince consort of England (1819–61) 27, 44, 145

Aldecoa, Gabriel de Benito de 206

Alexander II, tsar of Russia (1818–81) 10, 17, 157, 174; visits London 18; assassination and funeral 19-20

Alexander III, tsar of Russia (1845–94) 22, 27, 50, 64; death and funeral 35-6, 38

Alexander Mikhailovich, grand duke of Russia (1866–1933) 55, 142, 146

Alexander of Battenberg (Drino), marquess of Carisbrooke (1886–1960) 28, 41, 46, 116, 119, 155-6, 162, 169, 203

Alexander of Hesse and the Rhine, Prince (1823-88) 21

Alexander, king of Greece (1893–1920) 156, 158

Alexander, king of Yugoslavia (1888–1934) 161, 228

Alexandra ('Sandra'), princess of Hohenlohe-Langenburg (1878–1942), 40, 44, 47, 52, 73, 79, 82, 91, 145, 157, 300, 307; birth 19; at Queen Victoria's jubilee 24;

childhood 25; early life 27; betrothal and marriage 36; and Ducky's death 232; death 289

Alexandra Feodorovna (1872–1918), tsarina of Russia 47, 145, 157, 319; engagement and wedding 35; and coronation 40

Alexandra of Greece, later grand duchess of Russia (1870–91) 39

Alexandra of Kent, Princess (b.1936) 309

Alexandra, queen of England (1844–1925) 18, 22, 29, 34, 38, 67, 157, 161; coronation 49; death 174

Alexandrine, duchess of Saxe-Coburg Gotha (1820–1904) 26-7, 32, 57

Alexandrine, queen of Denmark (1879–1952) 50, 187-8

Alexei Alexandrovich, grand duke of Russia (1850–1908) 22, 35, 39, 64

Alexei Nicolaievich, tsarevich of Russia (1904–18) 57

Alfonso de Borbón y Borbón, Infante (1941–56) 318

Alfonso de Borbón, Infante, duke of Calabria (1901–64), 171, 200, 285

Alfonso de Orleans y Borbón, Infante (Ali) (1886–1975) 10, 108, 114, 124, 162, 169, 202-3, 219, 260; and civil war 11, 44; at Ena and Alfonso XIII's wedding 69, early life 70; Duchess of Coburg's views on 72; wedding plans announced by press 76, family discussions about wedding 77-8; officially betrothed 79, difficulties made about wedding 80-2, 87-9; military service 88-9; civil marriage ceremony 90; telegraphs Ena to tell her of wedding 92; deprived of titles, honours and cashiered from army 93-6; nursing duties 98; aviation interests and training 109-10, 113, 116, 118-20, 122; in Japan for funeral of Emperor Mitsohito 109; and outbreak of First World War 115; exiled to Switzerland 125-49; Alfonso XIII's alleged jealousy of 136-7; and aviation interests 140; military duties on Moroccan campaign 163, 165; in Romania for Ferdinand's coronation 164, aviation activities 164, 167-70, 172-3; writes to father 165; writes to Primo de Rivera 166; ill-health 171-2; and Carol II of Romania 174, 284-5; returns from England to Spain 176; offered command of Getafe Airport 176; treated for malaria 177; and George V 181; and university complex fund-raising American visit 182-6; and death of Primo de Rivera 198; and father's death 200; and Alfonso and Ena's departure after election results 205-12; working for Henry Ford 221, cruises around Greek islands 227; at wedding of duke and duchess of Kent 229; destroys diaries 232; longs to serve in war but offer to serve in army rejected 233-7, 245; told of Alonso's death 239; learns of Alonso's death and sails to England 240; returns to Spain 241; raised to lieutenant-colonel and rejoins army 248; appointed military commander in air force 249; writes to Kindelán 249; 263-4, 266, 273, 275, 277, 279; reports to Alfonso XIII on royal palace damage 270-1; in charge of 2nd Aviation Brigade 278; continues work for Bee's maternity home after her death 286-7; and brother Luis's finances 288; ill with typhus 289; informed of Sandra's death 290; named Juan's representative in Spain 291; visits Ena in Lausanne 292; dismissed from air force, diplomatic passport withdrawn and other activities restricted by Franco after Second World War 296-9; falsely alleged to be Pip's father 29;, at Pip's wedding 298; resigns as Juan's representative in Spain 302; and Barbazan's library work 308-11; shopping in London 330; last years and death 333

Alfonso de Orleans-Borbón y Ferrara Pignatelli, Don (b.1968) 329

Alfonso XII, King (1857–85) 98, 123, 152, 184, 209, 294

Alfonso XIII, king of Spain (1886–1941) 24, 46, 74, 77, 87, 109, 114, 118-121, 124, 144, 157-8, 164, 166-7, 184, 195, 196, 198, 200, 202, 219-20, 287-8, 293, 297, 303-4; and visit to England 61-3; and haemophilia concerns 64-5; wedding 66-9; and plans for Bee and Ali's wedding 79, 81-2, 84-5, 89; reaction to news of Bee and Ali's secret wedding 91; reaction to Bee and Ali's wedding 92; at funeral of Edward VII 99; and Ali's military service 101; and Ali's aviation interests 99-100; service in Morocco 100-5; rehabilitation and return to Spain 105-6; meets Bee and Ali on return to Spain 107, and accident at polo match 111, assassination attempt on 111, and outbreak of First World War 116; distances himself from Ena because of children's haemophilia 123; and Bee and Ali's exile 125-34; trying to blacken Ali's reputation because of his popularity in the army 136, growing estrangement from Ena 137, making 'advances' towards Bee 137; letter from Ali 152-4; visit to Paris 154; invites Princess Beatrice to Madrid 163, disliked by George V for treatment of Ena 167; and Carmen Moragas 179, annulment of marriage considered 179, ill-health 179; and Viana's death 180; and Gustav V's visit 180; disliked by George V 181; silver jubilee 181; and university complex fund-raising 184; and king and queen of Denmark's visit 187-9; and mother's death 188; and Queen Maria Cristina's acceptance of his marriage to Ena 190; depression 197, 201; at Antonio's funeral 201; and 1931 elections 203-4; departure after election results 205-8; in London 218; holiday in Austria 228; gives permission for Álvaro's wedding 240; at Alvaro's wedding 244; Te Deum after end of war 266; and telegram from Ali on war damage to palace 270; abdication in favour of Juan, death and funeral 285

Alfonso, prince of Asturias (1907–38) 73-4, 179, 197, 203; and reunion with duchess of Saxe-Coburg 151; problems with father 152; letter to Alfonso XIII 152-4; skiing accident 154; return to Madrid 154; at Esher 158-9; ill-health 161; marriage 227; death 260

Alfred of Saxe-Coburg Gotha, Prince (1874–99) 18, 23, 27; at Queen Victoria's jubilee 24; education 29; at Queen Victoria's diamond jubilee 41; death and funeral 42

Alfred, duke of Edinburgh and Saxe-Coburg Gotha (1844–1900), wedding 17; at Malta, 23, 25; at Queen Victoria's jubilee 24; at Devonport 28-9; and betrothal of Missy 30; succeeds as duke of Coburg 32; and betrothal and marriage of Sandra 36; silver wedding celebrations and son's death 41-2, death 44

Alice, countess of Athlone (1883–1981) 67; birth 21

Alice, grand duchess of Hesse and the Rhine (1843–78) 17, 33, 64

Almodóvar, Jaime, duke of 206

Alonso de Orleans-Borbón y Parodi Delfino, Don (1941–75) 206, 271, 288, 329

Alonso de Orleans-Borbón y Sajonia-Coburgo-Gotha, Prince (1912–36) 119, 150, 231, 237; birth 109; character 166; blows up door on last day at school 175; and cousin Cristina 177, 198; further education plans 198; skiing activities, 224-6; joins air force 237; killed, 239-40, 245; buried at Sanlúcar 251

Álvarez de Toledo, Martina, duchess of Santa Cristina 242 -3

Álvaro de Orleans-Borbón y Ferrara-Pignatelli (b.1970) 329

Álvaro de Orleans-Borbón y Sajonia-Coburgo-Gotha, Prince (1910–97) 100, 102, 107-8, 175, 177, 200, 202, 219-20, 223, 236-8, 241, 257, 277, 280-1, 295, 312, 316, 323; birth 98; and diphtheria 116-7; first flight with father 119; skiing activities 141, 224-6; character 165-6; further education plans 198; possibility of marriage to cousin Beatriz 198, 219-20; friendship with Parodi-Delfino family 230-1; Alonso's flying accident, and informs parents of his death 236-40; wedding 244; serves in air force 248, 253-4, 271; narrowly avoids air accident 251; in Italy 265-6, 287, 303, 319; represents parents at Alfonso XIII's funeral 285; at parents' golden wedding 321

Álvaro Jaime de Orleans-Borbón y Parodi Delfino, Don (b.1947), 10, 303, 321

Amadeo I, King (1845–90) 98, 118

Amedeo, duke of Aosta 225, 244

Anastasia Nicolaevna, grand duchess of Russia (1901–18) 50

Anastasia, grand duchess of Mecklenburg-Schwerin (1860–1922) 50, 53, 187

Andrei Vladimirovich, grand duke of Russia (1879–1956) 36, 39, 51

Andrew of Greece, Prince (1882–1944) 169

Andrew of Yugoslavia, Prince (1929–90) 161

Angulo y Suárez de Tangil, Fernando 243

Ansaldo, Juan Antonio, 258

Anton, Archduke of Austria, prince of Tuscany (1901–87) 195

Antonia of Portugal, *Infanta* (1845–1913) 30-1

Antonio of Orleans, *Infante* (1866–1930) 80, 93, 98, 103, 108, 152, 321; declared 'a prodigal' 163; death 200

Aranda Mata, Antonio 257

Arthur, duke of Connaught (1850–1942) 34, 42, 61, 169

Asquith, Herbert Henry (1852–1928) 193

Ataúlfo de Orleans-Borbón y Sajonia-Coburgo-Gotha, Prince (1913–74) 10, 116, 170, 177, 211, 216-7, 239-40, 250, 274-5, 291, 311, 315, 319-20, 323, 329-30; birth and baptism 112-3; skiing activities 141, 224; musical talent 222; serves in armed forces 245, 253; and Condor Legion 245, 247, 251, 254, 279-81; and Pip Scott-Ellis 245-6, 279-80; building activities and 'Villa Ataúlfo' 294, 307, 316; at parents' golden wedding 321; death 333

Aunós, Eduardo 198

Azaña, Manuel 232, 264

Azcárraga, Gen. 114

Aznar, Gen. (1860–1933) 111, 202, 204

Bagration-Mukhranski, Princess Leonida (1914–2010) 301

Barbazán, Julian 308-11

Beatrice (Bee) of Saxe-Coburg Gotha, *Infanta* (1884–1966) 9, 48, 60, 65, 73-4, 110, 116, 118-22, 164, 201-3, 216, 218, 220, 221-2, 225, 227-8, 261-2, 275-6, 278, 280, 303-6; early life 10, and civil war 11, birth, christening and childhood 20, 23-5; at Queen Victoria's jubilee 24; childhood 27, 36; and Missy's betrothal 31; early days in Romania 32-3, 41; in Russia 35; at Sandra's wedding 37; at Nicholas II's coronation, 40, at Queen Victoria's diamond jubilee 41, and brother Alfred's death 42-3, in England 43, love of sports 43, and Missy's return to Coburg 44, love of Wagner's music 44; and Queen Victoria's death 45; and landscapes and memories album 46; and romance with Misha 50, 52-4, 59; visits Egypt, 55-6; and relationship with Misha 60-1; in Nice with Ena 61, in London with Ena 61, and with Alfonso XIII in London 62-3, returns to Coburg 64; in Spain for Ena's wedding 66-7, 70-2; first meets Ali 70; wedding plans

announced by press 76, family discussions
about wedding 77-8; officially betrothed
79; difficulties made about wedding
80-2, 87-9; civil marriage ceremony 90;
intercedes with Alfonso XIII on Ali's
behalf 96-7; and Ali's lack of employment
98; birth and christening of Álvaro 98-9;
and Ali's military career 100, 103; letters
to and from Ena 101-3, 260, 292-5,
299-300, 312-4; nursing 104-5; return
to Spain with Ali 105-6; and birth of
Alonso, 109, and birth of Ataúlfo 113,
and outbreak of First World War 115; and
divided Spanish loyalties during war 117;
palace offensive to force her out of Spain,
123, suspected of being bad influence on
Ena, 124, exile in Switzerland 125-49;
'sharp tongue' 137, and Alfonso XIII's
advances, rumours about Bee trying to
exercise pro-German influence in Madrid,
no reason to take pro-German stance
during war, and plight of mother and
sisters during war 144-7, 149; reunion
with Missy after First World War 150;
and reunited with mother 151; return to
Madrid 154; on plight of Greek royal
family 156; at Esher 158-9; and Leopold
of Battenberg's death 162, in Esher 165,
167-8, 170; return to Spain 175; and
'injustices' against Ali 176; and George V
181, exhibition of paintings in Paris, and
university complex fund-raising American
visit 182-6; and death of Primo de Rivera
198; nursing and hospital work, 199; visit
to London 200; and departure from Spain
after election results 205-9, 211-3; letter
to Arnold Lunn 224-5; cruise around
Greek islands 227; at wedding of duke
and duchess of Kent 229; leaves Zurich
home 230; and Ducky's death 232; told
of Alonso's death 239; depression after
being informed of Alonso's death 239,
letter to Arnold Lunn 241, meets Ali on
arrival in England, returns to Spain, war
work, nursing and prisoner exchanges
241-5, 250, 252-6; and Missy's illness and
death 242, and Ali's military career, letter
to Missy 253; and Missy's death 259; and
Alfonso Prince of Asturias' death 260; war
relief work 263-4, 266; hopes for royal
restoration 265; nursing and prisoner
exchanges, 268; at Orleans Palace 269;
annoyed at she and family being treated
as foreigners 271; on Pip's work 276;
warned of likelihood of Second World
War 277; on possibility of Ataulfo and Pip
marrying 279; and birth of grandaughter

Gerarda 281; maternity home at Sanlúcar,
283, 285-7, 307; and brother-in-law Luis,
288; visits relations in Germany during
Second World War, 288; and Sandra's
death, 289; and Ena's continuing interest
in Spain and fears regarding restoration
289-91; disapproves of Grand Duke
Vladimir's marriage, 301; maternity home,
fund-raising and retirement to Sanlúcar
308, 322, 325-6; and Barbazan's library
work 308-11; and death of Carol II 311;
ill-health, last days and death 315-28;
funeral 329
Beatrice, Princess (Princess Henry of
Battenberg) (1857–1944) 34, 63, 65, 80,
88, 155, 168-9, 181; wedding 21; visits
Coburg 27-8; and Queen Victoria's death
46; visits Egypt 55; at Ena's wedding,
66-8; at Leopold of Battenberg's death
162; family visits to Spain 163, 179;
ill-health 201
Beatriz de Orleans-Borbon y Parodi Delfino
(b.1943) 13, 165, 222-3, 316, 321, 326-7,
329, 331; birth 291
Beatriz, *Infanta* (1909–2002) 111, 120,
168-9, 178, 181, 210, 227-9, 287, 304,
313, 321-3; birth 85; marriage to cousin
Álvaro discussed 219-20
Beatty, David (1871–1936) 24
Bemkart, Dr 42
Benito Ibáñez de Aldecoa, Gabriel 196
Benlliure, Mariano (1862–1947) 125, 197
Berenguer, Dámaso (1873–1953) 163,
199-200, 202
Berthelot, Henri (1861–1931) 146, 149
Bibesco, Prince 192-3
Blanca, *Infanta* (1868–1949) 195
Borbón y Pintó, Alfonso de, marquis of Santa
Fé de Guardiola 255
Bori, Lucrecia (1887–1960) 184, 187
Boris Vladimirovich, grand duke of Russia
(1877–1943) 36, 39-40, 48, 61, 144
Borrás, Rafael 205
Boyle, Joseph (1867–1923), 148
Bratianu, Ion (1864–1927), 139
Brown, John (1826–83) 22
Brun, Lucie 139
Buchanan, Sir George (1854–1924) 47
Bugallal Araújo, Gabino, count of Bugallal
(1861–1932) 204
Bülow, Prince Bernhard von (1849–1929)
48, 94
Bulygin, Alexander (1851–1919) 57
Bunsen, Sir Maurice de (1852–1932) 68
Burguete, Ricardo (1899–1934) 96, 126, 166

Calvo Sotelo, José 233

Calvo, Joaquín 271
Canalejas, José (1854–1912) 98-9, 106, 108, 110
Cantacuzino, Gheorghe (Zizi) (1869–1937), 43
Cantacuzino, Maruca, 151
Carla Parodi Delfino, duchess of Galliera (1909–2000) 316, 319, 321, 328
Carlos de Borbón, *Infante* and prince of the Two Sicilies (1870–1949) 115, 121, 154, 171, 188, 197, 265, 285
Carol I, king of Romania (1839–1914) 25, 29, 31, 44, 82, 114, 139; death 116
Carol II, king of Romania (1893–1953) 33, 36, 44, 114, 159, 174, 253, 268-9, 285; death 311-2
Casa Valencia, countess of 131
Castro, Miguel 303
Cavalcanti, marquis of 205
Caviedes, Antonio, marquis of (d.1959) 247
Ceballos, Leonor 138
Cecilia of Salm-Salm, Princess (1911–91) 191-2, 194-6
Cecilie, grand duchess of Mecklenburg-Schwerin, later crown princess of Germany (1886–1954) 50, 53
Chamberlain, Neville (1869–1940) 243, 261, 266
Chapin, Roy (1880–1936) 185
Charles, duke of Albany and of Saxe-Coburg Gotha (1884–1954) 44-5, 57, 67, 89, 96, 99; birth 21;
Charlotte of Wales, Princess (1796–1817) 26
Charlotte, hereditary princess of Saxe-Meiningen (1860–1919) 30
Chilton, Sir Henry 246
Christian X, king of Denmark (1870–1947) 50, 188
Churchill, Lady Randolph (1854–1921) 20
Cierva, Ricardo de la (1926–2015) 133
Constantin Constantinovich, grand duke of Russia (1891–1918) 148
Constantine I, king of Greece (1868–1923) 156, 158
Constantine II, king of Greece (b.1930) 322
Coolidge, Calvin (1872–1933) 183-4
Córdoba, Father Gonzalo de 328
Cotro Florido, Pepe 331
Cristina, *Infanta* (1911–96) 177, 181, 190, 227-8, 241, 266
Curzon of Kedleston, Lord (1859–1925) 155

Dato, Eduardo (1856–1921) 121
Delgado, Carlos 164
Denison, Lady Irene, marchioness of Carisbrooke (1890–1956) 162, 203
Díaz, Pastora 286

Dmitri Paulovich, grand duke of Russia (1891–1942) 39, 58, 142, 155, 229
Dolgoruki, Princess Catherine (1847–1922) 20

Echagüe, Gen. 87
Edward VII, king of England (1841–1910) 21-2, 34, 47, 61, 65, 66, 174, 210; coronation 49; critical of King Alfonso XIII and government 94, death and funeral 99
Edward VIII, king of England (1894–1972) 180
Edward, duke of Kent (1767–1820) 26
Edward, duke of Kent (b.1935) 322
Edwina, Countess Mountbatten of Burma (1902–60) 161
Elena of Greece, Princess (b.1963) 327
Elena Vladimirovna, grand duchess of Russia (1882–1957) 49, 50-1
Elena, queen of Italy (1873–1952) 252
Elisabeth of Hesse and the Rhine, Princess (1895–1903) 36, 42, 45, 48
Elisabeth of Romania, Princess, later queen of Greece (1896–1956) 35, 114-5, 150-1, 156; wedding 159
Elizabeth (Ella), grand duchess of Russia (1864–1918) 22, 34-5, 39, 41, 52, 57, 148
Elizabeth, queen of Romania (Carmen Sylva) (1843–1916) 31
Elósegui, Dr 206
Emanuel of Salm-Salm, Prince (1871–1916) 192
Ena (Victoria Eugenia), queen of Spain (1887–1969) 10, 12, 32, 96, 98, 109, 113, 118-22, 155, 164, 241, 261, 318, 322; and civil war 11; birth 25; visits Coburg 28; and Queen Victoria's death 45, 'Bee's best friend since her youth' 46; visits Egypt 56; with Bee in Nice and London 61, and Grand Duke Boris, 61, betrothal and marriage, 61-6, conversion to Roman Catholicism, renunciation rights to British throne, marriage and honeymoon 66-72; and Bee and Ali's betrothal 76-8, 80, and birth of Beatrice 85; informed of Bee and Ali's wedding 92, 94; and concerns about attitude to Ali 97; loyalty to Bee and Ali while officially in disgrace 101; Bee's letters to 102, 104; meets Bee and Ali on return to Spain 106-7; invites them on excursions 110; birth of Juan 111; and Elisabeth of Romania's visit 114; and outbreak of First World War 115; birth of Gonzalo 116; and divided Spanish loyalties during

war 117; and Alfonso's distancing himself from their children's haemophilia 123; Bee said to be bad influence on 124; and Bee and Ali's exile 125; growing estrangement from Alfonso 137, and *Infantes'* exile to Switzerland 139; and peritonitis 140, 179, 313; letters to Missy 144, 160; visit to England 154; and brother Leopold's death 163; ill-treatment of resented by George V 167; scolds marqis of Viana for his ill-treament 180; and mother in law's death 188-90; visits mother in London 201; international exhibitions and sons' ill-health, visits sick mother, and concern at election results 203-4; leaves Spain after election results 205-12; in London 218; at prince of Asturias's wedding 227; and Gonzalo's death 229; living at Fontainebleau 233; seeks help from National Red Cross with prisoner exchanges 243; at Alvaro's wedding 244; condolences to Bee on Missy's death 259; and birth of Juan Carlos 252; and letter from Bee on prince of Asturias's death 260; Bee writes to on hopes for royal restoration 265; warns Bee of likelihood of Second World War 277; and Alfonso XIII's death 285; leaves Rome as Italy at war with Britain 288; letter to Ali 290-1; letters to Bee 292-5, 299-300; disapproves of Grand Duke Vladimir's marriage 301; letters to and from Bee 312-4; at Juan Carlos's wedding 323; last visits to Madrid and death 330

Ernest II, duke of Saxe-Coburg Gotha (1818–93) 18, 26-7, 57; death 32

Ernest of Hohenlohe-Langenburg, Prince (1863–1950) 44; betrothal and marriage 36, 52

Ernest, duke of Cumberland (1845–1923) 62

Ernest, grand duke of Hesse and the Rhine (Ernie) (1868–1937) 57-8; betrothal and marriage 33; has smallpox 43; and divorce from Ducky, 47-8, and Elizabeth's death 48

Esperanza de Borbón y Orleans, Princess (1914–2005) 115, 265

Espinosa de los Monteros, Señor 206

Eugenia, empress of the French (1826–1920) 83

Eulalia, *Infanta* (1864–1958) 9, 70-2, 80, 83-8, 93, 107-8, 110, 128, 137, 156, 200, 243, 281, 287, 314, 316, 320; at Queen Victoria's jubilee 24; warns Alfonso XIII about threat of haemophilia 64-5; at Alfonso and Ena's wedding 69-72; death, 321

Farini, Tommasso, 327

Felipe de Borbón, prince of the Two Sicilies (1885–1949) 125

Felipe VI, King (1968–) 330

Feodora of Hohenlohe-Langenburg, Princess (1807–72) 36

Feodora of Saxe-Meiningen, Princess (1879–1945) 34

Feodora of Schleswig-Holstein, Princess (1866–1952) 90

Feodore Victoria, princess of Leiningen (1866–1932) 173

Ferdinand (Nando), king of Romania (1865–1927) 25, 79, 99, 160, 174-5; betrothal and wedding 30-1; illness 41; and First World War 139, 146, 149; coronation 164; death 181

Ferdinand of Bavaria, *infante* of Spain and prince of Bavaria (1884–1958) 70, 105, 109, 114, 154, 170, 187, 191, 103, 218, 301

Ferdinand, tsar of Bulgaria (1861–1948) 174, 289

Fernández de Henestrosa Luisa, *Infanta,* duchess of Talavera de la Reina (1870–1955) 198, 203, 218, 319

Fernando VII (1784–1833) 193

Ferrara Pignatelli, Emilia 329

Ford, Henry (1863–1947) 185, 187, 221, 228

Franco Bahamonde, Francisco, Dictator (1892–1975), 231, 233-4, 237, 240-1, 250, 252, 256-7, 265-6, 277-9, 290-4, 33; Bee's discussions with about exchange of prisoners 248; demands unconditional surrender of republican air force 270; fears influence of remaining royalty members in Spain 295-6; ill-health and death 332-3

Franco Bahamonde, Nicolás 241

Franco Bahamonde, Pilar 252

Franco Bahamonde, Ramón (1896–1938) 215

Franz Ferdinand, archduke of Austria (1863–1914) 115

Franz Joseph, emperor of Austria (1830–1916) 115

Frederica of Hanover, Princess (1848–1926) 65

Frederica, queen of Greece (1917–81) 322, 323

Frederick Francis IV, grand duke of Mecklenburg-Schwerin (1882–1945) 50, 187

Frederick III, German Emperor (1831–88) 24

Frederick VIII, king of Denmark (1843–1912) 99

Fredericks, Vladimir (1838–1922) 64
Friedrich Karl VI, prince of Leiningen (1898–1946) 173

Gapon, George ('Father') (1870–1906) 57
García Muñoz, Señor 288
García Pérez, Capt. A.131
García Pérez, Fausto (1884–1917) 95
Gaspari, Cardinal 281
Genaro de Borbón, prince of the Two Sicilies 169
Geoffray, Léon (1852–1927) 127-8
George Alexandrovich, grand duke of Russia (1871–99) 38, 50
George I, king of Greece (1845–1913) 51, 65, 99, 111
George II, king of Greece (1890–1947) 114, 156; wedding 159
George III, king of England (1738–1820) 32
George Mikhailovich, Count Brasov (1910–31) 189
George V, king of England (1865–1936) 25, 29, 31, 34, 99, 113, 115, 129, 133-4, 144, 147 229; wedding 32; at Alfonso and Ena's wedding 67; 'fears Bee's intrigues' 155, dislikes Alfonso XII for treatment of Ena 167; supportive of Bee and Ali 181; death 231
George VI, king of England (1895–1952) 313
George, duke of Kent (1902–42) 180, 229, 240-1, 243
Gerarda de Orleans-Borbón y Parodi Delfino, Doña (b.1939) 12, 239, 281
Gerardo Farini, Don (b.1967) 329
González Cornejo, Francisco 318
González Gallarza, Eduardo 296, 299, 301
González Gordon, Manuel María, marquis of Bonanza 318
Gonzalo, *Infante* (1914–34) 116, 178; death 229
Gottfried of Hohenlohe-Langenburg, Prince (1897–1960) 40, 321
Grahame, Sir George (1873–1940) 193, 211
Grandhome, Paul 182
Grey, Sir Edward (1862–1933) 130, 132
Gustaf V, king of Sweden (1858–1950) 144, 157, 180
Gustaf VI Adolf, king of Sweden (1882–1973) 57, 61
Gustav Adolf, prince of Sweden (1906–47) 229
Gwynne, G. F. 21

Haakon VII, king of Norway (1872–1957) 99
Haight, Edward M. (1896–1975) 186

Harcourt, Rey d' 251
Hardinge, Alexandra, Lady (d.1949) 113
Hardinge, Sir Arthur (1859–1933) 113, 123, 126-31, 133
Hardinge, Sir Charles, Baron Penshurst (1858–1944) 131
Harrison, Sir Richard (1837–1931) 29
Hauke, Countess Julia von, princess of Battenberg (1825–95) 21
Haya, Carlos 254
Helen, duchess of Albany (1861–1922) 20, 45, 159
Helen, queen of Romania (1896–1982) 159-60, 174, 284
Helena Augusta (Thora), Princess (1870–1948) 61
Helena of Schleswig-Holstein, Princess (Princess Christian) (1846–1923) 61
Helena Vladimirovna, grand duchess of Russia (1882–1957)
Henny, Lucy 224
Henry of Battenberg, Prince (1858–96) 21, 34
Hoyos, José Maria de (1874–1950) 203
Henry of Prussia, Prince (1862–1929) 34, 64
Heredia Spínola, countess of 171
Heredia, Conchita 122, 131
Herman VI of Hohenlohe-Langenburg, Prince (1832–1913) 36
Herrero, Carmelo 246, 316
Hildago de Cisneros, Ignacio (1896–1966) 172, 200
Hitler, Adolf (1889–1945) 261, 289

Ibáñez Martín, José 96
Ileana of Romania, Princess (1909–91) birth 82, 160, 174, 191-5
Ilundáin, Cardinal Eustaquio (1862–1937) 191, 318
Irene of Greece, Princess (b.1942) 322
Irene of Hesse, Princess Henry of Prussia (1866–1953) 34, 64
Isabel Alfonsa, *Infanta* (1904–85) 188, 191
Isabel II, Queen (1830–1904) 70, 72
Isabel, countess of Paris (1848–1919) 101, 106
Isabel, *Infanta* (1851–1931) 71, 111, 139, 154, 170-1, 203, 206, 219

Jaime, *Infante* (1908–75) 112, 178-9, 191, 194, 198, 228, 303-4
Jenner, Sir William (1815–98) 33
Johnson, Nicholas, 146
Jordana, Count of 292, 294
José Eugenio de Bavaria y Borbón, *Infante* Don 200
Juan Carlos I, King (b.1938) 314-5, 318, 332; birth 252;, engagement and

wedding, 322-3; proclaimed sovereign 333

Juan de Borbón y Battenberg, count of Barcelona, Don (1913–93) 178, 218, 252, 265, 268, 270, 288-90, 292-3, 297, 300, 304, 322, 325, 330, 332; birth 111-2; Alfonso XIII abdicates in favour of 285; barred from living in Spain and Italy 287; names Ali his representative in Spain 291; letter on organising a rupture with Franco discovered 294; thinks Nazi victory would be catastrophe for Catholic and Latin world, and moves with family to Portugal 295; manifesto 296; Ali resigns as his representative in Spain 302

Katharine, duchess of Kent (1933–) 322
Kaulbach, Friedrich August von (1850–1920) 47
Kerensky, Alexander (1881–1970) 144
Kindelán, Alfredo (1879–1962) 119, 173, 176, 201, 235, 239, 248, 250, 253, 270-1, 278, 280, 292, 294, 298-300, 302-3
Kindelán, Lola 294
Kindelán, Lolita, 253
Kindelán, Ultano 236, 244, 251, 284
Kira Kirillovna, grand duchess of Russia (1909–67) 169, 200, 241; at wedding of duke and duchess of Kent, and Ducky's death 231-2
Kirill Vladimirovich, grand duke of Russia (1876–1938) 39-40, 52, 79, 82, 98, 103, 113, 143-4, 157, 173-4, 241; at Queen Victoria's diamond jubilee 41; and attachment to Ducky 48-9; wounded in Russo-Japanese war 60, wedding 64; and claim to Russian throne 181; at wedding of duke and duchess of Kent 229, and Ducky's death 231-2
Kschessinska, Maria (1872–1971) 53
Kudashev, Alexander (1872–1917?) 127, 129, 131-2

Lambrino, Zizi (1898–1953) 160
Lansdowne, Henry, marquis of (1845–1927) 62-3
Larios, Ernesto 121
Lascelles, Henry, Viscount, earl of Harewood (1882–1947) 160
Leche, John 242-4
Lenin, Vladimir Illyich (1870–1924) 145, 148-9
Leopold I, king of the Belgians (1790–1865) 26
Leopold of Battenberg, Prince (1889–1922), 56, 64, 73, 82, 88, 91, 94, 99, 103-5,

110, 116, 124-5, 155-6, 181; death 162
Leopold Salvator, Archduke (1863–1931) 195
Leopold, duke of Albany (1853–84) 20, 44, 64, 159; death 21
Leopold, prince of Hohenzollern (1835–1905) 31
Leopoldine of Hohenlohe-Langenburg, Princess (1837–1903) 36
Lequerica, José Félix de 294
Lindbergh, Charles (1902–74) 183
Lloyd George, David (1863–1945) 146, 148
Lloyd, William 21
López Pinto, señor 233
López, Darío 206
Louis of Battenberg, marquis of Milford Haven (1854–1921) 21, 34, 161
Louis-Philippe, king of the French (1773–1850) 26, 158
Louis, Earl Mountbatten of Burma, (1900–79) 161
Louis, grand duke of Hesse and the Rhine (1837–92) 21, 33
Louise of Orléans, Princess (1882–1958) 115, 154, 265
Louise of Orléans, queen of the Belgians (1812–50) 26
Louise, duchess of Connaught (1860–1917) 34, 42, 169
Louro Viana, Ángel 310, 326
Lowther, Sir Cecil (1869–1940) 68
Luca de Tena, Juan Ignacio 321
Luis, *Infante* (1888–1944) 81-2, 85, 288
Luisa, *Infanta* (1882–1958) 112, 171, 197, 265, 291
Lunn, Arnold (1888–1974) 43, 225, 227, 239-41, 255-7
Lunn, Lady Mabel 225, 227
Lunn, Peter 227
Lunn, Sir Henry 225
Lupescu, Elena (1899–1977) 174, 311-2
Luque, Agustin de (1850–1937)

Maíz de Galíndez, Marcedes 304
Mallet, Marie (1862–1934) 42
Manuel II, king of Portugal (1889–1932) 85
Margaret (Daisy), crown princess of Sweden (1882–1920) 57, 61, 63
Marghiloman, Alexandru (1854–1925) 149
Maria Alexandrovna, duchess of Edinburgh and Saxe-Coburg Gotha (1853–1920) 38, 48, 49, 58, 60, 75, 97, 99, 103-4, 107, 130, 144, 173-4; wedding 17; first years in England 18; birth of children 19-20; at Malta 23, 25; at Clarence House 24; at Queen Victoria's jubilee 24; at Coburg 27; character 27-8, at Devonport 29,

and betrothal of Missy and Nando 30, and betrothal and marriage of Ducky and Ernie 33, and death of Alexander III 35-6; and betrothal and marriage of Sandra 36; at Nicholas II's coronation 40; silver wedding celebrations and son's death 41-2, 44; and deaths of husband and mother-in-law 44-5; commissions painting by Kaulbach 47; and Ducky's romance with Kirill 52-4; and Ducky's second wedding 64; at Ena and Alfonso's wedding 66, 69, and Bee's betrothal and marriage 79-86, 88-9; and *Infantes'* exile to Switzerland 135-6; anger with Alfonso XIII 136-7; on Bee's 'sharp tongue' 137; anger at Romania entering war on allies' side 140; and relations with daughters during war 144-6; reunion with Missy after war 151; last years and death 156-7; inheritance 160
Maria Alexandrovna, tsarina of Russia (1824–80) 17; death 20
Maria Amelia, queen of Portugal (1865–1951) 85
Maria Christina of Salm-Salm, Princess (1879–1962) 121, 191
Maria Cristina, *Infanta* (1911–96) 120-1, 168, 198, 201, 202, 211, 285
Maria Cristina, Queen (1859–1929) 67, 71, 76, 100, 108-9, 116, 134, 139, 154, 169-71, 173, 180, 184; during First World War 116; thought to be regetting disloyalty to Ena 139; death 187-8
Maria Kirillovna, grand duchess of Russia, later princess of Leiningen (1907–51) 73, 169, 173,
Maria Teresa, *Infanta* (1882–1912) 62, 70, 76, 77, 82, 92, 109, 154
Marie (Mignon), queen of Yugoslavia (1900–61) 151, 160-1, 228, 321; birth 44
Marie (Missy), queen of Romania (1875–1938) 12, 47-9, 79-83, 110, 195, 241; birth 19; at Queen Victoria's jubilee 24; betrothal and wedding 30-1; and birth of Carol 33; and birth of Elizabeth 35, at Nicholas II's coronation; 39; and Nando's illness 41; and affair with Cantacuzino 43; and birth of Nicholas 53; becomes queen 116; and Bee and Ali's exile 136 -8; and First World War 147-9; at Paris Peace Conference 150; reunion with mother 151; and Carol's wedding 159-60; letter from Ena 160; coronation 164; and death of Nando 181; exhibition of paintings in Paris 182; and Ducky's death 232; ill with suspected leukaemia 242; death 258-9

Marie Feodorovna (Minnie), tsarina of Russia (1847–1928) 34, 38, 40, 52, 66, 142, 148, 157, 161; disapproves of Ducky and Kirill's romance 54-5; refuses to accept Nicholas II and Misha are dead 181; death 189; funeral 229
Marie Pavlovna (Miechen), grand duchess of Russia (1854–1920) 34, 39, 54, 97, 137-8, 142; death, 157
Marie Pavlovna, grand duchess of Russia (1890–1958), 54
Marie-Amelie, queen of the French (1782–1866) 158
Marina, duchess of Kent (1906–68) 229, 240-1, 243
Martínez de Irujo, Luis, duke consort of Alba 301
Martínez Ramírez, Félix 201
Mary of Cambridge, Princess (1833–97) 32
Mary, princess royal of England, Viscountess Lascelles (1897–1965) 162
Mary, queen of England (1867–1953) 67, 181, 189, 241; wedding 32
Maura, Antonio (1853–1925) 79, 85, 92-3
Maurice of Battenberg, Prince (1891–1914) 46, 88, 103, 110, 116-7
Maza, Leopoldo, count of La 121
Mechtilde of Leiningen, Princess (1936–2021) 231
Medina Martínez, Fernando 270
Mercedes, princess of Asturias (1880–1904) 188
Mercedes, Queen (1860–78) 13, 321, 332
Mergelina, Pilita 284, 305
Merry del Val, Alfonso, marquis of (1865–1930) 155, 168, 200
Michael of Greece, Prince (b.1939) 323
Michael, grand duke of Russia (1878–1918) 36, 38, 58, 181; and romance with Bee 52-5, 59-60, 161-2; and Nicholas's abdication, 143, killed, 146
Michael, king of Romania (1921–2015), 160, 174
Mircea Lambrino of Romania, Prince (1920–2006) 160
Mircea of Romania, Prince (1913–7) 111, 140, 142, 150
Mitsohito, emperor of Japan (1852–1912) 109
Mola, Emilio, General 203, 233, 242-3
Montagu-Pollock, William H. 246
Montoro y Varela, Manuel de 330
Montpensier, Antonio of Orleans, *infante* of Spain, duke of (1824–90) 152, 269, 308-9
Mora, Fernando 290
Moreno Abella, Luis (1890–1940) 115, 163

Moreno y Gil de Borja, Luis 106
Moret, Segismundo (1833–1913) 98
Morral, Mateo (1879–1906) 68
Mountbatten, Edwina, Countess (1902–60) 161
Muguiro, Ignacio 311, 315
Mussolini, Benito (1882–1945) 287

Napoleon, emperor of the French
    (1769–1821) 26
Nicholas I, tsar of Russia (1796–1855) 35,
    156, 187
Nicholas II, tsar of Russia (1868–1918),
    34, 38, 50, 54, 57, 64, 66, 94, 102, 127,
    129, 142, 145, 182; betrothal, accession,
    wedding 34-6; coronation 38-40; and
    Ducky's divorce 47-8; ill with typhus 50;
    abdication 143, death 148, 157
Nicholas Nikolaievich, grand duke of Russia
    (1856–1929) 142
Nicholas of Greece, Prince (1872–1938)
    50-1
Nicholas of Romania, Prince (1903–78) 151,
    169, 292, 312; birth 53
Nozal, Leon 182

Olga Alexandrovna, grand duchess of Russia
    (1882–1960) 27, 38, 40, 66, 189
Olga of Greece and Denmark, Princess
    (1903–97), 240
Olga of Hanover and Cumberland, Princess
    (1864–1958) 62
Olga, queen of Greece (1851–1926) 51, 156
Ortega Morejón, José 152
Osorio de Moscoso y Moreno, Consuelo
    264, 326
Otaolaurruchi, Ramón 283
Ovin, Don Jacinto 283
Ozalla, Gloria 257

Pacelli, Cardinal 264
Padilla, Alejandro 184
Paléologue, Maurice (1859–1944) 143
Paley, Olga Karnovich, Princess (1865–1929)
    148
Papworth, Robert 135, 158
Parodi-Delfino, Carla, 223, 230-1, 254, 262,
    265, 281; wedding 244
Parodi-Delfino, Elena 223
Parodi-Delfino, Gerardo 222, 230-1, 236
Parodi-Delfino, Leopoldo 303
Parodi-Delfino, Marina 223
Parodi-Delfino, Paolo 222, 231, 236
Passavant, Sophie de 75
Patricia ('Patsy') of Connaught, Princess
    (1886–1974) 61
Paul Alexandrovich, grand duke of Russia
    (1860–1919) 22, 34, 39, 53-4, 58; death 157

Paul of Yugoslavia, Prince (1893–1976) 156,
    161, 169, 240
Paul, king of Greece (1901–64), 322-4, 327,
    332
Paz, *Infanta* (1862–1948) 69, 72, 82, 95,
    100
Perry, Sir Percival 222
Pétain, Henri-Philippe (1856–1951), 172
Peter, king of Yugoslavia (1923–70) 161
Petinto, Dr 210
Philipp of Saxe-Coburg Gotha, Prince
    (1844–1921) 28, 99
Picken, Hilda 29
Pilar of Bavaria, Princess (1891–1987) 170,
    201
Pilar, *Infanta* (1936–2020) 322, 324, 333
Pineda, Francesco de 173
Pius X, Pope (1835–1914) 73, 79, 115
Pius XI, Pope (1857–1939) 244, 267
Poincaré, Raymond (1860–1934) 112
Polo de Bernabé, Luis de (1857–1929) 62
Polo y Martínez Valdes, Carmen 293
Prieto, Indalecio (1883–1962) 133
Primo de Rivera y Orbaneja, Miguel
    (1870–1930) 166, 171-2, 189, 193,
    197-8, 211, 279, 331
Pyne, Percy R. (1857–1929) 183, 186

Queipo de Llano, Gonzalo, General 233
Quiñones de León, José (1872–1946)
    128-30, 153-4, 165

Ramsay, Alexander (1881–1972) 61
Ranieri, prince of the Two Sicilies, duke of
    Castro (1883–1973), 110
Rasputin, Grigori (*c.* 1859–1916) 142, 155
Reszke, Jean de (1850–1925) 83
Rich Paulet, Luisa 158, 167-8
Rich, Fernando 158, 167-8
Richter, Ernest von (1862–1935) 90
Richthofen, Wolfram 270-1
Riddell, Hutton 193
Rincón, count of 121
Rojas, Doña Belén 106
Rolfs, Dr 23
Romana, marchioness de la 187
Romanones, Álvaro de Figueroa y Torres,
    count of (1863–1950) 129, 134-5, 138,
    176, 204-5
Rubenstein, Anton (1829–94) 20
Ruiz de Somavía, Manuel 284, 305
Ruíz Moragas, Carmen (1898–1936) 179
Rüxleben, Hans Friedrich von 90

Saavedra y Collado, Carmen, dowager
    duchess of Peñaranda 244
Sacha, Ciriaco, Cardinal (1833–1909) 67

Sáenz de Santa María, César 106, 109, 163, 232, 317
Saint, Harry, 326
Sampedro y Robato, Edelmira (1906–94), 227
San Carlos, duchess of 155
San Martino di San Germano, Giovanna (b.1945) 333
Sánchez Guerra, José (1897–1964) 202
Sanjurjo, José, General (1872–1936) 172-3, 212
Santo Floro, Agustín de Figueroa, marquis of 138
Santo Mauro, Mariano Fernández de Henestrosa, duke of (1858–1919) 121, 123-4
Santoña, Juan, duke of (1865–1929) 121
Santos Suárez, Joaquín 121
Sazonov, Sergei (1860–1927), 127
Scott-Ellis, Bronwen (1912–2003) 169
Scott-Ellis, Elisabeth (1914–76) 169
Scott-Ellis, Gaenor (1919–2002) 169
Scott-Ellis, Priscilla (Pip) (1916–83) 169, 250-2, 262, 263, 269, 271; and Ataúlfo 229, 245-6, 279-81; nursing and relief work 246, 250-2, 263-6, 276-8, 291; and paratyphoid 259; awarded Military Cross 275; falsely said to be Ali's daughter 297; marriage to Vilallonga 298
Scott-Ellis, Rosemary (1922–) 169
Segura, Pedro, Cardinal (1880–1957), 189, 191-2, 317, 332
Sergei Alexandrovich, grand duke of Russia (1857–1905) 22, 34-5, 39, 52, assassinated 57
Sergei Mikhailovich, grand duke of Russia (1869–1918) 146
Sibylla, princess of Sweden (1908–72), 229
Silvestre, Manuel, General (1871–1921)
Smirnoff, Father Eugene (1846–1923) 64
Solchaga, José (1881–1953) 263
Sophia, queen of Greece (1870–1932) 156
Sophia, Queen, formerly princess of Greece (b.1938) 322
Sophie, duchess of Hohenberg (1868–1914) 115
Sorolla Bastida, Joaquín (1863–1923) 120
Sotomayor, duke of 290, 292, 301
Soveral, Luis Pinto de Soveral, marquis of (1850–1922) 49
Stanley, Arthur, dean of Westminster (1815–81) 17
Stirbey, Barbu (1872–1946) 149, 151, 167
Stuart, Timoteo 244
Sviatopolk-Mirskii, Peter, Prince (1857–1914) 57

Tomislav of Yugoslavia, Prince (1928–2000) 161
Torlonia, Alessandro, Prince di Civitella-Cesi (1911–86) 229, 287
Tornos, María Ángeles (d.1981) 211, 216, 332
Torrecilla, Andrés, marquis of La (1864–1925) 121
Torres, Father 180
Trepov, Dmitri (1850–1906) 57-8
Tuxen, Laurits (1853–1927) 24

Vacarescu, Helena (1864–1947) 29
Valdeiglesias, marchioness of 211
Vanderbilt III, Cornelius (1873–1942) 183
Vanderbilt, Mrs Graham Fair (1875–1935) 183, 186
Varela, José Enrique, General (1891–1951) 193-4, 233, 255
Vegas Latapié, Eugenio (1907–85) 138
Venizelos, Eleftherios (1864–1936) 158
Viana, marquis of (d.1927) 120-1, 125, 132, 179-80
Victor Emmanuel III, king of Italy (1869–1947) 40
Victoria Adelaide, duchess of Saxe-Coburg Gotha (1885–1970) 89, 97, 99
Victoria Melita (Ducky), Grand Duchess Kirill of Russia (1876–1936) 28, 52, 57, 60, 79, 82, 98, 103, 113, 168, 177; birth 19; early life 23-5; at Queen Victoria's jubilee 24; first betrothal and marriage 33-4; and birth of Elisabeth 36; and Ernie's smallpox 43, stillborn son 47; divorce 47-8; and Elisabeth's death and funeral 48; and attachment to Kirill 48, 53; second wedding 64; birth of Maria 73; in Madrid 113; and nursing activities 141; complains of being 'abandoned' 143-4; moves to France 160; Coburg Palace left to 173; exhibition of paintings in Paris 182; at wedding of duke and duchess of Kent 229; and Kirill's infidelity 229; illness and death 231-2
Victoria of Hesse and the Rhine, marchioness of Milford Haven (1863–1950) 21, 47, 161
Victoria, duchess of Kent (1786–1861) 26
Victoria, princess royal of England, later German Empress Frederick (1840–1901) 21, 24, 32, 34, 45
Victoria, queen of England (1819–1901) 10, 17, 22, 32, 36, 38, 42, 51, 56, 142, 159, 287, 322; first meets duchess of Edinburgh 18; jubilee 23; and betrothal and marriage of Ducky and Ernie 33-4; diamond jubilee 40-1, last weeks and death 45

Vigón Suero Díaz, Juan 296
Vilallonga y Cabeza de Vaca, José Luis,
    marquis of Castellbell (1920–2007) 297-8
Vilallonga, Carmen Susana Beatriz de 298
Vilallonga, John de 298
Villalobar, Rodrigo de Saavedra y Vinent,
    marquis of (1864–1926) 63, 64
Villamarciel, José, count of (1865–1940) 67
Villaurrutia, Wenceslao Ramírez de
    Villaurrutia, marquis of (1850–1933)
    62, 64
Villavieja, Manuel Escandón, marquis of
    (1857–1940) 10, 49, 61, 70, 183, 184,
    186
Vladimir Alexandrovich, grand duke of
    Russia (1847–1909) 22, 34-5, 39, 48, 64,
    66, 69, 113, 144
Vladimir Kirillovich, grand duke of Russia
    (1917–92) 144, 169, 241, 300-1; at
    wedding of duke and duchess of Kent
    229; and Ducky's death, 231-2

Wagner, Richard (1813–83) 28, 44, 107
Walden, John Scott-Ellis, Baron Howard de
    (1912–99) 169, 297
Walden, Margaret, Baroness Howard de
    (1890–1974) 169, 229, 245-6
Walden, Scott-Ellis, Thomas, 8th Lord Howard
    de (1880–1946) 100, 169, 229, 245
Wallington, Alice 246
Widener, Joseph E. 183
Wilhelm II, German Emperor (1859–1941)
    34, 47, 94, 128, 140, 156, 322; and
    courtship of Missy and Nando 30, 41, 45
Wilson, Woodrow (1856–1924) 150
Wohlparte, Georg 90

Xenia Alexandrovna, grand duchess of
    Russia (1875–1960) 38, 55, 142, 146,
    157, 160, 189

Zamoyski, Count Jan Kanty (1900–61), 188,
    190-1
Zubillaga, Gen. 209